APPLESCRIPT
IN A NUTSHELL

A Desktop Quick Reference

APPLESCRIPT
IN A NUTSHELL

A Desktop Quick Reference

Bruce W. Perry

O'REILLY®

Beijing • Cambridge • Farnham • Köln • Paris • Sebastopol • Taipei • Tokyo

AppleScript in a Nutshell
by Bruce W. Perry

Published by O'Reilly & Associates, Inc., 101 Morris Street, Sebastopol, CA 95472.

Editor: Troy Mott

Production Editor: Catherine Morris

Cover Designer: Ellie Volckhausen

Printing History:

June 2001:   First Edition.

ISBN: 1-56592-841-5

[M]

Table of Contents

Chapter 7—Flow-Control Statements 128

Part IV: Scripting Mac OS 9 Control Panels and Extensions

Preface

AppleScript continues to evolve on Mac OS 9 and Mac OS X as the ultimate scripting tool for the Macintosh. AppleScript's power to automate the operating system and complex applications such as graphics, desktop-publishing, and database programs, as well as a friendly English language dialect that helps ambitious scripters get up to speed quickly with their own applets, is not matched by any other platform's programming language. Yet, only a small percentage of Macintosh users are even aware that AppleScript is installed with their operating system. Those who are aware of AppleScript's presence on their machine often do not take full advantage of this tool to automate their daily computing activities, both on their local machine and over the Internet.

Who should and can use AppleScript? The following users come to mind right away: system administrators who are automating tasks with networks and applications; web and graphics professionals who want to control the development of web sites and publications; scientists, mathematicians, and engineers who require applets to make calculations and automate their own software tools, as well as day-to-day programmers and students who are designing and prototyping new programs. Not to mention everday users who want to automate their own computing tasks, such as file and folder backups.

If you are on a Macintosh, then you should be putting AppleScript to work for you.

The purpose of this book is primarily three-fold:

1. Describe AppleScript and its tools (Part I) and provide a core language reference (Part II) that all users can keep next to their computers as they write new scripts.

2. Provide detailed descriptions, examples, and reference information on how to script the numerous system-level programs on Mac OS 9 (Parts III and IV) and Mac OS X (Part V), such as the Finder on both OS versions, Sherlock, and Network Setup Scripting.

3. Give scripters general insight on how to approach the scripting of several programs that can be automated by AppleScript, such as Adobe Illustrator and Photoshop, FileMaker Pro, QuarkXPress, SoundJam MP, and OutLook Express. The mantra is, study the "application class" in the program's AppleScript dictionary and you'll be up and running with scripting that program before you know it. (Chapter 1 discusses the application class in general terms; while the application classes of all the various system components are described in detail throughout the book.)

Hopefully, this book will help reveal AppleScript to more Macintosh users, thus providing them with another outlet for creativity and productivity.

Organization of This Book

AppleScript in a Nutshell is structured in six parts.

Part I, *Introduction to AppleScript*

This section provides an overview of AppleScript and Script Editor, the free AppleScript development tool that installs with the Macintosh. Quick studies and experienced programmers will probably be able to develop their first AppleScripts (if you have never used AppleScript before) based on a reading of this introductory section alone. Chapter 1 describes how AppleScript is primarily used and also describes the relevance to AppleScript of *Apple events*, an internal messaging system that the Macintosh operating system uses for interapplication communication. The end of Chapter 1 summarizes AppleScript's core language features (Part II provides a more comprehensive language reference). You can use Chapter 2 as a helpful reference to Script Editor as you use this Apple Computer tool to develop your scripts.

Chapter 1, *AppleScript: An Introduction*

This AppleScript overview includes a description of how AppleScript is primarily used, an Apple-event tutorial, and a compressed language reference for those who want to dive right into scripting. Novice users should start here with the book, while very experienced AppleScripters may use this section as a review or skip over it.

Chapter 2, *Using Script Editor with OS 9 and OS X*

This chapter describes all of Script Editor's primary menu commands and controls. It also explains the various options for saving AppleScript files.

Part II, *AppleScript Language Reference*

If scripters need more information on specific language features, this is the place to look. The core-language information is presented with syntax examples, code examples, and text descriptions. Everything is arranged in alphabetical order to make things easy to locate. This includes the various data types (i.e., how AppleScript stores data in memory), operators (such as the common Math operators and the string-concatenation operator "&"), and how to set AppleScript variables and create user-defined functions, as well as advanced features, such as creating object-oriented script objects (Chapter 9).

Chapter 3, *Data Types*

This chapter describes the built-in AppleScript data types, including `string`, `integer`, `real`, `list`, and `record`. Comparisons with programming languages are made where it is appropriate (e.g., a `list` is like an array, and a `record` is an associative array).

Chapter 4, *Operators*

Use this chapter as a reference to the built-in symbols (e.g., &, +, *, -) that you can use in AppleScript expressions.

Chapter 5, *Reference Forms*

AppleScript provides several English-language terms to use when the script refers to objects on your computer system, such as files, folders, disks, and applications. This chapter is an alphabetical reference to these terms (e.g., `first`, `every`, `id`, `where`).

Chapter 6, *Variables and Constants*

AppleScript, like other languages, uses variables as placeholders that represent data (e.g., strings or numbers). This chapter describes the rules for naming and creating your own variables; it also provides a reference to AppleScript's constants and predefined variables (like `pi`).

Chapter 7, *Flow-Control Statements*

This chapter is an alphabetical reference to AppleScript's flow-control statements, such as `if`, `repeat`, `try`, `exit`, and `continue`.

Chapter 8, *Subroutines*

This chapter is a tutorial on creating user-defined subroutines, which are also called handlers, functions, or methods (in object-oriented parlance). The second part of this chapter describes five special handlers in AppleScript: *idle, open, quit, reopen*, and *run*.

Chapter 9, *Script Objects and Libraries*

AppleScripters can create script objects, which are user-defined types that can have their own attributes and methods. This chapter also describes function libraries, which are script objects that give other external scripts the ability to load and/or call the object's own functions.

Part III, *Scripting Mac OS 9 Applications*

This section is devoted to the scripting of system-level Mac OS 9 programs, such as Apple System Profiler, Keychain Scripting, the Finder, Network Setup Scripting, and Sherlock 2. The scriptable control panels and extensions are covered in the next section, Part IV. The programs that are covered in this section for the most part have comprehensive AppleScript dictionaries and can be used to extend your computer's capabilities (particularly with AppleScript!); however, they are not control panels or extensions. The exception to this scheme is Apple Guide, which is an extension but was included in this section so that the reader has access in a single chapter to a description of AppleScript and the help-related programs. Each chapter describes the purpose of the application, then describes each dictionary command and class in a reference-style form.

Chapter 10, *Apple Guide and Help Viewer*

This chapter describes the dictionaries and includes scripting tips for Apple Guide, the traditional automated Apple-help program, and the newer browser-based Help Viewer tool.

Chapter 11, *Apple System Profiler*

Accessible from the Apple menu, Apple System Profiler displays a wealth of information about the hardware and software on your system. This chapter describes its commands and classes and includes numerous code examples.

Chapter 12, *Keychain Scripting and Apple Verifier*

These are two Apple-security tools. Keychain Scripting is used to encrypt files and passwords, and Apple Verifier can verify digitally-signed files. This chapter tells where to find these applications and describes their commands and classes in reference form.

Chapter 13, *Desktop Printer Manager*

Scripters can use Desktop Printer Manager, a program introduced with Mac OS 8.5, to create and manage desktop icons that can be used for printing or otherwise processing documents and files. This chapter describes the proper syntax for controlling this application with AppleScript and also includes a reference to its dictionary commands and classes.

Chapter 14, *Mac OS 9 Finder Commands (MAC OS 9)*

The Finder is the Mac OS 9 application that controls the user's visual interface to the computer: its desktop controls as well as hard disks, network volumes, printers, and other devices. A lot of fun and useful AppleScripts deal with automating Finder activities, such as reading from and writing to files. This chapter covers the Finder commands, like *restart*, *shutdown*, *sleep*, and *make*, with detailed references to each command and any of their parameters.

Chapter 15, *Mac OS 9 Finder Classes*

This chapter covers the Finder classes, which are all the objects or things you are likely to control when scripting the Finder (e.g., files, folders, disks, and running applications). *Finder Classes* provides a detailed reference to each object's elements (if any) and properties.

Chapter 16, *Network Setup Scripting*

As the Macintosh becomes a sophisticated client and server on TCP/IP networks, *Network Setup Scripting* shows how you can use the commands and classes of this program with Open Transport to script a machine's various network configurations.

Chapter 17, *Scripting Sherlock 2*

You can automate sophisticated searches of local networks and the Web with AppleScript and Sherlock 2. *Scripting Sherlock 2* provides a description of this program and a reference, with code examples, to its commands (e.g., *index containers, search*) and classes.

Chapter 18, *URL Access Scripting*

URL Access Scripting describes the *download* and *upload* commands of this program, which can be used with the FTP and HTTP protocols to grab and save files off the Web.

Part IV, *Scripting Mac OS 9 Control Panels and Extensions*

This section is dedicated to the scripting of the Mac's control panels and extensions, which are located in the Control Panels and Extensions folders of the System Folder. Each chapter describes the purpose of this system software, then includes a reference to their dictionary commands and classes. Some of the more exciting new scriptable technologies are included in this section, including Apple Data Detectors, Folder Actions, and the Speech-related extensions in Chapter 30.

Chapter 19, *Appearance Control Panel*

This scriptable control panel lets you use AppleScript to set and change the visual and audible aspects of your computer, such as its background color, the font for desktop text, and how window title bars and scroll bars work. We show you how to do this and include a detailed reference to this software's commands and classes.

Chapter 20, *Apple Data Detectors Extension*

This chapter describes a powerful scripting technology by which you can assign an AppleScript to be triggered based on certain information that a user selects inside of a contextual menu, such as an email or web address. *Apple Data Detectors Extension* describes the Apple Data Detectors scripting-addition class and commands in reference form.

Chapter 21, *Apple Menu Options Control Panel*

This chapter describes how to use AppleScript to automate various menu items (e.g., Recent applications, documents, and servers) in the Apple menu (the drop-down menu in the upper-left part of the computer screen).

Chapter 22, *Application Switcher Extension*

The Application Switcher is the floating palette that the user can "tear" off of the Application menu (on the upper-right part of the computer screen). This chapter describes how to set various Switcher elements (e.g., its size, position, button order) with AppleScript and includes a reference to its extensive `application` class.

Chapter 23, *ColorSync Extension*

ColorSync Extension describes the AppleScript commands and classes for this built-in Macintosh software, which helps synchronize color-matching between the devices that create an image (e.g., scanners) and printers.

Chapter 24, *File Exchange Control Panel*

This chapter describes the File Exchange commands that you can use to create new extension mappings (i.e., a way to tell the Macintosh how to handle files with certain extensions like *.html*), for instance, or view the existing file-type mappings on a machine.

Chapter 25, *File Sharing Control Panel*

This chapter first summarizes file sharing on the Macintosh, which establishes the level of access network users have to a machine's disks and folders. Then it shows how to create new users or groups (or delete miscreants) with code examples and a reference section on File Sharing's dictionary commands and classes.

Chapter 26, *Folder Actions Extension*

Folder actions are AppleScripts that are triggered when items are added to or removed from a folder. Folder action commands constitute the Folder Actions suite of the Standard Additions osax and the dictionary commands that derive from the Folder Actions extension. This chapter describes both sets of commands.

Chapter 27, *FontSync Control Panel and Extension*

This chapter describes the dictionaries for the FontSync control panel and extension. They are used to synchronize the fonts between devices during image production and printing.

Chapter 28, *Location Manager Control Panel*

This chapter shows how you can use AppleScript to switch between the various computer and networking configurations that are displayed by the Location Manager control panel.

Chapter 29, *Memory and Mouse Control Panels*

This chapter describes the dictionary commands and classes for both the Memory and Mouse control panels. For example, the chapter shows how you can use an applet to find out about the computer's virtual-memory settings or disk-cache size.

Chapter 30, *Speech Listener and SpeakableItems Extension*

This chapter describes the different ways that you can integrate speech into your scripts, such as the *listen for* and *say* AppleScript commands. Speech listener is actually an application that is located in the Scripting Additions folder of the System Folder, but it will not work unless the Speech Recognition extension is installed and enabled.

Chapter 31, *Web Sharing Control Panel*

This chapter describes the functionality of the Web Sharing control panel and also gives an example of how to use AppleScript with a Common Gateway Interface (CGI) script. CGI scripts execute in response to web page requests, in order to process the incoming data from a form a web user has filled out, for instance. The Web Sharing control panel can be used to allow a computer to perform as a light-weight web server.

Part V, *Scripting the Mac OS X System*

AppleScript is in a state of flux and evolution on the new Mac OS X system. AppleScript also faces tremendous competition from the programming tools that come with (and can be installed on) Mac OS X, such as shell scripting tools, Perl, and Java. Nevertheless, this section will describe what you can do with Apple-Script and three Mac OS X programs that *can* be used with AppleScript: Mail, Terminal application (a command-line tool), and TextEdit. Part V begins with a discussion of AppleScript and scripting the new Mac OS X Finder, which is the OS 9 Finder after a major facelift.

Chapter 32, *Scripting the OS X Desktop*

This chapter explains some of the familiar Finder-like scripting that you can accomplish on Mac OS X, such as getting information about desktop items (e.g., files, folders, and disks) and making new files. This chapter compares the Mac OS X Finder dictionary to the Mac OS 9 Finder dictionary (and finds few differences, but that is likely to change with new OS X versions).

Chapter 33, *Scripting Mail*

This chapter describes the use of AppleScript with Apple Computer's new email application, aptly called "Mail." This chapter provides descriptions and code examples on setting up a new mail message and getting information about an email account.

Chapter 34, *Executing Scripts with the Terminal App*

Terminal application is the command-line tool or interface (a window or shell that you type script commands into) that comes with Mac OS X. This chapter shows how you can create, compile, and execute AppleScripts from the Terminal program.

Chapter 35, *Scripting TextEdit*

It is likely that the TextEdit's available AppleScript commands will change with new Mac OS X releases, so this chapter focuses on TextEdit's major commands (e.g., *count, open, save*) and text-related classes, such as `character`, `document`, `paragraph`, and `text`.

Part VI, *Appendixes*

Our AppleScript book would not be complete without a description and reference information on the many scripting additions or "osaxen" that veteran scripters use in almost every script (remember *display dialog* or *current date*?). Appendix A covers the Standard Additions (a group of scripting additions that Apple Computer bundles with the OS installation) that are installed with both Mac OS 9 and Mac OS X. This section describes each of the Standard Additions (e.g., *ASCII number, beep, choose application*) and any parameters that these osax commands use. Appendix B, *AppleScript Resources*, is a list of URLs that are relevant to AppleScript users.

Appendix A, *Standard Scripting Additions*

This appendix focuses on the several dozen Standard Addition scripting additions, which are installed along with Mac OS 9 and Mac OS X. These are extensions to the built-in AppleScript commands that you can use virtually anywhere in your script (Chapter 1 also discusses scripting additions). The Standard Additions are located in the *startup disk:System Folder:Scripting Additions* folder in OS 9 and, with Mac OS X, */System/Library/ScriptingAdditions/* (the primary location on OS X).

Appendix B, *AppleScript Resources*

This is an extensive list of web pages relating to Macintosh scripting and AppleScript.

Conventions Used in This Book

The following typographical conventions are used in this book:

`Constant width`
> Is used to indicate command-line computer output and code examples, as well as AppleScript class names, objects, parameters, data types, properties, methods, constants, variables, and flow-control statements like `repeat`.

Constant width bold

Is used to indicate user input in examples.

Italic

Is used to introduce new terms and to indicate URLs, user-defined files and directories, commands, file extensions, filenames, directory or folder names, and UNC pathnames.

Italic is also used to highlight chapter titles and, in some instances, to visually separate the topic of a list.

> This is an example of a note, which signifies valuable and timesaving information.

> This is an example of a warning, which alerts to a potential pitfall in the program. Warnings can also refer to a procedure that might be dangerous if not carried out in a specific way.

Keyboard Shortcuts

When keyboard shortcuts are shown (*Command-N*), a hyphen means that the keys must be held down simultaneously, while a plus means that the keys should be pressed sequentially.

Path Notation

We use a shorthand path notation to show you how to reach a given user interface element or option. The path notation is relative to a well-known location. For example, the following path:

Script Editor's File → Open Dictionary

means "Open the Script Editor's File menu, then choose Open Dictionary."

File path delimiters

AppleScript uses the colon to separate the directories in a file path, as in *MyStartupDisk:Desktop Folder:myfile*. The major scripting additions that deal with file paths, such as *choose file, choose file name* (Mac OS X and OS 9.1), *choose folder*, and *path to*, display their file paths in `alias` return values as colons. The chapters that deal with Mac OS X, however, will often identify the locations of files and folders with the Unix-style slash character / as the path delimiter (e.g., */users/bruceper/documents/*). This is the path delimiter used by Darwin, which is the core operating system for Mac OS X and has Unix origins. The opening slash character in the file path */users/bruceper/* sets the beginning of the path to the "users" folder on the disk or partition where Mac OS X is located. AppleScript on Mac OS X still generally uses colons as the path delimiter, however, which maintains consistency with older scripts (OS 8/9). One place where you can use the slash character to locate a path for AppleScript is in setting the `target` property for a Finder window, as in:

```
set the target of Finder window 1 to "/users/bruceper/"
```

Italic `Constant Width`

On occasion, you will find a command description such as *connect* `remote access configuration` object, which means that the *connect* command takes a `remote access configuration` object as a parameter.

How to Contact Us

We have tested and verified the information in this book to the best of our ability, but you may find that features have changed (or even that we have made mistakes!). Please let us know about any errors you find, as well as your suggestions for future editions, by writing to:

O'Reilly & Associates, Inc.
101 Morris Street
Sebastopol, CA 95472
1-800-998-9938 (in the U.S. or Canada)
1-707-829-0515 (international/local)
1-707-829-0104 (FAX)

You can also send us messages electronically. To be put on the mailing list or request a catalog, send email to:

info@oreilly.com

To ask technical questions or comment on the book, send email to:

bookquestions@oreilly.com

We have a web site for the book, where we'll list examples, errata, and any plans for future editions. You can access this page at:

http://www.oreilly.com/catalog/aplscptian/

For more information about this book and others, see the O'Reilly web site:

http://www.oreilly.com

Acknowledgments

Every book is a prodigious effort that could never be accomplished by the author alone. I would first like to thank my wife Stacy LeBaron and daughter Rachel, who have patiently and sympathetically waited for me to emerge from what has seemed, to them, a never-ending process of word- and code-crunching. Next I would like to gratefully acknowledge Anne and Robert Perry, my parents, who have instilled in me a love of books and the intellectual discipline it takes to digest and write them. The O'Reilly team has been indispensable: my editors Simon Hayes, for his insightful nudging and prodding when I first proposed the project, and the tireless efforts of Troy Mott and Bob Herbstman as the book entered the final production stages.

Chris Stone at O'Reilly also has made tremendous contributions to the shaping of this book. Thanks to Bill Cheeseman and Paul Berkowitz for helpful technical reviews of several chapters. Finally, I would also like to acknowledge all the AppleScript experts and engineers at Apple Computer who took time out from their busy schedules to comment on this book.

PART I

Introduction to AppleScript

CHAPTER 1

AppleScript: An Introduction

AppleScript is a scripting tool that installs with the Mac OS, including the newest release, Mac OS X. Programmers and power users use AppleScript to create scripts and applets, which are small Mac programs that can both accomplish useful tasks on their own and greatly extend the capabilities of other software systems.

This chapter covers the following topics:

- How AppleScript is used (for example, for software automation and the attaching of scripts within an application's menus).

- An overview of Apple events, a messaging technology that AppleScript uses to control scriptable applications. This section briefly describes (1) how AppleScript code sends Apple events, as well as (2) Apple event classes and objects.

- Two applications that you can use to access and run your scripts from the file system: Script Runner (for Mac OS X) and OSA Menu (Mac OS 9). Chapter 2, *Using Script Editor with OS 9 and OS X*, is completely devoted to Script Editor, which is the script development environment that installs with the Macintosh OS.

- AppleScript's language elements, such as data types, variables, handlers (i.e., subroutines or functions), and flow-control statements. This is a "quick reference" for the readers who want to dispense with narrative and dive right into scripting. Part II then covers all of these elements in detail.

How Is AppleScript Used?

AppleScript can be used for both simple, self-contained solutions, such as a program whose sole purpose is to monitor how much space is left on a disk, and comprehensive systems that automate or control a suite of software programs. Let's begin with a simple script type, a standalone applet that is not attached to or designed to automate another software program.

You generally create an applet by typing AppleScript source code into an Apple Computer scripting program called Script Editor. You then compile the script (if it does not have any errors) into a small program called a compiled script or an applet that can be double-clicked on the desktop. An AppleScript applet is a self-contained program with its own desktop icon, while a compiled script requires a host program like Script Editor or Script Runner (see "Using Script Runner with OS X" later in this chapter) to run it. Figure 1-1 shows an applet icon. Chapter 2 also explains the various options for saving an AppleScript.

sleep

Figure 1-1: An applet icon

AppleScript is a great tool for writing everyday utilities, such as managing files, folders, disks, and networking activities. The utility scripts provide all the functionality you need, without the necessity to automate another software program. These tasks, such as file backups or getting a browser to access certain web pages, would be time-consuming and tedious if they always had to be performed manually. Two examples of scripts that I run at least once every day are:

- A script that displays a dialog listing the names of all of the running programs on the Mac, including invisible background processes. I can select one or more of these programs and click a button on the dialog window to close them.

- An applet that calculates the remaining free space on all of the volumes that are mounted on the desktop, then displays the result for each volume and the total free storage space on all of the volumes put together.

 A single hard disk can be divided into several volumes, which the Mac OS represents as disk icons on the user's desktop.

By now you would probably like to see just what applet source code looks like. The script in Example 1-1 displays the largest unused block of Random Access Memory (RAM) remaining on the computer where the script is run.

Example 1-1: AppleScript Displaying the Largest Block of Free Memory

```
tell application "Finder"
    activate
    set memblock to (largest free block / 1024 / 1024)
display dialog "The largest free block is now about " & (memblock) & ¬
" megabytes."
end tell
```

This script asks the Finder application for a piece of data that the Finder maintains called "largest free block." This represents the size of the largest free memory block in bytes. The following script fragment:

```
(largest free block / 1024 / 1024)
```

divides this byte-size figure twice by 1024 to represent the result in megabytes, since most people convey the amount of computer memory they have using this measurement. *display dialog* is an often-used extension to the built-in AppleScript language called a scripting addition, which I explain later in this chapter (Appendix A, *Standard Scripting Additions*, of the book is devoted to descriptions of the standard scripting additions that are installed with Mac OS 9 and OS X). *display dialog* shows a dialog window containing the message label that you specify in the source code following the *display dialog* command, as in this part of Example 1-1:

```
display dialog "The largest free block is now about " & (memblock) & ¬
" megabytes."
```

The `tell` statement that opens the script, such as:

```
tell application "Finder"
```

is AppleScript's method of targeting an application to request some data from it or to control the program in some manner. Since the script displays some Finder information to the computer user, the *activate* command is used to make the Finder the frontmost program (i.e., its windows, if any are open, become the active desktop windows). `tell` statements, commands, and other syntax elements are described elsewhere in this chapter, as well as in detail in Chapters 3 through 8.

Automation

Along with creating a number of useful utilities, AppleScript has won a reputation as a premier tool for automating software workflows. In workflows, one or more separate software programs cooperate in a sequence of actions to complete a job. This means that launching an AppleScript can orchestrate several actions that involve software applications that are not otherwise designed to share data or call each other's menu commands. AppleScript does the calling of each program's commands (targeting them in a similar manner to how the Finder is targeted in Example 1-1), acting as a conductor for busy software medleys. AppleScript has earned the undying loyalty of many Mac scripters in the print and web publishing industries by its ability to simultaneously control applications such as QuarkX-Press, Adobe Illustrator, InDesign, and Photoshop, Canto Cumulus, FileMaker Pro, as well as the Microsoft Office members like Word and Excel.

As an example of automation, I designed an AppleScript in the summer of 2000 to convert thousands of text files to web pages. A company that publishes legal decisions wanted to make them available to a search engine on their web site. Since they were already plain text or Word files, and the page designs were very simple, we used an AppleScript to feed the pages to Word and to trigger its "Save as HTML..." menu command (which creates a simple, almost crude, web-page design at best). The company converted about 20,000 legal decisions in a matter of days, using this rather modest script that I developed in Script Editor.

Apple Computer has traditionally urged Mac software developers to make their programs "scriptable," and thus increase the market and following for those programs. It usually does. For example, Illustrator and Photoshop* are generally much more scriptable on the Mac platform than their Windows versions, which may influence some buyers to prefer the Mac versions (along with the fact that graphics professionals tend to prefer the Apple platform).

Similar to OLE automation on the Windows platform, many software programs allow themselves to be automated by exposing an object model to a scripting tool, in this case AppleScript. Conceptually, an object model is a tree-like diagram (see Figure 1-7 later in this chapter) showing the objects or "things" that the software represents as computer data (such as files, folders, or database records), as well as the objects' attributes or properties. AppleScript talks to these scriptable programs by exchanging *Apple events* with them. These are high-level operating-system events that are used for interapplication communication on the Mac. See the section "Apple Events" for more information.

With the release of Mac OS 9 and OS 9.1 in 2000 and early 2001, Apple Computer has made most of the computer's built-in software controllable by AppleScript. These are some of the scriptable OS 9 applications and control panels:

- Appearance control panel
- Apple Help Viewer
- Apple System Profiler
- Apple Verifier
- Application Switcher
- ColorSync extension
- File Exchange
- Memory control panel
- Sherlock 2 (the Find application)
- Speech Recognition

Some previously scriptable features have not been included in the Mac OS X installation, including preferences scripting, Folder Actions, printing scripting, and program linking. Future OS X releases will address these elements, according to Apple Computer, which adds that a number of Mac OS X applications are scriptable (with some qualifications):

- Finder (some Finder commands, such as *move* or *duplicate*, are not yet implemented or are not yet functioning)
- TextEdit
- Mail
- Sherlock

---

* Photoshop requires the licensing of the PhotoScripter plugin from Main Event Software (*http://www.mainevent.com*) to be extensively automated with AppleScript.

- QuickTime Player (the Pro version of this application is quite scriptable; visit *http://www.apple.com/applescript* to download the QuickTime scripts collection for Mac OS X)
- Apple System Profiler
- Stuffit Expander
- Internet Explorer
- ColorSync Scripting
- URL Access Scripting
- Image Capture Extension (a background application that works with the Image Capture program; its dictionary supports the scaling and rotating of image files)

In addition, the AppleScript engineers are apparently working on ways to let AppleScript interact with the command-line shells that come with OS X, such as the Bourne shell. OS X already permits the launching of AppleScripts from a shell (see Chapter 34, *Executing Scripts with the Terminal App*).

Attachability/Recordability

If an application is either attachable or recordable (or both), it is considered a near paragon of scriptability. Attachable means that you can create a script and then attach it to a program, so that the script is added to the program's internal menus. Applications usually implement attachability with Mac OS 9 by providing a folder for scripts and a menu item on their menubars that lists these available scripts. Figure 1-2 shows a menubar that contains a list of attached scripts for the BBEdit text editor.

Attached scripts will often run much faster than scripts that run as self-contained applets even if the script doesn't have anything to do with the application it is attached to (i.e., the script never sends Apple events to the host application). For example, I have an AppleScript that reads large web logs (more than 1 MB in size) looking for and recording for later display certain file paths. When attached to BBEdit 5.1, the script runs about six times as fast as it does when run as an applet outside of BBEdit (40 seconds as opposed to about 240 seconds). Try it with some of your own scripts.

A few applications allow themselves to be recorded by Script Editor, which is a great way to get started with scripting them. To do this, open Script Editor and click its Record button (see Chapter 2). You then activate an application and perform the actions that you are trying to record, or simply go in and manipulate its menus to see what happens. Once you click Stop in Script Editor, the Script Editor window will display the AppleScript source code representing the recorded actions. If the application is not recordable, the Script Editor window will be empty after you click Stop. Otherwise, you can then save the AppleScript as a macro that you can use and/or modify in the future. The Finder, BBEdit, and Microsoft Word are examples of recordable applications.

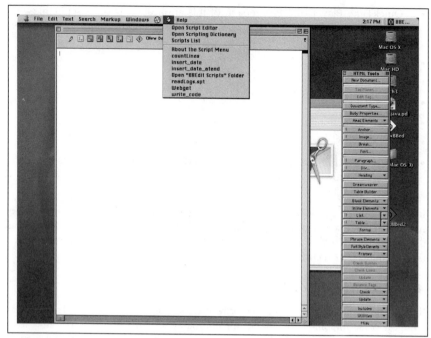

Figure 1-2: Attached scripts in BBEdit

Scripting Additions

Scripting additions are extensions to the AppleScript language. The Standard Additions and some others are written by Apple; however, there are hundreds of scripting additions the scripters can add themselves. They are added by placing the scripting addition file into the Scripting Additions folder. Once installed, scripting additions can be used by any script.

Another term for scripting addtion is osax (the plural form is osaxen), which stands for Open Scripting Architecture eXtention. The OSA is explained in an upcoming section of this chapter.

In Mac OS 9, the scripting additon files are stored in the *startup disk:System Folder:Scripting Additions* folder. They are stored in more than one location in Mac OS X, including */System/Library/ScriptingAdditions/*. Examples of two scripitng addition commands that are often used are *display dialog* (see Example 1-1) and *current date*. The latter command returns a **date** object that contains data about today's date and time. The Standard Additions are installed with the Mac OS.

 There is a large database of scripting additions at *http://osaxen.com.*

Apple Events

AppleScript and scriptable programs communicate with each other via Apple events or internal, invisible messages. This section provides an overview of how Apple events are implemented with AppleScript. As this information goes beyond basic script development, some readers may choose to jump ahead to the book's language-reference sections, do some scripting, and then revisit this section at another time.

OSA

The Open Scripting Architecture, which has been present on the Mac since the early 1990s, is Apple Computer's mechanism for making interapplication communication available to a spectrum of scripting languages. AppleScript is the OSA language that Apple provides, but there are other OSA-compliant languages, including UserLand Frontier and JavaScript.*

OSA accomplishes this "the-more-the-merrier" approach to scripting systems by using Apple events as the unifying technology. The situation is similar to Open Database Connectivity (ODBC) on the Windows platform, where any client application can talk to different database management systems using ODBC as a common conduit (as long as ODBC driver software exists for that particular database). In terms of OSA, the conduit (on Mac OS 9) is a scripting component that can convert whatever scripting language is used (AppleScript or JavaScript) into one or more properly constructed Apple events. Figure 1-3 shows the same Apple event being sent to an application in two different scripting languages.

Before AppleScripts or other scripting languages can be compiled and run, their corresponding extension files have to be installed (the AppleScript extension is included in an OS 9 installation) and then loaded into the computer's memory. The AppleScript extension or component is depicted in Figure 1-3.

Apple Event Registry

Along with scripting components, another important OSA element is the Apple Event Registry. The Registry is an Apple Computer-maintained database that maps all of the Apple events that the Mac OS standard software uses to a corresponding English-language command. This means that the *activate* AppleScript command is mapped to an *activate* Apple event, *quit* is mapped to a *quit* Apple event, and so on. You can use the Registry to discover the Apple event codes that are used by the Mac's standard software (such as the Appearance control panel, the ColorSync extension, or Sherlock 2). The section "Inside an Apple Event" describes what these codes are.

---

* Late night Software, Ltd.'s JavaScript for OSA tool, is accessible from *http://www.latenightsw.com.*

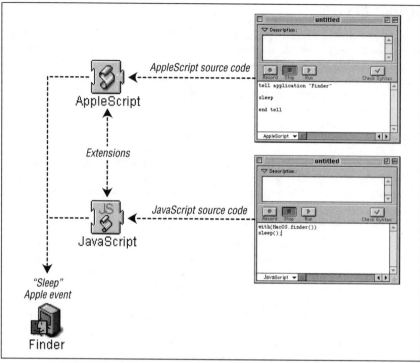

Figure 1-3: OSA scripting tools send Apple events

 The AppleScript software development kit (SDK) includes a File-Maker Pro file that contains the Apple Event Registry for AppleScript Version 1.3.4. Go to *http://developer.apple.com/sdk* for more SDK information.

To make them easier to understand and incorporate into applications, Apple events are logically grouped into suites or categories, such as the Database Suite, the Standard Suite, and the Text Suite. All Mac applications are required to support four Standard Suite events (*open, print, quit*, and *run*; this was the "Required Suite" prior to AppleScript 1.3). This does not mean that all Mac programs do support these events; software developers don't go to jail if they have not implemented these Apple events in their programs. However, this does mean that the vast majority of applications will reliably quit if, for example, your script sends them a *quit* Apple event.

Applications and scripting additions can (and usually do) define their own Apple events and corresponding human-language commands. For example, the BBEdit text editor supports a subset of the Standard Suite of Apple events that you can look up in the Registry database. BBEdit also contains a set of events and classes known as the BBEdit Suite, which is unique to BBEdit. Table 1-1 shows the Standard Suite Apple events and Apple event classes that BBEdit 5.1 supports. It also shows the Apple events and Apple event classes that are listed in the BBEdit Suite. (The section "Apple Event Classes and Objects" describes Apple event classes in more detail.)

Table 1-1: BBEdit 5.1's Standard Suite and BBEdit Suite

BBEdit Standard Suite Events	BBEdit Standard Suite Classes	BBEdit Suite Events	BBEdit Suite Classes
close	application	insert text	character
count	window	insert file	word
delete	document	insert folder	line
get	Recent file	insert project	text
make		find	text item
revert		replace	selection-object
save		find differences	hit
set		go to line	
		go to function	
		go to marker	
		select current paragraph	
		twiddle	
		change case	
		shift	
		hard wrap	
		insert line breaks	
		remove line breaks	
		unwrap	
		zap gremlins	
		entab	
		detab	
		insert glossary entry	
		get FTP file	
		put FTP file	

Client/Server

The application or applet that initiates an exchange of Apple events is called the client application. The client requests the help of the server ("do something for me!"). The client's Apple event(s) may request data (e.g., text, database records) or just a sequence of actions that the server should take ("Open a file and send me the paragraph that begins with 'Top-secret information.'"). The client can also be thought of as the Apple event "source," and the server can be thought of as a "target." An application can be both an Apple-event client and a target (if a client receives a reply Apple event, then it's the target of that event).

A machine can send up to about 2,000 Apple events per second (and can be as pokey as about 5 per second). This speed depends on factors such as how quickly the target application can process the Apple event(s).

How Many Apple Events Can Your Machine Send?

An Apple Computer engineer suggests that you use the following code to test how many Apple events a particular machine can send per second:

```
set start_time to current date
repeat 1000 times
    tell application "Finder"
        name -- gets the Finder's name, "Finder"
    end tell
end repeat
set elapsed_time to (current date) - start_time
display dialog "Average " & 1000 / elapsed_time & " events per ¬
second"
```

This code sends the Finder 1,000 Apple events, and then displays the event-per-second results. Running this as a compiled script out of Script Editor, my machine (a PowerMac 8500 upgraded to a G3 with plenty of memory) registered only 5 per second. However, when saved as an applet and attached to BBEdit, the speed improvement was 20-fold—100 Apple events per second!

Let's drill down further into Apple events. The upcoming section "Inside an Apple Event" shows you what an Apple event looks like at the system level, using the *sleep* Apple event, a Finder command, as an example.

Inside an Apple Event

Here's how it works when Script Editor compiles and executes the following code, which comprises a complete compilable script:

```
tell application "Finder" to sleep
```

This is what happens:

1. The AppleScript component has to find out which Apple event lies behind the *sleep* command. The component knows that the Finder is one of the places it should look for these details, because the Finder is targeted by the `tell` statement:

    ```
    tell application "Finder"...
    ```

2. Remember that sleep is an English-language term for putting the computer to sleep, but it is implemented as the *sleep* Apple event beneath the surface. Figure 1-4 shows the structure of the sleep Apple event.

    The AppleScript component discovers the attributes of the *sleep* Apple event (e.g., the event id) from a segment of the Finder file called the Apple event terminology extension (`'aete'`) resource. The `'aete'` resource maps the sleep script command to the Apple event depicted in Figure 1-4.

3. The component then sends that Apple event to the Finder, which responds to sleep by powering down the computer.

Here is an explanation of the structure behind the Apple event in Figure 1-4.

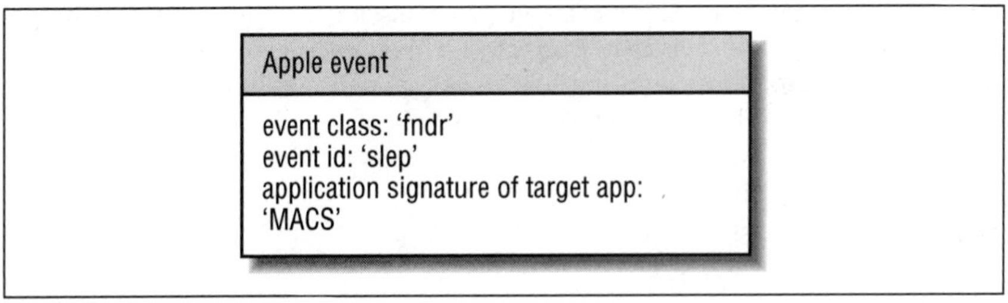

```
┌─────────────────────────────────────┐
│ Apple event                         │
├─────────────────────────────────────┤
│ event class: 'fndr'                 │
│ event id: 'slep'                    │
│ application signature of target app:│
│ 'MACS'                              │
└─────────────────────────────────────┘
```

Figure 1-4: A sleep Apple event

Every Apple event is comprised of unique four-character codes that represent the:

- Event class

- Event id

- Address of the target application

The event class represents a grouping of similar Apple events. The event id uniquely identifies the Apple event. The target address is a complex data structure that could contain the application's creator code or its Process Serial Number (PSN) or another piece of identifying information. For example, the *sleep* Apple event has event class 'fndr' and event id 'slep'. Table 1-2 contains the event classes and event ids for the Standard Suite in the Apple Event Registry. Apple events often get reorganized within different suites when Apple updates its Registry.

Table 1-2: Apple Event Codes for Standard Suite

Event	Event Class	Event Id	Class	Class Id
open	aevt	odoc	application	capp
run	aevt	oapp	document	docu
reopen	aevt	rapp	file	file
print	aevt	pdoc	alias	alis
quit	aevt	quit	selection-object	csel
close	core	clos	window	cwin
count	core	cnte	insertion-point	cins
delete	core	delo		
duplicate	core	clon		
exist	core	doex		
make	core	crel		
move	core	move		
save	core	save		

Most of the time, however, a scripter does not have to deal with event classes and event ids, just their AppleScript language equivalents.

Apple events specify the target programs that should receive the Apple event. Otherwise, your script would cause an execution or runtime error, because the operating system does not know where the Apple event is supposed to go.

The common way to specify the target programs for an Apple event in Apple-Script is to use a code such as in Example 1-2. You enclose the Apple events you will send to a program within the tell block, as in Example 1-2, which sends a quit Apple event to "FileMaker Pro".

Example 1-2: A Script Targeting FileMaker Pro

```
tell application "FileMaker Pro"
   quit
end tell
```

The value of the application signature attribute in Figure 1-4 is also a four-character code ('MACS' for the Finder), just like the event class and event id. You might recognize this code as the Finder's creator code.

 Each Macintosh file is distinguished by its file type (for example, a text file has file type "TEXT") and creator code (BBEdit's is "R*ch"). This is how the operating system knows which program to open when you double-click a desktop file. It examines the file's creator code.

Apple Event Parameters

Sometimes a lone Apple event like *quit* or *activate* will do the trick in a script. At other times, Apple events have to specify Apple event *parameters*. These are the data the receiver of the Apple event needs to carry out the Apple event's instructions. For instance, if the Example 1-3 script did not include the parameter:

```
file "mydocument"
```

then the OS 9 Finder would return an error, because its *open* Apple event requires a reference to the object(s) to open.

Example 1-3: A Finder open Command

```
tell application "Finder"
   (*open is the command; file "mydocument" is the parameter *)
   open file "mydocument"
end tell
```

 Examples in this book will usually include comments explaining code elements. Comment characters in AppleScript are two hyphens (--) for single-line comments and parentheses containing asterisk characters (* *) for multi-line or single-line comments.

Figure 1-5 illustrates the Finder's *open* Apple event with the reference to the *mydocument* file.

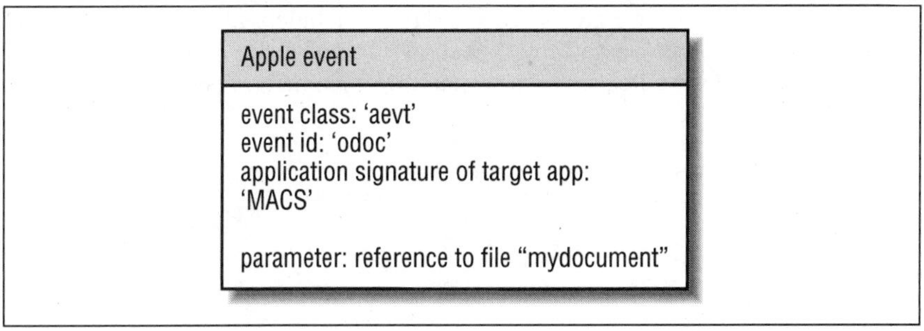

```
┌─────────────────────────────────────────────┐
│  Apple event                                  │
├─────────────────────────────────────────────┤
│  event class: 'aevt'                          │
│  event id: 'odoc'                             │
│  application signature of target app:         │
│  'MACS'                                        │
│                                               │
│  parameter: reference to file "mydocument"    │
└─────────────────────────────────────────────┘
```

Figure 1-5: The Finder's open Apple event

Apple event parameters can include standard data types (e.g., `integer` or `string`) or references to Apple event objects, such as a document file. Apple event objects are the items or "nouns" (e.g., a file, a folder, a database record) that some scripts interact with. See the following "Apple Event Classes and Objects" section for further explanation on handling objects in your scripts.

An Apple event can have more than one required or optional parameter. In another example, if you want your script to tell FileMaker Pro to create a new row in a database, then *create* is the Apple event (followed by the required keyword `new`). The *create* Apple event requires a parameter such as a `record` object (as in a database record or row). Otherwise, how would the database program know what you wanted to create?

The code in Example 1-4 opens a database file and then creates a new record with empty fields.

Example 1-4: Getting FileMaker to Create a New Database Row

```
tell application "FileMaker Pro"
   activate --brings the target application to the front
   open file "startupdisk:fm databases:myDB.fm4"
   create new record - "record" is the parameter
end tell
```

Example 1-4 could use the *create* command's optional `with data` parameter to fill the new row with data, thus creating a complete database record.

Apple Event Classes and Objects

You have read about Apple events, which are action words or verbs (*activate*, *delete*). Apple event classes (and the objects that are based on those classes) are the nouns that your script might want to manipulate in some manner (see Table 1-3). Example 1-2 told the Finder to open a file object (basically, a file on the desktop). Objects are the data or "things" that you are interested in querying or changing when you send an Apple event to a program.

For example, a script that controls a database program usually deals with database, field, record, or cell objects. An AppleScript that sends commands to a text editor works with character, word, paragraph, and document objects.

These Apple event objects are based on classes or blueprints, such as the `file` class or the **database** class. Table 1-3 shows some of the Apple event classes from the Apple Event Registry. The operating system represents these classes internally as four-character codes.

Table 1-3: Examples of Apple Event Classes in OS 9

Class	Four-Character Code
character	'cha '
disk	'cdis'
document	'docu'
file	'file'
folder	'cfol'
paragraph	'cpar'
text	'ctxt'
window	'cwin'
word	'cwor'

A class is a blueprint or data type for a noun or object that you can manipulate with a script.

When an architect creates a blueprint for a structure, all the homes that are subsequently built off of the blueprint are the offspring of her original design. The real wooden, brick, or metallic homes are "instances" (in object-oriented parlance) or objects of the blueprint or class. The architect creates a home class in her blueprint, then the builders generate real home objects based on the original class. For example, the BBEdit text editor defines a word class, which is a bunch of characters that are unbroken by a space, tab, or new-line character (e.g., "apple"). The five characters that make up the word (a,p,p,l,e) are all objects based on the BBEdit character class. So a word object constitutes a group of character objects. If you grouped together several separate character objects they might look like ("a", "p", "p", "l", "e").

For example, when you get the Finder to open a folder with a phrase like:

```
open folder "my_folder"
```

then you are telling the Finder to open the folder object (based on the folder class) whose name is "my_folder." This line of code will specifically create a Finder window showing the contents of the folder called "my_folder."

It is always important to describe an Apple event object in your script by its containment hierarchy, which is an exact specification of where an application like the Finder can find the object. Apple event objects are located in a similar manner to taking apart one of those wooden Russian dolls, where the dolls get smaller and smaller until you finally locate the last solid peanut-shaped doll inside of all the bigger ones. In other words, if you wanted to get information about the sender of the first message in your Outlook Express inbox folder, then you couldn't just tell Outlook to:

```
get the sender of the first message
```

because the emailer would not know where to look (i.e., in the "inbox" folder) for the email message. Consider Example 1-5, which *incompletely* describes the containment hierarchy for a file (assuming that the file is not located on the desktop).

Example 1-5: A File-Access Script That Causes an Error

```
tell application "Finder"
   open file "taxes2000"
end tell
```

The Finder cannot find this file because the script does not give a complete container reference, as in:

```
open file "taxes2000" of folder "Taxes" of startup disk
```

The script will therefore produce a dialog box reporting an error if it is run.

AppleScript has a number of ways to express containment relationships.

```
file "taxes2000" of folder "Taxes" of startup disk
```

(an "inside-out" reference). This is like describing the smallest Russian doll as "the tiny doll inside the slightly bigger doll that is contained by all the larger dolls." Or, you can use a possessive form such as:

```
startup disk's (folder "Taxes"'s file "taxes2000")
```

Using the possessive style with long container references like this one is usually less readable than the inside-out method.

Elements and Properties

Two other very important characteristics of Apple event objects are *elements* and *properties*. The class that these objects are based on defines the object's elements and properties. An object has zero or more of its defined elements, and exactly one each of its properties.

For example, SoundJam™ MP, a digital music player and encoder, defines a `playlist window` class. These objects are windows that contain lists of audio tracks that can play on the computer. Figure 1-6 shows the definition of the `playlist window` class from SoundJam's dictionary. (Chapter 2 explains a program's dictionary, which can be viewed by using Script Editor's File → Open Dictionary menu command.) A `playlist window` object has three elements: `track`, `file track`, and `URL track`. Further, `playlist windows` have a modified property (a `true` or `false` value depending on whether the window was modified since it was last saved). `playlist windows` also inherit several properties from SoundJam™ MP's `window` class. So a `playlist window` object can contain zero or more "track" elements, but it only has exactly one "modified" property value.

Rest assured that it is easy to grab the values of elements and properties in Apple-Script. You can use syntax such as:

```
tell app "SoundJam™ MP" to get first file track of first playlist window
```

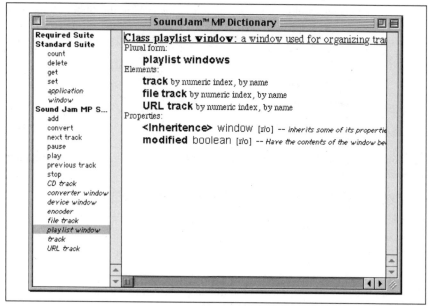

Figure 1-6: playlist window's elements/properties

This code sends SoundJam™ a *get* Apple event requesting a reference to an element, such as the first file track (an MP3 audio file) in the foremost playlist window that you see when SoundJam™ MP is open. The return value looks like:

```
'file track id 4 of playlist window id 5 of application "SoundJam™ MP"'
```

Once your script gets a reference to a track, it can then command SoundJam™ MP to play it with (you guessed it) the *play* Apple event that SoundJam™ MP defines.

Our introduction to Apple events concludes with a description of the all-important `application` class, which is the "king of the objects" in a scriptable program. The program that you script, such as application "SoundJam™ MP," is actually an object itself, an "instance" of the SoundJam™ MP `application` class.

Application Class

Many scriptable applications define an `application` class, which is the gem to study if you want to automate that program. Your quickest route to the `application` class is its description in the program's dictionary. We mentioned before that Mac programs can expose an *object model* to scripting components like AppleScript. An object model is a software abstraction, usually in tree-like form, showing the Apple event objects and Apple events that you can use with a program.

The `application` class is the root or top-level class in the program's object model. An Apple-event object model shows the `application` class and all of its elements and properties (if it has any defined elements). Figure 1-7 shows a simple object model for Sherlock 2, the Mac's fancy Find program. Sherlock 2 has three properties and contains zero or more `channel` elements. (I am sticking to the strict definition of an object's elements, which is that an object can have zero or more of them. In reality, Sherlock 2 always has at least one defined `channel`, which is the domain that it is searching.)

`channel` elements are themselves objects with their own properties: "all search sites" and "name" (e.g., the name of one `channel` is "Internet"). When in doubt about how to script a program, always use the program's dictionary to examine its `application` class. The elements and properties of the `application` class are the things that you will be able to control and derive values from with your AppleScripts.

If you are on friendly terms with an illustration tool, then it helps to sketch out an object model of a program you are trying to script.

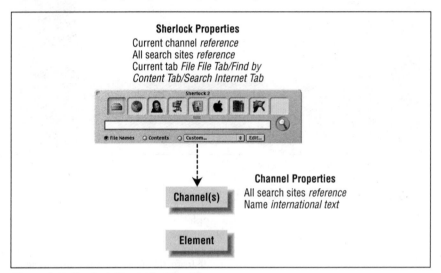

Figure 1-7: Sherlock 2's application class

Using Script Runner with OS X

OS X has a little application called Script Runner that you can use to run your scripts. Figure 1-8 shows what the open Script Runner looks like on the OS X desktop. You can find Script Runner in the AppleScript folder inside the Applications folder. Open the program by double-clicking it. If you want to add your own scripts to the Script Runner menu, choose "Open Scripts Folder" from the Script Runner menu. This opens a Finder window on to the following directory: */Users/ yourname/Library/Scripts/.* Then drag any compiled scripts (they have to be saved as compiled scripts) into this window. You can of course add compiled scripts to this */Scripts* folder by navigating to it yourself (i.e., not using the Script Runner "Open Scripts Folder" menu command). After you close and restart Script Runner, you can run these scripts by choosing them in the Script Runner menu. If you create folders in the */Scripts* folder, then Script Runner will display these folders as sub-menus. This is a good way to categorize and present lots of different scripts in the Script Runner menu.

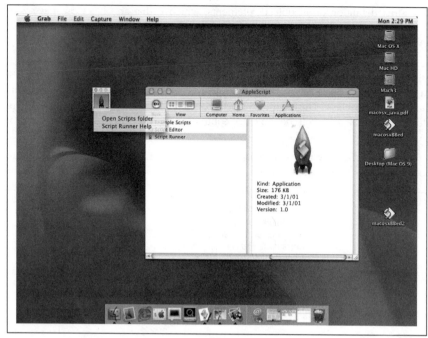

Figure 1-8: Script Runner on OS X

Using OSA Menu with OS 9

I mentioned previously that you can run AppleScripts from within Script Editor or save them as applets that can be double-clicked. In Mac OS 9, an application called OSA Menu gives you a third script running option. OSA Menu is a non-Apple system extension that you can install from the OS 9 installation CD-ROM (you can find it in the folder *CD Extras:AppleScript Extras*). OSA Menu adds its own menu to the upper-right corner of the OS 9 Finder or desktop. Figure 1-9 shows the OSA Menu after it has been activated.

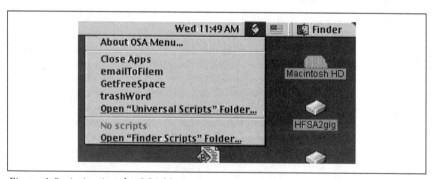

Figure 1-9: Activating the OSA Menu

The OSA Menu shows a list of compiled scripts that can be run straight from the desktop by choosing their filenames from the menu. OSA Menu will show the scripts that are stored in the following folder in OS 9: *startup disk:System Folder:Scripts:Universal Scripts*. To run properly from this menu, however, the AppleScripts have to be saved in Script Editor as compiled scripts, not applets. Chapter 2 contains more information on these script-saving options.

Checking Your AppleScript Version

This introduction would not be complete without mentioning how important it is to check which version of AppleScript is running on the machine executing your scripts. This is particularly true if your script is used on computers that might not be running Mac OS 9 or later. New versions of AppleScript are generally released along with the latest generation of the operating system. Mac OS 9 contains Apple-Script Version 1.4 (an updated version of AppleScript, Version 1.4.3, also runs on OS 9). In the Spring of 2001, Mac OS 9.1 and Mac OS X used AppleScript 1.6.

There is an extremely simple way to find out which version of AppleScript is installed on the machine where the script is running. Checking the value of the version property in Script Editor will return the version number, as in `1.4` in Mac OS 9 or `1.3.4` in Mac OS 8.5. If you do not understand certain aspects of this script, Part II of the book is a detailed AppleScript language reference.

Your script can check the version property with code such as that shown in Example 1-6.

Example 1-6: Checking the AppleScript Version Number

```
set ASversion to version as string -- initialize ASversion to a string
set ASversion to (characters 1 thru 3 of ASversion as string) as real (*
coerce ASversion to a real number like 1.4 *)
if ASversion is greater than or equal to 1.4 then (* test whether the version
value is ≥ 1.4 *)
    display dialog "Good, you're running at least AppleScript 1.4" (* give the
user some feedback with a dialog box *)
else
    display dialog "You're running AppleScript " & ASversion
end if
```

Example 1-6 first gets the AppleScript version property as a **string** value (e.g., `"1.4"`) and stores it in an **ASversion** variable. The first three characters of this variable (such as `1.3` if the version was `1.3.4`) are then coerced to a **real** type, as in `1.3`. We had to take just the first three characters of the **string** because a **string** with two decimal points in it, as in `1.3.7`, cannot be coerced to a **real** value (since a **string** with two dots in it is an invalid representation of a number). Chapter 3 discusses the **real** data type.

This numerical value is then checked to see if the user is running at least Apple-Script 1.4. The script uses the *display dialog* scripting addition to display information to the user about the found *version* value. You can also check the version property of the Finder, and other applications that have this property, by first targeting the application in a **tell** statement, as in Example 1-7.

Example 1-7: Displaying the Finder Version Number

```
tell application "Finder"
    set fVersion to version as string
    display dialog "You're running Finder version " & fVersion
end tell
```

Diving In

No doubt there are readers who are eager to dive into AppleScripting before they go on to this book's upcoming language reference. This section summarizes the important AppleScript language elements you need to know before you start coding:

- Case sensitivity
- Statement termination
- Line continuation character
- Naming identifiers or variables
- Variable declaration
- Comments
- Data types
- Operators and reference forms
- Flow-control statements
- Subroutines
- Script objects and libraries

All of these language elements are described in more detail in Part II (except for case sensitivity and statement termination, which are taken care of adequately in the following sections).

Case Sensitivity

Unlike other scripting languages such as JavaScript and Perl, AppleScript is not case-sensitive. In other words, MYVAR is the same as myvar, or *myfunc* is the same as *MyFunc* in terms of function definitions. Script Editor will not let you define two functions with the same name, even if their letters are different combinations of upper- and lowercase characters. The numerous AppleScript constants and reserved words (case, current application, and other constants are covered in Chapter 6, *Variables and Constants*) cannot be reused as your own variable or method names. A script can change the values of predefined variables such as pi or space; however, scripters are better off using these predefined variables for the variables' intended purpose and creating their own variable names. Script Editor sees "pi" and "PI" as the same thing ("PI" would be corrected to "pi" when you compile the script). Class and command names within applications, while mostly lowercase, are corrected when you compile the script to the spelling that is specified in the app's dictionary. (Chapter 2 explains an application's dictionary.) For instance, if you typed the class name tcpip v4 configuration into Script Editor, inside of a *tell app "Network Setup Scripting"* block, it would be corrected to "TCPIP v4 configuration" when the statement was compiled.

Statement Termination

You don't have to terminate an AppleScript statement using any special characters, as you do with Perl (the semi-colon character). You do, however, have to
complete each statement on a line before you go on to the next statement, unless
you use the continuation character (¬).

Line Continuation Character

You can split a very long statement into several lines by typing *Option-Return* on
the Macintosh. This produces a continuation character (¬). This character only
affects how the code looks in Script Editor and is not part of the compiled code. If
you store a `string` literal in a variable, however, and add a continuation character to the middle of the literal `string`, then this character becomes a visible part
of the compiled `string` of characters (you usually want to avoid this). Splitting
long code statements with the continuation character makes the script more readable. You will use this character often.

Naming Identifiers or Variables and Functions

The names that you create for variables and functions have to begin with a letter
or underscore character (_), but subsequent characters can include letters,
numbers, and underscores. In variables or function names, you cannot include
AppleScript's reserved words and operators such as *, &, ^, or + (covered in
Chapter 4, *Operators*) or special characters such as $, @, or #. An exception to this
AppleScript rule allows for the creation of weird variable or function names if you
use vertical bars (|) to begin and end the identifier, as in: `set |2^$var| to 25`.
The variable `|2^$var|` is actually valid. If you wanted to create the equivalent of
a Perl scalar variable in AppleScript, you could use: `set |$perlVar| to 25`.
There is no practical limit to the size of AppleScript variable names; that is, you
can have a variable name that has up to 251 characters, but you would never want
to deal with variable names that long. In my OS 9 testing, a variable name that
exceeded 251 characters produced the error dialog in Figure 1-10.

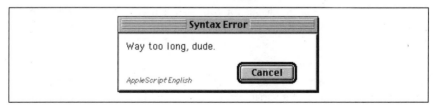

Figure 1-10: Script Editor signals a variable name that's too long

Variable Declaration

You can use either the `set` or `copy` keywords to declare a variable and assign a
value to it, as in the following examples:

```
set myvar to (5 * 25)
copy (5 * 25) to myvar
```

Both of these statements produce the same result; they store the integer 125 in the myvar variable. The set version however is more intuitive and is used more often to declare variables. set and copy furthermore have different results when you use the variable to contain a list, record, or script object. (Chapter 9, *Script Objects and Libraries*, discusses this AppleScript feature.) The copy keyword, as in:

```
copy listVar to newListVar
```

will make a new copy of the list value stored in listVar and store this new list in newListVar. If you used:

```
set newListVar to listVar
```

the list stored in newListVar will still refer to the original list (i.e., listVar). The newListVar variable will not get a new copy of the list when you use set. Chapter 6 goes further into this set and copy subject.

Comments

Comments are the descriptions that you add to the code as reminders to yourself and guidance to other coders; they are not part of the executable script. Apple-Script uses two or more dashes (--) preceding the comment text for single-line comments and (* *) surrounding the comment text for single- or multi-line comments. Using dashes, you can have a comment on the same line as some code, such as:

```
set myvar to 10 -- initialize myvar to 10.
```

AppleScript does not use the popular slash-slash (//) single-line comment characters of Java or C++.

Data Types

Like most scripting tools, AppleScript is a "loosely typed" programming language. This means that for the most part you do not have to specify exactly how the computer will store some data when you set a variable to a value. AppleScript takes care (or tries to) of the details for you. So when you use the code fragment: [set num to 75], AppleScript knows that num is an integer or number. If you use:

```
set numstr to "I'm a string"
```

numstr is automatically stored as a string. This feature does not forbid you from specifying the data type of a variable, which is a good idea in many situations and creates more readable code. If you want to explicitly set a variable to an Apple-Script data type, use the as keyword, as in get current date as string. If you want to ensure that a number will be stored as a real data type, use code such as:

```
set num to 75.0
```

This code sets the variable num to a real data type, which is a very large number that can include a decimal point, similar to a double type in Java. A program can now increment or increase the variable num to a much higher number than it could if it were left as an `integer`, which has a range of –536,870,911 to 536,870,911, inclusive. What if you wanted to have a variable keep track over time of the number of people on Earth who are connected to the Web? This number would eventually exceed one billion, so you would want to use a variable of a `real` data type.

However, explicitly setting data types in AppleScript is also a potentially error-prone strategy if you are not careful in your script planning. For example, the code: `set num to 1.5 as integer` will compile but raise an error once the script is run. The error message is "Can't make 1.5 into an integer." If you left the `as integer` part out of the code fragment, then AppleScript would automatically set num to a `real` data type and no error would occur.

The following list briefly describes the other principal data types that Apple-Scripters should be aware of (these are all covered in more detail in Chapter 3):

boolean
> The literal words true or false, or an expression that evaluates to true or false. AppleScript does not treat other types of "true- or false-type" values, such as 0 or 1, as boolean values. Example 1-8 shows two ways to derive and store boolean values in AppleScript.

Example 1-8: Boolean Values in AppleScript

```
set bool to false -- bool is a boolean data type
set bool to (5 > 3)
(* bool is a boolean because the expression "(5 > 3)" evaluates to true *)
```

date
> Set a variable to a date value with code such as:
>
> > `set theDate to date "12/5/2000"`
>
> Remember to use the `date` keyword followed by the `date string` ("12/5/ 2000"), or the `theDate` variable is stored as a `string` type. A common error is to type something like `set the Date to "12/5/2000"`, which stores a `string` data type in `theDate`, not the `date` value that the scripter is aiming for. A lot of scripts get an initial date value from the useful scripting addition *current date*. When this command is used in a script, it returns a `date` object representing the current date and time, as in:
>
> > `date "Tuesday, December 05, 2000 12:00:00 AM"`
>
> Appendix A, *Standard Scripting Additions,* describes the *current date* command.

String
> A series of letters, spaces, numbers, or other characters delimited by double-quote marks, as in "c" or "Here is a longer string" or "" (an empty string, but a valid string nonetheless). Suffice it to say, you deal with strings all the time in AppleScript as you read data from or write data to files, database records, and other storage media. AppleScript does not allow you to define a string with single quotation marks; you have to use double quotes. Once you have a string type, then you can get its length property (an integer), which is the

number of characters that are in a string. You can use a phrase such as current date as string whose return value looks like:

```
"Tuesday, December 05, 2000 2:59:30 PM"
```

A `string` also has several elements such as words. The code fragment:

```
words of "four score and seven years ago"
```

returns a `list` type of all the words in the string (i.e., `{"four"`, `"score"`, `"and"`, `"seven"`, `"years"`, `"ago"}`). You can concatenate two strings to make one string using the concatenation character ("&").

List

Called an array in other languages like Perl or Java. In AppleScript, you can store values of several different data types, including strings, numbers, and other lists, in the same list. Example 1-9 stores a string, a number, a list, and the pi predefined variable in the same list. You can see how incredibly useful this data type is; you will deal with lists *all* the time as an AppleScripter.

Example 1-9: AppleScript List Type

```
set myString to "A list that stores a string, a number, a list, and a ¬
constant."
set myList to {myString,75.0,{1,2,3},pi}
(* Return value of this script:
{"A list that stores a string, a number, a list, and a constant.", 75.0,
{1, 2, 3}, 3.14159265359}
*)
```

Lists are surrounded by curly braces (`{ }`), and a comma separates each list member. Variables that contain values, such as `myString` in Example 1-9, can also be stored in lists. Lists have three properties: `length`, `rest`, and `reverse`. `length` returns the number of list members, as in 4 for the list in Example 1-9. `rest` returns all the list members except for the first one, so the return value of `rest` of `myList` (from Example 1-9) would be `{75.0, {1, 2, 3}, 3.14159265359}`. Finally, `reverse` gives you the list with all of its members displayed in reverse order, as in:

```
{3.14159265359, {1, 2, 3}, 75.0, "A list that stores a string, a
number, a list, and a constant."}
```

You can obtain a member of a list by using the syntax item and the indexed position of the list member, as in:

```
item 4 of myList
```

This code returns the value 3.14159265359. Lists are one-based, meaning that the first list member is located at position 1, not 0 as in other languages' array implementations. Finally, you can concatenate or combine two lists by using the & operator. In Example 1-9, the code:

```
myList & "Another string"
```

attaches `"Another string"` to the `myList` list variable and makes it the last list member.

Record

A record consists of a series of name/value pairs separated by commas and surrounded by curly braces. Perl would call this an associative array, or Visual Basic would call it a collection. Examples are {name: "AppleScript In a Nutshell", subject:"AppleScript"} and {first:"Bruce"}. You can refer to the members of a record by the property name, as in:

```
subject of {name: "AppleScript In a Nutshell", subject:"AppleScript"}
```

This returns "AppleScript". Records do not have item elements, so you cannot use the code item 1 of {first:"Bruce"}. You can change or coerce a record into a list, thus altering the data type of the value. An example is:

```
set nw to {name: "AppleScript In a Nutshell", subject: & ¬
"AppleScript"} as list
```

The return value loses all the property names from the original record: {"AppleScript In a Nutshell", "AppleScript"}.

Operators and Reference Forms

An operator is a symbol or token that is used with values or variables in an Apple-Script expression. An example is the well-worn expression 2 + 2 = 4 (if you just dropped this expression into a Script Editor window, it would return a boolean value of true). The operators in this expression are "+" and "=". AppleScript has most of the operators that you would expect a scripting language to make available to the programmer. AppleScript also allows the scripter to use very readable English expressions for operators, such as:

```
if 5 is greater than 3 and 6 equals 6 then set bool to true
```

The principal symbolic operators are demonstrated in Example 1-10. All operators, including the English forms, are described in Chapter 4.

Example 1-10: AppleScript Operators

```
(* & concatenates one string to another, or combines two or more lists or
records *)
set twoPhrases to "One phrase " & "connected to another phrase."

(* the following code returns {"a string inside of a list", "added at the end
of a sentence."} *)
set twoLists to {"a string inside of a list"} & {"added at the end of a
sentence."}
(* & also combines two records to make one record. *)
set twoRecs to {firstn:"Amanda"} & {secondn:"Smith"}

(* parentheses and Math operators do what you would expect them to *)
set int to (5 * 6) - 8 -- returns 22

(*If you use / or ÷ the result is always a real data type. If you use div the
result is always an integer *)
set n1 to 50 / 26   -- returns 1.923076923077
set n2 to 50 ÷ 26   -- returns 1.923076923077
set n3 to 50 div 26  -- returns 1; div only returns integer data types
```

Example 1-10: AppleScript Operators (continued)

```
(* < ≤ > ≥ ≠ = are used to test equality *)
set bool to 50 < 26 -- bool is false
set bool to 50 > 26 -- bool is true
set bool to 50 = 26 -- bool is false
set bool to 50 ≠ 26 -- bool is true


(* ^ is the exponentiation operator *)
set n1 to 50 ^ 2 -- n1 is 2500.0, a real data type


(* mod returns the fractional part and throws out the rest of the integer
part, the opposite of div which throws out the fractional part *)
set n2 to 7 mod 3 -- n2 is 1


(* not, or, and are boolean operators; they are used to combine two
expressions
to produce a boolean result *)
set bool to true and false -- bool is false
set bool to true or false -- bool is true
set bool to not true -- bool is false
set bool to (2 + 2 = 4) and (not (2 ^ 2 = 4)) (* you can combine expressions
to get a result; bool is false in this case because the second part of the
expression (i.e., (not (2 ^ 2 = 4)) ) evaluates to false *)
```

A *reference form* is an English or symbolic expression that describes where a value is within its container. As an AppleScripter, you will often find yourself describing contained objects in order to accomplish your task, such as "get the first record in the database named myDB" or, "get the second paragraph of the last document in the folder named January Stuff." AppleScript offers numerous ways to refer to these contained items. Chapter 4 goes into great detail in describing these methods, which are demonstrated in short by Example 1-11. For example, you can describe contained items by referring to the first-tenth item, then with anything that requires a reference that exceeds 10 you use the number, as in: get the 1000th word of document "Mydocument".

Example 1-11: Different Ways to Refer to Contained Items

```
tell application "Finder" to get the folder after (the 20th folder of startup
disk)
(* gets the folder object after the 20th folder on the startup disk *)
tell application "Finder" to get the folder after the 20th folder of ¬
startup disk
tell application "Finder" to get the folder before the 20th folder of ¬
startup disk
```

You can create very useful and detailed scripts using AppleScript's numerous reference forms. Example 1-12 gets only one part of a list of numbers (i.e., the numbers 3 through 6) and stores this sub-section in another list variable. The following section briefly describes the repeat and if...end if statements that appear here.

Example 1-12: Using the Range Reference Form

```
set list1 to {1, 2, 3, 4, 5, 6}
set list2 to (numbers 3 thru 6 in list1) -- returns only {3,4,5,6}
```

Flow-Control Statements

AppleScript includes syntax that you can use to test expressions and only have some code execute if certain conditions are met, as well as loop through code statements and then exit from the loop. These programming constructs are often called *flow-control statements*. These statements are covered extensively in Chapter 7.

Like many other programming languages, AppleScript uses an if...then... else...end if statement to test various expressions. AppleScript also has an if simple statement and an if compound statement (one that extends over several lines). For example, you can use code such as:

```
if numVar > 1000 then return 1000
```

on one line without including any end ifs. Example 1-13 includes both types of if statements.

AppleScript uses several variations of the **repeat** statement to loop through code (see Example 1-13). **Repeat** is AppleScript's version of the for (;;;) or while… or foreach… loops of other languages like Perl or Java. AppleScripters often use **repeat** to loop through the values of a list. For example, the code:

```
repeat with m in listVar...end repeat
```

will loop through all of the list members stored in the variable listVar. Within the loop, the iterator variable m will sequentially contain each list-member value. Example 1-13 includes several versions of the **repeat** and if...end if statements.

Example 1-13: AppleScript if and repeat Statements

```
set userNum to 75.66
 (* compound if statement *)
if the class of userNum is real then
   display dialog "It's a real number."
else if the class of userNum is integer then
   display dialog "It's an integer."
else
 (* you can include a final else as part of the test; in this case it is not
necessary *)
end if

(* simple if statement *)
if userNum is greater than 100 then display dialog "The value exceeds 100."

(* various repeat loop variations *)
repeat 10 times
   set userNum to userNum + 1
end repeat
```

Example 1-13: AppleScript if and repeat Statements (continued)

```
(* endless loop without 'exit repeat' *)
repeat
   exit repeat -- this loop only iterates once because of exit
end repeat

repeat while userNum < 10000
   set userNum to userNum * 2
end repeat

(* if the statement following 'until' evaluates to 'true' then the repeat
statements are not executed *)

repeat until userNum >100000
   exit repeat (* this exits from this loop right away; you could do
something else if you wanted to *)
end repeat

set myList to {1,2,3,4}
(* repeat statement that iterates over list contents *)
repeat with mem in myList
   set userNum to userNum + mem
end repeat

(* A different kind of repeat loop *)
repeat with loopVar from 2 to 10 by 2 (* loop circles five times; loopVar
is 2,4,6,8,10 *)
   --do something here
end repeat
```

Another important statement construct in AppleScript provides the language with error-trapping capability. It is called the `try` statement, and looks like `try...on error...end try`. `try` is similar to Java's `try...catch()` statement. If you enclose a series of AppleScript statements in a `try` block and one of them raises an error, AppleScript will "catch" the error and allow you to deal with it in a responsible manner. Without using a `try` statement, a run-time error will cause a script to display an error message, and then terminate the script execution. Example 1-14 demonstrates how to use the `try` block. Again, Chapter 7 thoroughly describes these statements and others.

Example 1-14: Trapping Errors with try

```
try
   set aNum to (text returned of (display dialog ¬
      "Enter a number." default answer ""))
   set aNum to aNum as real
on error errmsg
   display dialog "It looks like you did not enter a number: " & errmsg
end try
```

Subroutines

Subroutines are code units that can be used over and over again throughout the script once they are defined in the AppleScript program. They are essentially user-defined commands. Subroutines or handlers in AppleScript can be called with or without parameters, similar to functions in other languages. The subroutine can return a value to the calling script or simply perform a task and exit without returning a value. You can do almost whatever you want in a subroutine (except define another subroutine within it), including declare and initialize variables and call other functions. Example 1-15 creates a simpler way of producing a character from its ASCII decimal number equivalent. It calls the *ASCII character* scripting addition to produce the value.

Example 1-15: Simple AppleScript User-Defined Subroutine

```
set let to chr(67)-- the variable is set to 'C'
on chr(int)
    return ASCII character int
end chr
```

To define a subroutine in AppleScript, use the keyword on followed by the subroutine name, an opening parenthesis character, one or more optional variables that represents any subroutine arguments, and a closing parenthesis. If you have more than one parameter, then separate them with commas. Subroutines that do not have any parameters require empty parentheses, as in on chr(). The end chr part, or simply end, is also required (Script Editor will automatically add the name of the subroutine after end if you forget to do it yourself). Whatever you want the subroutine to do is defined within the on char()...end block. A return statement will immediately return from the subroutine, and it will optionally return a value, as in return "finished" (the subroutine would return a string "finished"). You can pass objects (such as dates) to a subroutine as parameter values. Example 1-16 returns the difference in days between two dates.

Example 1-16: Getting the Difference Between Two Dates

```
set dayDiff to getDiff(current date, date "Sunday, January 1, 1984 12:00:00
AM")
on getDiff(date1, date2)
    if date1 > date2 then
        return ((date1 - date2) / (24 * 60 * 60))
    else
    (* if the dates are equal then the subroutine returns 0.0 *)
        return ((date2 - date1) / (24 * 60 * 60))
    end if
end getDiff
```

Subtracting one AppleScript date object from another returns the difference between the two dates in seconds. This subroutine processes the seconds to return the difference in days (the result is a real data type, so it might look like 6185. 835706018518, which is almost 6,186 days). Example 1-15 and Example 1-16 both show that you can call a subroutine higher up in a script than where its definition appears.

Script Objects

Script objects give AppleScript very basic object-oriented features, including inheritance. A script object is defined in a script-code block that looks a little like a subroutine definition. Script objects are created within a script with the `script` [script name]...end script syntax. Example 1-17 contains a simple script object definition. The object has two methods: one returns a property value and the other method increments the value of the property by one. The bottom of the script creates two copies of this object then calls its methods and displays the results.

Example 1-17: Creating a Script Object

```
(* begin the script object definition *)
script Test
    property myval : 0 -- one integer property
    on getVal() -- define a method
        return myval -- return the prop value
    end getVal
    on upVal() -- define another method
        set myval to myval + 1 -- increment myval property  by one
    end upVal
end script -- end script object definition
copy Test to t1 -- create new Test object
copy Test to t2 -- create another, different Test object
(* two ways to call an object's methods *)
tell t1 to upVal()
t2's upVal()
t2's upVal() (* t2's upVal method is called twice, setting its myval property
to 2 *)
set theMessage to "t1: " & (t1's getVal() as string) (* find out the two
object's property values *)
set theMessage to theMessage & return & "t2: " & (t2's getVal() as string)
display dialog theMessage
```

You may have noticed the use of the keyword `copy` to create the two `Test` objects in Example 1-17. The `copy` keyword creates a new copy of the object and stores it in the named variable, as in [copy Test to t1]. If the script used set t1 to Test and set t2 to Test, then the variable t2 would not have a new copy of the Test object. It would refer to the same Test object (and the same myval property) as the t1 variable.

Libraries present a real-world use of script objects. A library, which is a type of script object, can be one or more method definitions stored as a compiled script. To use the library's methods, load it into the script with the *load script* scripting addition (Example 1-18 and Example 1-19 demonstrate this).

Example 1-18: Defining a Library

```
(* define some methods and save as an applet or compiled script;
the file name of the script is "farewell"
*)
on sayGoodbye()
```

Example 1-18: Defining a Library (continued)

```
    display dialog "Goodbye"
end sayGoodbye
on sayCiao()
    display dialog "Ciao"
end sayCiao
```

Now load the library into any old script by providing its file path (where the script is saved on the computer) as a parameter to the *load script* scripting addition.

Example 1-19: Using a Library

```
set bye to load script "macintosh hd:desktop folder:farewell"
  (* call library methods *)
bye's sayGoodbye()
bye's sayCiao()
```

Chapter 9 goes into much greater depth on script objects.

CHAPTER 2

Using Script Editor with OS 9 and OS X

Unless you decide to use a commercial development environment to create scripts, the free Script Editor will be your principal AppleScripting tool.* This is fine; many AppleScript purists have clung to Script Editor and still find it easy to use, even though it hasn't changed that much in years. Besides, it's free with the Mac OS 9 and OS X installation. You can find Script Editor in the */Applications/AppleScript* folder in Mac OS X; in OS 9, this application is located in *startup disk:Apple Extras:AppleScript.*

Script Editor is particularly useful for creating the first versions of scripts using the Finder in OS 9. You can record most tasks involving the Finder (such as an action involving a file, folder, or disk), and then make any manual changes later in Script Editor. Chapter 1, *AppleScript: An Introduction,* describes the recording of scripts.

The rest of this chapter is devoted to explaining the principal commands and controls of this program. I will also describe some basic scripting mechanics such as file-saving options and describe how to view dictionaries. The chapter concludes with an example applet that turns around and controls its creator.

Figure 2-1 shows what the Script Editor and its Results window (which displays the return values for its executed code) look like on the OS X desktop. The Script Editor includes controls and menus to:

- Compile, save, and run AppleScripts
- Record Apple events from recordable applications
- Debug scripts with the Event Log and Result window
- View other application's dictionaries (see the section "Dictionaries")

---

* Smile is a free AppleScript tool that can be downloaded from *http://www.tandb.com.au/ smile*. Three commercial development environments are Digital Technology International's FaceSpan, Main Event Software's Scripter, and Late Night Software Ltd.'s Script Debugger. Script Editor 1.6 has also been made available for Mac OS 9.1.

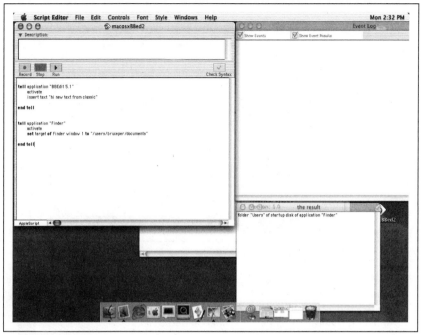

Figure 2-1: Script Editor on OS X

Script Editor Controls/Commands

The Script window, shown in Figure 2-2 (from the OS 9 desktop) is where you edit and compile code. The other windows that are displayed and used by this program are dictionary windows, Event Log, and Result window (all these are discussed later in this chapter). The title bar of the window contains the name of the script next to a script icon that indicates which file type you saved it as (e.g., compiled script, applet). In Mac OS 9.1 and Mac OS X (i.e., AppleScript 1.5 and later), if you drag that icon to a disk folder the script will be moved to that folder.

 All menu commands and windows attributed to Script Editor for OS 9 are replicated without any changes in OS X, except for the fact that the OS X Script Editor has been redesigned for the Aqua interface.

The following list describes the parts of the Script window:

1. *Description field.* The text area at the top of the script window is called the description field. This space assumes the role of a global comment area for the script. You can use this area to type in information about a script's purpose, its properties, its functions, the scripting additions it may use, and any other helpful reminders to yourself or other script users. In addition, when creating a script to use an Apple Data Detector (ADD), use the

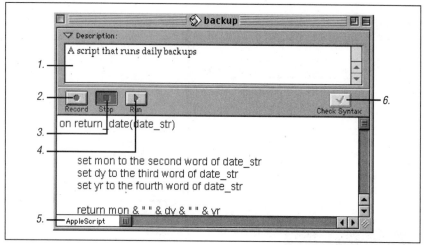

Figure 2-2: Script Editor window in OS 9

description field to contain the type of detector that will be referenced in the script and other values. ADD is an intriguing Apple technology that allows you to run scripts that respond to contextual menu selections. Chapter 20, *Apple Data Detectors Extension*, is devoted to ADD.

2. *Record*. Pressing this button or typing *Command-D* turns on Script Editor's Apple-event recording capability. A cassette-tape icon will begin blinking in the upper left part of the computer screen on OS 9. Script Editor will only record Apple event code that originates from recordable apps, such as the Finder.

3. *Stop*. Clicking this button or typing *Command-.* stops recording. The Apple events that are recorded are converted from Apple event code into Apple-Script terms and displayed in the script window. Only a few applications other than the Finder are recordable (see Chapter 1 for a description of recording a script). If you have turned on recording for a program and it is not recordable, then clicking the Stop button results in a blank script window.

4. *Run*. This button attempts to compile and run the script statements. Typing *Command-R* also executes this control. Any syntax errors in the script will cause an error dialog to be displayed.

5. *Lower left pop-up menu*. The pop-up menu button on the lower left of the script window (in Figure 2-2, where you see the label "AppleScript") allows you to choose which scripting component will be used to compile and execute your script. This pop-up button identifies only installed scripting components (see Chapter 1 for a description of scripting components). Apple-Script is selected by default in this button (it might be the only selection if this is the only scripting component you have installed on your machine).

6. *Check Syntax*. Clicking this button compiles or fails to compile the code in the script window. The first syntax error this feature encounters is highlighted in the window. Check Syntax does not run or save the script. If the syntax is okay, then Script Editor will format the code by indenting it (such as indenting the code inside of `tell` statement blocks).

Dictionaries

Before scripting an application, first find out which AppleScript commands it supports. The scripter also has to know which of the target application's objects, such as files, paragraphs, or database records, can be manipulated by a script. You can accomplish this task by selecting the program from Script Editor's File → Open Dictionary menu command. This command displays the dialog box depicted in Figure 2-3. Figure 2-4 shows what the same dialog box looks like in Mac OS X. Just choose the application icon of the program that you want to examine to view its dictionary in a dictionary window.

 You can open a program's dictionary by dragging the program's icon in the Finder to the Script Editor's icon.

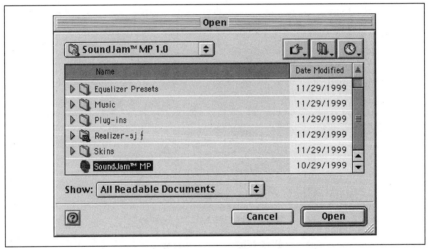

Figure 2-3: Open Dictionary dialog box in OS 9

The application's dictionary specifically lists the sets, or suites, of script commands and classes that the program supports (for example, the Standard Suite, AppleScript suite, or Text suite). Figure 2-5 shows the Finder's dictionary window in OS 9. The left panel of the dictionary window lists the application's commands in plain text and its classes in italics. Remember that commands are the messages or Apple events that a script sends an application in order to get it to do something (e.g., *sleep*). Classes or objects are the things that a script may try to change or get information about (e.g., a file or folder).

If a system application, extension, or control panel does not show up in their folder when you use File → Open Dictionary, then they do not have a dictionary; they are minimally scriptable or not scriptable at all. Some control panels in OS 9, for instance, do not have a dictionary but respond to a "run" AppleScript command (such as Energy Saver). In Mac OS X, for example, if the application icon is dimmed in the Open Dictionary dialog window, then the app does not (yet) have a viewable dictionary.

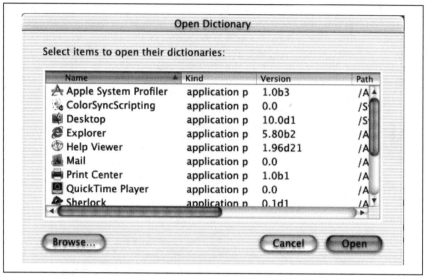

Figure 2-4: Open Dictionary dialog in OS X

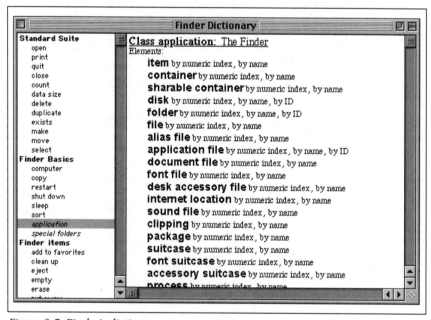

Figure 2-5: Finder's dictionary

Special Edit Menu Items

The Edit → AppleScript Formatting menu item allows the scripter to determine the font type and size inside the script window of various AppleScript language elements such as uncompiled text, operators, and comments. A pop-up menu button at the bottom of the dialog box produced by this command identifies the dialect that Script Editor will use (e.g., "AppleScript English").

Script Editor's Edit → Paste Reference menu item will add to the script window a reference to any objects (such as files or disks) that you have selected and copied from the desktop. For instance, if you select and copy a disk called "scratch" on your desktop, then choosing this menu item will paste `disk "scratch"` within the script window.

Script Saving Options

You have four different options for saving a file in Script Editor; however, Mac OS X does not support the stationery option of OS 9. These options are available from the File → Save or File → Save As menu choices.

 A droplet is by definition saved as an applet, but AppleScript gives it a different icon due to the enclosure of its code in an **on open** handler.

Figure 2-6 shows the icons for AppleScript file types. Mac OS X supports all of these icon types except the stationery one.

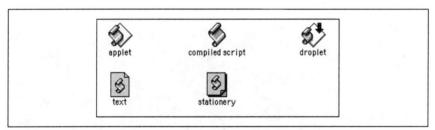

Figure 2-6: Icons for AppleScript file types

Script text file

If a script cannot compile without errors, or you just want to save it as plain text, then use the script text saving option. The text option saves the file as file type `'TEXT'` and creator type `'ToyS'`. In OS X, Script Editor tries to compile a script first when you save it, then displays a dialog window if the script cannot be compiled without error, giving the user the option of saving the script as a text file. If you are not finished with the script and therefore do not yet want to try compiling the source code, then you can skip the compilation stage by holding down the Shift key and choosing Script Editor's File → Save menu item. The file will only be saved as a text file.

Compiled script file

Script Editor will try to compile the source code before saving it. After a script is saved as a compiled script, double-clicking it opens the script in Script Editor, rather than executing it. These scripts have a file type of 'osas' and creator type 'ToyS'. You can run these scripts from within Script Editor.

 The Mac OS distinguishes different kinds of files by giving them unique four-character file types, such as 'osas' for a compiled script, 'TEXT' for an ASCII text file, and 'APPL' for an application that can be double-clicked to launch in the Finder. The four-character creator type identifies the application that handles the file when it is double-clicked (for example, 'ToyS' for Script Editor).

Classic applet

These file icons represent an applet that the user can double-click in the Finder to execute. An applet is a self-contained Macintosh application, independent from Script Editor. Classic applets have a file type of 'APPL' and a creator type of 'aplt'. You can still edit these files within Script Editor by choosing File → Open Script, then selecting the applet, or by dragging and dropping the applet icon on to the Script Editor icon. A classic applet is designed to run on Mac OS X but only within the classic environment. Figure 2-7 shows the classic (OS-9 type) dialog produced by executing an applet that was saved as a classic applet on an OS X machine.

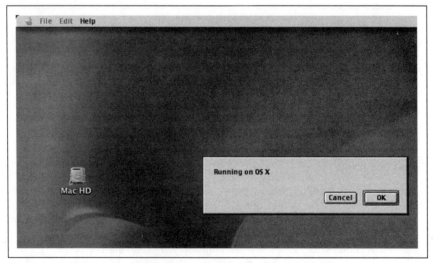

Figure 2-7: A classic applet executes within the confines of the classic environment

There are a few instances when you would want to run a classic applet inside OS X. One of them is that you want to automate a program that is running in the classic environment on OS X. Another reason is if you are developing an applet for an organization that is using OS 9. If you want to do any Mac OS X scripting, just create and test the applet using the latest version of Script Editor on OS X.

MacOS X applets

These applets are intended to work on a computer running Mac OS X (and future OS versions) or on an OS 9 machine that has the CarbonLib extension installed. However, the "MacOS X applet" saving option only works with AppleScript Version 1.5.5 or later, which installed with Mac OS 9.1, so only the MacOS X applets that are created on OS 9.1 machines will run on Mac OS X machines (running the Mac OS X for instance). MacOS X applets are also self-contained applications, independent from Script Editor.

Unraveling Classic and MacOS X Applets on OS X

A classic applet that targets a Mac OS 9.1 application (e.g., BBEdit 5.1) does what you would expect it to when double-clicked within Mac OS X. It runs within Mac OS X's classic environment (and opens the classic environment if that has not yet been launched by the operating system), launches the OS 9.1 program, and performs the applet's actions with that program. A MacOS X applet that does not target an OS 9.1 program does not use the classic environment.

But what about a MacOS X applet that targets an OS 9.1 program? My testing with Mac OS X indicates that a script saved as a MacOS X applet can still be used to script a program that is running within the classic environment. A MacOS X applet that inserts some text in a BBEdit document file will launch BBEdit in the classic environment and perform the script's actions, just like an applet saved as "classic" will. Strangely enough, I found that both the MacOS X applet and the same applet saved as a classic applet were also able to script elements of the OS X Finder. This is the simple script that I used to test the behavior of both classic and MacOS X applets. It first sends commands to a program that is running within the classic environment, then it scripts the Mac OS X Finder:

```
tell application "BBEdit 5.1"
    activate
    insert text "some more text"
end

(* Now script the OS X Finder *)

tell application "Finder"
    activate
    set target of Finder window 1 to "/users/"
end tell
```

The File → Save dialog box in OS 9 also presents you with a Stationery Option, which gives you the option of saving the file as a template (a stationery pad in Macintosh parlance) or as a document file. If you choose the stationery option, then every time you open the file a new document will be created with the template's contents.

You can prevent the further editing of either a compiled script or an applet by choosing File → Save As Run-Only. A run-only compiled script will not reopen in Script Editor if double-clicked, unlike compiled scripts that are not saved as run-only. The applets saved as run-only will execute when double-clicked, but you cannot open them in a new script window for further editing. If you want to prevent users from opening up the application to view its source code, then this is one reason for saving it as run-only.

When you save a script as an applet (classic or Mac OS X), you have two other checkbox options in the Script Editor's File → Save As dialog box:

Stay Open
Check this option and the script will not quit after it has completed its job. It will remain one of the running processes on the computer and will even show up in the Mac's About This Computer window. This window displays (on OS 9) a list of running applications and how much RAM they are using; it is accessible from the Apple menu in the upper left corner of the screen. You have to manually quit these scripts from their menu bars, or send them a *quit* Apple event in some other manner, such as from another script. A Common Gateway Interface (CGI) script on a Mac web server is an example of an application that should be saved using the Stay Open option.

Never Show Startup Screen
Unless this option is checked, executing an applet will cause the display of a startup screen or window, which offers the user the option to run or quit the applet. The top of the startup screen also displays any text that you included in the script window's description field before you saved the applet. In OS 9, this option is checked by default. In other words, running the applet will *not* produce a window before the applet does anything else.

Applets versus droplets

A script application or applet behaves differently in the Finder than script *droplets*.

A script applet acts like any other Mac application—it performs its operations when the user double-clicks it. And if you display the Application Switcher palette, the applet's icon shows up there. Unless the scripter chose the Stay Open option of the File → Save As menu command when she saved the applet, the script process quits after it has completed all of its statements (and after the user has dismissed any dialog boxes the applet displays).

You can also save your script as a droplet. Droplets execute when files, folders, or other objects are dragged and dropped on to the droplet's icon on the Mac desktop. The dropped objects are then passed as an object of value type list to the droplet's *open* handler. (See Chapter 8, *Subroutines*, for a description of handlers or subroutines.)

To save a script as a droplet, you have to nest the script inside of an *on open...end open* handler. When you save the script as an applet with one of these handlers, it has a different icon than other script applications. See Figure 2-6 for an example.

Droplets are very handy for the drag-and-drop processing of entire folders. For example, you could create a droplet that uploads to a web site directory the entire contents of whatever folder is dragged to the droplet. When you drop an item (such as a file, folder, or disk icon) on to the droplet, the droplet automatically executes its *open* handler. The parameter to the *open* handler stores whatever is dropped on the droplet as a `list` object containing objects of value type `alias`. (An `alias` looks like a pathname when converted to a `string`, as in "Macintosh HD:Desktop folder:myfile.txt.") You have to include a parameter with your *open* handler definition if you want the droplet to deal with the objects that are dropped on it.

If you only drag one file to this droplet, such as a single text file, then the parameter will consist of a `list` with one `alias` object in it. If the droplet cannot handle whatever object is dragged and dropped on it, then the droplet icon will not highlight when you drag the item over it.

For example, the script in Example 2-1 displays a dialog box that reveals the `file type` and `creator type` of the first item that is dropped on the droplet. If you do not understand several aspects of this program, rest assured that the rest of the book goes into great detail on variables, `tell` statements, and other AppleScript syntax elements.

Example 2-1: Droplet Displaying File and Creator Types

```
on open (list_of_aliases)
    (* the parameter to the 'open' handler is a list of aliases*)
    tell application "Finder"
        (* stores the first item that is dropped on the droplet in a variable
called 'an_item'    *)
        set an_item to (first item of list_of_aliases)
        set amessage to "File type is: " & (an_item's file type as string) & ¬
        return & "Creator type is: " & (an_item's creator type as string)
        (* use the 'display dialog' scripting addition command to show
information to the user *)
        display dialog amessage
    end tell
end open
```

Debugging with Event Log and Result Windows

Script Editor has two minimal debugging tools on OS 9 and OS X: Event Log and Result windows.

Event Log

You can open the Event Log by typing *Command-E* or by choosing it under Script Editor's Controls menu. If you select the Show Events and Show Event Results checkboxes in the Event Log window, then running the current script will display the result of each Apple event after a (-->) symbol (Chapter 1 discusses Apple events). You can use Event Log to follow along with a program and make sure that the results of each operation are what you expect them to be. Figure 2-8 shows the Event Log window in OS 9.

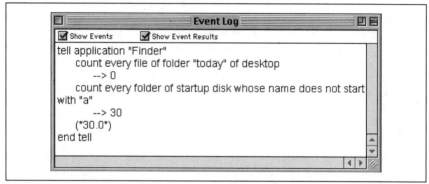

Figure 2-8: Event Log window

You can use the log keyword in your program and uncheck Show Events and Show Event Results if you just want to track the value of a certain variable in your program. For example, the log window depicted in Figure 2-8 is associated with the program in Example 2-2 (an OS 9 applet).

Example 2-2: Using the log Keyword in Event Log

```
tell application "Finder"
    set todayFiles to
        (count of every file of folder "today" of desktop) as real
    set filecount to
        (count of (every folder of startup disk whose name does not start ¬
        with "a")) as real
    log (filecount)
end tell
```

If you unchecked the checkboxes in Event Log, then the Event Log window will only show the result of the log (filecount) statement bracketed by AppleScript comment symbols (* *). In this case, the result of the log (filecount) statement is the value of the filecount variable. If you had 30 folders on the desktop that did not start with "a", then the Event Log window would display (*30.0*).

You can suppress and restart event-logging activity by using the stop log and start log statements. Here is how event-logging works in OS 9: checking the Show Events checkbox sets a log-level value to 1—whenever this value is greater than 0, the Event Log displays Apple events. The start log statement increases this value by 1. The stop log statement decreases the log-level value by 1. So if the log-level value was 1 to begin with, using the stop log statement will stop displaying Apple events until the code reaches a start log statement.

The following OS 9 program in Example 2-3 stops logging Apple events until the final two statements of a `tell` code block.

Example 2-3: Using stop log and start log

```
tell application "Finder"
   stop log
   count (every file of folder "today" of desktop)
   start log
   set filecount to ¬
      (count of (every folder of startup disk whose name ¬
      does not start with "a"))
         as real
   log (filecount)
end tell
```

Since the `stop log` statement reduces the log-level value to 0, it prevents Event Log from displaying Apple events until the `start log` statement appears.

Result window

Typing *Command-L* or using the Controls menu displays the Result window. The sole purpose of this window is to display the result of the last operation in a script you execute. Sometimes this is the only information a programmer needs. An example of a Result window is shown in Figure 2-9.

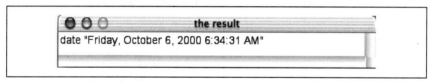

Figure 2-9: Result window in OS X

For example, type **current date** by itself in a new script window, then run the script. The Result window will display something like:

```
date "Saturday, October 7, 2000 3:18:20 PM"
```

Scripting the Script Editor

You can also use Script Editor as the target application for the Apple events sent from your script. If you are like me, you might want to begin your script in a more robust programmer's editor, such as BBEdit. Once you are ready to test and compile the code, the following script in Example 2-4 copies the text from BBEdit, and then pastes it into a new Script Editor window. This applet is for demonstration purposes only and performs marginal error-trapping for the sake of brevity (it only checks to see if BBEdit has an open window). The applet has been developed under Mac OS 9 and uses the *open for access, write,* and *close access* scripting-additions commands from the Standard Additions. (Scripting additions are covered in Appendix A, *Standard Scripting Additions.*) Presumably, a tweaked version of this script could run on OS X; however, BBEdit had not yet released an OS X version of its text editor at the time of this writing.

Example 2-4: An AppleScript That Moves Script Code into a Script Editor File

```
(* this variable will store the BBEdit text and is initialized to a string *)
set allCode to ""

(* this variable will store the path to the Desktop folder and is initialized
to a string *)
set deskPath to ""
tell application "BBEdit 5.0"
    try
        activate
        set allCode to (window text of document 1)
    on error errMessage
        display dialog "Looks like BBEdit does not have any open windows" & ¬
        return & return & "Error: " & errMessage & return & return & ¬
        "Exiting applet"
        return -- this return statement exits the applet's run handler
    end try
end tell

(* ask the user for a new filename then create a Script Editor file on the
desktop *)
tell application "Finder"
    set frontmost to true
    display dialog ¬
        "What name do you want to give the new script?" default answer ""
    set newScript to (the text returned in the result) as string
    make file at desktop with properties ¬
    {name:newScript, file type:"TEXT", creator  type:"ToyS"}
    set deskPath to (desktop as string)
end tell

(* Use the 'write' scripting addition to write the code to the Script Editor
file *)
tell application "Script Editor"
    activate
    set script_file to (deskPath & newScript) as alias
    open for access script_file with write permission
    write allCode to script_file
    close access script_file
    open script_file
end tell
```

Another solution to some of the limitations of using Script Editor as a text editor (e.g., no line numbering, bookmarks, and very little customization capabilities) is to not use Script Editor! See the footnote at the beginning of this chapter for a short list of alternative AppleScript development environments. Each of these programs, particularly the commercial ones, have many more features than Script Editor and are updated often.

PART II

AppleScript Language Reference

CHAPTER 3

Data Types

In Chapter 1, *AppleScript: An Introduction*, I touched on data types, but now I will delve deeper! A data type describes how a programming system stores data in memory, and it is similar to the types used by other languages such as Java or Visual Basic. AppleScript data types specify the type of value that a variable stores (e.g., `date`, `integer`, `string`, `real`) or that an AppleScript command or scripting addition returns (see Appendix A, *Standard Scripting Additions*). The data type that a variable stores determines what the script can do with it afterward, such as perform a math operation on an `integer` type or find out the `length` property (the number of characters) of a `string` type.

This chapter only describes the built-in AppleScript data types; however, a variable could also store a reference to an object such as a file, a web URL, or a database record (see Chapter 1 and its discussion of Apple event objects). Table 3-1 lists the data types described in this chapter, which also includes the correct syntax to use when storing a certain data type in a variable and the other data types to which a variable can allowably be cast or coerced.

Table 3-1: AppleScript Data Types

alias	real
boolean	record
class	reference
constant	RGB color
data	string
date	styled Clipboard Text
file specification	styled Text
integer	text
international Text	Unicode text
list	unit of measurement classes
number	

With some exceptions such as the **date** data type, you do not have to declare a data type when you declare a variable. When you declare a variable and store a **string** in it, such as:

```
set theString to "I am a string"
```

AppleScript will naturally enough store the literal value "I am a string" as a **string**. (The **set** keyword is used to store values in variables; this is summarized in Chapter 1 and explained in more detail in Chapter 6, *Variables and Constants*.)

The same is true with **boolean** value types, such as:

```
set theTruth to false
```

AppleScript knows that **theTruth** is storing a **boolean** value. When you store a number with a fractional part in a variable, AppleScript automatically sets that variable to a **real**. There are several exceptions, however, to this loosely-typed nature.

Consider Example 3-1 of a **number** and a **string** (**number** is just a synonym for a **real** or **integer**). When you run the example, you'll find that the **number** starts out as a data type **integer**, then takes part in a math operation that uses the / division operator. The results of operations that use this operator are always of type **real**.

 A **real** can store the decimal portion of a number and an **integer** cannot.

Similarly, in Example 3-1, what starts out as a **string** (which otherwise looks like a **date**) is coerced to a very different **date** object. By "coerced" I mean the variable's data-storage method is altered to that of another data type. This is sometimes called "casting" from one data type to another in other programming languages such as Java. In AppleScript, there are some casts that are allowed (for example, from a **number** to a **string**) and others that are not allowed (a **real** to an **integer** if the real has a fractional part). The reference sections for each data type later in this chapter include an "allowed coercions" section, which describes the casts or coercions that are allowed for each data type.

Example 3-1: An Example of Coercion

```
set theNumber to 25
log class of theNumber -- theNumber is an integer type
set theDate to "December 12, 1999"
log class of theDate -- theDate is a string
set theNumber to (theNumber / 3) (* theNumber is result of / operation so
it's coerced to a real*)
log class of theNumber -- class is now real
set theDate to date theDate -- theDate string is coerced to a date value type
log class of theDate
```

In the second-to-last line, the `theDate` variable that stores a `string` is coerced to a `date` object. The `class of theDate` part of this example returns the `class` property of the `date` object, which is a nice way to look at which value type it is storing.

The following sections describe each AppleScript data type in alphabetical order, including the other data types to which they can be coerced.

alias

Allowed coercions

```
list with one item, as in: {alias "Macintosh HD:Desktop
Folder:newfile.txt"}
string
```

Syntax

```
set theFile to alias "Macintosh HD:Desktop Folder:newfile.txt"
```

Description

An `alias` type is a representation of a disk, folder, or volume. An alias is a form of referring to an object such as a file (as in the syntax example), which is very similar to the "alias files" that you can create in the Finder.

 An `alias` file is a Finder object that can be referred to in tell statements that target the Finder. An `alias` (such as the `alias` in the syntax example), on the other hand, is a built-in AppleScript class or type.

Nearly everyone who has used a Macintosh is familiar with making alias files (i.e., select the file and type *Command-M* or choose File → Make Alias from the Finder's menu in Mac OS 9). For example, if you have a file called *new.txt* and you make an `alias` out of it, then the Finder creates a new file in the same location that looks like Figure 3-1. This file refers to the original file by using a unique identifier. Even if you move the original file around within the volume (which is represented by a disk icon on OS 9's desktop), but not outside of the volume, the `alias` file will still find it. An `alias` value type is similar to an `alias` file. Every time you change and recompile a script that refers to an `alias`, AppleScript will attempt to find the file or other object that the `alias` refers to. A lot of commonly used commands take `alias`es for arguments (such as *open for access*) or return `alias`es (e.g., *choose file*). See Appendix A for more information on these commands.

One way to create an alias in AppleScript is by preceding a valid file path with the keyword `alias`:

```
alias "Macintosh HD:Desktop Folder:newfile.txt"
```

new.txt alias

Figure 3-1: An alias file icon

If the file path, a `string`, does not point to a valid file, folder, disk, or volume, the script will not compile in Script Editor. For example, if you use the code:

```
set theFile to alias "Macintosh HD:Desktop Folder:newfile.txt"
```

and the file *newfile.txt* does not exist, then Script Editor will not allow a compilation to an applet or compiled script.

Another way to create an `alias` in AppleScript is to use the keyword `as` with a `string`:

```
set theFile to "Macintosh HD:Desktop Folder:newfile.txt"as alias
```

The `string` used with `as` (e.g., "Macintosh HD:Desktop Folder:newfile.txt"), however, has to be a valid file path or the script will not compile. Other ways to get aliases to files or folders are the *choose file*, *choose folder*, and *path to* scripting additions. See Appendix A for a description of these commands. All three commands return `alias` types that refer to files, folders, or to special folders such as control panels. The examples elsewhere in this chapter include the use of these scripting additions.

Examples

Aliases are particularly useful in AppleScript for getting the path to files or folders as strings. The first example shows how to use the *path to* scripting addition to get a `string` that represents the Desktop Folder ("Macintosh HD:Desktop Folder:"). The *path to* osax returns an `alias` type, which is then coerced to a `string`:

```
(* this line returns something like "Macintosh HD:Desktop Folder:" *)
set dpath to (path to desktop) as string

(* this returns an alias like alias "Macintosh HD:Desktop
folder:today:index.html", but only if the "index.html" file exists *)
set theFile to alias (dpath & "today:index.html")
set dt to (path to desktop) as string (* returns (depending on the
startup disk name) "Macintosh HD:Desktop Folder:" *)
set fileAlias to (choose file with prompt "Choose a file if you please.")
(* presents a dialog box to the user and returns an alias type that looks
like alias "myStartupDisk:Web Files:search.html".*)
set folAlias to (choose folder with prompt "Choose a folder to store ¬
the new file in.") (* this time returns an alias type that points to a
folder. The return value looks like alias "myStartupDisk:Web Files:".
Notice that the folder path (i.e., "myStartupDisk:Web Files:") ends with
a semi-colon (":"), which is the character used to delimit file paths on
the Macintosh. *)
```

```
set theApp to (choose file with prompt "Choose an app to launch") (* You
can then launch the chosen application with code such as tell application
(theApp as string) to run. *)
```

boolean

Allowed coercions

list with one item, as in {true}
string

Syntax

set theTruth to true

Description

boolean data types can only be one of two values: true or false. When setting
a variable to a literal boolean value, just type true or false without quotation
marks. Expressions that include comparison operators return boolean values (see
the following Examples section).

Two of the examples in the "Examples" section demonstrate that AppleScript does
not consider case by default when comparing string values. If you enclose the
string comparison in a considering case...end considering block,
however, the case of the characters (upper- or lowercase) matters. Therefore, the
last expression in "Examples" returns false because of the uppercase "I" in the
first operand and the lowercase "i" in the second operand.

Three of the examples use three logical operators: and, or, and not. These are
AppleScript language elements that you will use all the time to test or alter boolean
values. For example, the following phrase finds all files that are *not* gif files:

get (every file in folder "images" whose not (name ends with "gif"))

If you have to, you can set the value of a boolean variable to the return value of
an expression:

set theBool to ("I am" is equal to "i am")

The theBool variable evaluates to true. The parentheses are there to make it
more readable; they are not necessary in this case.

You cannot use numerical values (such as 0, 1, or -1) as boolean values, unlike
Perl. If you try to write

if (-1) then display dialog "hey!"

then you will get a pithy error message on the order of "can't make -1 into a
boolean value." In Perl, lots of different values evaluate to true. Any number is
true except 0, including 1 and -1; string values other than the "empty string" ("")
evaluate to true. Not so with AppleScript—boolean values are either true, false,
or a boolean return value from a comparison expression, AppleScript command,
or application-property value.

Examples

This expression returns true, because 35 is greater than 25:

```
35 > 25
```

This expression also returns true because the math is correct:

```
25 is less than 35
```

This expression returns false because the not operator reverses the value of true:

```
not true
```

With and, both operands must evaluate to true for the expression to be true:

```
true and false -- returns false
```

This expression returns true because the first operand is true and the expression "short circuits" (i.e., returns true without evaluating the second operand):

```
true or false -- returns true
```

AppleScript doesn't consider case by default and finds two strings to be equal:

```
"I am" is equal to "i am" -- returns true
```

This expression returns a false value because case sensitivity is taken into account:

```
considering case ... "I am" is equal to "i am" ...end considering
(* returns false *)
```

---

class

Allowed coercions

```
list with one item, as in {integer}
string
```

Syntax

```
set theClass to class of theString
```

Description

The class value type is used to describe the data type of a variable or object, such as: boolean, class, integer, real, record, or string. It is used most often to check the value type of a variable or return value:

```
set theString to "I am a string"
set theClass to class of theString -- returns string
```

Getting the class property of a string returns an object of type class, which is just the word string (or whatever the class is) without quotation marks. If you want to twist your tongue into further knots, follow the prior example with the statement:

```
get class of theClass
```

It returns, you guessed it, the term class with no quotation marks.

Examples

To make sure they are of the proper data type, check the `class` property of any parameters that are passed to functions:

```
on MultiplyByTwo(aNumber)
    if (class of aNumber is not in {integer,real}) then
        return 0
    else
        return aNumber * 2
    end if
end MultiplyByTwo
MultiplyByTwo(45)
MultiplyByTwo("woops")
```

The first call to the *MultiplyByTwo* function will result in "90." The second call will produce "0" because the parameter is a `string`, instead of the required `integer` or `real` value type.

The `class of aNumber` part of the previous example returns an object of type `class` (it will return `integer` from the first call to *MultiplyByTwo* and `string` from the second call). The segment:

```
(class of aNumber is not in {integer,real})
```

of the function call is a `boolean` expression. It will return `false` if the class of the parameter is either an `integer` or a `real`.

---

constant

Allowed coercions

> `list` with one item, as in `{constant}`
> `string` (beginning in AppleScript Version 1.3.7)

Syntax

```
set theVar to pi (*theVar is set to the value of the pi constant, which
is about 3.14159265359 *)
```

Description

AppleScript and scriptable applications include several constants or pre-defined variables that are based on the `constant` class. Chapter 6 includes more information on these constants.

Examples

`case` is a `constant` that in the following example will determine how strings are compared:

```
considering case
    set compString to ("I am" is equal to "i am")
end considering
```

This code sets the variable `compString` to `false` because the two strings are not equal considering the case of the `string` characters. The AppleScript constant `case`, if you test it using the code class of case, returns the `constant` class.

Many applications have defined their own constants using the constant value type. For example, Sherlock 2's current tab property will return one of the following Sherlock 2-defined constants (Find File Tab, Find by Content Tab, or Search Internet Tab):

```
tell application "Sherlock 2"
    set sh_tab to (get current tab)
    class of sh_tab -- returns constant
end tell
```

 The return value of the current tab property is a constant identifying the Find File Tab, for instance. You can coerce this constant return value to a string, however, if you had to display the result using the *display dialog* scripting addition, which takes a string for a parameter (among other parameters). To coerce the return value of the previous example to a string you could use the code:

```
get current tab as string
```

data

Allowed coercion

list with one item, as in {«data utxt0065006100720074068»}

Syntax

```
Set theVar to "earth" as Unicode text (* returns «data
utxt0065006100720074068» *)
```

Description

data is a value type that can be used to store data that cannot be stored using any of the other AppleScript value types.

The Script Editor Result window displays raw data surrounded by double-arrow or guillemet characters ("« »"). You can produce these symbols on the Macintosh keyboard by typing *option-backslash* ("«") and *option-shift-backslash* ("»").

For example, in OS 9 Unicode text is an AppleScript value type that is displayed as raw data in the Script Editor Result window (even though it is still stored as type Unicode text). However, AppleScript 1.6 with Mac OS 9.1 and OS X can display Unicode text as regular strings (as in "Hello"). The following example displays a lowercase "u" character as Unicode text:

```
set ucode to "u" as Unicode text
```

The Script Editor Result window will return the value as "«data utxt0075»."

Unicode text uses two bytes (16 bits) per character to store strings. (See later in this section for more details on the Unicode text class.)

Within the guillemets, the word "data" is followed by a space then a four-character code representing the Unicode text class ("utxt"). The actual data representing the lowercase "u" precedes the closing guillemet character ("0075»"). The lowercase "u" is represented in the ASCII table as the number 75 in hexadecimal form (117 in decimal). It only takes one byte to store a "u"; the one byte is represented by the "75" portion of the data return value ("«data utxt0075»"). The rest of this data ("00"), representing the unused extra byte, is two zeros.

Raw Syntax

You can also use *raw syntax* to represent data and commands in your own scripts. For example, AppleScript recognizes the term «class cfol» as the equivalent of the word folder, which is the Apple event object that represents a folder on your computer. The class part of this data structure stands for the data type, and cfol represents the four-character code for folder (remember our Chapter 1 discussion of four-character codes for class types?).

It is normally preferable to use natural language terms ("folder") for these objects, except for when a built-in AppleScript term or a term from an application's dictionary does not exist for a command you want to execute. While these situations are rare or nonexistent, one of them occurs when you want to send an Apple event to a program, and you do not know the human-language command to use for the event (or there isn't an AppleScript term for the command). For example, you might have developed an application that handles certain Apple events, but the program doesn't have a dictionary yet. However, you still want to test how it deals with Apple events sent by AppleScript. You could then use the following raw syntax to send a *get* Apple event to the program "myapp" requesting its version property:

```
tell application "myapp" to «event coregetd» version
```

This expression encloses the word "event" in guillemets ("«»") followed by a space and the *get* command's event class ("core") and event id ("getd") pushed together. Recall from Chapter 1 that every Apple event is distinguished by its event class (the suite or category of events that it is part of) and its individual event id. In other words, the previous example uses raw syntax instead of the conventional coding style:

```
tell application "myapp" to get version
```

In another example, you could substitute the raw syntax:

```
«class cdis» "scratch"
```

for the AppleScript code reference:

```
disk "scratch"
```

representing a mounted volume on the desktop with the name "scratch." The four characters "cdis" represent the Apple event object code for the disk class.

Where do you find out about all of these event and class codes? The AppleScript software development kit (SDK) includes a FileMaker Pro file that contains event and class codes for all events and objects associated with Mac OS 8.5 (this SDK had not been updated as of January 2001). Go to *http://developer.apple.com/sdk* for more SDK info.

Examples

You can use raw syntax to represent data, as in the following examples (the question is, do you really want to?):

```
«class file» "bigfile.txt" (* a form of file "bigfile.txt" that refers to
a file called "bigfile.txt" *)
«data utxt0025» as string -- returns the percent sign ("%")
«event aevtodoc» file "bigfile.txt" (* In AppleScriptese, open file
"bigfile.txt" *)
```

date

Allowed coercions

> list with one item
> string

Syntax

> set dateVar to date "January 1, 2000"

Description

You can use strings to express several different forms of **date** expressions. But AppleScript will not store the value as a **date** object unless you precede the **string** with the **date** keyword:

> set theDate to date "1/1/2000"

It is very easy to forget to include the **date** keyword; if you leave it out, the variable will be set to a **string** and will not contain any of the **date** object's properties (e.g., **Time String**).

This example uses the *current date* scripting addition to return a **date** object. The script shows the code's return value within comment characters ("(* *)"):

> set theDate to current date
> (*date "Friday, November 12, 1999 8:22:11 AM" *)

Once you have a valid **date** object, then you can obtain the values of several properties from it:

Class
> date

Date String
> The date not including the time value ("Friday, November 12, 1999")

Day

An integer that represents the day of the month, as in 12 for "November 12"

Month

Represents one of the following constants:

January	July
February	August
March	September
April	October
May	November
June	December

Time

An integer representing the number of seconds since midnight

Time String

Gets the time from the date object in string form ("8:22:11 AM")

Weekday

Stored in one of the following constants:

Monday	Tuesday
Wednesday	Thursday
Friday	Saturday
Sunday	

Year

An integer representing the year

If you create a date object from a literal string, then AppleScript will always fill in a default property value (such as for the Time property) if the literal string does not provide one. Here's an example of a bare-bones date value and what the object actually looks like under the surface after AppleScript has filled in the default values:

```
set myDate to date "1/1/2000"
return myDate -- looks like date "Saturday, January 1, 2000 12:00:00 AM"
```

If you do not supply a time value, then AppleScript will set the time as midnight for that day ("12:00 AM"). If you create a date object but supply only a time value, but not the date:

```
set myDate to date "17:00"
```

then AppleScript will set the date of the object to the date when the script was compiled. In other words, the date object always has a property value for the date or time, even if you have not provided one upon object creation.

AppleScript allows you to use the following constants in date calculations:

days

Equals 24 * hours

hours

Equals 60 * minutes

minutes

Equals 60 * `seconds`

weeks

Equals 7 * `days`

AppleScript Pivot Dates

As everyone learned from the Y2K furor, it is not a good idea for an application to accept the year portion of dates as two digits (e.g., "01") instead of four ("2001"). Always use four digits when you create AppleScript `date` objects. However, imagine that you are using an AppleScript to pull date strings from an old text or database file that represents dates such as "09/09/87." What is "87"—1987" or "2087"? Here is how AppleScript handles the so-called pivot dates, where the two-digit century is interpreted relative to the current year:

- If the current date is between 0 and 10 (as it is now, 2001), a two-digit date with a year value between 00 and 90 is considered in the current century. A date with a year value from 91 to 99 is represented as in the previous century. So the year portion of "1/1/10" is represented as "2010," and the year of "1/1/95" is considered "1995."

- If the current two-digit year falls between 11 and 90 (as in 2011), then any year in the 00 to 99 range is considered in the current century. In 2011, then, the year part of the date string "1/20/45" would evaluate to "2045."

- If the current year is late in the century, as in "1999," then any two-year dates from 00 to 10 are considered in the next century. All the other two-year dates are represented as in the current century.

Examples

If you compiled and saved the expression:

```
set myDate to date "17:00"
```

on January 20, 2000, then the `myDate` `date` object would look like this:

```
date "Thursday, January 20, 2000 5:00:00 PM"
```

Scripters work a lot with `date` objects. You can perform addition and subtraction with dates, for instance. The following example tells you when a project with a six-month deadline is due, based on the date when you signed the project contract:

```
set userInput to (display dialog "When did you sign the contract?" ¬
default answer ((current date) as string))
set contractDate to date (text returned of userInput)
set projectDue to date (contractDate + (180 * days))
set amessage to "Brace yourself, your project is due on " & projectDue
display dialog amessage
```

It first asks the user for the contract-signing date by using the *display dialog* scripting addition. The code then displays a text field to request user input. In this case, I use a date `string` returned from the *current date* scripting addition (the return value is coerced to a `string`) as the default answer. For the sake of clarity and keeping the example short, I have not tested what the user has entered into the text field to make sure that the value is a valid date `string`. Any final program should test the input value for validity. The `contractDate` variable takes the `string` returned from the *display dialog* window (`text returned` of `userInput`) and coerces it to a `date` object. Then the script roughly calculates six months as: 180 * days (`days` is a constant that equals 24 * `hours`). This calculated value is added to the `contractDate` `date` object to get a date representing six months from the contract date. It stores this value in the `projectDue` `date` variable. The final two lines create and display a message dialog box notifying the user when their project is due. The following segment:

```
set amessage to "Brace yourself, your project is due on " & projectDue
```

shows how the scripter can concatenate a `date` object to a `string`, and Apple-Script will coerce the `date` object to a `string` for you.

A scripter can also use the `Time` property of a `date` object to calculate elapsed time in seconds. The next example uses the `Time` property to calculate how long it takes the prior example to run (including how long the user takes to fill in and dismiss the dialog box). A code-timing function using the `Time` property of `date` objects is a useful addition to a scripter's function library:

```
set codeStart to (time of (current date))
set userInput to (display dialog "When did you sign the contract?" ¬
default answer ((current date) as string))
set contractDate to date (text returned of userInput)
set projectDue to date (contractDate + (180 * days))
set amessage to "Brace yourself, your project is due on " & projectDue
display dialog amessage
set codeEnd to (time of (current date))
set timeDif to (codeEnd - codeStart) as string
display dialog ("This code took " & timeDif & " seconds to run.")
```

Here are more examples of creating `date` objects:

```
set myDate to date "12/1/2000"
set myDate to date "December 1, 2000"
set myDate to date "12/1/2000 5:00 PM"
set myDate to date "12/1/2000 17:00"
set myDate to date "17:00"
```

file specification

Allowed coercions

List with one item
string

Syntax

```
set fSpec to (new file default name "urlfile")
```

Description

The file specification class can reserve the name and path for a file, even if the file has not yet been saved to the hard disk. The *URL Access Scripting* scripting addition takes a value of type file specification for both its *download* and *upload* commands.

Examples

This code requests the user to name a file and choose its saving location (with the *new file* scripting-addition command) then downloads a web page to the file:

```
set fspec to (new file default name "urlfile")
tell application "URL Access Scripting" to download "http://www. ¬
parkerriver.com" to fspec
```

new file displays a dialog box that allows the user to name and choose the location for a file, but it doesn't actually save the file. It returns the file information as a file specification data type.

The following code gets a file specification, and then sends a *save* Apple event to the text editor BBEdit. The text editor then saves its front window to the file specification the applet user had previously created:

```
set newFileSpec to ¬
    (new file with prompt "where would you like the future file saved?")
(* returns a file specification object *)
tell application "BBEdit 5.1"
    save window 1 to newFileSpec
end tell
```

The *info for* scripting addition takes a file specification parameter. It gives you a substantial amount of information about a file that's been saved to disk, including the name, size in bytes, file type, and creator type. However, the *info for* command will return an error if the file specification data has not yet been saved:

```
set filespec to ¬
(new file with prompt "Where do you want a new file saved?")
tell application "BBEdit 5.1"
    save window 1 to filespec
end tell
set fileInfo to (info for filespec)
display dialog "name: " & (name of fileInfo) & return & "size: " & ¬
    (size of fileInfo)
```

---

integer

Allowed coercions

list with one item
string
real

Syntax

```
set myInt to 12 as integer
```

Description

An `integer` value type is a positive or negative number that does not have a decimal part. You can use `number` as a synonym for `integer`, but the class of the variable remains `integer`, as in:

```
set aNum to 30 as number
```

If you get the `class` property of `aNum`, it will be `integer`.

If you need a very high number, such as for a variable that will hold the U.S. national debt, you will have to use a `real` data type. An `integer` has a range of -536870911 to +536870911. If you're going to work with very high numbers, particularly if the script will increase the value of those numbers, then you should use a `real` value type to hold the value.

Examples

Here are some examples of numbers that AppleScript will store as integers, as well as numbers that AppleScript will end up storing as reals because they are too big or have a fractional part:

integer class

```
set bigInt to 500000000
```

integer class

```
set bigInt to -500000000
```

The variable `bigInt` is stored in a `real` data type because of the size of the number:

```
set bigInt to 600000000
```

The variable `bigInt` is converted to the `real` class because it has a fractional part:

```
set bigInt to 6.1
```

AppleScript automatically sets a data type for a variable depending on the size of the number or whether it has a decimal point. In the following code, the number starts out as an `integer`, has a number with a decimal point added to it, then is converted to a `real` value type to accommodate the fraction:

```
set int to 1
log class of int -- integer
set int to int + 1.2
log class of int -- real
```

You cannot depend on AppleScript to always assign the *intended* value type to a number. This example code will reach the limits of a positive `integer` (in this case +536870911 on my machine) then begin assigning negative numbers to the `int` variable. Its class remains `integer` while it is processed. This was a problem with integer data types in AppleScript 1.3 through 1.4.3 (see the following note).

```
set int to 536870909
log class of int
repeat 3 times
    set int to int + 1
    log int
    log class of int
end repeat
```

Changing the opening line of the last example to:

```
set int to 536870909 as real
```

will solve the problem and allow the positive number to increase in value by one during each iteration of the loop. (See Chapter 7, *Flow-Control Statements*, for an explanation of repeat loops.)

 In AppleScript 1.5 and later, integers will be converted to reals when the integer exceeds 536870911. This obviates the necessity to originally store the incrementing number as a real (but this might be a good idea anyway if you expect the number to grow very large).

---

international text

Allowed coercions

> List with one item
> string
> Unicode text
> integer or real if text depicts a valid number

Syntax

```
set intText to "The World" as international text
```

Description

The international text class stores string data differently than a standard string. Each chunk of international text begins with a four-character language code and a four-character script code, both of which determine the format of subsequent bytes of text. A variable declared as type international text can be used to store text that is comprised of Chinese characters, for instance, but only if the Macintosh computer running the script has the proper language kit installed.

---

list

Allowed coercion

string, if the data type of each item in the list can legally be coerced to a string

---

 A single-item list (such as {44}) can be coerced to any data type that the item could be coerced to if it were not in a list. For example, {44} could be cast or coerced to a string, because 44 is an integer, and AppleScript permits that data type to be coerced to a string.

Syntax

```
set theList to {"Mercury","Mars",pi,3.14} as list
```

Description

An AppleScript list is close to what other languages such as Perl or Java would call an array. In AppleScript, you can store items of any data type in a list, even other lists. You can mix data types among list items (store strings, numbers, and other objects in the same list). The items as a group are surrounded by curly braces and separated by commas. For example:

```
set theList to {"Mercury","Mars",pi,3.14}
```

includes two **strings**, the **pi** predefined variable (which AppleScript will evaluate to about 3.14159265359), and a **real** number.

A list is a data type that you will encounter often in AppleScript. Several AppleScript commands return lists, such as getting every item in a container (e.g., *get every folder of desktop*) You can use the following properties with a list:

class
> Always returns list. Test a return value or variable to find out if it is a list by using this property, as in:
>
> ```
> class of theList
> ```

length
> Returns the number of items in a list, as in:
>
> ```
> length of theList
> ```

rest
> Returns a value of type list containing every item but the first one.

reverse
> Returns a value of type list containing all the items of the original list but in reverse order (e.g., reverse of theList—returns {3.14, pi, "Mars", "Mercury"}).

Examples

You can use several different reference styles to grab individual items from a list, such as the **first**, **last**, or **middle** reference methods (e.g., **first item** of theList—**Mercury**). You can use integers as reference methods, such as:

```
1000th item of theList
```

(if the list included at least 1000 items). You can also access subgroups within a list by referring to them as a range. For example:

```
items 1 thru 3 of theList
```

returns a list containing the first, second, and third entries in the theList variable. You can refer to any list value by referencing its list position, as in item 3 of theList. Lists are not "zero indexed" by default in AppleScript. The first position in an AppleScript list is occupied by item 1.

AppleScript lists are very supple; you can "concatenate" two lists to make a bigger single list. The following code uses the concatenation operator (&) to combine two lists:

```
set theList to {"Mercury", "Mars", pi, 3.14} as list
set secondList to {"Neptune", 2000, "NutShell"}
set comList to theList & secondList
-- results in {"Mercury", "Mars", 3.14159265359, 3.14, "Neptune", 2000,
"NutShell"}
```

If you concatenate a list data type with a string, integer, real, or boolean data type, AppleScript adds the value to the end of the original list. For instance:

```
set theList to theList & "Let me in"
```

results in a new list with the "Let me in" string added to the end of it. This makes it very simple to dynamically add data to an existing list, whether the data are other lists, strings, numbers, or different classes.

You get a different result when you try to concatenate a list of values to a string. AppleScript first coerces theList to a string. All of the list items are jammed together and separated by AppleScript's default text item delimiters, which is the empty string (""). Thus when list items are converted to a string the result is often unreadable—a string of characters with no spaces separating them. This example is one solution to prettying up a string that was formerly a list:

```
(* save a reference to AppleScript's default text item delimiter, which
is an empty string, "" *)
set defaultDelim to text item delimiters
set text item delimiters to return
tell application "Finder"
    set folList to (name of (items of desktop whose kind is "folder")) ¬
as list
    set folList to folList as string
end tell
set text item delimiters to defaultDelim
display dialog folList
```

The best solution to coercing a list to a string is to temporarily change Apple-Script's text item delimiters. The prior example first saves the default text item delimiters in a variable, so we can return AppleScript to its default string behavior after the script runs. Then the text item delimiters value is changed to the return predefined variable, which, when used in this manner, is a return character (displaying the string following it on the next line). The script then tells the Finder to get a list of all the names of the desktop's folders and coerce the list to a string. Since I changed the text item delimiters to a return character, this will create a string that lists each folder name on a separate line. This string, or at least a portion of it (depending on how cluttered the desktop is with folders), is displayed to the user using the *display dialog* scripting addition. Finally, the script also resets the text item delimiters to the Apple-Script default (an empty string, "").

number

Allowed coercions

```
String
list with one item
integer to real
real to integer (unless real has a fractional part)
```

Syntax

```
set theNumber to 25 as number
```

Description

number is a synonym for real or integer. However, the class for a number with a decimal point will be a real, and the same goes for a whole number (its class will be integer). Here are some illustrations of this:

theNum is of class integer
```
Set theNum to 25 as number
```
theNum is of class real
```
Set theNum to 25.1 as number
```

In other words, the number data type can be used in AppleScript, but its actual class will be either integer or real.

---

real

Allowed coercions

```
String
list with one item
integer (if there is no fractional part)
number (a synonym)
```

Syntax

```
set theNumber to 25.6 as real
```

Description

A real is a positive or negative number that can include a decimal point, such as -512.5 or 3.14159265359 (the value of the pi predefined variable is a real value type). Use real when you want a variable to store a very high number. The largest positive value that a real number can reach with AppleScript 1.4.3 on OS 9 is 1.797693E+308. This very large number, however, can safely be exceeded with real data types under AppleScript 1.5.5/1.6 (Mac OS 9.1 and OS X).

Examples

The second line of this example raises an error in AppleScript Version 1.4.3 and Script Editor: "The result of a numeric operation was too large":

```
set theVar to 1.797693E+308

set theVar to theVar + 1
```

At any rate, this is a giant number. To use scientific notation, follow the `real` or floating-point number with the letter "e" (upper- or lowercase) along with an `integer` like 20 (e.g., 2.0e20 or 2.0e+20; the "+" is optional, any "−" sign is not). If the `integer` is a positive n, then the number is equal to *real number * 10^n*; if n is negative then the number is equal to *real number * 10^{-n}*. AppleScript converts to scientific notation the `real` numbers that are greater than or equal to 10,000.0 when the script is compiled. My machine also converts to scientific notation numbers that are less than or equal to 0.001, but the *AppleScript Language Guide for AppleScript 1.3.7* ascribes this behavior to numbers less than or equal to 0.0001.

 AppleScript will automatically use the `real` value type for all numbers with decimal points. The results of math operations that use the / or ÷ operators are always `reals`. The results of calculations using *, +, −, ^, and mod operators are `reals` or `integers` depending on the magnitude of the results or whether the operands are `reals` or not. (Operators are covered later in Chapter 4, *Operators*.)

You can coerce an `integer` to a `real`, and AppleScript will drop a ".0" on the end of the number. However, you cannot coerce a `real` to an `integer` if the `real` has an actual fractional part. For instance, 6.3 cannot be coerced to an `integer`, but 6.0 can. In other words, AppleScript does not automatically chuck out the fractional part of a `real` when coercing it to an `integer`. It first determines whether the coercion is legal or not. This code is an illustration of this process:

```
set theVar to 6.3
set theVar to theVar + 0.7 (* theVar is now 7.0 so it can be coerced to
an integer *)
set theVar to theVar as integer
log theVar
log class of theVar -- the class is integer
```

---

record

Allowed coercions

`list` (but all the names from the name/value pairs are thrown out)

Syntax

```
set theRec to {name: "AppleScript in a Nutshell", subject: ¬
"AppleScript"} as record
```

Description

A `record` value type is close to what a Perl programmer knows as a hash or associative array and what a Java programmer would recognize as the HashMap class. This is a powerful data type that lets you store name/value or property/value pairs in a variable. These values are then accessible by the property name (not the item number). For instance:

```
get name of theRec
```

---

from the preceding syntax example returns "AppleScript in a Nutshell." But:

```
get item 1 of theRec
```

raises an error; you just cannot use the latter reference method.

Examples

You can find out how many property/value pairs there are in a record by getting its length property, as in:

```
length of theRec
```

(which returns 2). You can change values by referring to the property name (unless the record is a read-only application property). You can also add to a record by concatenating another record to it:

```
get length of theRec -- returns 2
set subject of theRec to "AppleScript language"
set theRec to theRec & {users:"Mac scripters"}
get theRec (* returns {name:"AppleScript in a Nutshell",
subject:"AppleScript language", users:"Mac scripters"} *)
```

You can coerce a record to a list type, but the record (now a list) will lose all of the property names. For example:

```
get theRec as list
```

will return:

```
{"AppleScript In a Nutshell", "AppleScript language", "Mac scripters"}.
```

Records can have expressions or variables as property values, as in the following example (however, you cannot use variable values for property names):

```
set myVar to "A variable"
set twoRec to {calc:(2 + 2.5), var:myVar} as record (* returns {calc:4.5,
var:"A variable"} *)
set twoRec to {calc:(2 + 2.5), var:myVar,myVar: 7} as record (* returns
{calc:4.5, var:"A variable",myVar: 7} and doesn't evaluate the myVar
variable at the end of the record*)
```

You cannot use two-word property names when creating your own record. You will have to use capital letters or underscore characters to create more descriptive property names:

```
set climberName to {FirstName: "Edmund", last_name: "Hillary"}.
```

as opposed to:

```
set climberName to {First Name: "Edmund", Last Name: "Hillary"}.
```

---

reference

Allowed coercion

string depending on the nature of the reference

Syntax

```
set theRef to a reference to (the name of file 1 of desktop)
```

Description

The reference class *points to* an object or value. In the syntax example, `theRef` points to `the name of file 1` on the desktop, no matter which file becomes the first file on the desktop over time. In other words, the value of this reference can change. If you just set `theRef` to `name of file 1 of desktop` as opposed to a *reference* to `name of file 1 of desktop`, then `theRef` would contain a `string` (such as "myfile.txt") rather than a reference to the name. The next time you referred to the variable `theRef` in the script, it would still have the `string` value "myfile.txt," even if this file were no longer `file 1 of desktop` (i.e., it might now be file 2 or file 3 because the desktop files got changed around). A *reference* to the `name of file 1`, however, would continue to provide the name of the desktop's first file, even if that file had changed since the `theRef` variable was initialized.

Examples

To set a variable to a `reference` class, you use the **a reference to** operator, or **a ref to** for short. Some references, such as Finder references to files or folders, can be coerced to strings:

```
tell application "Finder"
    set theRef to a reference to the name of file 1
    get theRef as string -- returns "filename.txt"
end tell
```

RGB color

Allowed coercion

```
list
```

Syntax

```
set myRGB to {0,0,0} as RGB color (* returns the color black as an RGB
Color value *)
```

Description

RGB color values are lists of three integers (between 0 and 65535) that represent the red, green, and blue components of a color. The script commands for a graphics application may take or return RGB color values, for example. The class of an RGB color is actually a `list` value:

```
set myRGB to {0,0,0} as RGB color

get class of myRGB -- returns list
```

You can change the values in an RGB color object by referring to its `item` property:

```
set item 3 of myRGB to 10000.
```

string

Allowed coercions

list with one item; numbers as long as the string is a valid integer
real
international text
Unicode text

Syntax

```
set myString to "Good old string" as string
```

Description

AppleScript strings are like strings in other languages (arrays of characters), except that they have to be surrounded by double quotation marks; you do not have the option of using single quotation marks. You can get the number of characters in a string, including spaces, by using a string's length property:

```
length of myString
```

AppleScript strings have the following built-in elements:

characters
paragraphs
text
words

Examples

The statement:

```
words of myString
```

or:

```
every word of myString
```

will return a list of strings containing each of the words in the original string ({"Good","old","string"}). This is handy if your script wants to examine or otherwise process each of the words in a string. The same goes for the other elements; characters of myString returns a list of strings, with each item in the list being a single-character string ({"G", "o", "o", "d", " ", "o", "l", "d", " ", "s", "t", "r", "i", "n", "g"}). The following example iterates through this list and returns the number of non-space characters in the string. Items in lists are one-based, meaning that the first character in a string is character 1. These statements would make a nice subroutine for a string-handling library:

```
set myString to "Good old string"
set noSpaceCharCount to 0
repeat with c from 1 to (length of myString)
(*space is a string constant representing a space character *)
    if not (character c of myString is space) then
        set noSpaceCharCount to noSpaceCharCount + 1
    end if
end repeat
get noSpaceCharCount
```

The **text** element of a **string** allows you to grab ranges of characters in a **string** and return the value as a **string** rather than a **list**:

```
characters of myString
```

or:

```
characters 2 thru 8 of myString
```

returns a value of type **list**. For example:

```
get text 6 thru 15 of myString
```

would return "old string."

Use a backslash or escape character ("\") to produce double quotation marks, tabs, or returns in strings.

You might want to use escape characters in the window produced by the *display dialog* scripting addition command. The following example shows how to use the escape character in an AppleScript **string** value. If you then write the **string** to a file, for instance, the escape character ("\") will not appear in the written out **string**, just the characters that it "escaped," such as double quotation marks:

```
set myString to "\"Two words \t \ttwo tabs and \ra return character\""
(* returns "\"Two words → → two tabs and
a return character " *)
```

The AppleScript concatenation character (&) can connect two strings. For example:

```
"String one " & "String two"
```

results in "String one String two." Make sure to include spaces in the connected strings to ensure readability. This is an operator that you will be using with strings all the time.

A **string** can be coerced to a **number**, and vice versa, as long as the **string** looks like a **number**. You can convert "55" or "3.14" to a **number**, but you cannot coerce "1.3.7" or "1.4Stephanie" to a **real** or **integer**. You can coerce and then perform math on a **string** that is a valid **number**, for instance. This code finds out if a user has AppleScript version 1.4 or greater on their machine:

```
set ASversion to version as string
if ((text 1 thru 3 of ASversion) as real) ≥ 1.4 then (* string coerced to
real *)
    display dialog "good, you're running at least AppleScript 1.4"
else
    display dialog ("Maybe you should consider upgrading to AppleScript ¬
    1.4 or 1.5;You" & " are now running " & ASversion)
end if
```

If you poke around in the various scripting additions, you will find many that work with strings. For example, as part of the Standard Additions, the *offset* osax will find the position of one `string` inside of another (Appendix A is devoted to scripting additions):

```
set theString to ¬
"Robert Cohn was once middle-weight champion of Princeton."
offset of "Princeton" in theString
(*returns the character position where 'Princeton' begins which is the
integer 48 *)
```

Styled Clipboard Text

Allowed coercions

`list` with one item

Syntax

```
set myClipText to "Styled clipboard text" as Styled Clipboard Text
```

Description

`Styled Clipboard Text` is a special value type for applications that can cut and paste styled text between them. Styled text is text that contains font and style information, such as a chunk of text that is 14-point Arial and bold. `Styled Clipboard Text` can only be displayed in the Result window as raw data (see the `data` data type description).

Styled Text

Allowed coercions

`list` with one item; numbers as long as the `string` is a valid `integer` or `real`

Syntax

```
set myString to "Styled string" as Styled Text
```

Description

`Styled Text` is a `string` that can but does not have to contain font and style information. `Styled Text` has all of the elements and properties of a `string`. In fact, the `class` of `styled Text` is `string`. This data type also has a `length` property, which returns the number of characters in the `string`. `Styled Text` strings have `character`, `paragraph`, `text`, and `word` properties. Some word-processing applications, such as AppleWorks, return the styled-text value when you get the text from a document.

The various font and style characteristics of `Styled Text` are incorporated into the `string`, but you cannot change them with built-in AppleScript code (as in `set font of styledTextVar...`). In addition, you can coerce strings back and forth between `Styled Text` and `string`. But a literal `string` ("I am a string") that is coerced to `Styled Text` does not actually have any style or font information; it is just plain text.

text

Allowed coercions

list with one item; numbers as long as the string is a valid integer or real

Syntax

```
set myString to "text is just a string" as text
```

Description

text is a straightforward synonym for string, with no differences (see the string data type). Make sure not to mistake the text class for the string class's text element (you can get text 1 thru 10 of a string to return the first 10 characters as a string). This AppleScript shows how you can store strings as text, but its class remains string:

```
set myString to "text is just a string" as text
set len to length of myString -- text has the same properties as string
log len -- find out the string length in Event Log
class of myString -- returns string
```

Unicode Text

Allowed coercions

list with one item; strings or international text, but some text information may be lost

Syntax

```
set worldlyStr to "A Unicode string" as Unicode text
```

Description

Unicode text values reserve two bytes of memory for each character. This allows Unicode text to represent up to about 65,000 characters from languages throughout the world (Version 3.01 of the Unicode Standard defined more than 49,000 characters), including Arabic, Chinese, Japanese, Korean, and numerous others. The Unicode Standard is an evolving standard for international character encoding (see *http://www.unicode.org*).

Prior to AppleScript Version 1.5.5, the Script Editor can only display Unicode text as raw data, but its class is preserved as Unicode text.

 AppleScript 1.6 on OS X and OS 9.1 can display Unicode text as a string, as in "A."

Examples

This AppleScript shows what a returned Unicode text value looks like in Apple-Script Version 1.5.5 and later, and in AppleScript Version 1.4:

```
set UnicodeStr to "Hi" as Unicode text
(* returns «data utxt00480069» in AppleScript version 1.4; and "Hi" in
version 1.5.5 and later*)
```

The raw-data return value is comprised of the word «data» and the actual Unicode text data enclosed in guillemet symbols (« »). The Unicode text data begins with a four-character code representing the Unicode text class ("utxt") and then a hexadecimal representation of the characters in the string. These characters are represented as "00480069" inside of the raw-data return value.

Unit of Measurement Classes

Allowed coercions

integer, real, and string

Syntax

```
set theMeters to 6000 as meters
```

Description

AppleScript provides six categories of classes for representing area, length, temperature, cubic volume, liquid volume, and weight measurements. These data types are very handy for converting measurements within the categories:

Area value types
> square feet
>
> square kilometers
>
> square kilometres
>
> square meters
>
> square metres
>
> square miles
>
> square yards

Length value types
> centimeters
>
> centimetres
>
> feet
>
> inches
>
> kilometres
>
> kilometers
>
> metres

```
meters

miles

yards
```

Temperature value types
```
degrees Celsius

degrees Fahrenheit

degrees Kelvin
```

Cubic volume value types
```
cubic centimeters

cubic centimetres

cubic feet

cubic inches

cubic metres

cubic meters

cubic yards
```

Liquid volume value types
```
gallons

litres

liters

quarts
```

Weight value types
```
grams

kilograms

ounces

pounds
```

---

 degrees Kelvin and quarts began with AppleScript Version 1.3.7, along with the coercion of miles to other length-measurement types.

Examples

You can only coerce back and forth between measurement classes within the same category. The return values for these classes are the name of the data type followed by a space and its value. The return value of:

```
set theMeters to 6000 as meters
```

is "meters 6000.0" and its class is meters. The following code illustrates what is and is not permitted in terms of using these classes. The end of the code example shows the results from Script Editor's Event Log window:

```
set theMeters to 6000 as meters
set theFeet to theMeters as feet
log theFeet
set theReal to (theFeet as inches) as real
log theReal
set cubYards to theReal as cubic yards
log cubYards
set cubYards to cubYards as yards
```

```
Event log:
(*feet 1.96850394E+4*) -- meters to feet returns as class 'feet'
(*2.362204728E+5*)-- feet to inches to real returns as class 'real'
(*cubic yards 2.362204728E+5*) -- real to cubic yards returns as class
'cubic
yards'
--> Can't make cubic yards 2.362204728E+5 into a yards. (* returns an
error, because you cannot coerce a 'cubic yards' class into a 'yards'
class.
*)
```

You can convert **meters** to **feet** (6000 meters is equivalent to about 19,685 feet), because both of these classes are in the "length" category. The previous example then converts **feet** to **inches** (also permitted because they are both length units) and stores that result as a **real** value type (i.e., a floating-point number that represents the number of inches in 6,000 meters). Then, since the number (stored in the variable **theReal**) is a **real** value type rather than a length-unit type, it can be coerced to **cubic yards**. **cubic yards** is in the cubic-volume category. But **cubic yards** cannot be coerced to **yards**, which is in the length category, thus giving rise to the error in the prior example.

These groups of data types make it very easy to create utility functions for calculating measurements. The next example is a subroutine that converts meters to feet or feet to meters (see Chapter 8, *Subroutines*). The second parameter to the *ConvertMe* function is a **boolean**. If it's **true**, then the conversion is from **meters** to **feet**. If **false**, then the conversion is from **feet** to **meters**. Another way to accomplish this task is to check the class of a single parameter (i.e., **val**). If its class is **feet**, then convert it to **meters**, and vice versa. If its class is neither, then write the subroutine to return an error code such as -1.

```
on ConvertMe(val, toFeet)
    if toFeet then -- 3.2808399 feet equals one meter
        set conResult to val * 3.2808399
        set replyToUser to "Converting " & val & " meters to feet equals: ¬
        " & (round conResult) & " feet" -- use round scripting addition
        display dialog replyToUser    (* display the conversion result using
display-dialog scripting addition *)
    else -- one foot equals 0.304799999537 meters
        set conResult to val * 0.304799999537
        set replyToUser to "Converting " & val & " feet to meters equals: ¬
        " & (round conResult) & " meters" -- use round scripting addition
        display dialog replyToUser   (* display the conversion result using
display-dialog scripting addition *)
    end if
end ConvertMe
```

CHAPTER 4

Operators

Operators are symbols that programmers use to perform operations in AppleScript code, such as in mathematical expressions or equality tests. Operators (e.g., =, +, −, *) are familiar to programmers in other languages (such as Java and Perl), as well as young math students. In the following AppleScript code fragment, the * and the = characters are the operators:

```
2 * 10 = 20
```

With the exception of parentheses, AppleScript's operators (listed in Table 4-1) are *binary operators*, meaning that each operator takes an operand, such as a number, variable, or expression, on either side of it. In the previous code fragment, the 2 is the left-hand operand and the 10 is the right-hand operand for the * operator. Operators can also be used to test two expressions for equality or to combine two strings into one string, as in these two code fragments:

```
Set eq to (56.5 >= 56) (* the eq variable is set to true; the >=
("greater than or equal to") operator is used to test two values for
equivalence *)
Set twostrings to ("two strings" & " are now one string.") (* using
the & string-concatenation operator *)
```

Table 4-1: AppleScript Operators

&	As
( )	Begins with
*	Contains
+	Does not contain
−	Does not equal
/ ÷ div	Ends with
<	Is contained by
<= ≤	Is not contained by
=	Mod

Table 4-1: AppleScript Operators (continued)

>	Not
>=	Or
A reference to	
And	

A distinguishing element of AppleScript is that its operators can be either symbols, such as &, =, +, or , or human-language words such as `equals`, `does not equal`, or `is greater than`. As a scripter, the choice is entirely up to you whether to use `is less than` or the < symbol, for instance. The latter two operators are synonyms and have the same meaning in code. Table 4-1 lists the operators that are covered in this chapter, but not all of the possible synonyms (e.g., `is less than`, `comes before`, `is not greater than`). The synonyms for each operator are listed in the Synonyms heading of the sections (described in alphabetical order in the remainder of this chapter) on each operator.

&

Syntax

```
"Use this operator  " & "to concatenate two strings."
```

Return value

A `string` if the left operand is a `string`; a `record` if the left operand is a `record`; a `list` if the left operand is another value type

Description

The concatenation operator can be used to combine two values to produce a single third value combining the operator's two operands. You will mostly use this operator for `string` concatenation. However, it is also often used to add to records or lists. Make sure not to confuse this operator with the + symbol, which is the concatenation operator of Java and JavaScript that is only used for addition and scientific notation (e.g., 1.2e+6) in AppleScript.

Examples

```
"My age is dare I say " & 43 (* combining a string and a number returns a
string as in "My age is dare I say 43" *)

{"apples","oranges"} & {"bananas"} (*combine two lists to make one list:
{"apples","oranges","bananas"} *)

{name: "Pedro Martinez",record: "23-4"} & {award:"Cy Young"} (*add a new
item to a record, returning {name:"Pedro Martinez", record:"23-4",
award:"Cy Young"} *)

1.4 & 2 (* returns {1.4,2}. Looks weird, but you might want to store a
long list of numbers in a list value type, then it doesn't seem so weird.
*)
```

Operators

```
"Your AppleScript version is " & version (* Some concatenation operations
fail and need some massaging; "Your AppleScript version is " & (version
as string) will solve this problem *)
```

( )

Syntax

```
35 - (15 + 42)
```

Return value

The result of the expression that is stored within the parentheses, which can be
any valid AppleScript expression, identifier, or return value from a subroutine or
command.

Description

Using parentheses with expressions forces the parenthetical operation to be evaluated first, hopefully producing the result you intended. The syntax example that
begins this section would produce 62 if the parentheses were not there (35 − 15
+ 42), whereas with the parentheses the result is -22. Each nested parenthetical
expression is evaluated before any outer parenthetical expressions are evaluated.

To a lesser extent, the use of parentheses makes complex statements more readable, even if the placement of the parentheses does not change the result of the
expression.

Examples

```
35.6 * (7 / (round realVar)) (* a complex expression, including the
'round' scripting addition, looks a little clearer when parentheses are
used, even though the result is the same compared with leaving the
parentheses out *)

set herReply to (display dialog ¬
"Do you love me?" default answer ¬
"Of course I do!" buttons {"answer him", "cancel affair"}) (* use
parentheses to encapsulate, at least visually, the return value from a
scripting-addition command (these parentheses are not strictly necessary)
*)
```

*

Syntax

```
10 * 3.14
```

Return value

An integer if the left-hand operator is an integer and the right-hand operand is
either an integer or can be coerced to an integer (for example, 3.0 can be
coerced to 3); otherwise a real. Finally, if both operands are integers but the result
will exceed the numerical limit of an integer type (536,870,911 to -536,870,911),
than the return result is a real.

Description

The multiplication operator is used to multiply two integers, two reals, or an integer and a real. The return result is an integer or a real, depending on the factors explained in the previous paragraph. The lessons that you learned in your early math classes apply to this operator as well; AppleScript will evaluate a multiplication expression before it will evaluate addition or subtraction. For example, the expression 10 + 7 * 5 results in 45, not 85.

You can multiply a number times a string if the string looks like a number. AppleScript first coerces the string to an integer or real (depending on whether the string has a decimal point), and then performs the multiply operation.

Examples

```
10 + 7 * 5 -- results in 45 not 85; (10 + 7) * 5 results in 85

set aNum to 10 * 3.0 (* aNum is an integer type, because left-hand
operand is an integer and right-hand operand can be coerced to an integer
*)

set aNum to 10.0 * 3.0 -- aNum is a real type

set aNum to 30000000 * 20 (* aNum is a real, because the result exceeds
the storage capacity of an integer, even though both operands are
integers *)

set aNum to 10 * "4.1" (* aNum is a real; a string like "4.1" is a valid
operand if it can be coerced to a number *)
```

+

Syntax

```
set aNum to 10 + 3.14
```

Return value

An integer if the left-hand operator is an integer and the right-hand operand is either an integer or can be coerced to an integer; a real if either operand is a real; a date if the left-hand operand is a date object

Description

This operator is used to add two operands together or to add time to a date value. It is also used in scientific notation to denote a real that is greater than or equal to 10,000.0, as in 1.0E+9 (this number is one billion; see the description of the real value type in Chapter 3, *Data Types*). The addition operator is not used to concatenate two strings (& is responsible for that); neither does AppleScript provide anything like a ++ operator. The following is an example statement for incrementing a numerical variable in AppleScript:

```
set aNum to aNum + 1
```

Here are some examples of adding time to dates.

Examples

```
set mydate to (date "Saturday, January 1, 2000 12:00:00 AM") ¬
+ 1000 (* adds one thousand seconds to the date *)

set mydate to (date "Saturday, January 1, 2000 12:00:00 AM") + (30 * ¬
days) (* adds 30 days to the date (you can also use the constants
minutes, hours, or weeks) *)
```

–

Syntax

```
set aNum to 10 - 3.14
```

Return value

An integer if the left-hand operator is an integer and the right-hand operand is either an integer or can evaluate to a whole number (for example, 3.0 can evaluate to 3); a real if either operand is a real. If the left-hand operator is a date, then the result is of class date.

Description

This operator subtracts one operand from another or makes a number negative if there is only one operand. This operator can also be used to subtract time from dates, either in the form of an integer (representing seconds) or the constants minutes, hours, days, and weeks. The minus (–) symbol is also used in Apple-Script to denote small real numbers, as in 1.0E-9 (this number is 0.000000001; see the description of the real value type in Chapter 3). AppleScript does not provide anything like a –– operator. The following is an example statement for decrementing a numerical variable in AppleScript:

```
set aNum to aNum - 1.
```

Here are some examples of subtracting time from dates.

Examples

```
set mydate to (date "Saturday, January 1, 2000 12:00:00 AM") - 1000 (*
subtracts one thousand seconds from the date *)

set mydate to (date "Saturday, January 1, 2000 12:00:00 AM") - (30 * ¬
days) (* subtracts 30 days from the date (you can also use the constants
minutes, hours, days, or weeks) *)
```

/ ÷ div

Syntax

```
set aNum to 10 / 3.14
```

Return value

If you use / or ÷ the result is always a `real` value type. If you use `div`, the result is always an `integer`.

Description

The three division operators differ in that / and ÷ produce `real` value types, whereas `div` always returns an `integer`. `div` is the opposite of `mod`. For example, 10 div 3 results in 3 and the remainder of 1 is ignored; 10 mod 3 results in 1 (the remainder) and the 3 result is ignored. You produce the ÷ character by typing `option-/`. Remember not to confuse the / division operator with the \ escape character that is used to produce string characters such as a `tab` (\t) or `return` (\r).

Examples

```
10 / 3 -- returns 3.333333333333

10 div 3 -- returns 3

10 mod 3 -- by way of comparison, returns 1
```

<

Syntax

```
10 is less than 11 -- returns true
```

Synonyms

`[is] less than`

`comes before`

`is not greater than or equal [to]`

`isn't greater than or equal [to]`

Description

These operators, either the symbols or human-language versions, return `true` or `false` from the expression where they are used. You can use `dates`, `integers`, `reals`, or `strings` with these operators. Both operands should be of the same class. If they are not then AppleScript tries to coerce the right operand to the class of the left operand.

Scripters who swear by AppleScript's plainspokenness can stick with `is less than`, `comes before`, and their other alternatives (as opposed to just "<").

Examples

```
35.29 is less than 35.3 -- returns true

"animal" < "boy" -- returns true

date "1/1/1970" comes before date "1/1/2000"-- returns true.
```

≤ <=

Syntax

    10 is less than or equal to 11 -- returns true

Synonyms

[is] less than or equal [to]

is not greater than

isn't greater than

does not come after

doesn't come after

Return value

 boolean; true or false

Description

This binary operator returns true if the left operand is less than or equal to the right operand. You can use dates, integers, reals, or strings with this operator. If both operators are not of the same class, then AppleScript attempts to coerce the right operand to the class of the left operand.

Examples

    100 <= 200 -- returns true

    300.536 is less than or equal to 300.537 -- returns true

    12 isn't greater than 11 -- returns false

=

Syntax

    integerVar is equal to 50

Synonyms

equal[s]

is

[is] equal to

Return value

 boolean; true or false

Description

This operator tests whether two operands are equal and returns a true or false value. You can use the symbol = or the human-language versions (e.g., equals) interchangeably. You can also use any of the operators to test the equivalence of

---

boolean values, lists, numbers, dates, strings, and other classes. Remember, AppleScript does not use = for variable assignment; it uses statements of the form:

```
set var to 50
```

Chapter 6, *Variables and Constants*, discusses AppleScript variables and assignments. This operator syntax allows the scripter to use very readable statements:

```
if a does not equal b then display dialog "inequality!"
```

Examples

```
50 equals "50" -- returns false

50 is equal to ("50" as integer) (* true since "50" is coerced to 50
prior to the equality test *)

"animal" is equal to "AniMaL" (* true if you do not enclose this
statement in a considering case...end considering block *)

(8 div 3) = (8 mod 3) -- both expressions evaluate to 2 so true

{65,75} equals {65,(65 + 10)} -- true, you can compare lists
```

>

Syntax

```
102 > 101 -- returns true
```

Synonyms

comes after

[is] greater than

is not less than or equal [to]

isn't less than or equal [to]

Return Value

boolean; true or false

Description

These operators, either the symbols or human-language versions, return true or false from the expression where they are used. You can use dates, integers, reals, or strings with these operators (both operands should be of the same class). If the operands are not of the same class, then AppleScript attempts to coerce the right operand to the class of the left operand.

In AppleScript, you can also use the contraction isn't less than or equal [to], along with the other English language versions of the > operator. You can compare a lot of things in AppleScript to test for equality, as the following examples show. But you have to break up lists or records, or extract properties from them, before their contents are compared with the greater than variations. You can say:

```
{65,75} equals {65,75}
```

---

but you cannot use the expression

```
{65,75} is greater than {65,75}
```

Examples

```
1500.0 is greater than 1500.1 -- returns false

pi > 3 -- returns true, because pi evaluates to about 3.14159265359

date "1/1/2050" comes after date "1/1/2000" -- true
```

≥ >=

Syntax

```
500 ≥ 500 -- returns true
```

Synonyms

≥

```
[is] greater than or equal [to]

is not less than

isn't less than

does not come before

doesn't come before
```

Return value

boolean; true or false

Description

This binary comparison operator returns true if the operand on the left is greater than or equal to the right operand. You can use dates, integers, reals, or strings with these operators (both operands should be of the same class). If the operands are not of the same class, then AppleScript attempts to coerce the right operand to the class of the left operand.

In AppleScript, you can also use the contractions doesn't come before and isn't less than, along with the other English language versions.

Examples

```
1500.0 is greater than or equal to 1500.1 -- returns false

pi ≥ 3 -- returns true, because pi evaluates to about 3.14159265359

date "1/1/2050" does not come before date "1/1/2000" -- true
```

^

Syntax

```
set bigNum to 3^30
```

Return value

`real`

Description

This binary arithmetic operator raises the operand to its left to the power on its right. It always returns a `real` value type. The operands can either be `integers` or `reals`.

Examples

```
set intNum to 10 ^ 2 -- intNum evaluates to 100, an integer

set realNum to 10.1 ^ 2 -- realNum is returned as a real type, 102.01
```

[a] reference to

Syntax

```
set myRef to a ref to (file 1)
```

Synonyms

```
[a] ref to
```

Return value

`reference`

Description

You can set the variable on the left of this operator to a reference to the object or value on its right. The variable is then "pointing" to this object or value. For example, if you tell the Finder to:

```
set myRef to a ref to file 1
```

then `myRef` will refer to the first file on the desktop. If file 1 on the desktop changes, then `myRef` will still refer to file 1, even if that file is now different from the first one. This is best illustrated by the code in the following Examples section.

The script in the Examples section first creates a variable called `myRef` and sets it to the first file on the desktop. That file is then moved into a different folder; in other words, it is no longer the first file on the desktop. Another file now has that distinction. Since `myRef` was set to:

```
a reference to file 1
```

it now refers to the new file 1 (the old file 1 was moved into a different folder). As indicated by testing the:

```
name of myRef
```

a second time, `myRef` now points to a different file. This operator could be used in scripts that necessitate a variable that always points to a certain location in a container, such as to the last record in a database. Even though the database may change (records are dynamically deleted and added), you can always get information about the last record, such as its id number, because you have a variable that points *to that position* in the database, not just to a particular record.

Examples

```
tell application "Finder"
    set myRef to a ref to file 1
    set f1 to name of myRef
    log f1 -- look at value of the variable in Event Log window
    move file 1 to folder "today" (* original file 1 is now in a different
location *)
    set f2 to name of myRef
    log f2 -- look at value of the variable in Event Log window
end tell
```

and

Syntax

```
set myBoolean to (firstVal and secondVal)
```

Return value

boolean; `true` or `false`

Description

`and` is a logical operator that takes two operands. Both operands have to be boolean values, `true` or `false`. Both operands have to evaluate to `true` for the entire `and` expression to return `true`. If the first operand (the one on the left of the `and` operator) evaluates to `false`, then the second operand is not evaluated, because the `and` expression returns `false` if any of its operands is `false` (the expression is "short-circuited"). The `and` operator does not have any equivalent symbols ("&," "&&"), as in Perl or JavaScript. Table 4-2 shows the different combinations that you can use with `and` and the resulting expression values.

Table 4-2: Return Values of Expressions Using the and Operator

and Expression	Return Value
true and true	true
true and false	false
false and true	false; second expression is not evaluated
false and false	false; second expression is not evaluated

as

Syntax

```
set myReal to "3.14" as real
```

Return value

Class identifier to the right of operator, if valid

Description

The **as** operator is used to coerce or cast values or variables to certain class types. The operand to the right of the **as** operator has to be a class identifier, such as `boolean`, `integer`, `list`, `real`, `record`, `string`, or some other object type. The expression will fail if the value in the first operand cannot be coerced to the class identified in the second operand (in fact you will find these statements raising a lot of errors as you experiment with coercing values from type to type). See Chapter 3 for a discussion of which types can be coerced to different classes.

---

begin[s] with

Syntax

```
set mybool to ("zoology" starts with "zoo") -- returns true
```

Synonyms

`start[s] with`

Return value

`boolean`; `true` or `false`

Description

The operands for these operators must be strings or lists. If the operand to the left contains the operand to the right, then the expression returns `true`. If the operands do not evaluate to the same class, then AppleScript attempts to coerce the right operand to the class of the left operand. You can combine strings and lists in these statements. For example:

```
set mybool to ( {"string", "twine"} starts with "string" )
```

returns `true`, because AppleScript coerces the right operand to a single-item string (`"{"string"}"`) before it makes the `starts with` comparison. This operator and its synonym are designed to compare operands that are either both strings or both lists, however. This operator and its sibling `ends with` are very handy for identifying portions of strings within larger strings. For example, if you prefixed the characters "db_" to all of your database files, then you could distinguish those files by using the `begins with` operator, as in the following example.

Examples

```
tell application "Finder"
    get count of (files whose name begins with "db_")
end tell
```

contains

Syntax

```
set mybool to ({"apples","oranges","peaches"} contains "peaches")
(* returns true *)
```

Return value

boolean; true or false

Description

The contains operator can take lists, records, or strings as operands. You can use this operator to search for an item in a list, a record, or a part of the string. If the operand to the right of the contains operator is of a different type than the left operand, then AppleScript attempts to coerce the second operand to the class of the first one. This is an operator to get to know well. A lot of commands return lists, strings, and records; contains is a very useful tool for finding certain values within these value types.

You cannot use contains directly to search the contents of a folder, but there is a workaround for this task. The example in this section illustrates returning a list with a command and then using the contains operator to search the list. You can use contains to search a record too:

```
{name:"Bruce W.", state:"MA"} contains {name:"Bruce W."}
```

Examples

```
tell application "Finder"
    tell folder "new images"
        set fJpgs to files whose name contains ".jpg" (* returns list of
jpeg files, if any *)
        if length of fJpgs > 0 then (* if the list is not empty then display
count of jpegs *)
        display dialog ((length of fJpgs) as string)
    end if
    end tell
end tell
```

---

does not contain

Syntax

```
set mybool to ({"apples","oranges","peaches"} does not contain ¬
{"peaches"}) -- returns false
```

Return value

boolean; true or false

Description

does not contain, or doesn't contain, is the opposite of contains. It returns true if the list, record, or string operand does not contain the second list, record, or string operand. See contains in this chapter for a further discussion.

---

does not equal

Syntax

```
if intVarOne ≠ intVarTwo then beep
```

Synonyms

≠

is not

isn't

is not equal [to]

isn't equal [to]

doesn't equal

Return value

boolean; true or false

Description

These operators are the opposite of the equals operator and its variations. They return true if the operands, which can be of any class, are unequal. You can use the symbol interchangeably with the human-language versions (isn't) with strings, numbers, and other classes.

ends with

Syntax

```
"index.html" ends with ".html" -- returns true
```

Return value

boolean; true or false

Description

This operator is invaluable when searching a disk or folder for files with certain file extensions (e.g., *.html*, *.gif*) and then doing something only with those found files. The ends with operator works with lists and strings. If you use this operator to compare a string with a list or vice versa, then AppleScript tries to coerce the string or list to the type of the left operand.

Examples

```
{"apples", "oranges"} ends with "oranges" -- returns true

"oranges" ends with {"n","g","e","s"} (* true, after AppleScript coerces
the right operand from list to string, after which it looks like "nges"
*)
```

```
{"img1.gif", "img2.gif"} ends with ".gif" -- false

{"img1.gif", "img2.gif"} ends with "img2.gif" -- true
```

is contained by

Syntax

```
"html" is contained by "index.html" -- returns true
```

Synonyms

```
is in
```

Return value

boolean; true or false

Description

This operator can take lists, records, or strings as operands. If the left-hand operand is not of the same class as the second operand, then AppleScript will attempt to coerce the first operand to the second operand's class before evaluating the expression. You cannot use this operator alone to find out if a file is contained by a disk or folder (see the discussion of contains) because the folder, file, and disk classes are not lists, records, or strings.

is not contained by

Syntax

```
"html" isn't contained by "index.html" -- returns false
```

Synonyms

```
is not in
isn't contained by
```

Return value

boolean; true or false

Description

These operators return the opposite result of the is contained by and is in operators. They return true if the left operand—a list, record, or string— cannot be found in the list, record, or string operand on the right. If the left operand is not of the same class as the second operand, then AppleScript attempts to coerce the first operand to the second operand's class before evaluating the expression. The use of is not in and its variants is a good way to delineate the strings that do not contain certain substrings.

Examples

```
tell application "Finder"
    (* get a list of desktop files whose names do not contain '.jpeg' *)
    get files where ".jpg" is not in name of files
end
```

mod

Syntax

```
set theMod to 63 mod 20 -- returns 3
```

Return value

integer or real

Description

The mod operator divides its left operand by the right operand and returns any remainder (otherwise zero), rather than returning the division result. See the section on the div operator, which does the opposite; it returns the division result and throws out the remainder.

Examples

```
set theMod to 63 mod 20.0 -- result is an integer 3

set theMod to 63.0 mod 20 -- result is a real  3.0

set theMod to 63 mod 20.1 -- result is a real 2.7

set theMod to 63.0 mod 20.0 -- result is an real 3.0
```

not

Syntax

```
set theTruth to not ("index.html" contains ".html") -- returns false
```

Return value

boolean; true or false

Description

not is a logical operator that reverses the boolean value of a variable or expression. If the variable or expression is true then the not return value is false, and vice versa. AppleScript does not have the (!) symbolic alternative for the not operator as Perl and other scripting languages do.

Operators

or

Syntax

```
set theTruth to (intVar1 > intVar2) or ("index.html" contains ".html")
```

Return value

boolean; true or false

Description

or is a logical operator that takes two boolean operands, true or false. The or expression returns true if either operand evaluates to true. If the first operand (the one on the left of the or operator) evaluates to true then the second operand is not evaluated, because the or expression returns true if any of its operands is true (the expression is "short-circuited"). The or operator does not have any equivalent symbols (|, ||), as in Perl or JavaScript. Table 4-3 shows the different combinations that you can use with or and the resulting expression values.

Table 4-3: Return Values of Expressions Using the or Operator

or Expression	Return Value
true or true	true
true or false	true; second expression is not evaluated
false or true	true
false or false	false

CHAPTER 5

Reference Forms

This chapter describes the AppleScript reference forms, or the ways that you can specify or refer to one or more objects in AppleScript code. First we will describe the ten different reference forms, then the rest of the chapter provides a reference to the actual AppleScript reserved words (e.g., **every, thru, whose**) that you can use to identify or refer to objects in your code.

Here are the ten different reference forms:

Arbitrary Element

Using the reserved word **some**, AppleScript code can grab a random object in a container. Here is an example:

```
tell application "Finder"
    (* get a random image file from a desktop folder *)
    set randomImage to some file of folder "jpegs"
end tell
```

See the section on **some**.

Every Element

This type of reference form specifies every object of a certain class type in a container, such as:

```
tell application "Finder"
    set allFiles to every file in folder "today" (*   returns a list
    of file objects *)
end tell
```

See the section on **every**.

Filter

The Filter reference form specifies objects based on certain attributes, such as all files whose name ends with *.txt*. The **where** and **whose** reserved words are used in Filter references. See the **whose** section.

ID

The ID reference form can be used to grab an object based on the value of its ID property (if it has an ID property, that is.) The ID reference form is expressed in code with the AppleScript `id` reserved word. See the `id` section.

Index

The popular Index reference form specifies an object based on its numbered or indexed position in a container. The following example shows two ways to get the first file on a disk:

```
tell1 application "Finder"
    get file 1 of disk "backup"
    get first file of disk "backup"
end tell
```

See the sections on `first` and `last`.

Middle Element

The Middle Element reference form is designed to get the middle object of a certain class type in a container or the middle item of a list. See the section on `middle`.

Name

The Name reference form identifies an object by its name, as in `"application 'Finder'"`. See the `name` section.

Property

Using the Property reference form, your script can grab the value of a property and store it in a variable, for instance. The property may derive from an `application`, a `date` object, a `script` object, or a `record` value. Here are three examples of using the Property reference form.

```
(* get the Finder's largest free block property *)
tell application "Finder"
    set freeMemory to largest free block
end tell
(* returns the month property of a date object *)
set mon to the month of (current date)
(* gets the lastName property of a record object *)
set prezName to lastName of ¬
{firstName: "Abraham", lastName: "Lincoln"}
```

Range

The Range reference form specifies a subset of objects within a container. The return value is a list, or the code raises an error if the container does not contain the specified range of objects. See the `every...from...to` section for some examples.

Relative

The Relative reference form describes an object based on its position compared with another object, such as in this example:

```
tell application " Finder"
    get the folder before the last folder in the startup disk
end tell
```

See the sections on `after`, `back`, `before`, and `beginning`.

Table 5-1 shows the reserved words that you can use to specify objects in Apple-Script code, but not all of the English language synonyms that you can use with these forms. The synonyms are included under the Synonyms heading for each reserved word's section. The reference form is identified in parentheses.

Table 5-1: Reserved Words for Use with AppleScript Reference Forms

after (Relative)	id (ID)
back (Relative)	last (Index)
before (Relative)	middle (Middle Element)
beginning (Relative)	name (Name)
first (Index)	some (Arbitrary Element)
every (Every Element)	whose (Filter)
every...from...to... (Range)	

after

Syntax

```
tell app "FileMaker Pro" to get ID of record after (current record of ¬
database "myDB.fm4") (* returns ID of the record after the currently
active record *)
```

Synonyms

[in] back of

behind

Description

The reserved word after indicates a Relative reference form. Use this reference syntax to identify an object based on its position relative to another object. after is a synonym for in back of and behind. Unlike some other reference methods, this one needs object references on either side of it (when targeting the Finder), such as:

```
folder after folder "Apple Extras" of startup disk
```

The "folder" indicates which class type or value the script is specifying; after is the reserved word indicating Relative reference form, and folder "Apple Extras" of startup disk refers to the object position on the startup disk where AppleScript will start looking for the folder. The following code refers to the object position on the startup disk where AppleScript will start looking for the folder:

```
(folder "Apple Extras" of startup disk)
```

back

Syntax

```
tell app "AppleWorks"
    move paragraph 1 of text body of document 1 to the back of text body¬
    of document 1
```

```
(* or, move paragraph 1 of text body of document 1 to the end of text
body of document 1 *)
end tell
```

Synonyms

end

Description

The back and end reserved words are Relative reference forms that can refer to
the last insertion point in a container, such as a text document. The end word can
also refer to the end of a list, as in:

```
get end of {1,2,3,4,5} -- this returns 5
```

They can also refer to the last *insertion point* in a container, such as a text document. The insertion point is the place in a text document where your cursor is
positioned. You can use beginning and front to refer to the *first* insertion point
of a container. You can also use back to refer to open application windows (at
least in terms of the BBEdit text editor):

```
tell application "BBEdit 5.0" to close back window
```

last might be more readable if you are getting the last item in a container, such
as a folder (see last).

---

before

Syntax

```
tell app "Finder" to get folder before system folder
```

Synonyms

[in] front of

Description

Both Relative reference forms, before or in front of allows the scripter to grab
or refer to items that are located just before a known object, such as a file, folder,
or database record. Similar to a binary operator, before and in front of take
references both before and after it:

```
file before last file
```

To get the database-record id just before the currently active one, you could tell
FileMaker Pro to do the following:

```
get (ID of record before current record)
```

---

beginning

Syntax

```
set list1 to {1,2,3,4,5}
set the beginning of list1 to 10 -- list1 is now {10,1,2,3,4,5}
```

Synonyms

`front`

Description

`beginning` and `front` are reserved words that specify an insertion location in the beginning of a text file, for instance. Like `back` and `end`, `beginning` and `front` are Relative reference forms; however, they point to the first insertion point rather than the last insertion point of a container. You can also use `beginning` and `end` with lists, in the manner of the Syntax example.

---

first, second, third, fourth, etc.

Syntax

```
tell app "Finder" to get 75th file of extensions folder
```

Synonyms

`Index`

`[-]integernd, [-]integerrd, [-]integerst, [-]integerth`

Description

You can identify an object by its numerical position in a folder or other container. For numbers 1–10 you can use the word forms (`first`, `second`, `third`), such as `eighth file of startup disk`. For numerical positions greater than 10, you have to use an `integer` (optionally preceded by the minus sign) followed by any one of the four suffixes (e.g., "rd"), even if it doesn't sound right. Telling the Finder to:

```
get 75rd file of extensions folder
```

is legal. A negative `integer` searches the container in the opposite direction, from its last item to its first. For example, `get file -1` (when targeting the Finder) gets the last file on the desktop. You can also use the index reference style in the following manner:

```
disk index 2
```

The `index` reserved word is optional; mostly you will just use the `index`-less style:

```
folder 3 of Startup disk
```

Examples

```
tell app "BBEdit 5.0" to get -1000th word of document 1 (* gets 1,000th
word searching from the document end *)

tell app "Sherlock 2" to get third channel (* channel surfing Sherlock 2
returns 'channel "Internet" of application "Sherlock 2"' *)

tell app "Sherlock 2" to get tenth channel (* will raise an error if the
container (e.g., the Sherlock 2 app) does not have ten of the objects, in
this case channels *)
```

every

Syntax

```
tell app "Finder" to get every file of extensions folder
```

Description

Using the every syntax returns a list of items in a container, such as files in a folder, words in a document, or cells in a database record. You can get the equivalent return value by dropping the every keyword and making the object plural, as in words of document 1. This statement returns a value of type list whose items are all the words from document 1. You have to check an application's dictionary, however, to make sure that the plural form is allowed for the particular object.

The every form is very useful for grabbing the property values of a group of objects and storing them in a single list. Telling the Finder to:

```
get physical size of every file in extensions folder
```

or:

```
get physical size of files in extensions folder
```

returns the amount of disk space in bytes that each extensions folder file is taking up.

Examples

```
tell app "FileMaker Pro" to get cells of current record (* returns a list
containing the values in each column of the currently active record or
row in an open database *)

tell app "FileMaker Pro" to get name of every cell of current record
(* returns the field names for the currently active database *)
```

every ... from ... to ...

Syntax

```
tell app "FileMaker Pro" to get every record from 1 to 5 (* returns a
list, with each item in the list being another list encompassing the
values for each database record *)
```

Synonyms

... from ... to ...

through

thru

Description

These reserved words represent the Range reference form. These reference methods allow the scripter to select a range of objects:

```
words 10 thru 41 of document 1
```

The return value depends on which objects you select. Telling FileMaker Pro to get a range of database records returns a list value; but telling BBEdit to get a range of words from a text document returns the string containing those words. The example code shows all four of these forms, which produce an equivalent result.

Examples

```
tell application "BBEdit 5.0"
    set w1 to (every word from 10 to 41) of document 1
    set w2 to (words from 10 to 41) of document 1
    set w3 to (words 10 through 41) of document 1
    set w4 to (words 10 thru 41) of document 1
end tell
```

id

Syntax

```
set fileID to id of file "mydocument"
```

Description

Disks, folders, and files, when accessed through the Finder, have a unique id property, even if you change the name of the item. The id is an integer such as 297774 (disks often have negative numbers for ids, such as -1). You can only use the id reference style with objects that have an id property. This property is identified in their dictionary (Chapter 2, *Using Script Editor with OS 9 and OS X*, discusses dictionaries). The following example code shows how to use the id reference.

Examples

```
tell application "Finder"
    set tid to id of folder "today" -- returns an integer such as 277000
    set name of folder "today" to "yesterday" (* changes name of original
folder *)
    open (the first folder whose id is tid) (* still opens original folder
using its id property *)
end tell
```

last

Syntax

```
tell app "FileMaker Pro" to get last record (* returns a list containing
the values from the last record in the currently active database *)
```

Description

last returns the last item in a container, such as files in folders, records in databases, or cells in records. You must test the return result, however, because the ordering scheme to determine which object is last may differ depending on the container. In folders, the last item may be the farthest back in alphabetical order. In a database, the last cell is usually the last column in a database schema or layout. last, when used in the manner of last record or last file, is a synonym of back.

---

middle

Syntax

```
get middle folder of startup disk
```

Description

The middle reference style gets the middle object in a container, including a list. For example, the return value of:

```
middle item of {"apples","oranges","peaches"}
```

is "oranges." If there is an even number of items in the container then AppleScript essentially adds one to the count of container items, then uses the div operator to divide the new count by two. For example, to calculate the middle item of {0,1,2,3,4,5,6,7,8,9}, AppleScript adds one to the count of items in this list (making it now 11 items), and then evaluates 11 div 2 to reach 5 (or the fifth item). In this example the middle (or fifth) item evaluates to 4.

 AppleScript 1.5 and later has fixed a problem that appeared in AppleScript 1.4.3 and earlier, whereby code that references the middle item of an empty list ("{}") could crash AppleScript. Now the code (middle item of {}) will compile in AppleScript Version 1.5.5 or 1.6 but raise a runtime error if the code is executed.

---

name

Syntax

```
get folder named "today" -- gets folder object by its name property
```

Description

When you use the common AppleScript parlance of:

```
tell app ApplicationName
```

you actually use the name reference form. You can use either form of specifying an object by its name property:

```
tell app named "Sherlock 2"
```

or:

```
tell app "Sherlock 2"
```

Scripters often reference files, folders, and disks by their **name** property, if they know the name. There is a difference, however, between getting an object's name and getting an object by name, as these examples indicate.

Examples

```
get folder "today" (* returns a folder object using the name reference
form; could also write 'get folder named "today"' *)

get name of folder "today" -- returns a string, "today"
```

some

Syntax

```
tell app "Sherlock 2" to get some channel
```

Description

some returns a random object from a container. This might be useful if you are randomly selecting images for display from a directory. The script could state:

```
set ranImg to some file of folder "images" where (name ends with ".gif")
```

The **ranImg** variable would then be set to a random *.gif* file that is stored in the *images* folder. The return results are in any event far less predictable than specifying files by name or property values.

whose

Syntax

```
set fJpegs to every file in folder "images" whose name ends with ".jpg"
```

Synonyms

where

Description

The **whose** and **where** reserved words represent the Filter reference forms. These reference styles allow the scripter to select objects based on characteristics that can be tested with a **where** or **whose** reserved word. To use **where** or **whose**, the statement first refers to an object such as a document file, disk, database record, or image file, which is followed by **where** or **whose**, and then a boolean expression. As the following examples indicate, you can create Structured Query Language (SQL)-type **where** statements that narrow the number of objects returned from a statement based on certain criteria.

Examples

```
get files where (creator type is not "MSWD") (* targeting the Finder,
returns only files that are not Microsoft Word files *)

get disks whose name is not (get name of startup disk) (* targeting the
Finder, returns disks other than the startup disk *)
```

CHAPTER 6

Variables and Constants

This chapter describes the rules for AppleScript variables, including `variable scope` and the special variables that you can add to your script called *properties*. The second part of this chapter is devoted to AppleScript's predefined variables such as `pi` and `current application` (a constant). These AppleScript variables are called *constants* because their value is predefined, and you mostly cannot use the same words for your own script variables. You could name one of your own variables `pi` (a predefined variable) and get away with it, but this would only confuse the readers of your code.

Variables

Here are two ways that you can create your own variables in AppleScript:

```
set int to 20 -- one way to set a variable to an integer

copy 20 to int -- another way
```

A variable is a word or identifier that the scripter creates to store a script value. An example is the `int` variable in the statement `set int to 20`. Along with `copy`, the `set` reserved word is used to set a variable name to a value, in this case an `integer`. AppleScript variables can store any value, including booleans, lists, numbers, records, strings, and application-defined classes. AppleScript variables have to begin with a letter or underscore (_) character, but subsequent characters can include numbers and underscores. You cannot include operators and other symbols that AppleScript reserves for different uses (such as *, &, ^, or +) or special characters (such as $, @, or #). An exception to this rule in AppleScript allows the creation of memorable variable names if you use vertical-bar characters (|) to begin and end the identifier:

```
set |2$var*&^%#| to 2
```

AppleScript is not a case-sensitive language, so the variables that include the same characters but in varying case are treated as the same identifier. In other words, myname, myName, and MYNAME are all considered the same variable. Variable names can be one to several characters long, depending on your stylistic preferences.

This AppleScript gives several examples of valid and invalid variable names, as well as how to use the set and copy keywords to declare a variable and store a value in it:

```
set l to {"a", "legal", "var"} as list (* a variable name can be one
letter *)

set a_veryLong_but_legal30_variable500_name to "Too long in my opinion"

copy 500 to int (* using the copy keyword instead of set has the same
effect on integers *)

copy "A string" to str -- creating a string variable with copy

set $perl_string to "Can't imitate perl without pipe characters" (* this
will raise a compiler error *)

set |$perl_string| to "Recreate a perl scalar variable if you use pipe ¬
characters"

set 2str#in/g to "You can't start a variable with a number or use ¬
special  symbols in it" (* another error, unless you enclose the
characters in pipe symbols *)
```

In most cases, you do not have to declare a data type (e.g., integer, string) when you set a value to a variable. You will want to set a variable to a real using the code:

```
set largeNum to 500000000.0
```

when further processing will increase it in value beyond an integer's storage capacity (see Chapter 3, *Data Types,* for a discussion of the real and integer data types). In addition, date variables have to be declared as dates in the manner of set myDate to date "1/1/2000". Sometimes, the code is a lot clearer to its originator and other programmers when you explicitly set variables to the intended class, even if AppleScript does not require explicit typing (except for date strings).

The reserved word copy has a different effect than set when the value is a list, record, or script object. In other words:

```
copy 500 to int --or copy "A string" to str
```

has the same result as:

```
set int to 500 --or set str to "A string"
```

With lists, records, or script objects, however, copy creates a new copy of the object in the variable:

```
set list1 to {"the", "first", "list"}
set list2 to list1 -- list2 refers to list1
copy list1 to list3 -- list3 has a whole new copy of list1
set item 2 of list1 to "different"
```

```
log (list2) -- changes to list1 also effect list2
log (list3) (* changes to list1 do not affect list3; it's a different
copy of the first line *)
```

The first list (list1) is a list of three strings. The list2 variable is set to the
same list. But the third declared variable (list3) receives a copy of the first
list. Afterwards, a change to the second string of the first list alters the value
of the list2 variable, because it is actually pointing to the changed list. The
log (list3) code indicates that the third list, whose list copy was not
changed by the set item 2 of list1 to "different" statement, still
contains the original list value. Again, this behavior is only true for using copy
with a list, record, or script object. (Chapter 9, *Script Objects and Libraries*,
discusses script objects.)

 The log command is used to view the values of variables in Script
Editor's Event Log. Chapter 2, *Using Script Editor with OS 9 and OS
X*, is devoted to Script Editor.

Variable Scope

Variable scope refers to the location in a script where variable values can be
accessed. A variable that can be accessed anywhere in the script is known as
global and has to be declared as such in the script:

```
global aVariable
```

AppleScript variables are local by default, meaning that if a script contains both
script statements and function or subroutine definitions, then the variables that are
declared inside of the function(s) are local (i.e., trying to access them outside of
a function raises an error) unless declared as global outside the routine. This
element is best illustrated by an example:

```
set aNum to 7
display dialog (do_it(aNum) as string) (* call the do_it function and
display its result *)
log avar (* avar variable is not visible at this location; this causes an
error *)
  (* subroutine definition *)
on do_it(v)
    set avar to 0 -- avar is local to the subroutine
    set avar to v + 1
    return avar
end do_it
```

This script sets an integer variable to 7, then displays the results of a function call
using the *display dialog* scripting addition. The *do_it* function is defined inside the
script. It has an avar variable that is initialized to 0 then used to add 1 to the
integer argument that is passed to the function. Though the avar variable
provides the return value for the *do_it* function, it is only known inside the function.
The third line of this example, which tries to log the avar value in the Script-Editor

---

Event Log window, raises an error because the **avar** variable's scope is **local** to the *do_it* function. The error dialog reads: "The variable **avar** is not defined."

The next example solves this problem by declaring **avar** as **global** (initializing the variable at this script location, as in **set avar to 0**, would have the same effect). Then the function call sets the variable to 8, and the Event Log has no trouble logging its value because **avar** is visible at the top-level of the script:

```
set aNum to 7
global avar
display dialog (do_it(aNum) as string)
log avar -- avar evaluates to 8
on do_it(v)
    set avar to 0
    set avar to v + 1
    return avar
end do_it
```

Use the reserved word **local** to give a variable **local** scope. In another variation of our script, the **avar** variable inside the function is first declared as **local**. This means that there are now two different **avar** variables, one at the top level of the script and another local **avar** version that is restricted to the function (outside of an illustrative example like this, you usually wouldn't give two different variables the same name):

```
set aNum to 7
global avar
set avar to 0 -- global avar is initialized to 0
display dialog (do_it(aNum) as string) -- return value is from local avar
log avar -- global avar still is 0
on do_it(v)
    local avar
    set avar to v + 1
    return avar (* returns the integer 8 but doesn't affect global avar
end do_it *)
```

Properties

A **property** is a variable that retains its value after a script has run. Even after you have quit and launched a script again, the script retains its **property** value. A **property** has global scope throughout a script. You have to define a **property** with the **property** keyword (**prop** for short), followed by a space, a variable name, a colon character (**:**), and its initial value:

```
prop runval : 0
```

The colon can be preceded and followed by a space, which improves code readability. The following AppleScript creates a **howmany property**, then increments it by one and displays its value each time the script is run:

```
property howmany : 0
set howmany to howmany + 1
display dialog (howmany as string)
```

howmany starts out as 0, then keeps a count of how many times the script has been run. It will not be reinitialized to 0 unless the script is recompiled (optionally altered then saved again). You can set a property to any value type, including booleans, lists, records, and strings. It is good form to declare all properties at the top level of a script, since they are global variables that persist from script execution to execution. You cannot declare a property inside of a handler, as the following example shows. The script successfully displays the value of the aPi property (which is the value of the pi predefined variable, a real number), even though the property is declared beneath the *display dialog* command. It is better practice to declare all properties at the top of a script:

```
property aList : {"a", "list"}
property aString : "A string"
property aRecord : {name:"A record", type:"record class"}
display dialog (aPi as string)
property aPi : pi
on init()
    property initvar : "I'm inside" (* raises an error and prevents
    script from compiling *)
end init
```

You can also declare a parent object for the script by using the syntax property parent : *scriptObject* or *Application*. In place of the *scriptObject* or *Application* placeholder you include a script object or application. The script with the parent property then inherits the properties, elements, and commands of the parent object. See "current application" in the section *"Constants and Predefined Variables"* in this chapter and Chapter 9 for more information on inheritance in AppleScript.

In sum, you can declare a variable as global at the script's top level if you want to use it throughout the script. The next AppleScript declares a global called initv and then uses it in both the script's run handler and in a user-defined subroutine called *init*. (Chapter 8, *Subroutines*, describes the run handler.) The initv variable is visible inside both subroutines. The as string portion of the (init() as string) fragment is not strictly necessary, but otherwise included to make it clear that an integer return value is coerced to a string before it is included in the display dialog text:

```
global initv
on run
    set initv to 0
    display dialog "Function return value is: " & (init() as string) & ¬
    return & "Value of initv is: " & initv
end run
on init()
    set initv to initv + 1
end init
```

Constants and Predefined Variables

Constants are reserved words that AppleScript has given a predefined value that you cannot change. There are boolean constants (true or false), date constants (e.g., April, May), and considering or ignoring constants (e.g., case, white space), among others. Predefined variables, on the other hand, have a changeable value. In other words, you can use code such as set pi to 5 and the pi predefined variable will no longer have the value of about 3.14159 in your script! You cannot change the value of the boolean constant `false`, however (`set false to 3` will not compile). The constants are listed in Table 6-1, and the Predefined Variables are listed in Table 6-2. Certain date and time values (i.e., `minutes`, `hours`, `days`, `weeks`) are changeable in a script like predefined values; however, they are grouped with other date constants for convenience.

Table 6-1: AppleScript Constants

all caps	all lowercase
application responses	ask
bold	case
condensed	current application
date and time constants (e.g., January, February)	diacriticals
expanded	expansion
false	hidden
hyphens	italic
no	outline
plain	punctuation
shadow	small caps
strikethrough	subscript
superscript	true
underline	white space
yes	

Table 6-2: AppleScript Predefined Variables

anything	it
me	missing value
pi	result
return	space
tab	version
my	

all caps

Syntax

```
{class:text style info, on styles:{plain, all caps}, off styles:{italic,
underline, outline, shadow, condensed, expanded, strikethrough,
superscript, subscript, superior, inferior, double underline}}
```

Description

`all caps` is a text-style constant that represents all capital letters. Some applications return text values that encapsulate the style information, such as font and point size, instead of leaving it as plain ASCII text. The syntax example shows the return value from an application command that gets the style of a chunk of text. The return value is of type `record` and contains the list of text-style constants that are on or off for the text. The AppleWorks command is:

```
get style of text body of document 1
```

Along with all caps, the text-style constants (italic, underline, outline) are reproduced as literal words without quotation marks.

all lowercase

Syntax

```
{class:text style info, on styles:{plain, all lowercase}, off
styles:{italic, underline, outline, shadow, condensed, expanded,
strikethrough, superscript, subscript, superior, inferior, double
underline}}
```

Description

This is a text-style constant that represents all lowercase text characters. Some Mac applications return text that encapsulates one or more of these text-style characteristics (e.g., italic, bold, underline). See all caps for an expanded description of text-style constants.

anything

Syntax

```
set myBasket to anything
```

Description

anything is a predefined variable of type class that can incorporate other classes. In other words, if a command's parameter type is anything then the command will accept more than one value type, as opposed to a command like *display dialog* that only takes one data type as its direct parameter, a string. The AppleScript Language Guide recommends the following usage of anything as an example. If you want a script to monitor a variable to determine if the variable's value or data type has changed, you can set a variable to anything. Then later on in the script test the variable to determine if its value has changed, as in set bool to (myBasket is equal to anything). If the bool variable is true, then the myBasket variable has not been changed, as in set to a string.

application responses

Syntax

```
Ignoring application responses
    (* do some scripting here *)
end ignoring
```

Description

The constant application responses can be included in an ignoring...end ignoring statement block to ignore an Apple event response from a program. This ignoring statement would usually take place in a repeat loop that is querying several different running programs for some purpose. Chapter 7, *Flow-Control Statements*, discusses ignoring and repeat.

Examples

This code tells the Finder to send the script a list of running processes on the computer. process is an element of the Finder application (check the application class in Finder's dictionary and you will find "process" listed under "elements"). The code every process returns a list of process objects, which are otherwise known as running applications on the computer:

```
tell application "Finder"
    (* procs contains a list of running processes on the computer *)
    set procs to every process
    repeat with p from 1 to 4 (* do something with the first four listed
    processes *)
        ignoring application responses -- ignore any reply Apple events
            (*script will try to get name of each process but ignore the
            response, and 'myname' will not get a value *)
            set myname to (name of (item p of procs))
            try
                tell application myname
                    display dialog myname
                end tell
            end try
        end ignoring
    end repeat
end tell
```

If you look at Script Editor's Event Log while this program is running, you'll see a sequence of Apple events sent to each process to retrieve its name (i.e., get name of process "Folder Actions"), but the script will ignore any of the application responses sending the app's name. As a result, the myname variable will not be set to a valid value. Consequently, the tell application myname statement will raise an error (handled by the try...end try block), and no dialogs will ever be displayed.

 Error handling with try blocks is covered in detail by Chapter 7.

If you substitute considering...end considering for ignoring...end ignoring (considering application responses is the default behavior for scripts, so you do not actually have to include it), then the script will do what it's supposed to. It displays four dialogs one after the other containing four of the running process's names.

ask

Syntax

```
Close document 1 saving ask
```

Description

ask is a constant parameter to the *close* command or Apple event, as in close document 1 saving ask. If this parameter is included, in lieu of its alternatives no or yes, then the closing application must produce a dialog asking the user whether to save the document before closing it.

Examples

This AppleScript shows how to use this command. If you use no then the document is closed, whether or not any unsaved changes have been made to it. If you use yes then the app closes the document and saves it using its present filename:

```
tell application "BBEdit 5.0"
    activate
    close document 1 saving ask (* other options are 'saving no' and
    'saving yes' *)
end tell
```

---

bold

Syntax

```
{class:text style info, on styles:{plain, all caps}, off styles:{bold,
italic, underline, outline, shadow, condensed, expanded, strikethrough,
superscript, subscript, superior, inferior, double underline}}
```

Description

bold is a text-style constant that represents a boldface rather than plain character. Some applications return text values that encapsulate the style information, such as font and point size, instead of leaving it as plain ASCII text. See all caps in this section for a further discussion.

---

case

Syntax

```
Considering case
    "Colorado" is equal to "colorado" -- returns false
end considering
```

Description

case can be used in a considering...end considering statement block to take into account upper- or lowercase when making a string comparison. AppleScript does *not* consider case in string comparisons by default. The considering case statement block will consider character case in all the statements within its block.

Examples

The following program will run silently, because the boolean expression "animal" is equal to "aNiMal" returns false considering case:

```
considering case
    if "animal" is equal to "aNiMal" then beep 1
end considering
```

condensed

Syntax

```
{class:text style info, on styles:{plain, all caps}, off styles:{italic,
underline, outline, shadow, condensed, expanded, strikethrough,
superscript, subscript, superior, inferior, double underline}}
```

Description

condensed is a text-style constant that represents the condensed style in a text-editing application such as AppleWorks. The condensed style reduces the space between words. Some applications return text values that encapsulate the style information, such as font or point size, instead of leaving it as plain ASCII text. See all caps in this section for a further discussion.

current application

Syntax

```
set ap to current application
```

Description

The current application is the default application that receives script commands, in the absence of explicit tell statements. Chapter 7 discusses the tell statement. You can set the default application for an entire script by declaring a parent property:

```
property parent : application "Finder"
```

This statement establishes the Finder as the target of any script commands that are not located in a tell statement.

Examples

The upcoming example uses some Finder commands (the Finder is the default or current application). Then the script sends *activate, set,* and *get* Apple events to the text editor BBEdit. The last two lines show that you can use the current application constant to set a variable to the script's default target application. The last line:

```
tell ap to get my name
```

returns "Finder." my is a built-in AppleScript reference to the script object itself, whose parent is the Finder. my name returns "Finder" (Chapter 8 discusses script objects):

```
property parent : application "Finder"
open file "events.html"
get name -- returns "Finder"
tell application "BBEdit 5.0"
    (* BBEdit receives activate, set, and get Apple events *)
    activate
    set mytxt to (get line 1 of document 1)
end tell
set ap to current application
tell ap to get my name
```

date and time constants

Syntax

Months

January, February, March, April, May, June, July, August, September, October, November, December

Days

Sunday, Monday, Tuesday, Wednesday, Thursday, Friday, Saturday

time constants

minutes, hours, days, weeks

Description

The month constants are returned by getting the month property of a date object, as in get month of mydate. You can also use them to test which month is represented by a certain date object:

```
set mydate to date "Friday, January 1, 2000 12:00:00 AM"
if day of mydate is 1 and month of mydate is January then display dialog
"Happy New Year!"
```

The day constants are the day-related values that are returned by a date object's weekday property.

These constants, normally used with dates, represent the following values:

minutes

60

hours

60 * minutes

days

24 * hours

weeks

7 * days

Examples

To calculate how many minutes are in a day (1440), you could write:

```
set dayMinutes to days / minutes
```

These constants contain `integer` value types. A common way to use them is to add or subtract time from `date` objects:

```
set newdate to (date "January 1, 2000") + (20 * weeks)
```

This example adds 20 weeks to the first day of the last year of the millennium (yes, I'm strictly Gregorian in my view of which year represents the last one of the millennium). If you wanted to, you could use these reserved words as `integer` constants. For example, minutes returns 60 and weeks returns 604800 (or, 7 * 24 * 60 * 60). You have to be exact in your usage of these constants, if not in your grammar. If you want to add one week to a date, for instance, you have to use code similar to the following:

```
mydate + 1 * weeks
```

You cannot write:

```
mydate + 1 week
```

---

diacriticals

Syntax

```
Ignoring diacriticals
    (* do some scripting here *)
end ignoring
```

Description

These accent characters are ignored in `string` comparisons that use an `ignoring diacriticals...end ignoring` statement block. By default, AppleScript considers diacriticals when comparing strings.

Examples

This AppleScript shows that by default the strings that have diacritical marks do not return `true` when compared with the same `string` without the marks. The result is reversed when the `diacritical` constant is ignored (`hasDiacritical` returns `false` and `hasDiacritical2` returns `true`):

```
set hasDiacritical to ("spät is late in German" is equal to "spat is late
in German") -- returns false
ignoring diacriticals
   set hasDiacritical2 to ("spät is late in German" is equal to "spat is
   late in German") -- returns true
end ignoring
log hasDiacritical -- is false
log hasDiacritical2 -- is true because the diacritical in "ä" is ignored
```

expanded

Syntax

```
{class:text style info, on styles:{plain, all caps}, off styles:{italic,
underline, outline, shadow, condensed, expanded, strikethrough,
superscript, subscript, superior, inferior, double underline}}
```

Description

expanded is a text-style constant that represents the expanded style in a text-editing application such as AppleWorks. The expanded style increases the space between words in a sentence. (Some applications return text values that encapsulate the style information, such as font or point size, instead of leaving it as plain ASCII text. See all caps in this section for a further discussion.)

expansion

Syntax

```
Ignoring expansion
    (* include string comparison here *)
end ignoring
```

Description

If expansion is included in strings that are located in an ignoring expansion...end ignoring statement block, then AppleScript considers the characters Æ, æ, Œ, and œ to be single characters and not equal to AE, ae, OE, and oe. By default, AppleScript considers the string "Æ" to be equal to the string "AE." Chapter 7 is devoted to AppleScript statements such as ignoring...end ignoring.

false

Syntax

```
Set falseBool to false
```

Description

false is the boolean constant that equals false or not true. Chapter 3 discusses the boolean data type.

hidden

Syntax

```
{class:text style info, on styles:{plain, all caps}, off styles:{bold,
italic, underline, outline, shadow, condensed, expanded, hidden,
strikethrough, superscript, subscript, superior, inferior, double
underline}}
```

Description

hidden is a text-style constant that represents the hidden style in a text-editing application such as AppleWorks. Some applications return text values that encapsulate the style information, such as font or point size, instead of leaving it as plain ASCII text. See all caps in this section for a further discussion.

hyphens

Syntax

```
Ignoring hyphens
    "A hyphen" is equal to "A-hyphen"
end ignoring
```

Description

AppleScript considers hyphens in strings by default during string comparisons. You can change this behavior by enclosing the string-comparison statement in an ignoring hyphens...end ignoring statement block. This code shows that hyphens will not be considered when comparing strings in this manner:

```
ignoring hyphens
    set theTruth to ("burning-hot pavement" is equal to "burninghot ¬
    pavement") -- theTruth is true
end ignoring
```

it

Syntax

```
Tell it to get its name
```

Description

it is shorthand for a script's default target. The following example returns the string "9.0," which is the Finder's version in Mac OS 9. The script's default target was previously set to the Finder by declaring the Finder as a parent property (see current application in this chapter or Chapter 3 for more information on parent properties). Therefore, it is a reference to the Finder:

```
property parent : application "Finder"
tell it to get its version (* returns the value of the Finder's version
property *)
```

italic

Syntax

```
{class:text style info, on styles:{plain, all caps}, off styles:{italic,
underline, outline, shadow, condensed, expanded, strikethrough,
superscript, subscript, superior, inferior, double underline}}
```

Description

`italic` is a text-style constant that represents the italic style in a text-editing application such as AppleWorks. The italic style places one or more characters in a `string` in italics. Some applications return text values that encapsulate the style information, such as font or point size, instead of leaving it as plain text. See `all caps` in this section for a further discussion.

---

me

Syntax

```
Set returnVal to MyScriptFunc() of me
```

Description

me is used to specify a script-defined subroutine or property, to distinguish it from the properties or functions of other applications that the script uses. me is most often used in the form *propertyname* or *functionname* of me. In the following code, the me predefined variable is used inside a `tell...end tell` statement block to identify the *getMegabytes* function as a script subroutine, not a Finder command. If you left out the *of me* part of *getMegabytes(b)* of me then the script would raise an error, because it would tell the Finder to call its *getMegabytes* handler, but the Finder doesn't define this command. In the absence of the me or my constants, all commands inside of a `tell...end tell` block are directed to the application targeted by the `tell` block or to scripting additions (Chapter 7 discusses `tell` blocks). The script identifies *getMegabytes* as its own subroutine, which is an elegant way to call this useful routine anywhere you want in the script:

```
tell application "Finder"
    set b to largest free block -- returns free memory block as bytes
    set mb to getMegabytes(b) of me
    display dialog mb
end tell
(* subroutine definition; converts bytes to megabytes *)
on getMegabytes(byteVal)
    if (class of byteVal) is in {integer, real} then
        set megValue to (byteVal / 1024 / 1024)
        return megValue
    else
        return 0
    end if
end getMegabytes
```

---

missing value

Syntax

```
{"192.168.0.1", "0.0.0.0", missing value}
```

Description

`missing value` is a predefined variable that takes the place of a missing property value in return values that involve lists, for instance. The following code asks the Network Setup Scripting system app for the IP address of each network configuration on the computer. Since not all configurations use the TCP/IP protocol (some use the AppleTalk protocol), some of them are not associated with an IP address. The return value for this example looks like `{"192.168.0.1", "0.0.0.0", missing value, "0.0.0.0", missing value, missing value, "0.0.0.0", missing value}`, where missing value takes the place of the return value for the configurations that do not have an IP address:

```
tell application "Network Setup Scripting"
    open database
    get IP address of every configuration (* returns list of IP addresses
    and missing values *)
    close database
end tell
```

my

Syntax

```
Set megValue to my getMegabytes(bytes)
```

Description

`my` is a reserved word that has the same effect as using the reserved words of me in a script (see me in this chapter). There is no difference between the two predefined variables; you can use whichever one appears more readable to you (my gets my vote). In the following example, you replace the statement:

```
set mb to getMegabytes(b) of me
```

with:

```
set mb to my getMegabytes(b)
```

This tells AppleScript that you are calling the script's *getMegabytes* subroutine, as opposed to an osax or custom application command. In other words, my denotes script ownership of a property or subroutine.

no

Syntax

```
Close document 1 saving no
```

Description

`no` is a constant parameter to the *close* command or Apple event:

```
close document 1 saving no
```

If this parameter is included, in lieu of its alternatives **ask** or **yes**, then the closing application closes the document without saving it, whether or not the document has been changed. See "ask" earlier in this chapter.

outline

Syntax

```
{class:text style info, on styles:{plain, all caps}, off styles:{italic,
underline, outline, shadow, condensed, expanded, strikethrough,
superscript, subscript, superior, inferior, double underline}}
```

Description

`outline` is a text-style constant that represents characters that are outlined in black (or some other text color), and white in the middle, rather than appearing as plain text. Some applications return text values that encapsulate the style information, such as a font and point size, instead of leaving it as plain literal text. See `all caps` in this section for more discussion of text-style constants.

pi

Syntax

```
Return pi * (radius^2)
```

Description

`pi` is a predefined variable that returns a **real** value of about 3.14159. You can use this predefined variable in geometry calculations, as in the following example. This script has a *getArea* subroutine that returns the area of a circle when passed the circle's radius as an argument. Chapter 8 discusses how to create your own functions.

```
set circleArea to getArea(12)
on getArea(radius)
    if (class of radius) is in {integer, real} then (* check to make sure
    parameter is a valid number *)
        return pi * (radius ^ 2) -- this calc returns the area of a circle
    else
        return 0
    end if
end getArea
```

plain

Syntax

```
{class:text style info, on styles:{plain, all caps}, off styles:{italic,
underline, outline, shadow, condensed, expanded, strikethrough,
superscript, subscript, superior, inferior, double underline}}
```

Description

`plain` is a text-style constant that represents plain text. Some applications will return text values that encapsulate the style information, such as its font or point size, instead of leaving it as plain ASCII text. See `all caps` in this section for more discussion of text-style constants.

---

punctuation

Syntax

```
Ignoring punctuation but considering case
    (* do string comparison *)
end ignoring
```

Description

AppleScript considers punctuation marks such as commas and periods in strings by default when it compares strings for equality. If you enclose the string comparison in the statement `ignoring punctuation...end ignoring`, however, AppleScript will ignore the punctuation when evaluating a string comparison. `punctuation` comprises the following characters in AppleScript:

```
.
?
:
;
!
\
,
"
`
```

The next example uses the `punctuation` constant to ignore any commas in the numbers entered into a dialog box by a user. If the script did not use the `ignoring punctuation` statement, and the user entered a number with one or more commas (such as 1,000,000), then the statement:

```
if inputNum as real ≤ 1000
```

would raise an error. This is because by default the strings with nonnumber characters in them cannot be coerced to integers or `reals` (with the exception of strings like "1.0e + 4," which would evaluate to the `real` type in scientific notation—1.0e + 4). In the case of the following script, the punctuation marks can be ignored, allowing "1,000,000" to be coerced to a `real` data type (which would look like 1.0e + 6). Chapter 3 discusses the `real` type.

```
set inputNum to text returned of (display dialog "Enter a number larger ¬
than 1,000" default answer "")
ignoring punctuation
    if inputNum as real ≤ 1000 then
        display dialog "Remember it has to be bigger than 1,000"
```

```
        else
            display dialog "Your number is: " & inputNum
        end if
    end ignoring
```

result

Syntax

```
Set lastExpr to result
```

Description

result is a handy predefined variable that contains the value of the last statement evaluated in a script. You can set variables to result as in:

```
set finalVar to result
```

or use the following code to display the result:

```
display dialog result
```

If there is not a valid result from an expression, as in the top of the next example,
then trying to get the value of result will raise an error. The bottom tell block
in the following code stores the value of the last expression (i.e., 2 * 2) in the
result predefined variable:

```
tell application "Finder"
    activate -- this Apple event doesn't return a value to AppleScript
    get result -- this statement raises an error
end tell
tell application "Finder"
    2 * 2
    get result -- returns 4
end tell
```

return

Syntax

```
Set theStr to "one line" & return & "another line"
```

Description

The return predefined variable represents a return character. You will use this
predefined variable a lot with the concatenation character (&) in order to make
strings more presentable:

```
"a long sentence divided into" & return & "two lines with the return
character"
```

Make sure not to confuse the return statement with the return predefined variable. AppleScript also uses return as a statement inside of subroutines. If you use
the return statement, the subroutine or function will return to the part of the
script that called the function. The return character is a predefined variable while

return, as used in functions, is a flow-control statement (see Chapter 7). This code illustrates the difference between the two:

```
set aString to "String with " & return & "one return character." (* use
the return constant *)
run_it(aString) -- call the function
on run_it(str) -- function definition
    display dialog str ¬
        buttons {"okay", "Big deal", "cancel"} default button 2
    (* use return statement to return the value of the button the user
clicked to dismiss the dialog box *)
    return (button returned in the result) (* return statement, not
constant *)
end run_it
```

shadow

Syntax

```
{class:text style info, on styles:{plain, all caps}, off styles:{italic,
underline, outline, shadow, condensed, expanded, strikethrough,
superscript, subscript, superior, inferior, double underline}}
```

Description

shadow is a text-style constant that represents the display of characters with a drop shadow behind them. Some applications will return text values that encapsulate this style information, such as font and other embellishments, instead of leaving it as literal plain text. See all caps in this section for more discussion of text-style constants.

small caps

Syntax

```
{class:text style info, on styles:{plain, small caps}, off
styles:{italic, underline, outline, shadow, condensed, expanded,
strikethrough, superscript, subscript, superior, inferior, double
underline}}
```

Description

small caps is a text-style constant that represents the display of characters with small capital letters. Some applications will return text values to an AppleScript that encapsulate this style information, such as font and other embellishments, instead of leaving it as literal plain text. See all caps in this section for more discussion of text-style constants.

space

Syntax

```
"string with" & space & " an extra space"
```

Description

space represents a space character in a string. You can use it when building your own strings:

```
"String with " & space & space & "two extra spaces."
```

You can also use the tab and return predefined variables to exert more control on string appearance.

---

strikethrough

Syntax

```
{class:text style info, on styles:{plain, small caps}, off
styles:{italic, underline, outline, shadow, condensed, expanded,
strikethrough, superscript, subscript, superior, inferior, double
underline}}
```

Description

strikethrough is a text-style constant that represents the display of characters with a line drawn through them, as though someone editing the document had crossed them out. Some applications will return text values to an AppleScript that encapsulate this style information, such as font and other embellishments, instead of leaving it as literal plain text. See all caps in this section more discussion of text-style constants.

---

subscript

Syntax

```
{class:text style info, on styles:{plain, small caps}, off
styles:{italic, underline, outline, shadow, condensed, expanded,
strikethrough, superscript, subscript, superior, inferior, double
underline}}
```

Description

subscript is a text-style constant that represents the display of characters with a lower-than-normal baseline, as in subscript. Some applications such as AppleWorks will return text values to an AppleScript that encapsulate this style information, such as font and other embellishments, instead of leaving it as literal plain text. See all caps in this section for more discussion of text-style constants.

---

superscript

Syntax

```
{class:text style info, on styles:{plain, small caps}, off
styles:{italic, underline, outline, shadow, condensed, expanded,
strikethrough, superscript, subscript, superior, inferior, double
underline}}
```

Description

superscript is a text-style constant that represents the display of characters with a higher-than-normal baseline, as in superscript. Some applications such as Apple-Works will return text values to a script that encapsulate this style information, such as font and other embellishments, instead of leaving it as literal plain text. See all caps in this section for more discussion of text-style constants.

tab

Syntax

```
"A string" & tab & tab & "with two tabs in it."
```

Description

tab is a predefined variable that places a tab in a string:

```
"Here is a string" & tab & tab & "with two tabs in the middle of it."
```

You can also insert return and space characters into your strings.

true

Syntax

```
Set boolVal to true
```

Description

true is the boolean constant that equals true or not false. Chapter 3 discusses the boolean value type.

underline

Syntax

```
{class:text style info, on styles:{plain, small caps}, off
styles:{italic, underline, outline, shadow, condensed, expanded,
strikethrough, superscript, subscript, superior, inferior, double
underline}}
```

Description

underline is a text-style constant that represents the display of characters that are underlined, as in underline. Some applications will return text values to an Apple-Script that encapsulate this style information, such as font and other embellishments, instead of leaving it as literal plain text. See all caps in this section for more discussion of text-style constants.

version

Syntax

```
Get version as string
```

Description

AppleScript's **version** property returns a **version** value (yes, **version** objects are based on the **version** class) that can be coerced to a **string**, as in "1.4." The number is the version of AppleScript that the machine running the script has installed. The following code shows how you can test for AppleScript's **version**. (Other applications, such as the Finder, also have a **version** property. Check the application class in the program's dictionary to find out if they do.)

```
set ASver to version as string
(* grab the "1.4" part of the value and coerce it to a number so that it
can be tested *)
if (text 1 thru 3 of ASver as real) ³ 1.4 then
display dialog ¬
"Good, you're running at least AppleScript version 1.4"
else
display dialog ¬
"Perhaps you should consider upgrading to a newer AppleScript version"
end if
```

white space

Syntax

```
Ignoring white space
    (* do string comparison *)
end ignoring
```

Description

If you enclose a **string** comparison in an **ignoring white space...end ignoring** statement block, then AppleScript ignores any spaces, tabs, or return characters when comparing strings. Otherwise, AppleScript takes these characters into account during **string** comparisons. **Ignoring white space** might be useful when checking for certain content strings seized from textually complex sources like web pages. The following code shows what happens when you ignore white space:

```
set string1 to "a spread" & tab & tab & return & "out string."
set string2 to "aspreadoutstring."
ignoring white space
    return (string1 is equal to string2) -- returns true
end ignoring
```

yes

Syntax

```
Close document 1 saving yes
```

Description

yes is a constant parameter to the *close* command or Apple event:

```
close document 1 saving yes
```

If this parameter is included, in lieu of its alternatives **ask** or no, then the closing application saves the document, if it has been changed, before closing it. Depending on the application's default behavior, it usually prompts you for a filename (if the document does not have a valid filename) before closing it. Therefore, you should use the *activate* command to bring the target application to the foreground, so that the user can see any dialog box. See "ask" in this chapter for more info.

CHAPTER 7

Flow-Control Statements

The flow-control statements in AppleScript orchestrate the "flow" or the order in which the code statements execute in your scripts. Programmers will be familiar with AppleScript's if conditional statements, which are very similar to the syntax of Visual Basic, Perl, and other languages. These statements execute code only if the tested conditions are true. AppleScript handles loops in script code with several variations of the repeat statement, similar to the "for," "foreach," or "for each" statements in other languages. The repeat flow-control construct repeats the execution of code a specified number of times or for each member of a container, such as a list type. Or, it repeats a code phrase a specified number of times:

    repeat 100 times...end repeat

You will be pleased to know that AppleScript has more than adequate error-trapping capabilities. This is accomplished by enclosing the statements that may raise errors in a try...end try statement block. In addition, you have already seen dozens of examples of the tell..end tell statement in earlier chapters. These statements specify the objects, usually application objects, that receive the commands or Apple events that your script sends. You specify the targets of different script commands by using these tell statements.

You can nest flow-control statements within other flow-control statements. Most of these statements end, appropriately, with the reserved word end, optionally followed by the statement identifier, such as tell or repeat. An example is:

    tell app "Photoshop 5.5"...end tell

The if and tell statements allow "simple" rather than "compound" usage, such as:

    if (current date) > date "1/1/2001" then display dialog "Welcome to 2001"

These simple statements appear on one line, they do not contain other code statements, and they do not need to be completed with the **end** reserved word. This code shows some nested flow-control statements and simple statements:

```
tell application "Finder"
    set freeMemoryBlock to largest free block
    (* Here's a simple statement; no 'end' is necessary *)
    if freeMemoryBlock < 10000000 then display dialog ¬
    "Memory is getting low"
    set listOfProcesses to name of processes
    if "BBEdit 5.0" is not in listOfProcesses then (* compound 'if'
statement *)
        tell application "BBEdit 5.0" to run -- simple 'tell' statement
    end if
end tell
```

Suffice it to say, flow-control statements are how AppleScript derives much of its power and complexity. You will develop very few scripts that do not use at least one flow-control statement. Table 7-1 lists the statements that this chapter describes.

Table 7-1: Flow-Control Statements

considering	repeat with *loop variable*
continue	repeat *integer* times
error	return
exit	tell *simple statement*
if *simple statement*	tell *compound statement*
if *compound statement*	try
ignoring	using terms from
repeat	with timeout
repeat until	with transaction
repeat while	

---

considering [but ignoring] end [considering]

Syntax

```
Considering case
    "animal" is equal to "AniMal" -- returns false
end considering
```

Description

Use **considering** statements to specify the elements that should be considered during string comparisons and communications with other applications. The statements that constitute the comparison are enclosed in the **considering...end considering** block. This statement block affects how each of its enclosed statements is processed. The **considering** statement can also alter AppleScript's default behavior for the code that is executed prior to the end of the **considering** statement (signaled by an **end** or **end considering** phrase). For example, if you wanted to compare two strings and take upper- or lowercase characters into account, but ignore any white space in the strings, then you would use the statement: **considering case but ignoring white space...end** considering. AppleScript's default behavior is to consider elements such as case, white space, and punctuation when it compares strings for equality. The following constants can also be used in the considering statement (Chapter 6, *Variables and Constants*, discusses AppleScript's constants):

- `application responses`
- `case`
- `diacriticals`
- `expansion`
- `hyphens`
- `punctuation` (i.e., `. , ? : ; ! \ ' " ` `)
- `white space`

AppleScript considers by default an application's responses to any Apple events that your script sends them. You can use the `ignoring` statement to ignore responses from an application, as in considering case but ignoring application responses.

There are a few instances when ignoring application responses might make sense, such as when you are sending *quit* commands to several running processes. If one of the processes responds to the command with an error, then the script ignores its response (as well as any other application response) and thus prevents it from disrupting the execution of the rest of the script. See "ignoring" in this chapter for more details.

Examples

This code shows how to use this statement with a fairly complex string comparison:

```
tell application "Finder"
    considering case but ignoring punctuation, white space and hyphens
        set theTruth to ("voracious appetite" is equal to "voracious, ¬
        appetite") --returns true
    end considering
end tell
```

The example tells AppleScript which elements to consider and ignore when executing the string comparison within the `considering` statement block. Since white space, hyphens, and punctuation should be ignored in the comparison, the two strings turn out the same. Therefore, the `theTruth` variable is set to `true`. If you are wondering why you would ever ignore these elements in a string comparison, programs often deal with a lot of junk characters and tokens, such as markup-language elements, which are returned from applications or web pages. The `considering` statement allows you, in a minimal way, to filter out elements that you do not want to include in string comparisons (unfortunately, you will have to write custom functions or use an HTML-parsing osax to filter out the common < > characters in hypertext markup language [HTML], as AppleScript does not consider them to be "punctuation").

continue

```
On parMethod(int )
    If somethingTrue then
        (* code statements here *)
    else
        continue parMethod(int) -- call parent script's parMethod version
    end if
end parMethod
```

Description

The continue statement is used to call a parent script's method from a child script. In AppleScript, a child script can inherit properties and methods from a parent script. This topic is covered in Chapter 9, *Script Objects and Libraries*. The child script specifies its parent (if it has one) by declaring a parent property at the top of the script:

```
property parent : NameOfScript
```

The *NameOfScript* part can be either the name of a script object or an application, such as:

```
application "Finder"
```

A child script inherits the methods of a parent; it does not have to define these methods. However, the child script can "override" the parent method(s) by redefining them in the body of the script. Within these redefined methods, it can use the continue statement to call the parent method. The following example constitutes a child script that calls its parent's version of the *parMethod* function based on the magnitude of the numerical argument passed to the method. The child object handles **real** numbers and the parent handles integers.

Examples

```
On parMethod(int )
    If (class of int is real) then
        Return (int * 2)
    Else
        continue parMethod(int) (* it's an integer so call the parent
        parMethod *)
    end if
end parMethod
```

error

Syntax

```
error myErrText number 9000 -- myErrText contains the error description
```

Description

The error statement allows you to raise an error based on certain script conditions. Why would you ever want to raise an error? You may want to catch an error in a function but handle the error in the part of the code that called the function, higher up in the call chain. So you would use the **error** statement to pass the error up to the calling function, such as in the following example. This is similar to "throwing" an exception in Java.

Examples

This example uses a *getNumber* method to get a number from the user, but it does not bother (for the sake of demonstration) to check the entry to ensure that the user has entered a valid number. If the user enters data that is not a number then the statement:

```
return (theNum as number)
```

causes an error, because AppleScript cannot coerce non-numeric characters to a number. To be specific, this is AppleScript error number –1700. The *getNumber* method catches the error and uses an **error** statement to pass the original error's error message and number back to the calling handler (in this case the script's *run* handler), which then catches the "re-raised" error and displays a message:

```
on run
    try
        display dialog "Your number is: " & (getNumber() as text)
    on error errmesg number errn
        display dialog errmesg & return & return & "error number: " & ¬
            (errn as text)
    end try
end run
on getNumber()
    set theNum to (text returned of (display dialog ¬
    "Please enter a  number:" default answer ""))
    try
        return (theNum as number)
        on error errmesg number errnumber
        error errmesg number errnumber
    end try
end getNumber
```

The **error** statement also gives the scripter more control on how program errors are handled. For example, you can catch an error in a script with a **try** block (see "try" later in this chapter), examine the nature of the error, then re-raise the error with the **error** statement providing a more lucid error message to the user. This is best illustrated with the following code, which catches an error caused by coercing a non-numeric string to a **real** data type:

```
(* use the display-dialog scripting addition to ask the user to enter a
number *)
set aNum to the text returned of (display dialog "Enter a number" ¬
default  answer "")
try
    set aNum to aNum as real (* non-numeric string like "10ab" will raise
an error *)
on error number errNumber
    set myErrText to "Can't coerce the supplied text to a real: " & ¬
```

```
      return & "The AS error number is " & errNumber
      error myErrText number 9000 -- add your own error number
   end try
```

The code first asks the user to enter a number, using the *display dialog* scripting addition. This produces a dialog box with a text-entry field. If the user enters some text that cannot be coerced to a number, such as 10ab (the included letters ab cause the coercion to fail), the expression:

```
set aNum to aNum as real
```

causes the script to raise an error. The try block catches the error, and then processes the statements following the on error code. These statements include:

```
error myErrText number 9000
```

which produces an AppleScript error-dialog box and adds the scripter's custom message (stored in the variable myErrText). It also provides a custom error number of 9000. You can create your own groups of error numbers or variables for certain error conditions, which your script can then identify and respond to with more accuracy and clarity than if the scripter only relied on AppleScript's error numbers.

The next two examples illustrate the setup and usage of custom error variables. The first example is a script that contains several user-defined error variables for some common errors that occur in AppleScripts. This script is loaded into the current script using the *load script* scripting addition (Appendix A, *Standard Scripting Additions*, discusses scripting additions, or osaxen). The example only contains three constants, but it could define dozens of them to accommodate most or all of the possible script errors that could occur. The constants are set to the actual values that AppleScript assigns to the errors that represent, for example, the failure to coerce data from one type to another (i.e., error number -1700):

```
set FAILED_COERCION to -1700

set MISSING_PARAMETER to -1701

set TIMEDOUT_APPLEEVENT to -1712
```

You can then test for certain errors and, if you discover them, display more informative messages or take some other appropriate action. For example, the script in the following code sets the variable objErrors to the script object defined in the prior example. It then uses the FAILED_COERCION and TIMEDOUT_APPLEEVENT constants from that object to test for these error conditions. In other words, the TIMEDOUT_APPLEEVENT variable contains AppleScript's actual error number for Apple events that time out (-1712), but it is easier to remember if it is stored in a variable with a coherent name. If either of these errors is detected, the error statement is used to produce a dialog box with your own error message:

```
set objErrors to (load script file "HFSA2gig:nutshell book:demo ¬
scripts:scr_0504")(* this script object contains the user-defined error
variables *)
set userReply to the text returned of (display dialog ¬
 "Please enter a number" default answer "")
try
```

```
    set aNum to userReply as real (* if the user doesn't provide a number
    this statement will fail and the try block will catch the error *)
    on error errM number errNumber
    if errNumber is equal to (objErrors's FAILED_COERCION) then
    (* FAILED_COERCION is a property of the script object stored in
objError *)
        error "The number you provided was not a valid integer or real."
    else if errNumber is equal to (objErrors's TIMEDOUT_APPLEEVENT) then
        error "For some reason AppleScript timed out."
    else -- default error message for all other errors
    set defMessage to "Sorry, AppleScript error number: " & errNumber & ¬
    "occurred in the script. Here's AppleScript's error description: " & errM
    error defMessage
    end if
    end try
```

The **error** statement includes a number of optional parameters. It is important to remember that you supply the values for these parameters (if you want to use them). With **try** blocks and on **error** statements, AppleScript itself will fill these parameters with values (see "try" later in this chapter):

- A non-labeled parameter that contains the text describing the error, as in **error "The Apple event timed out"**.

- A labeled parameter that identifies the error number, such as **error "The Apple event timed out" number** 9000. You use the keyword **number** followed by the **integer**. If you do not include an error number, AppleScript gives this parameter a default value of −2700.

- A labeled parameter that identifies the object that caused the error, as in **error "The Apple event timed out" number 9000 from userReply**. You use the keyword **from** followed by a reference to the object, in this case the variable that caused the coercion error.

- A labeled parameter that involves the reserved words **partial result** followed by a value of type **list**. If the command that caused the error involved the receipt of return values from multiple objects (e.g., a command sent to several database files to get some data), then the **list** value contains any of the values that were successfully received before the error halted the operation. AppleScript gives this parameter a default value of the empty list ({ }).

- A **to** keyword or label followed by a word that identifies a class type, such as **boolean**, **string**, or **integer**. If the command that caused the error received the wrong type of parameter value, then the **to** labeled parameter will identify the correct data type that the parameter expected.

The following example demonstrates how to pass the information about an Apple-Script error to an **error** statement. The script intentionally raises an error by using a **string** instead of a **boolean** expression in an **if** statement. Then it passes the error data as a long **string** to an **error** statement:

```
try
    if "not a boolean" then (* this causes an error, caught in the try
    block *)
        beep 2
```

```
        end if
    on error errMessage number errNum from errSource partial result ¬
    errList  to class_constant -- various variables store information about
    the error
        set bigmessage to "The error is: " & errMessage & return & ¬
        "The number is: " & errNum & return & "The source is: " & errSource
        error bigmessage -- error statement displays dialog box to user
    end try
```

exit [repeat]

Syntax

```
repeat 2 times
    exit repeat
end repeat
```

Description

The **exit** statement causes the flow of script execution to leave the **exit** statement's **repeat** loop. The execution then resumes with the script code following the **repeat** loop. **exit** can only be used inside of a **repeat** loop, regardless of the **repeat**-loop variation. Using **exit** is the conventional way to exit a **repeat** loop that has no conditional statement associated with it, as shown in this example. In other words, this form of **repeat** is an infinite loop:

```
repeat
    set userReply to the text returned of (display dialog "Want to get ¬
    out of this endless loop?" default answer "")
    if userReply is "yes" then exit repeat
end repeat
```

This endless loop can also be exited by clicking the Cancel button on the dialog produced by *display dialog*, which terminates the execution of the script.

if simple statement

Syntax

```
If theBool is true then exit repeat
```

Description

AppleScript supports the simple **if** statement that is similar to Perl's. You can use a statement such as the following:

```
if (current date) is greater than or equal to date "1/1/2001" then ¬
display dialog "Welcome to 2001"
```

You do not have to "close" this statement with an **end** or **end if**, as you do with more wordy compound statements. You just include the reserved word **if** followed by a **boolean** expression (returns **true** or **false**), the reserved word **then**, and whichever statement you would like to execute if the **boolean** expression returns **true**. This example has several different versions of the **if** statement.

Since there are two different versions of the same date-test expression, this script will create two of the same dialog boxes:

```
if (current date) is greater than or equal to date "Saturday, January ¬
1, 2000 12:00:00 AM" then display dialog "Welcome to 2000" (* simple if
statement *)
if (current date) is less than date "Saturday, January 1, 2000 12:00:00 ¬
AM" then display dialog "Enjoy end of 1999" -- simple if statement
    set yearCount to 0
    if (current date) ≥ date "Saturday, January 1, 2000 12:00:00 AM" then
    --compound if statement
    display dialog "Welcome to 2000"
    set yearCount to yearCount + 1
else if (current date) ¬
 < date "Saturday, January 1, 2000 12:00:00 AM" then
    display dialog "Enjoy end of 1999"
end if
```

Use a simple if statement if the script only has to execute one line of code in the event that the boolean expression tests true. Otherwise use a compound if statement.

---

if [then] [else if] [else] end [if]

Syntax

```
If theBoolean then
    (* code statements *)
else if anotherBool then
    (* code statements *)
else
    (* code statements *)
end if
```

Description

The compound if statement can be used to test several boolean expressions and only execute subsequent script code if the enclosing expression is true. The syntax of the if compound statement is almost exactly the same as Visual Basic's, JavaScript's, and Perl's, with some minor differences (for example, VB pushes the else and if together to make "elseif"). A plain-English pseudocode translation of this statement would be, "if this happens then run this code; else if that happens then run this code; else (if neither of the first two things happen) then run this default code." You do not have to include any curly-brace characters ({ }) to enclose the conditional script code that the if statement contains. As long as you place different lines of code on separate lines, then the then part of if...then and the if part of end if are optional, as in the following code. The compiler puts the "thens" and "end if" in the right places.

Examples

In the following example, the (current date) date "1/1/2001" is the tested boolean expression. If it's false, then the else statement(s) will execute.

```
Set yearCount to 0
if (current date) ≥ date "1/1/2001"  -- compiler will fill in 'then'
    display dialog "Welcome to 2001"
    set yearCount to yearCount + 1
else
    display dialog "Enjoy the end of 2000"
end -- 'if' is optional
```

ignoring [but considering] end [ignoring]

Syntax

```
ignoring application responses
end ignoring
```

Description

You can use this statement block to control **string** comparisons. The **ignoring** statement is used with **application responses** to disregard any responses from the apps that receive the script commands:

```
ignoring application responses...end ignoring
```

The following AppleScript constants are the parameters to the **ignoring** statement. They are all considered by default:

- **application response**
- **case**, as in upper- or lowercase
- **diacritical**, like the two dots in ü.
- **expansion**; if ignored, then æ, Æ , œ, and Œ are equal to ae, AE, oe, and OE, respectively. These letters are by default not equal to each other.
- **hyphen**, as in "-"
- **punctuation**; these marks are ignored by the statement ignoring punctuation: . , ? : ; ! \ ' " `
- **white space**

Examples

This code shows how to use **ignoring...end ignoring**. Believe it or not, the code:

```
"j'u-n,k t?'ext" is equal to "junk text"
```

returns **true**, because the enclosing **ignoring** block tells AppleScript to ignore punctuation and hyphens when making the string comparison:

```
ignoring punctuation and hyphens but considering case
    return ("j'u-n,k t?'ext" is equal to "junk text") (*returns true
because punctuation is ignored in the comparison *)
end ignoring
```

If you want to ignore more than one constant, just separate them with the **and** operator:

```
ignoring punctuation and white space and hyphens and expansion.
```

You can also use the but considering parameter followed by one of the specified constants (e.g., hyphen, white space) to ignore some elements but consider others:

```
ignoring punctuation but considering white space
```

repeat end [repeat]

Syntax

```
repeat
    if someTrueCondition then exit repeat
end repeat
```

Description

repeat without any conditional statements associated with it results in an infinite loop. In most cases, you need to use an exit statement to terminate the loop and resume execution with the statement that follows end repeat. This statement begins with repeat on its own line and finishes with an end or an end repeat (the repeat part of end repeat is optional). All of the statements that should execute within the loop appear between the repeat and end repeat lines. You can nest repeat loops within each other.

Examples

This AppleScript shows one repeat loop nested within another. It also illustrates that the exit statement only exits the repeat statement in which exit is contained. So the example actually needs two exit statements to emerge from its repetition purgatory:

```
repeat -- outer repeat loop
    repeat -- beginning of inner repeat loop
        set userReply to the text returned of ¬
        (display dialog ¬  -
            "Want to get out of inner endless loop?" default  answer "")
    if userReply is "yes" then exit repeat
    end repeat
    set userReply to the text returned of ¬
    (display dialog "Want to get out of outer endless loop?" default  ¬
    answer "")
    if userReply is "yes" then exit repeat
end repeat
```

repeat until end [repeat]

Syntax

```
Repeat until trueBoolean
    (* code statements *)
end repeat
```

Description

This form of repeat takes the until keyword and a boolean expression, as in: repeat until countVar is true. The statements that are contained within repeat until...end repeat will continue to execute until the boolean conditional expression is true. If the expression following until is true, the repeat loop is terminated and execution resumes with the statement following end repeat. You could also exit this repeat loop using the exit statement (see exit). Note that when repeat until encounters a true value, the loop is immediately ended; its enclosed statements are not executed.

Examples

This AppleScript shows a repeat until statement that also contains an exit statement:

```
set theCount to 0
repeat until (theCount = 5)
    if theCount = 4 then exit repeat
    set theCount to theCount + 1
    log theCount
end repeat
```

This code increments a theCount integer variable by one with each cycle through the loop. The code includes a simple if statement that exits the repeat loop once the theCount variable reaches 4. Without the exit statement, the variable would reach 5; the expression: theCount = 5 would return true, and the repeat until loop would terminate. We keep track of the value of theCount with a log theCount statement. This displays all of the theCount values in Script Editor's Event Log window.

repeat while end [repeat]

Syntax

```
Repeat while trueBoolean
    (* code statements *)
end repeat
```

Description

repeat while keeps executing its enclosed script code as long as the boolean expression following while is true:

```
repeat while theTruth is true...end repeat
```

If the boolean expression that follows while returns false, then the repeat while loop is terminated, and its enclosed script code will not execute anymore. Script execution then resumes after the end repeat part of the repeat while statement. repeat while has the opposite effect of repeat until; it keeps executing as long as some boolean expression is true, whereas repeat until keeps executing *until* something is true. You can also use exit within repeat while to leave the loop. In general, Repeat loops can contain nested repeat loops, as well as other flow-control statements such as if and tell.

Examples

This code shows how to use **repeat while**:

```
set theCount to 0
repeat while (theCount < 5)
    set theCount to theCount + 1
    log theCount
end repeat
```

The two code lines within this **repeat while** statement block will continue executing (thus increasing the value of **theCount** by one) while **theCount** is less than 5. Each cycle through the loop tests the **boolean** expression:

```
theCount < 5
```

and, as long as this expression returns **true**, the enclosed code will execute again. The variable **theCount** actually reaches 5 in the following code. This is because it is eventually incremented to 4, then the:

```
repeat while (theCount < 5)
```

executes and, since **theCount** is still less than 5, the enclosed script code executes once more, increasing the variable's value to 5.

---

repeat with {loop variable} from {integer} to {integer} [by stepVal] end [repeat]

Syntax

```
Repeat with loopVar from 1 to 10
    (* code statements *)
end repeat
```

Description

This form of the **repeat** loop executes a specified number of times over a range of values. A loop variable keeps track of how far the **repeat** loop has progressed in cycling over its range of loops. The loop variable increments by the value of **stepVal** (or one by default if the **stepVal** variable is not specified) throughout each loop. This makes the **repeat with** statement much more flexible and powerful than **repeat {integer} times**. You can take the value of the loop variable and use it in the executing code, as in the following example. Once this **repeat with** statement reaches the end of its range, as in:

```
repeat with loopVar from 1 to 10
```

(10 is the end of the range here), then the **repeat** loop terminates and code execution resumes with the statement following **end repeat**. You can also use the **exit** statement to terminate this loop (see "exit"). **repeat with** is similar to the famous:

```
for (i=0; i < rangeVar; i++)
```

variation of the loop statement that JavaScript, Java, and C++ programmers are very familiar with.

Examples

This AppleScript loops through each character of a word to see if any character is repeated. It uses the loop variable to determine which character in the word to examine. This example also shows how you can specify any of the range values with expressions that return integers, instead of just literal integers:

```
repeat with loopVar from 2 to (2^2)
    set theString to the text returned of (display dialog ¬
    "Enter a word and I'll tell you which letter, if any, repeats first" ¬
    default answer "")
    set len to (length of theString) (* len is set to the number of
characters in string *)
    tell application "BBEdit 5.0"
        repeat with loopVar from 1 to len (* repeat from char 1 to length
of string *)
            if loopVar is equal to 1 then set charList to {} (*create a list
to hold the examined characters *)
            set tempChar to (character loopVar of theString) (* tempChar is
a single character in the string like 'o' *)
            if tempChar is in charList then (* if it's already in the list
            then it appears more than once in the string *)
                display dialog "Your repeating character is " & tempChar
                exit repeat (* exits the repeat loop; finishes executing the
                script *)
            end if
            set charList to charList & tempChar (* no repeating chars yet so
add the current char to the list *)
            if loopVar is equal to len then (* if this is true then we did
not find any repeaters *)
                display dialog "You had no repeating characters!"
            end if
        end repeat
    end tell
end repeat
```

This script uses the BBEdit text editor because this app is good at examining text. The script gets a word from the user using the *display dialog* scripting addition (Part IV of the book discusses scripting additions). Then it uses a repeat with loop to get each single character in the string and store it in a variable of type list (i.e., charList). This is how the script keeps track of the characters it has already examined. The loopVar of the repeat with statement identifies individual characters of the string with an index reference form, as in character loopVar. If loopVar were 3 then the expression would evaluate to character 3, which is the third character in the string. The code then checks the charList list of characters to see if the currently examined character is already in there. If the character is already in the list then it appears more than once in the string. Then the script tells the user which character repeated and exits the loop:

```
display dialog "Your repeating character is " & tempChar
```

This example shows this repeat with loop with a specified step value:

```
set theString to "Kindly give me every other word."
set allWd to words of theString -- returns list of words
```

Flow-Control Statements

```
set len to length of allWd
set userMsg to ""
repeat with indx from 1 to len by 2 -- repeat loops over the list by two
    set userMsg to userMsg & return & (item indx of allWd)
end repeat
display dialog "Here's every other word on its own line: " & return & ¬
userMsg
```

repeat with {loop variable} in {list} end [repeat]

Syntax

```
Repeat with listVar in myList
    (* code statements *)
end repeat
```

Description

This variation of the **repeat with** statement iterates over a **list** of values, storing the current value in the loop variable. Once the last **item** in the **list** has been stored in the loop variable, the statement terminates and code execution resumes after **end repeat**. If you have to examine a **list**'s contents, this statement is a crucial part of your code. You can also use the **exit** statement inside this **repeat with** statement to stop executing code inside the loop. After any call to **exit**, code execution resumes after the **end repeat** part. You do not have to declare the loop variable in any way; AppleScript creates this temporary reference variable for you. You can also get the loop variable's value later in the script, after the repeat loop has completed executing. The value will be a reference to the last item in the list:

```
item 6 of {"Each", "word", "on", "a", "different", "line"}
```

Using this form of repeat loop, you can get inaccurate results if the script is trying to compare the value of the loop variable with another value (such as a **string** or **integer**). Instead, one of our technical reviewers recommends that you use syntax such as:

```
set booleanVar to ((contents of loopVar) equals 1)" (* note the "contents
of" part *)
```

The value used in the part of the statement following the **in** reserved word must be a **list**.

Examples

This code takes each of the items of a **list** and concatenates them to a **string**, which is then displayed to the user:

```
set theString to "Each word on a different line"
set theList to words of theString -- returns a list of words
set displayString to "" -- initialize this string
repeat with wd in theList
    set displayString to displayString & return & wd
```

```
end repeat
display dialog displayString
wd as string -- this will return "line"
```

AppleScript does not destroy the loop variable (wd in the prior example) after the repeat loop is finished. Getting the value of wd in the last example, after the repeat with statement has done its job, returns:

```
item 6 of {"Each", "word", "on", "a", "different", "line"}
```

---

repeat {integer} times end [repeat]

Syntax

```
Repeat 10 times
    Display dialog contriteStatement
End repeat
```

Description

This loop statement begins with the reserved word repeat, followed by an integer representing the number of times the loop should cycle, then the reserved word times and an end repeat. (The repeat of end repeat is optional.) You can use this variation of repeat if you do not need the finesse of the two more complex but powerful repeat constructs, such as:

```
repeat with loopVar in list
```

Once this loop has executed its enclosed script statements integer number of times, it terminates and the script execution resumes after the end repeat. You can also short-circuit this repeat loop by using the exit or exit repeat statement. This causes the script flow to proceed to after end repeat, regardless of whether the loop has cycled integer number of times.

Examples

The following code does exactly what the last repeat example did; it works with each word in a list, finally displaying each of them on a different line. However, it uses the "repeat {integer} times" variation instead. The example also shows that you can use the return value of an expression for "{integer}" including an integer variable, instead of just a literal integer such as 9:

```
set theString to "Each word on a different line"
set theList to words of theString
set len to length of theList
set displayString to ""
set counter to 0
repeat len times -- len resolves to the length of the word list
    set counter to counter + 1
    set displayString to displayString & return & (item counter of ¬
    theList)
end repeat
display dialog displayString
```

In this example, the line `repeat len times` uses the `len` variable's `integer` value to specify how many times the `repeat` loop should execute. `len` represents the length of the `list` of words that the code reassembles into another `string`.

return [return value]

Syntax

```
Return true
```

Description

The `return` statement returns values from functions or subroutines, just as it does in Perl and JavaScript. If you finish a function definition with just `return`, with no subsequent return value, then the function will return to where it was called in the script without returning an actual value. You can return any value, such as a `number`, `string`, `boolean`, or `list`:

```
return true
```

If you do not use `return` at all in a function then the return value of the function will be the result of its last statement, if the statement returns a result. (Chapter 9 is devoted to developing functions in AppleScript.)

If you define a function with just `return` without a value and then try to set a variable to the return value of that function, the script will raise an error.

Make sure not to confuse the `return` statement with the `return` predefined variable, which is a return character in a string such as:

```
set theString to return & "Start a new line"
```

tell simple statement

Syntax

```
tell app "SoundJam MP" to run
```

Description

You use the `tell` statement to identify the target of an AppleScript command:

```
tell app "Photoshop 5.5" to run
```

In this case, *run* is the Photoshop application's command. The `tell` simple statement only takes up one line of code and does not need to be completed with an `end tell`. You use the reserved word `tell`, followed by a reference to an object, such as the application "Finder," then the reserved word to preceding the actual command that you want to send to the object. `tell` statements can be nested within each other, such as using a `tell` simple statement inside a compound `tell` statement (one that involves several lines of code and finishes with `end tell`).

Examples

This code tells the Finder to open Photoshop only if a certain amount of memory is available to the computer:

```
tell application "Finder"
    (* largest free block is converted from bytes to megabytes then
rounded off with the round scripting addition *)
    set freeMem to (round (largest free block / 1024 / 1024))
    if freeMem > 50 then (* only open PS if there is a free memory block >
    50 meg *)
        tell application "Adobe® Photoshop® 5.5" to activate (* tell simple
        statement *)
    else
        display dialog ¬
"Freemem = " & freeMem & " Not enough memory for gluttonous Photoshop!"
    end if
end tell
```

This example occurs within a compound **tell** statement that targets the Finder. If the **largest free block** property of the Finder (which identifies the largest free block of available RAM on the computer) exceeds 50MB, then Photoshop receives an *activate* command as part of a **tell** simple statement.

 If you are running AppleScript 1.4 or higher, you can create easy-to-remember aliases to invoke your favorite apps with the **tell** statement. For example, create an alias file for the SoundJam MP application, name this alias "SJ," and then store it in *startup disk:System Folder:Scripting Additions*. Now, when your AppleScripts include the code: **tell app "SJ"** the enclosed code statements direct their Apple Events to SoundJam MP. This saves a lot of typing!

---

tell end [tell]

Syntax

```
Tell app "SoundJam MP"
    (* code statements *)
end tell
```

Description

The **tell** compound statement identifies the target of an AppleScript command or Apple event (as in **tell app "Photoshop 5.5"**) followed by other AppleScript statements and an **end tell**. The **tell** compound statement can enclose any number of AppleScript statements, including other **tell** statements and flow-control structures such as **if** or **repeat**. You can identify any object in a **tell** statement, but unless the object is an **application** object such as FileMaker Pro or QuarkXPress, it has to be nested within another **tell** statement targeting the object's parent application. For example, if you want to use a statement such as:

```
tell window 1 to close
```

then you would have to first target the application that "owns" the window, as in the following example:

```
tell application "BBEdit 5.0"
   (* hasChanged will be true or false *)
   set hasChanged to (front window's modified)
   if hasChanged then
      tell front window to close saving yes
   else
      tell front window to close
   end if
end tell
```

This script first finds out whether the front BBEdit window has been modified, and it stores this boolean value (true or false) in the hasChanged variable. If true, then a tell simple statement sends the front BBEdit window a *close* command (with a parameter instructing BBEdit to save the changes). If this tell statement was not nested within the tell app "BBEdit"... statement, then AppleScript would not know which application's window the script was talking about, and an error would be raised. You could also write the program without a nested tell statement, as in this code:

```
tell application "BBEdit 5.0"
   set hasChanged to (front window's modified)
   if hasChanged then
      close front window saving yes  (* send BBEdit the close command
      without another tell statement *)
   else
      close front window
   end if
end tell
```

With a feature that was new to AppleScript 1.4, you can add aliases to applications in the *Scripting Additions* folder of the *System Folder.* Give these aliases a short, easy-to-recall name like "fm" for FileMaker Pro, and you no longer have to spell out the app's name in the tell statement. You can just use the syntax tell app "fm"..., and AppleScript will find the application.

You can also use the predefined variables me, my, and it within tell statements. AppleScript assumes that any command such as *activate, close,* or *open* within a tell statement should be directed to the application that is identified in the tell statement. The exceptions are:

- A nested tell statement that targets a different application; in this case, any commands that are issued within *this* nested tell are directed to *its* target app.

- A scripting addition or osax command, such as *display dialog* or *round,* can be issued within a tell statement in most cases without any qualifying or accompanying code requirements.

- Commands that are qualified with the my or of me reserved words. This tells AppleScript that the command is a script command, as in:

  ```
  set theTruth to my func()
  ```

- Commands that target the app identified in the `tell` statement.

- Commands that are associated with a script object.

Examples

The script at the end of this section calls the script's own function inside of a `tell` statement. It also calls a function defined by a script object. `it` is an AppleScript reserved word that refers to the default target of Apple events, which is normally identified in a `tell` statement (Chapter 1, *AppleScript: An Introduction*, describes Apple events). This script is a little bigger than most included in the chapter, and I apologize to those like me who are partial to the use of only code fragments as examples. But it illustrates an important element of how you work with `tell` statements—the visibility of commands.

The script first identifies the text editor BBEdit in the compound `tell` statement, then tells this app to make a new window. The next line sets a `firstLine` variable to the return value of a function call:

```
InnerScript's getIntro()
```

Without the reference to the script object `InnerScript`, AppleScript would assume that the *getIntro* function was a BBEdit command, because *getIntro* is called inside of a `tell app "BBEdit 5.0"` statement. However, the script code indicates that this is the *getIntro* function of the `InnerScript` object. The following code would also work:

```
set firstLine to getIntro() of InnerScript
```

If you look down to the definition of the `InnerScript` script object, you see that it defines a function (*getIntro*) that returns the value of InnerScript's `Intro` property, which is a `string`: "I'm the first sentence." A lot is going on in the `if` statement in the next example:

```
if (my addLine(firstLine)) then display dialog "Text added ¬
successfully: " & its name
```

The script calls its own function (as opposed to a BBEdit command) called *addLine*. The reserved word `my` distinguishes this function (*addLine*) as defined by the script, not BBEdit, so AppleScript looks for the function definition in the script itself, rather than in BBEdit's dictionary. The following phrase would also work:

```
addLine(firstLine) of me
```

The function inserts text into a BBEdit document and returns `true` if successful. The `if` statement responds to any `true` return value from the *addLine* function by displaying a message `string` that includes `its` name. It is an AppleScript constant that refers to the default target for commands, which, inside this `tell` statement, is BBEdit. So `its name` returns "BBEdit 5.0":

```
tell application "BBEdit 5.1"
    make new window with properties {name:"Front Win"}
    (* the InnerScript script object is defined beneath this code *)
```

```
    set firstLine to InnerScript's getIntro()
    (* addLine is the 'outer script's' function, not InnerScript's *)
    if (my addLine(firstLine)) then display dialog ¬
"Text added  successfully: " & its name
end tell

(* user-defined function addline() *)
on addLine(txt)
    try
        tell application "BBEdit 5.1" to insert text txt
    on error
        return false
    end try
    return true
end addLine
(* script object definition *)
script InnerScript
    property Intro : "I'm the first sentence."
    on getIntro()
        return Intro
    end getIntro
end script
```

try [on error] [number | from | partial result | to] end [error | try]

Syntax

```
Try
    (* code statements here *)
    on error errText
    display dialog "An error:" & errText
end try
```

Description

try represents AppleScript's all-important error-trapping capability. If any of the statements that are enclosed in a try...end try statement block raise an error, then AppleScript catches the error and prevents it from taking down the whole script. After try catches the error (similar to Java's try...catch exception-trapping syntax), the script has the option of adding inside the try block the reserved words on error followed by any code that should execute in response to the error.

 on error is optional inside of try statements beginning with AppleScript 1.4.

The program will then resume following the end try part of the try block, as though nothing happened. Without a try block, AppleScript's default error behavior is to display an error message in a dialog box then cancel the running script. try only catches one error at a time. By using the on error statement and its numerous parameters, you can uncover all kinds of details about the error, but you do not have to use it. In the OS versions previous to Mac OS 9, Script Editor does not compile a script that includes a try block without an on error statement.

Examples

This example traps any errors caused by invalid data entered by the user, and then goes on its merry way without explicitly responding to any errors. try statements can be used inside and outside of your own subroutines, script objects, and libraries; they can nest other statements such as if, repeat, and tell. In fact, your entire script can run inside of a try statement, and the try block can contain other try statements:

```
try
    set userReply to the text returned of ¬
        (display dialog "Try your best to enter a number." default answer ¬
        "")
    set invalidNum to false
    set userReply to userReply as real
on error
    set invalidNum to true
end try
if invalidNum then
    display dialog "That's the best you can do?!"
else
    display dialog "thanks for entering: " & userReply
end if
```

This script politely asks the user for a number; it sets the reply to the variable userReply. This variable is then coerced from a string to a real type, which raises an error if userReply is not a valid number. For example, "a10" couldn't be converted to a valid number. AppleScript displays this error and stops running the script if we do not catch it in the try block. If the error is raised, the statements that appear between on error and end try execute. In this case, the script sets a boolean variable invalidNum to true. Remember, the script does not have to use the on error statement part of try in Mac OS 9 or OS X. It can simply use a try block to prevent any errors from crashing the script, then go on blithely executing the rest of the code. The error handler of the try statement contains five variables from which you can obtain information about any errors. The following code shows two of the many ways that you can use try. The first demonstration catches but then skips over any errors that might be raised while it executes its code. The second use of try deploys the on error handler to grab all the data that it can about the error and display it to the user:

```
tell application "SoundJam™ MP"
    try
        activate (* will raise an error if SoundJam isn't on the computer,
        but the program will just keep going *)
    end try
    try
```

```
        set allPlay to playlist windows -- a list of playlists
        repeat with pl in allPlay
            if (name of pl) is "tranceControl" then set mainPlay to pl
        end repeat
        set trackNameList to name of (tracks of mainPlay)
        set trackMsg to ""
        on error errMsg number errNum from objErr partial result errList ¬
        to  errClass
        (* display the error message, error number, the object that is the
        source of the error, any partial results, and class information *)
            display dialog errMsg & ": " & errNum & return & "Source of ¬
            error  was: " & objErr & return & "Here are any partial ¬
            results: " &  errList & return & "If coercion failure it ¬
            involved a coercion to: " & errClass
        return -- exit the program
    end try
    repeat with nam in trackNameList
        set trackMsg to trackMsg & return & nam
    end repeat
    display dialog "The MP3 track names in the main playlist are: " & ¬
    return & trackMsg
end tell
```

In the prior example, if any statements in the second try block raise an error, then the on error handler displays error information using all five parameters of on error. AppleScript gives these parameters a value (e.g., the error description and number) for you if any errors are raised. The values for the partial list and to parameters are empty lists if there are no partial results or coercion problems associated with the error. Here's a rundown of the five optional on error parameters:

- The first nonlabeled parameter is a string describing the error, as in on error errMsg. The variable errMsg, which you create, contains the error message.

- The number parameter contains the error number, as in on error number errNum. Use the number label followed by your own variable to contain the number.

- The object that was the source of the error is labeled with the keyword from. An example is on error from objErr. You create the variable following the reserved word from, and if AppleScript can identify the object source of the error, it will store the name of the object in that variable.

- If the error-causing operation involved getting a list of values, and it was successful in getting *some* of the list values, then this list is stored in the variable labeled with the reserved words partial list. The content of this variable is of type list.

- If the error was caused by a faulty coercion, than the class that the script failed to coerce some value to is identified in the variable following the reserved word to, as in on error to errClass. The identifier errClass contains the word describing the class, such as boolean, list, or real.

using terms from end [using terms from]

Syntax

```
Tell app "Finder" of machine "eppc://192.168.0.2"
    Using terms from app "Finder"
        Get largest free block
    End using terms from
End tell
```

Description

This block structure allows the scripter to compile a script using local applications and to have the option to run the script on remote machines using a TCP/IP or AppleTalk network. Chapter 25, *File Sharing Control Panel*, describes how to use the Mac's powerful new program linking technology to run distributed Apple-Scripts over TCP/IP networks. using terms from is new to AppleScript 1.4. Similar to the tell block, it takes an application object as a parameter, as in:

```
using terms from app "Finder"
```

You use this construct to help avoid the display of the Script Editor dialog box that asks for the location of the target application in a tell block. This dialog box usually displays when the script is first compiled and then whenever the script is executed on a different machine. If you have not encountered this dialog box yet during AppleScript hacking, then you are either lucky or just haven't done very much AppleScripting.

Examples

using terms from is best illustrated with this example, which dynamically targets whatever machine you want, but compiles using terms from the local machine:

```
set theMachine to "eppc://" & the text returned of ¬
(display dialog "Enter your IP address:" default answer "")
try
    tell application "Finder" of machine theMachine
        using terms from application "Finder"
            set freeMem to (round (largest free block / 1024 / 1024)) as ¬
            string
            display dialog freeMem
        end using terms from
    end tell
on error errMsg
    display dialog errMsg
end try
```

This script targets the Finder on a particular Apple machine (depending on what the script user enters as the machine name or IP address). The script compiles, however, using its local Finder app. If the user enters an invalid or nonexistent IP address, then an error is raised and reported at the end of the try block. When targeting applications over a TCP/IP network, you have to precede the IP address with the protocol `"eppc://"`, which stands for "event program to program communications":

```
tell application "Finder" of machine "eppc://192.168.0.2"
```

with timeout [of] {integer} second[s] end [timeout]

Syntax

```
With timeout of 15 seconds
End timeout
```

Description

The `with timeout` statement allows you to alter AppleScript's default 60-second time limit for the Apple events that are sent to applications. Normally, if an application fails to respond to an Apple event within 60 seconds, AppleScript raises an "Apple event timed out" error and stops running the script. You can make this time limit shorter, say 30 seconds, by using the syntax:

```
with timeout of 30 seconds...end timeout
```

You enclose the `with timeout` structure in a `try` block to trap and report any timeout errors (see "try"). `with timeout` only applies to the following types of commands. In other words, the `with timeout` limit is ignored unless the command is one of these types:

- Commands sent to applications targeted in `tell` blocks

- Scripting addition commands that have application objects as parameters (not too many osaxen have application objects as parameters)

- Scripting addition commands that are called inside of `tell` statements that target other applications

Examples

The following example times out if you just let the *display dialog* dialog box sit there for over five seconds. This happens because the *display dialog* scripting addition is positioned inside the `tell` block targeting the Finder. Pull the scripting-addition command outside the `tell` block, and the script does not time out. Again, `with timeout` does not work with scripting-addition commands unless the command is part of a `tell` block targeting another application, or it takes an application object as a parameter:

```
try -- catch any timed out errors
    with timeout of 5 seconds
        tell application "Finder"
            get version
            display dialog "fast" (* let this sit for about 5 secs and raise
            an error *)
        end tell
    end timeout
on error -- will be called if 'with timeout' block times out
    display dialog "Sorry, the operation timed out"
end try
```

If an AppleScript that sends an Apple event to another application times out, the Apple event itself is not cancelled (with or without a with timeout statement). So the script might have timed out, but the application could still eventually respond to the Apple event that the script sent to it.

with transaction [session object] end [transaction]

Syntax

```
With transaction
    (* code statements here *)
end transaction
```

Description

with transaction is designed to group together its enclosed statements and commands by assigning each of them a single transaction id. If a database application supports with transaction, for instance, than it knows which Apple events or commands share a transaction and can initiate an appropriate response, such as locking the particular table from other users until the transaction is complete. What is a transaction? A transaction gathers together a group of operations and declares, in essence, that, "we're all in this together—if one of us fails, then we all fail. We won't signal a successful completion until we all succeed."

The with transaction statement itself, beyond assigning the transaction id, does not have any other transactional-related capabilities such as rolling back all of the statements if one of the statements (e.g., a statement that updates or alters a database file) within the transaction fails. Any behavior that commits or rolls back database changes that are part of a single transaction would have to be initiated by the database system itself (the database program that AppleScript is scripting). with transaction only works with the database programs that support this statement.

Examples

To show what the with transaction statement looks like, the following Apple-Script requests the first database record from an open FileMaker database. It encloses this request in a with transaction block:

```
tell application "FileMaker Pro"
    with transaction
        get the first record in the database named "Mydatabase"
    end transaction
end tell
```

In this case, if you watch the Script Editor Event Log window as you run the script, FileMaker converts the with transaction statement to its own begin transaction command. This command returns an integer, the transaction id, such as 2812565. You can include an optional session-object parameter with the with transaction block, but not all applications support it. If you want to use AppleScript, transactions, and databases, then you have to evaluate the particular database system's support for with transaction.

CHAPTER 8

Subroutines

A subroutine is a piece of code or sequence of statements that is defined in a program or script and can be used repeatedly throughout that script. Apple-Scripters traditionally refer to this programming construct as a "handler." When the script calls the subroutine, the flow of code execution branches to the statements in the subroutine. Those statements are executed and may or may not return a value to the segment of the script that called the subroutine. Then the script execution resumes at the statement following the subroutine call.

AppleScript subroutines are not that much different than they are in other programming languages. AppleScript supports the creation of subroutines with *positional parameters*. This means that the subroutine definition begins with the keywords on or to and a subroutine name that does not clash with any of Apple-Script's other predefined names (such as **anything** or **pi**), and then a set of parentheses that optionally lists any parameters or values that should be passed to the subroutine. The subroutine in Example 8-1 is called *myfunc*.

Example 8-1: Simple Subroutine Definition

```
on myfunc(s1,s2)
return (s1 & s2)
end myfunc"
```

This example concatenates or combines two strings that are passed to the subroutine as parameters (for the sake of brevity I have left out the typical checks that you would include for whether the parameters are valid strings). When calling *myfunc* in code, the parameters have to be in the same order as they are in the subroutine definition:

```
myfunc("one string ", "connected to another")
```

AppleScript also supports an unwieldy (my humble opinion, of course) form of subroutine that includes labeled parameters (see the section "Subroutines with

Labeled Parameters"). This chapter concludes with a discussion of the five special built-in Apple-event handler types listed in Table 8-1.

Table 8-1: Five Built-in AppleScript Handlers

idle handler
open handler
reopen handler
quit handler
run handler

Subroutines with Positional Parameters

The AppleScript subroutines with positional parameters are simple to design and use, as long as you meet certain guidelines. The keywords on or to are required in the subroutine definition, followed by the name of the subroutine, and any parameters separated by commas and contained in parentheses. You have to use empty parentheses following the subroutine name if the subroutine will not take any parameters. The subroutine's name must comply with AppleScript's rules for identifiers. In AppleScript, the names that you create for variables and subroutines have to begin with a letter or underscore (_) character, but subsequent characters can include letters, numbers, and underscores. Unless you begin and end the subroutine name with a vertical bar (|), you cannot include AppleScript's reserved words and operators such as *, &, ^, or +, or special characters such as $, @, or #.

The end keyword is required to signal the end of the subroutine definition. You can follow end with the subroutine name for the sake of readability:

```
On Squared(n1)...end Squared
```

This is not required, however; the compiler, Script Editor, does it for you. You can declare and give values to variables in AppleScript subroutines, and use the various flow-control statements such as:

```
if...then...end if
```

and:

```
repeat...end repeat
```

However, you cannot define another subroutine inside of a subroutine definition.

To call a subroutine, use the subroutine name followed by its parameters inside of parentheses:

```
Squared(7)
```

With subroutines that take positional parameters, you have to code the arguments in the same order as they appear in the subroutine definition. You have to include all of the specified arguments—the arguments in AppleScript subroutines are not optional (nor can they be declared as optional). Use empty parentheses with subroutine calls if the routine does not take any arguments. You can also use

Subroutines

expressions, other variables, and other subroutine calls to give the parameters values, as in:

```
Squared((7*2))
```

or:

```
Squared(DividedBy(8))
```

If you use a subroutine to give a parameter a value, that subroutine must return a value. Example 8-2 is a complete subroutine definition that takes one number as its parameter and returns that number squared. The first set of comments, beneath on squared(num), describe how to call the method, as well as its parameters and return value.

Example 8-2: AppleScript Subroutine Definition

```
on squared(num)
    (*
    call method as: Squared(number)
    parameters: an integer or real type
    returns: the parameter squared, or zero if the param is not a valid
    integer or real
    *)
    if class of num is in {real,integer}  AND num ≠ 0 then
        return num ^ 2
    else
        return 0
    end if
end squared
Set big_number to Squared(2345)
```

When you are creating subroutines with positional parameters, you can design them to return a value to the part of the script that called the subroutine in the first place. You can use the **return** keyword, with or without a literal value or expression:

```
return 0 -- or just 'return' alone, without a specified value
```

Using **return** with a **Boolean** value (e.g., **return true**) allows you to signal the successful or failed execution of the subroutine. Using **return** without a value stops execution of the subroutine and returns the flow of execution to the part of the script that called the subroutine. If you do not use the **return** statement in a subroutine, the routine returns the value of the last expression that was evaluated in the subroutine (if the last expression returns a value). If the last expression in the subroutine does not return a value, and if the subroutine does not use the **return** statement followed by an expression or value, then the routine does not return a value. See Example 8-2 and Chapter 6, *Variables and Constants,* or Chapter 7, *Flow-Control Statements,* for other examples and discussions of the **return** statement.

By default, any variables declared inside the subroutine are local to the routine. This means that the scope of the variables is restricted to the routine; if you try to access the variable outside of the subroutine, the script will fail to compile. You can explicitly declare a variable as local by using the **local** keyword, as with the variable dstring in Example 8-3. This is good practice for using local variables, as it makes the subroutine definition easier to understand.

A variable can also be declared as global inside of the routine. This is accomplished by using the keyword global followed by the name of the variable:

```
global myvar
```

This means that the variable is visible outside of the subroutine. Chapter 6 discusses local and global variable scope.

Example 8-3 takes a date object as an argument and returns a "month day year" string such as "August 3 1999." If the argument is not a date object such as:

```
if class of theDate is not date
```

then the subroutine returns the string "invalid argument." You could return 0 or raise an error dialog box as an alternative. The local dstring line declares a dstring variable whose scope is restricted to the *ReturnDate* subroutine; it is not "visible" outside of the routine. The local dstring declaration is not strictly necessary since first declaring the dstring variable inside of a subroutine definition automatically makes it a local variable, unless the global keyword is used ("global dstring"). But using the local keyword in this manner makes the subroutine definition more readable.

Example 8-3: A User-Defined date Subroutine

```
on ReturnDate(theDate)
    if class of theDate is not date then return "invalid argument"
    local dstring
    set dstring to (theDate as string)
    (*
    call method as: ReturnDate(current date)
    parameters: theDate is a date (not a string) such as date "Tuesday,
    February 6, 2001 12:00:00 PM" returns: A string that looks like
    "February 6 2001"
    *)
    set mon to the second word of dstring
    set dy to the third word of dstring
        set yr to the fourth word of dstring
return mon & " " & dy & " " & yr
end ReturnDate
```

If you call one of your own subroutines inside of a tell statement, such as:

```
tell app "Finder"...end tell
```

AppleScript responds to the subroutine call as an application command (in this case, of the Finder) unless you use the my or of me keywords. Example 8-4 calls the script's *squared* subroutine (instead of looking in the Finder's dictionary for a *squared* command), because the script uses the my keyword in calling the routine. This is just a demonstration script; you would only use a tell statement if the script were also sending the Finder some commands.

Example 8-4: Using the my or of me Keywords

```
tell application "Finder"
   my squared(7)
end tell
on squared(num)
   if class of num is in {real, integer} and num ≠ 0 then
      return num ^ 2
   else
      return 0
   end if
end squared
```

Subroutines with Labeled Parameters

These subroutine types are a slightly different animal than the subroutines with positional parameters, but they have some of the same rules. The keywords on or to are required in the labeled-subroutine definition, followed by the name of the subroutine, and optionally a nonlabeled parameter called a *direct parameter*. If the subroutine has a direct parameter (it does not have to), then the subroutine name has to be followed by the keyword of or in:

```
On Square of intOne...
```

Subroutines with labeled parameters are unwieldy to design compared with subroutines with positional parameters, but they make more subroutine calls resembling human language possible. The two different types of AppleScript subroutine designs are also a matter of personal taste, I suppose. Example 8-5 shows a labeled subroutine definition.

Example 8-5: Labeled Subroutine Definition

```
on Square of intOne above intLimit given Intclass:theClass
   if (intOne > intLimit) and (theClass is integer) then
      return intOne ^ 2
   else
      return 0
   end if
end Square
Square of myint above 0 given Intclass:(class of myint)
```

Example 8-6 redesigns the preceding subroutine using positional parameters instead.

Example 8-6: A Redesigned Subroutine Using Positional Parameters

```
on Square(intOne,intLimit,theClass)
   if (intLimit > 0) and (theClass is integer) then
      return intOne ^ 2
   else
      return 0
   end if
end Square
```

The rules on naming the subroutine (using local and global variables) and ending the subroutine definition are the same as those that apply to naming subroutines with positional parameters (see the previous section). In the following example, the direct parameter is followed by the first labeled argument, `above intLimit`:

```
on Square of intOne above intLimit given Intclass:theClass
```

Along with `above`, you can use the following AppleScript reserved words: `about`, `against`, `apart from`, `around`, `aside from`, `at`, `below`, `beneath`, `beside`, `between`, `by`, `for`, `from`, `instead of`, `into`, `on`, `onto`, `out of`, `over`, `since`, `through`, `thru`, and `under`. These words have no meaning in the context of calling labeled routines except to make the subroutine call more readable. Instead of writing:

```
on Square intOne above intLimit given Intclass:theClass
```

you could substitute:

```
on Square of intOne apart from intLimit given Intclass:theClass
```

and the subroutine, as long as its other elements were legal, would run the same.

If the subroutine with labeled parameters has a direct parameter (they do not have to), then the definition must also include either one of the aforementioned labels (e.g., `thru`), a `given` labeled argument, or both of these parameter types. The `given` label takes a `variable:value` pair as a parameter, which can be used to find out whether a value is `true` or `false`:

```
given theBool:boolVal
```

In Example 8-5, `given Intclass:theClass` is used. You then give `Intclass` a value when calling the routine:

```
Square myint above 0 given Intclass:integer
```

The body of the subroutine evaluates the value of `Intclass`.

To call one of these subroutines, you have to include the direct parameter if one has been defined for the routine. If the routine defines any of the parameters that use AppleScript's reserved words (such as `thru` or `above`), they come next (if there are more than one, then these parameters may be called in any order). Any `given` parameters must come after the other labeled arguments. You have to include all the arguments defined by the subroutine—the arguments defined in AppleScript subroutines are not optional when the routine is called. Unlike the routines with positional arguments, when you call a subroutine with labeled parameters, you do not surround the arguments with parentheses. But you have to include the labels and parameter values (or any variables containing the values) in the subroutine call.

idle handler

Syntax

```
on idle
    return 600 -- idle is called every 10 minutes
end idle
```

Description

AppleScripts can be saved to stay open after they have been executed, instead of completing their tasks and quitting. Chapter 2, *Using Script Editor with OS 9 and OS X*, discusses the nuances of saving AppleScripts. These scripts may define an *idle* handler, essentially a subroutine that AppleScript calls by default every 30 seconds when the script has been launched and is open. You can change this time interval by returning a positive number (a `real` is legal but an `integer` makes more sense) from the *idle* handler. The syntax example returns 600, or the equivalent of 10 minutes, which will be the new time interval for AppleScript's execution of this *idle* handler. If the handler returns any value other than a positive number then the time interval is kept at the 30-second default. The *idle* handler should have some purpose other than altering the interval by which it is run, as in the code in the following Examples section. Another example that typifies an *idle* handler's role is to lurk in the background monitoring the usage of a folder that network users have access to. When the folder's content changes, the handler can note that in a log entry, for instance.

Examples

The following *idle* handler example makes the Netscape browser the front window every 10 minutes and reloads or forces a fresh reload (that is where the `flags 3` labeled parameter for Netscape's *OpenURL* command comes in) of the URL *http://my.yahoo.com*. You can see how an *idle* handler would come in handy if you wanted to do more complex web processing, such as periodically seizing data from the Web and storing it in your desktop or network database.

 An intriguing use of stay-open scripts is to use them as live subroutine libraries that are stored in memory and can be called from other scripts. Take a bunch of useful subroutines that other scripts could use, and save them together in a stay-open applet. Execute the applet. Then call the subroutines using a `tell` statement that targets the name of the applet. These subroutines that are stored in open applets can even return values to the calling script, as in the following example. You do not have to define an *idle* handler inside a stay-open script or library, unless this stay-open applet has to do some processing itself.

```
on idle
    tell application "Netscape Communicator™"
        activate
        (* the 'flags 3' param forces a reload of the document from the
server *)
        OpenURL "http://my.yahoo.com" flags 3
    end tell
    return 600 -- call idle every 10 minutes, if Yahoo doesn't mind
```

```
end idle
  (* here are two subroutines defined in a stay-open applet called
  'RunningLib' *)
on timesTwo(num)
    return num * 2
end timesTwo

on divTwo(num)
    return num / 2
end divTwo

(* Here's another applet that calls RunningLib's subroutines and gets
values from them *)
set mynum to 0
tell application "RunningLib"
    set mynum to divTwo(timesTwo(75))
end tell
mynum -- value is 75.0
```

To quit a script that has been saved to "stay open" and contains an
idle handler, you can choose Quit from the File menu on its menu
bar (yes, stay-open scripts have a menu); select the script icon in the
Application Switcher and type *Command-Q*, or send the app a *quit*
command from another script.

open handler

Syntax

```
on open(list_of_aliases)
    set item1 to the first item of list_of_aliases as string
    display dialog "Here's the path of the first object you dragged over ¬
    me: " & item1
end open
```

Description

An *open* Apple event is sent to any Mac application when you drag file, folder, or
disk icons on to its own icon in the Finder. If an icon is not highlighted when you
drag the object over it, then the application or other object associated with that
icon is not designed to handle these drag-and-drop events. If you drag files and
other icons over an AppleScript applet, the applet receives an *open* command that
triggers any *open* handlers that are defined in that applet. They look like this:

```
on open(list_of_aliases)...end open
```

The *open* handler has one parameter—a `list` type containing `alias` objects for
all the items that were dragged to the applet. If the user only drops one item on

the applet icon, then the *open* subroutine's parameter will contain a `list` with one item in it. You can code the *open* handler to take purposeful actions with files and folders that are dropped on the applet in any way you see fit. Example 2-1 in Chapter 2 shows a script that displays the file type and creator type of any valid object that is dropped on the applet.

 If the applet does not have an *open* handler or has an empty *open* handler, then the applet does not take any actions when you drop an object on it; it just opens then quits simultaneously.

reopen handler

syntax

```
on reopen
    display dialog "I am already running; you do not have to double-click
    me!"
end reopen
```

Description

The *reopen* handler is designed for the occasions when a user double-clicks a stay-open applet that is already running. This action executes the *reopen* handler. So anything that you want to happen when the user tries to "reopen" a script that is already running should be defined within the reopen handler. All this example does is display a dialog to users when they double-click a running applet that contains this *reopen* handler.

quit handler

syntax

```
on quit
    display dialog "Sure you want to quit?"
    continue quit -- quits the applet
end quit
```

Description

Scripters can add *quit* handlers or subroutines to stay-open applets in order to process code statements whenever the applet receives a *quit* Apple event. The syntax example displays a dialog whenever its applet receives a *quit* command, and then it quits when the user dismisses the dialog box because the code includes the `continue quit` statement. If the code did not include this statement then the applet, in response to a *quit* command, would call its *quit* handler and stay open.

Make sure to include the `continue quit` statement in *quit* handlers, unless you want the applet to stay open until the next computer restart. A *quit* handler without a `continue quit` causes the applet to intercept and nullify the user's efforts to quit the app from its File menu. To bypass the *quit* handler, choose Quit from the applet's menu while holding down the Shift key, or press the *Command-Shift-Q* key combo while the applet is the active or front application.

The *quit* handler is only necessary for stay-open applets, because the applets that are not saved as stay-open will process their statements and immediately quit (see Chapter 2 for more on the nuances of saving applets).

run handler

Syntax

```
on run
  (* do major scripting here *)
end run
```

Description

Whether you like it or not, most of your scripts contain a *run* handler implicitly or invisibly. What Apple Computer calls an "implicit run handler" involves all the statements in a script except for property definitions, subroutine definitions, and any script objects (see Chapter 9, *Script Objects and Libraries*). This means that all of these statements are enclosed in an invisible `on run...end run` subroutine block. This implicit *run* handler is called each time:

- The applet icon is double-clicked.

- The user chooses the applet from the Apple menu.

- The user chooses the applet from the Apple Menu Items folder.

- The applet is placed in *startup disk:System Folder:Startup Items* and the computer is restarted.

You can explicitly code the *run* handler to clarify to readers of your code exactly what happens when the applet receives a *run* command, as in the next example. If this script did not include the `on run...end run` statements, then its implicit *run* handler would still encompass the statements:

```
add()
```

and:

```
display dialog "I received a run command " & howmany & " times"
```

The applet property howmany increments by 1 each time this applet receives a *run* command:

```
property howmany : 0
on run
  add()
  display dialog "I received a run command " & howmany & " times"
end run

on add()
  set howmany to howmany + 1
end add
```

Sending a *run* command to an application, as in `tell  app "Photoshop 5.5" to run`, loads the application if it is not already running. Use *activate* to gain the focus of the application (i.e., highlight the program on the desktop) when it is already running. Sending a *run* command to an AppleScript causes its implicit or explicit *run* handler to execute.

CHAPTER 9

Script Objects and Libraries

A script object is a template or class from which you can create AppleScript objects. Objects are self-contained script code that can have their own properties, methods, and variables. See Chapter 1, *AppleScript: An Introduction,* for details on using objects in AppleScript.

When a script object is created in memory, that object is considered an instance (in object-oriented parlance) or copy of the template on which the object was based. The script object can be a collection of properties, a group of methods defined together (as a *library*, which is discussed in the section "Libraries"), or a bunch of properties, methods, and statements that comprise a single object. Script objects can inherit the properties and methods of a parent object simply by defining a parent property at the top of the script:

```
prop parent : MyParent
```

MyParent in this case is a variable that refers to another script object.

In summary, script objects represent a limited form of object-oriented programming in AppleScript. Considering that you can define objects and libraries on one machine, and create new instances of those objects or call methods in the library on another machine that shares a TCP/IP network, what you can achieve with AppleScript objects is limited only by the breadth of your imagination. This exciting new form of distributed computing on the Mac is called "program linking via IP".

Script Objects

You define an AppleScript script object using the basic syntax that Example 9-1 illustrates.

Example 9-1: Syntax for Creating a Script Object

```
script MyScript
  (* define properties, methods, variables here *)
end script
```

Use the syntax `script...end script` to define a script object within another script. For example, a single script could involve its own properties, subroutines, *run* handler, and one or more script objects. Used in this manner, a script object can be like a "type" that you define. Example 9-2 defines a *Collection* type within another script. A Collection involves one to several property/value pairs and methods that can return Collection values as well as add a new property/value pair to the Collection. In this case, the Collection object or type is defined at the top of the script and then demonstrated beneath the script-object definition. The example Collection involves the names of some planets followed by their diameters in kilometers.

Example 9-2: A Collection Script Object

```
script Collection
   property col : {} (* an empty list type until it is initialized as a
record *)
   (* return the collection *)
   on getCol()
      return col
   end getCol
   (* set the collection value(s) *)
   on setCol(rec)
      if (class of rec is record) then
         set col to rec -- collection object's col property is set to rec
      else
         return
      end if
   end setCol
   (* add a member to the collection *)
   on add(mem)
      if (class of mem is record) then
         set col to col & mem
      else
         return
      end if
   end add
   (* get the value of a member as in '4880' for Mercury; mem has to be a
reference to one of the collection items as in 'Mercury of col' (the
'Mercury' value of the Collection or record) *)
   on getMem(mem)
      return mem
   end getMem
end script
(* create a Collection object *)
set objCol to Collection
tell objCol to setCol({Earth:"12756", Mercury:"4880"})
(* add a member to it *)
```

Example 9-2: A Collection Script Object (continued)

```
tell objCol to add({Venus:"12104"})
(* set a variable to the Collection object's col property *)
tell objCol to getCol()
set myCol to the result
(* getmem takes as an argument a reference to one of the Collection's members
*)
tell objCol to getMem(Earth of myCol)
set retVal to the result -- retVal is set to "12756"
set mesg to "Earth is " & retVal & " kilometers in diameter."
display dialog mesg
```

You could add other methods to the Collection object, such as a method that deletes a property/value pair from the "col" property (there's a programming challenge). You can also define this script object as a separate compiled script, without including the

```
script Collection...end script
```

syntax. Give the saved script the filename *Collection*. Example 9-3 does the same thing as Example 9-2, except that Example 9-3 gains access to the external script object (which has a filename of *Collection*) by using the *load script* scripting addition.

Example 9-3: Loading an External Script Object File

```
(* set a variable to the Collection script object using 'load script' osax *)
set objCol to (load script "macintosh hd:desktop folder:Collection")
tell objCol to setCol({Earth:"12756", Mercury:"4880"})
tell objCol to add({Venus:"12104"})
tell objCol to getCol()
set myCol to the result
tell objCol to getMem(Earth of myCol)
set retVal to the result
set mesg to "Earth is " & retVal & " kilometers in diameter."
display dialog mesg
```

You call the methods of AppleScript objects using the `tell` statement, assuming that the script object referred to by the `objCol` variable has a *getName* method:

```
tell objCol to getName()
```

See Chapter 7, *Flow-Control Statements,* for details on the `tell` statement. You can also use the possessive form to call an object's method, as in

```
objCol's getName()
```

or, use the `of` keyword

```
getName() of objCol
```

AppleScript doesn't use the "dot" syntax of other languages such as Java or JavaScript (i.e., you cannot use the syntax objCol.getName()).

You create several copies of the same script object by using the `copy` keyword, as opposed to the `set` keyword. For example, let's say you defined the Collection script object in the same script as the one in which you will use this object to do something (such as create instances of the object in memory). The code fragment in Example 9-4 creates separate instances of the Collection object in the variables cObj1 and cObj2.

Example 9-4: Creating Separate Instances of a Script Object

```
(* create two separate instances or objects from a user-defined Collection
type *)
copy Collection to cObj1 -- this var refers to one Collection object
copy Collection to cObj2 -- this var refers to another Collection object
```

In the case of cObj2, if you used the code set cObj2 to Collection instead, then cObj2 and cObj1 would point or refer to the same Collection object. Using the copy syntax allows the scripter to create separate objects.

You can create a child script object from a parent object by giving the child object a parent property. Example 9-5 creates a child object from the Collection object that I defined in Example 9-2. This new object inherits all of the properties and methods of the parent; you do not have to include those properties or methods in your definition of the child object. If you define a method with the same name as your parent's method, AppleScript overrides the parent method and calls the child's method. In this example, the child object defines a name property and getName method; only the child object will have this property and method, not its parent Collection object. The example also demonstrates the use of the continue statement inside of a method that you are overriding. If you use the continue statement followed by the name of the parent's method, then Apple-Script calls the parent method. For Java programmers, if you were overriding a method called setCol, then the AppleScript continue statement is like calling the following inside of the overridden method:

```
super.setCol() (* in Java, calling the base-class method inside a
derived-class method that is overriding the parent method *)
```

You use the continue statement when you want to add new functionality to a parent object's method *and* still have the parent method execute. In other words, you can also override a parent object's method by completely changing the method's behavior and never calling the parent method.

Example 9-5: Using Child and Parent Script Objects

```
script NewCollection
(* use 'load script' osax to populate the parent property *)
property parent : (load script "macintosh hd:desktop folder:Collection")
(* give child object two new properties: name and version *)
property name : "NewCollection"
property version : "1.0"
on getName()
    return my name
end getName
on getVersion()
    return my version
end getVersion
```

Example 9-5: Using Child and Parent Script Objects (continued)

```
(* override the setCol method then just call parent's method; you could do
more
if you wanted to *)
on setCol(rec)
    continue setCol(rec)
end setCol
end script

(*create child object *)
set obj to NewCollection
tell obj to getName()
display dialog result -- display 'NewCollection'
obj's setCol({Mars:"6794"})
display dialog "Mar's diameter is: " & (Mars of obj's getCol())
```

You can intercept the calling of a scripting addition by using a script object and the `continue` statement. In other words, you can override some osax commands (you must test them first however), just as a `child` object might override a `parent` object's methods. The script object in Example 9-6 has a *delay* method that displays a dialog box asking the user if they really want to delay the script. If the user dismisses the dialog box with the Okay button, then the following code calls the *delay* scripting addition (whose `integer` argument determines how many seconds the script will pause): `continue delay 10`.

Example 9-6: Overriding a Scripting Addition

```
script delayer
    on delay
        display dialog "Do you really want to delay the script?" buttons ¬
        {"okay", "no"} default button 2
        if button returned in result is "okay" then continue delay 10
        -- calls delay osax
    end delay
end script
tell delayer to delay (* if 'okay' button is pressed then the script is
delayed by 10 seconds *)
```

Libraries

A library is a type of script object that represents a group of methods that are stored in a compiled script. Just define several useful functions in Script Editor then save them with a meaningful name, like *WebLib*. You can then call these functions from other scripts by using the *load script* osax:

```
set wlib to (load script "macintosh hd:ASlibraries:WebLib")
```

Let's say the *WebLib* library has a method called *httpGet*. The `wlib` variable now refers to the *WebLib* script object, so you could call this method with the code:

```
wlib's httpGet()
```

You could also save *WebLib* as a stay-open applet. As long as the library applet is running (with few performance implications as a small applet will only use several hundred bytes of memory), you could call its functions from another applet with code as spare as:

```
tell app "WebLib" to httpGet("my.yahoo.com")
```

AppleScript will be able to "find" the *WebLib* applet a lot easier when you try to compile the latter code fragment if *WebLib* is already a running process.

There are several good reasons why you might want to have code libraries running on your machine, with a principal one being code reuse. Let's say you have five separate applets that each performs various mathematical calculations. Instead of defining the same math subroutines inside of each applet, you can keep these subroutines stored inside a single library, from which the various applets can use these methods after loading the library themselves. It is inefficient to include the same subroutine definition inside five different applets. Another reason to consolidate code inside of libraries is to "separate the things that change from the things that stay the same."* For example, a system administrator might have created several applets that occasionally have to be updated to accommodate the changing requirements of their network users. In designing the scripting system, the scripter places all subroutines and/or properties that *do not* change inside a library, which can be called from the applets that *do* have to be rewritten and compiled once in a while. It is inefficient to keep recompiling the unchanged source code, except in response to the rare occasions when it has to be changed. So the rule of thumb when designing large AppleScript systems is to take the things that do not change and put them in a library that will be loaded by other applets.

Remote Script Object and Library Access

Script objects and libraries can also be accessed remotely over TCP/IP networks. This is a very powerful feature of Mac OS 9 and later versions called "program linking via IP." For example, if the *WebLib* library were running on another Mac on the network, you could call its methods from a script on another machine as long as you knew the library machine's IP address. Here's the code:

```
tell app "WebLib" of machine "eppc://192.168.0.2" to httpGet("my.
yahoo.com")
```

The protocol "eppc:", by the way, stands for "event program to program communications." The possibilities are limitless. Chapter 25, *File Sharing Control Panel*, is devoted to scripting the File Sharing control panel and program linking.

---

* I derived this nice principle of program design from the very good book, *Thinking in Java* by Bruce Eckel.

Libraries are AppleScripts that can feed their functionality into other applets. Along with user-defined subroutines, you can also place code that automates certain programs inside of libraries so the code can be used by all applets. For example, you might define a library subroutine that will tell Photoshop 6 to open and save an image file. Any time any other applet needs to save an image file in Photoshop, it just uses this external library function, instead of having to define the method itself.

PART III

Scripting Mac OS 9 Applications

CHAPTER 10

Apple Guide and Help Viewer

With Mac OS 8.5 and beyond, Macintosh users have two pieces of system soft-ware to rely on for getting help on the Mac OS and programs: the Apple Guide extension and the new browser-based Help Viewer. Apple Guide (see Figure 10-1) is the tool that can be launched from the Help menu command of several programs. It usually provides the most basic software help, allowing the user to search a small help database and spawning little animations that circle and choose menu items for you. Mainly in response to the Web, Apple's system has since moved to a browser-based help system with the Help Viewer system application. Compared with Apple Guide, Help Viewer more closely integrates the operating-system help documents with web protocols and Sherlock 2. (Sherlock 2 is covered in Chapter 17, *Scripting Sherlock 2.*) You can find the Help Viewer in the following directory if you're running Mac OS 8.5 or later: *startup disk:System Folder:Help:Apple Help Viewer:Help Viewer.* This chapter describes the Apple Guide's and Help Viewer's dictionaries and gives some examples of how to script your own help systems.

The scriptable Apple Guide extension is located in *startup disk:System Folder:Extensions.* You normally cannot open an application's Apple Guide file from outside the app, unless you are using trusty AppleScript. Example 10-1 opens up the BBEdit Guide file, goes instantly to the Look For help panel, and places the search term "grep" in that panel's search edit field. An AppleScript can be used as a software-testing device for new Mac help systems that use Apple Guide.

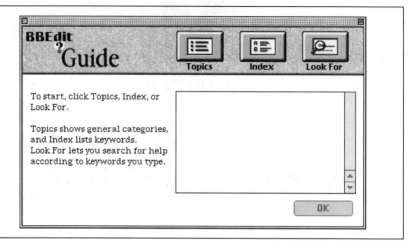

Figure 10-1: An Apple Guide window

Example 10-1: Opening the BBEdit Guide File

```
(* Apple Guide's 'open' command can take a file specification type for a
parameter *)
set filespec to ¬
   "macintosh hd:BBEdit 5.0:BBEdit 5.0:BBEdit Guide" as file specification
tell application "Apple Guide"
   (* Use the 'string' labeled parameter and the 'ViewNumber' parameter
   that takes an integer type *)
   open database filespec string "grep" ViewNumber 4
end tell
```

Apple Guide

Syntax

```
tell application "Apple Guide"
   GoViewTopicAreas (* when a Guide window is open, go to the topics
   panel *)
   (* do other stuff with an open Apple Guide *)
end tell
```

Dictionary commands

Animate

If an animation object like a QuickTime movie exists in the open Apple Guide window, then this command is a signal for it to execute its animation. The following is an example of *animate*:

```
tell app "Apple Guide" to animate
```

Your script raises an error if you use this command and the open Apple Guide window does not have an animation.

Close

This command closes all the Apple Guide windows and the running database of help files. But it doesn't close the Apple Guide program, which is still running invisibly in the background. You can still send the program an Apple event to open another application's Guide files, for instance. Use *Quit* if you want to completely quit the Guide program so that it doesn't use the machine's memory anymore.

DoCoach

This command draws the coach mark that is defined for the current Apple Guide window, or it has no effect if the current panel has not defined a coach mark. If any of the Topics, Index, or Look For Apple Guide panels are active then this command raises an error.

CoachID integer

This optional parameter draws the coach mark associated with a particular id number, if any is defined for the active Guide panel or window.

DoHuh

If the beveled button with the "Huh?" label is active in the lower left corner of the Guide window, then issuing this command is the equivalent of clicking the "Huh?" button:

```
tell app "Apple Guide" to DoHuh
```

GoBack

This command closes an "oops" topic and returns to the Guide window that preceded the active oops panel. What's an oops topic, you ask? When the Apple Guide instructs the user to initiate a command such as File → Print and the user moves to the next instructive panel without doing the requested command, then Apple Guide usually displays another panel with the oops label and some text that repeats the instructions.

GoNext

This command moves to the next Apple Guide window.

GoNextUnconditionally

Unlike *GoNext*, this command goes to the next window regardless of whether the user has followed the previous panel's instructions.

GoNextToPanel

This command goes to the next numbered panel, as in:

```
tell app "Apple Guide" to GoNextToPanel PanelNumber 5
```

Specify the panel number with the **PanelNumber** labeled parameter. If there is not a panel number 5 (because the active set of Apple Guide windows only has four panels), then Apple Guide ignores the command.

GoNextToFirst

This command goes to the first panel in the Guide sequence.

GoNextToLast

This command goes to the last panel in the Guide sequence.

GoPrevious

This command goes to the window preceding the active Guide panel; it's the same as clicking the left arrow button in the lower region of an Apple Guide panel.

GoPreviousUnconditionally

This goes to the window preceding the active Guide panel, but doesn't evaluate any of the help program's qualifiers such as whether the user followed on-screen instructions. This command has the same effect as clicking the left arrow button in the lower region of an Apple Guide panel.

GoStart

This goes back to the beginning of a help sequence, such as an Apple Guide Topics window.

HidePanel

This minimizes a help window (makes it smaller on the desktop).

ShowPanel

This command expands or maximizes a minimized guide window. The command is ignored if the panel is already maximized.

TogglePanel

If the panel is minimized this command maximizes it, and vice versa. It has the same effect as clicking the zoom box (first control in upper right corner) on the Guide panel.

GoViewIndex

This command goes to the access window's Index view, which has the same effect as clicking the Index button. If the access window is not open then this command raises an error. The access window is the upper level Guide window. See *GoViewLookFor* and *GoViewTopicAreas*.

GoViewLookFor

This command goes to the access window's Look For view (which is the same as clicking the Look For button). If the access window is not open then this command raises an error. See *GoViewIndex* and *GoViewTopicAreas*.

`string string`

The `string` labeled parameter for this command forces a search for the `string` and presents some topic results:

```
GoViewLookFor string "grep"
```

GoViewTopicAreas

This goes to the access window's Topics view, which also happens when you click the Topics button in the access window. If the access window is not open then this command raises an error. See *GoViewIndex* and *GoViewLookFor.*

Open

Use the *Open* command, followed by a *database* `file-specification` labeled parameter, to open a new Apple Guide help system. Save the path to the Guide file in a `file specification` variable, and then follow the *open database* syntax with the variable and any of the two optional parameters.

Here's a syntax example:

```
tell app "Apple Guide" to open database filespec string "grep"
ViewNumber 4
```

This command forces a search of the `filespec` Guide file for the term "grep" and presents the results in a Look For access window. Notice that the target application for the example's command is "Apple Guide", not "BBEdit 5.0." When you use AppleScript, the program's Guide file is controlled through the Apple Guide application. BBEdit's dictionary does not identify any Apple events for controlling help files.

Database file specification

The database labeled parameter uses a `file specification` object, which contains the file path to an Apple Guide file.

string string

The labeled parameter *string* (which takes a `string` type) allows the script to force a database search for the particular `string` term. Using this parameter with the *open* command is the equivalent of the user going to the Look For access window, entering the `string` in the edit field, and clicking the search button. So a single AppleScript command substitutes for at least three manual interactions with the Apple Guide.

ViewNumber integer

Follow this labeled parameter with an `integer` representing one of six choices of views that will be displayed: 1=Full Howdy, 2=Topic Areas, 3=Index, 4=LookFor, 5=Single Howdy, 6=Single Topics. For example, Figure 10-1 represents the Full Howdy view.

OpenPanelOnly

This command opens the presentation window (as opposed to an access view such as Index) associated with the panel id number provided with the `panelId` labeled parameter. You also have to provide the `database` labeled parameter with this command if a Guide database isn't already open.

PanelId integer

This is a number representing the id of the panel to open:

```
OpenPanelOnly PanelID 4.
```

Database file specification *or* string *pathname:*

Include this labeled parameter if Apple Guide is not already running or if you are changing Guide files:

```
OpenPanelOnly PanelID 4 Database filespec
```

Apple recommends that scripters use a `file specification` type rather than a `string` type for identifying the Guide file.

OpenPanelOnlyAnother

You can open a panel in a new window using this command, as long as a Guide file is already open. In other words, an already opened presentation window will not close as a result of *OpenPanelOnlyAnother.*

`PanelId integer`
> Identify the panel to open in a new Guide window with this labeled parameter:

```
OpenPanelOnlyAnother PanelID 4
```

OpenPanelOnlyReplacement
> This replaces any existing windows with the presentation window identified with the *PanelId* labeled parameter. The parameter is required, as shown in the following:

```
OpenPanelOnlyReplacement PanelId 4
```

`PanelID integer`
> Include the id of the panel that will open.

OpenWithSequence
> If you know the sequence id of a particular sequence of Guide presentation windows, then you can use this command to test it:

```
OpenWithSequence Database filespec SequenceID 4
```

`Database file specification`
> Save the Guide file's path (a **string** such as "macintosh hd:BBEdit 5. 0:BBEdit 5.0:BBEdit Guide") to a variable of type **file specification**, then use the variable for the *Database* labeled parameter:

```
OpenWithSequence Database filespec SequenceID 1
```

`SequenceID integer`
> This is a required labeled parameter whose **integer** represents the id of the sequence of panels to launch.

`PanelNumber integer`
> Optionally, include the id of the panel that starts off the sequence:

```
OpenWithSequence Database filespec SequenceID 1 PanelNumber 2
```

OpenNamedSequence
> This is like the previous command, except that you name the sequence with a **string**, rather than providing a sequence id number. The following is a syntax example:

```
OpenNamedSequence Database filespec SequenceName "printhlp"
PanelNumber 2
```

`Database file specification`
> Save the Guide file's path (a **string** such as "macintosh hd:BBEdit 5. 0:BBEdit 5.0:BBEdit Guide") to a variable of type **file specification**, then use the variable for the **Database** labeled parameter:

```
OpenNamedSequence Database filespec SequenceName "printhlp"
```

`SequenceName string`
> This is the name of the sequence to initiate on the desktop.

`PanelNumber integer`
> Optionally, include the id of the panel that will start off the sequence:

```
OpenNamedSequence Database filespec SequenceName "printhlp"
PanelNumber 2
```

OpenWithSequenceAnother

> This is designed to display a sequence of panels without closing any existing windows, but a Guide file or database must already be open.

> `SequenceID integer`
>
> > This is a required labeled parameter whose `integer` represents the id of the sequence of panels to launch.

> `PanelNumber integer`
>
> > Optionally, include the id of the panel that starts off the sequence:
> >
> > `OpenWithSequenceAnother SequenceID 1 PanelNumber 2`

OpenWithSequenceOops

> This command initiates a new sequence of panels in an open Guide window, hiding but not closing the original window. A *GoBack* command returns the user to the prior window. The particular Guide database must already be open.

> `SequenceID integer`
>
> > This is a required labeled parameter whose `integer` represents the id of the sequence of panels to launch.

OpenWithSequenceReplacement

> This closes any existing access or presentation windows and starts a new sequence in another presentation window. A syntax example is:
>
> `OpenWithSequenceReplacement SequenceID 1 PanelId 2`

> `SequenceID integer`
>
> > This is a required labeled parameter whose `integer` represents the id of the sequence of panels to launch.

> `PanelNumber integer`
>
> > Optionally, include the id of the panel that starts off the sequence:
> >
> > `OpenWithSequenceReplacement SequenceID 1 PanelId 2`

PlaySound

> This sends the open Guide file a *PlaySound* Apple event and includes the id of the sound data as a labeled parameter:
>
> `tell app "Apple Guide" to PlaySound SoundId 4`

> *SoundId* `integer`
>
> > This is a number representing the id of the sound data in the database. This labeled parameter is required.

Quit

> This closes any open windows and terminates the Apple Guide app. Unlike *close*, *Quit* does not leave Apple Guide silently running in the background, using its megabyte or so of memory.

QuitFront

> This is similar to *Quit*, but it leaves Apple Guide running if there is more than one Guide window open. In other words, *QuitFront* closes the front Guide window but leaves the next window intact and does not shut down Apple Guide. If only one window is open then *QuitFront* has the same effect as *Quit*.

Help Viewer

Since Help Viewer (see Figure 10-2) is essentially a browser, you can open up any local hypertext markup language (HTML) file with it (see the *open* command for Help Viewer). AppleScripters can thus use this program to either provide their scripts with their own HTML-based help systems or provide an alternate and perhaps quicker avenue to the Mac OS's help files.

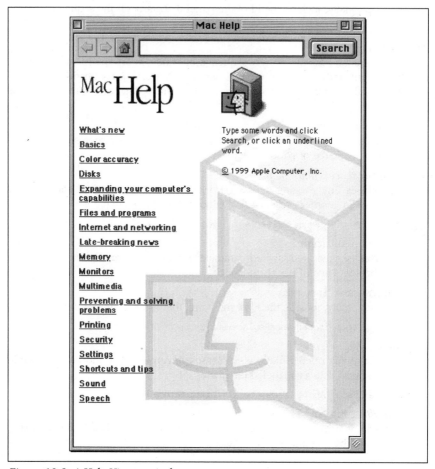

Figure 10-2: A Help Viewer window

Syntax

```
tell app "Help Viewer"
    (* get the app to print various help topics or open HTML files here *)
end tell
```

Dictionary commands

Open `alias list`

One of the ways to open up a help file in Help Viewer is to send it an *open* Apple event with a `list` of aliases as a parameter (one alias, representing the file path to the page you want to open). The following example opens a page on Help Viewer search tips. You can also use *open* to open your own HTML files in Help Viewer, as long as you make sure to save the file path as an `alias` inside of a `list` (as in `{my_alias}`) before passing this parameter to *open*:

```
tell application "Finder"
    (* path to the Help Viewer tips file *)
    set tips to
        ((system folder as string) & "help:apple help viewer:hvtps.¬
        htm")
        as alias
end tell
tell application "Help Viewer"
    activate -- bring it to the fore
    open {tips} -- use open followed by a list with one alias
end tell
```

Print `alias list`

You can use code similar to the prior example to send a *print* command to Help Viewer. Create an `alias` to the HTML file, or have the user choose the file to print using the *choose file* scripting addition. (Appendix A, *Standard Scripting Additions*, is devoted to scripting additions.) This could be accomplished with the following code, which returns an `alias` type pointing to the file:

```
choose file with prompt "Choose the Help Viewer html file" of type
{"TEXT"}
```

Then pass a `list` containing the `alias` to the *print* command:

```
print {the_alias}
```

Quit

This quits the Help Viewer app.

Run

This command opens Help Viewer so that you can send Apple events to it:

```
tell application "Help Viewer" to run
```

Close

This command also quits Help Viewer, like *Quit.*

Search `string`

This searches the help files using a particular search term:

```
tell app "Help Viewer" to search looking for "AppleScript"
```

If you want to search just one "book," such as QuickTime Help, then pass the *search* command a `string` parameter:

```
search "QuickTime Help" looking for "AppleScript"
```

looking for string

Follow the *looking for* labeled parameter with a `string` containing your search term, as in the following:

```
search looking for "QuickTime" -- or ...
```

```
search looking for "QuickTime or AppleScript"
```

Help Viewer allows the use of the following boolean operators: and, +, or, |, not, !, and grouping with parentheses ( ). An example of grouping is searching for files containing "file type" or "file sharing" but not "file exchange":

```
search looking for "file + (type | sharing) ! exchange"
```

handle url string

An easy way to open up a file in Help Viewer is to use the *handle url* command followed by a `string` containing the file path. You can use file paths that are relative to the *startup disk:System Folder:Help* folder:

```
handle url "Apple Help Viewer:hvtps.htm"
```

The latter command opens up the Help Viewer tips file. Using the *open* command appears to work better if you want to use absolute paths (e.g., "Macintosh HD:Desktop Folder:myfile.html") or open up your own HTML files using this program (see *open* earlier in this chapter).

Dictionary classes

application

The Help Viewer `application` class has one element, a `window` object, and one property, which is an `alias` type of the current file that the Help Viewer window is showing at the time. You can access the `window` element by using this code:

```
tell app "Help Viewer" to get name of window 1
```

This would return a `string` such as "Help Viewer Tips." You can get the file path of whatever file happens to be displayed in Help Viewer at the moment with code such as the following:

```
get current file as text
```

This code returns something like "Macintosh HD:System Folder:Help:Apple Help Viewer:hvtps.htm."

window (window *object*)

You can get properties of the current Help Viewer window (see the `window` class description) by seizing this element with code such as:

```
tell app "Help Viewer" to get name of window 1
```

The element can be referred to by either its `name` (window "Help Viewer Tips") or its `index` (window 1).

Current file (alias)

Use this property to get the pathname of the file that Help Viewer currently displays.

window

A Help Viewer window has several common AppleScript window properties, but you cannot use the Help Viewer app to make a new window, as in the following:

```
make new window ...
```

You can get the value of any of these properties with code such as:

```
get bounds of window 1
```

collapsed (boolean)

You can hide all but the Help Viewer title bar by using this code:

```
set collapsed of window 1 to true
```

bounds (bounding rectangle)

This property returns the bounding rectangle for the window. This is a list of coordinates (which you can change), such as {50, 79, 668, 611}. For instance, this Help Viewer window's upper left corner is 50 pixels from the left edge of the screen and 79 pixels down.

closeable (boolean; *read-only*)

This is a true/false value that indicates whether the window has a close box (the little box in the upper left corner of the window).

titled (boolean; *read-only*)

If the window has a title in the title bar, this property is true.

index (integer)

This is the index property of the open Help Viewer window. Help Viewer loads new help files and search results into the same window, so this property is almost always 1:

```
window 1
```

floating (boolean; *read-only*)

Most Help Viewer windows are not floating; in other words, you can place them behind other document windows on the desktop. This property value is false if the window is not floating.

modal (boolean; *read-only*)

A modal window (such as an Alert dialog message) has to be dismissed by the user before they can do anything else with their desktop objects. The main Help Viewer window returns false for this property.

resizable (boolean; *read-only*)

If the window can be resized then this property returns true.

zoomable (boolean; *read-only*)

This returns true if the Help Viewer window has a zoom box, as does the main Viewer window.

zoomed (boolean)

This returns true if the user has clicked the Help Viewer's zoom box.

name (international text)

This gets the name of the window, which appears in its title bar. An example of the return value is "Mac Help."

visible (boolean; *read-only*)

> If the Help viewer window is open, which it is when the program is running, then this property returns true.

position (point; *read-only*)

> This returns the upper-left corner coordinates of the window as a list type. An example of the return value is {29, 175}. The first number represents the number of pixels from the left side of the screen along the x-axis.

Examples

```
tell application "Help Viewer"
    activate -- make Help Viewer the active window
    set myhelp to "macintosh hd:desktop folder:machowto.htm" as alias
    -- open up your own html file
    open {myhelp}  -- open command takes a list of aliases (or alias)
end tell
```

It is easier to use *open* rather than *handle url* if you want to use absolute file paths to open up different HTML files in Help Viewer.

If you want to create uniformity with the Mac OS's help system, you can generate your own software program's help files in HTML form, then use Help Viewer to display the files.

CHAPTER 11

Apple System Profiler

Apple System Profiler is a system program that gathers and displays everything you ever wanted to know about your software, hardware, and networking features, including a few things you wish you didn't know, such as how many extension files reside on your machine. The ASP is located in *startup disk:System Folder:Apple menu Items*; it is accessible from the Apple menu. A system administrator who is responsible for a lot of Macs could use AppleScript and ASP to print out customized reports on all the machines they are responsible for. Figure 11-1 shows the System Profile tab of the Apple System Profiler. The following dictionary reference applies to ASP Version 2.4.4, which is installed with Mac OS 9.04.

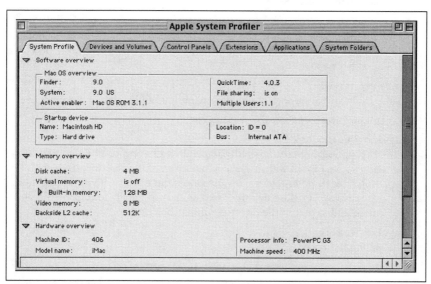

Figure 11-1: Apple System Profiler

187

Apple System Profiler

Syntax

```
tell app "Apple System Profiler"
    (* get the machine's IP address *)
    get TCPIP address
end tell
```

Dictionary commands

open object or list of objects

This command opens an ASP report, as in the following example:

```
set rep to "macintosh hd:desktop folder:ASP report" as alias
tell application "Apple System Profiler"
    activate bring ASP to the front
    open rep
end tell
```

print object or list of objects to print

This prints a report, as in print `ASPreportFile` displaying print dialog true as text.

`displaying print dialog (boolean)`

This is an optional `true`/`false` value. If it's `true`, it displays a dialog for setting printing preferences prior to printing the ASP report.

as (text/shown on screen)

This is an optional labeled parameter involving whether to print out the report as text or as it is laid out on screen in the ASP document.

quit

This command quits ASP.

run

This command sends a *run* Apple event to ASP, which is the same as double-clicking the program's icon on the desktop. This opens the application if it is not already open.

close reference to object

This closes an ASP report, optionally saving it in a file. Here is example code:

```
close report "ASPreport" saving ask
```

`saving yes/no/ask`

The optional *saving* labeled parameter takes one of three constants. *yes* saves the report with a default name in ASP's directory (which is the *Apple Menu Items* folder), *no* just closes the report without saving it, and *ask* displays a dialog that the user can use optionally to rename the document and save it in the directory of his choice.

`saving in alias`

Using the code

```
close report report 1 saving in aliasFile
```

saves an open report in the `alias` contained in the variable `aliasFile`.

count reference to object

This command counts the number of open reports or ASP windows and returns an `integer`:

```
count each window
```

each class

The `each` labeled parameter, as in `count each report`, is not required; you can use syntax such as `count reports` instead.

exists reference to object

This finds out whether a report or window exists:

```
exists report 1
```

This command returns a `boolean` value, `true` or `false`.

make

This command makes a new report:

```
make new report at "macintosh hd:desktop folder" with properties
{report contents: {system profile} }
```

A report is the only object that ASP can use *make* with.

new (class)

Follow the `new` labeled parameter with the `report class` type:

```
make new report
```

at (location reference)

Follow the `at` labeled parameter with a `string` indicating where you want to save the report:

```
at "macintosh hd:desktop folder"
```

with data (anything)

This labeled parameter does not appear to add any value in this context beyond what you can accomplish with the `with properties` labeled parameter. At any rate, follow this labeled parameter with an `anything` value.

with properties (record)

The `with properties` parameter is followed by a `record` type that contains the new report's properties. Chapter 3, *Data Types*, describes the `record` data type. Here is the example code:

```
tell application "Apple System Profiler"
    make new report at
        "macintosh hd:desktop folder" with properties
        {report contents:{hardware overview},
        report view format:text}
end tell
```

save reference to report

You can save an ASP report to a file with code such as:

```
save report 1 in "macintosh hd:desktop folder:new.txt"
```

in (alias)

If you pass in a valid `string` pathname with the `in` labeled parameter, then ASP saves the report in a new file.

backup *(boolean)*

The **backup true** labeled parameter is not necessary; if you continually save the same report but with different filenames, the original saved report is not overwritten. These actions will just create several different files of the same ASP report.

Dictionary classes

application

This class represents the Apple System Profiler app. It includes the **window** and **report** elements, as well as numerous properties that contain information on the computer's memory, such as volumes (disks), files, networking protocols, and other features. Scripters can set non–read-only ASP properties with code such as:

```
tell app "Apple System Profiler" to set report contents to ¬
    memory overview
```

You can get information about the machine with code such as the following:

```
get QuickTime version or get file sharing
```

This is **true** or **false** if file sharing is enabled. The phrase "(report class)" in the following definitions means that the **report** class shares this property with the **application** class, and the property has the same definition. The following are **application** elements:

report

The application can have one or more open ASP reports. See the **report** class.

window

The application can have one or more open ASP windows. See the **window** class.

The following are **application** properties:

properties

The code:

```
tell app "Apple System Profiler" to get properties
```

returns a **record** type containing the names and values of the vast majority of the application's properties. To get a specific property value from this **record** type, use code such as:

```
get AppleTalk address of properties
```

This useful property returns the hardware address of your Ethernet card as a **string**, such as "08.00.07.00.00.00."

clipboard *(a* list *of anything)*

This returns a **list** of whatever items are in the clipboard.

name *(international* text*)*

The name is "Apple System Profiler."

frontmost *(boolean)*

This value is **true** if ASP is the frontmost app on the desktop.

version *(version)*

> This returns the ASP version number, which is a string like "2.4.4." Version 2.4.4 comes with Mac OS 9.04 and includes the dictionary described in this chapter.

gathers at launch *(list of constants)*

> This property tells ASP which machine data to gather when it starts up or launches. You can also set this property by choosing ASP's menu command *Edit-Preferences*. The constants are any of the following:

all	network overview
applications	printing overview
control panels	production information
devices and volumes	software overview
extensions	system folders
hardware overview	system profile
memory overview	

> Here is example code:

```
set gathers at launch to {network overview, system folders}.
```

gathering *(boolean)*

> This is a **boolean** value that returns **true** if the application is in the process of collecting data on the machine.

remembers window size *(boolean)*

> This sets the "save window location and size" checkbox in the Preferences window of the app.

report view format *(text/shown on screen)*

> You can set this property to either of the two constants. There are slight differences in the way the two constants display the ASP data (for example, **text** is better for printing the document).

preferred report contents *(a list of constants)*

> You can set this property to any of these constants:

all	network overview
applications	printing overview
control panels	production information
devices and volumes	software overview
extensions	system folders
hardware overview	system profile
memory overview	

The setting determines the default manner in which ASP gathers machine data.

control panel volumes *(list of aliases or the constants **startup/attached/all/preferred**)*

> Usually ASP just gathers information that derives from the startup disk, but your computer might mount more than one volume on the desktop. This property determines whether you gather data on the control panels of only the startup disk or of several other volumes. You can use a **list**

of aliases to the various volumes or one of the constants to give this property a value:

```
set control panel volumes to attached
```

extension volumes (list *of aliases or the constants* startup/attached/ all/preferred)

Using this property, you can control where ASP gathers information from on extension files. Use a list of aliases to the volumes or one of the four constants to give this property a value.

application volumes (list *of aliases or the constants* startup/attached/ all/preferred)

Usually ASP just gathers information that derives from the startup disk, but your computer might mount more than one volume on the desktop. You can control where ASP gathers information on applications. Use a list of aliases to the volumes or one of the four constants to give this property a value.

system folder volumes (list *of aliases or the* startup/attached/all/ preferred)

Scripters can specify the system folders that ASP gathers data on by setting this property to either a list of aliases pointing to the system folders or one of four constants. The default is **startup**.

system info (record)(report *class*)

This property returns a **record** containing data from the **system overview** section of the System Profile panel. An example return value is:

```
{file sharing:true, finder version:"9.0", system version:"9.0.4
US", active enabler:"PowerPC Enabler 9.0.4 9.0.4", AtEase
version:"1.1", QuickTime version:"4.0.3",
StartupDiskName:"Macintosh HD", MacOS info:true,
StartupDiskType:"Hard drive", StartupDiskLocation:"ID = 0",
StartupDiskBus:"SCSI Bus 0", disk cache size:"6.50 MB", startup
info:true, system info:true}.
```

MacOS info (record)(*report class*)

This gathers all of the information from the Mac OS overview section of the System Profile panel. This property returns a **record** type. Chapter 3 describes the **record** data type.

finder version (string)(*report class*)

This returns the version of the Finder from the frontmost ASP window or report.

system version (string)(*report class*)

This property returns a **string** containing the system version (e.g., "9.04") from the frontmost ASP window or report.

active enabler (string)(*report class*)

This property returns the version of the active enabler system software or an empty string if there isn't one installed.

`AtEase version` (string)(*report class*)

This is the version of the software At Ease, if it's installed.

`MultipleUsers user name` (string)(*report class*)

This returns the current username if Multiple Users is installed and a user is logged in.

`MultipleUsersEnvironment` (string)(*report class*)

This property returns information on the Multiple Users environment if Multiple Users is installed and a user is logged in.

`QuickTime version` (string)(*report class*)

This property finds out which Quicktime version the machine is running with code such as:

```
set qt to QuickTime version
```

`file sharing` (boolean)(*report class*):

This is a `true` or `false` value indicating whether file sharing is enabled.

`startup info` (record)(*report class*)

This property returns a `record` containing useful system information such as your machine's disk-cache size. The return value from `get startup info` looks like:

```
{StartupDiskType:"Hard drive", StartupDiskLocation:"ID = 0",
StartupDiskBus:"SCSI Bus 0", disk cache size:"6.50 MB", startup
info:true}
```

`StartupDiskName` (string)(*report class*)

This property returns the name of your startup disk.

`StartupDiskType` (string)(*report class*)

This returns a `string` such as "Hard drive."

`StartupDiskLocation` (string)(*report class*)

This property returns a `string` such as "ID = 0."

`StartupDiskBus` (string)(*report class*)

This returns a string from the startup device section of the System Profile panel, such as "SCSI Bus 0."

`memory info` (string)(*report class*)

This is a `record` type whose return value looks like:

```
{video memory size:"", memory cache size:"Not installed", VM
info:true, VM size:"209 MB", VM storage:"scratch", physical RAM
size:"208 MB", memory info:true}
```

`disk cache size` (string)(*report class*)

This property returns the disk cache `string` from the memory overview section of the System Profile panel. An example is "6.50 MB."

`video memory size` (string)(*report class*)

This property returns the video memory size or an empty `string` if the data is not available.

`video note` (string)(*report class*)

This property returns nothing on my machine, but returns a `string` if Video note information is available.

memory cache size *(string)(report class)*

This property returns "Not Installed" if the external L2 cache is disabled on your motherboard, as is true for my CPU-upgraded machine.

VM info *(boolean)(report class)*

This is a true/false value indicating whether virtual memory is turned on.

VM storage*(string)(report class)*

This property returns the name of the volume or disk that is storing the virtual-memory file, if virtual memory is turned on.

VM size *(string)(report class)*

This returns a string representing the amount of virtual memory the machine is using; it returns an empty string otherwise.

physical RAM size *(string)(report class)*

This property returns the amount of memory the machine has.

hardware info *(record)(report class)*

This returns a record type containing the information that is found in the hardware-overview section of the System Profile panel. Here's a sample return value:

```
{logicboard num:"69", unique logicboard num:"69", model
name:"Power Macintosh 8500 series", keyboard type:"Apple
Extended Keyboard", hardware attributes:"Not available",
processor type:"PowerPC G3", rated speed:"400 MHz",
processors:"1", nanokernel version:"2.13", free pools:" 0",
scheduled processors:" 1", hardware info:true}.
```

logicboard num *(string)(report class)*

This represents a subset of the hardware-info value (see the example return value under "hardware info").

The following 10 properties represent a subset of the hardware info value (see the example return under "hardware info"):

unique logicboard num (string)(report class)
rated speed (string)(report class)
model name (string)(report class)
keyboard type (string)(report class)
hardware attributes (string)(report class)
processor type (string)(report class)
processors (string)(report class)
nanokernel version (string)(report class)
free pools (string)(report class)
scheduled processors (string)(report class)

network info *(record)(report class)*

All of the available AppleTalk, Ethernet, modem, and other networking information (including TCP/IP address and subnet mask) is returned as a record type. In other words, this is a very useful value for anyone who is dealing with networked Macs. The data derives from the network-overview section of ASP's System Profile.

Ethernet information *(record)(report class)*

    This property returns a `record` type containing the values for Ethernet link, duplex, and speed.

Ethernet link *(string)(report class)*

    This returns the Ethernet link value from the network-overview section of ASP's System Profile tab.

Ethernet speed *(string)(report class)*

    This returns the Ethernet speed value from the network-overview section of ASP's System Profile tab.

Ethernet duplex *(string)(report class)*

    This returns the Ethernet duplex value from the network-overview section of ASP's System Profile tab.

modem info *(string)(report class)*

    This property returns the modem info value from the network-overview section of ASP's System Profile tab.

modem name *(string)(report class)*

    This property returns the modem name value from the network-overview section of ASP's System Profile tab.

modem protocol *(string)(report class)*

    This property returns the modem protocol value from the network-overview section of ASP's System Profile tab.

modem version *(string)(report class)*

    This property returns the modem version value from the network-overview section of ASP's System Profile tab.

modem status *(string)(report class)*

    This property returns the modem status value from the network-overview section of ASP's System Profile tab.

Open Transport info *(record)(report class)*

    This property returns a `record` type containing information derived from the network-overview section of the System Profile tab. The following is a sample return value:

```
{Open Transport installed:true, Open Transport status:true, Open
Transport version:"2.6.1", Open Transport info:true}.
```

Open Transport installed *(boolean)(report class)*, Open Transport status *(boolean)(report class)*, Open Transport version *(string)(report class)*

    These properties return a subset of the Open Transport info value. See Open Transport info for a sample return value.

AppleTalk info *(record)(report class)*

    This value is a `record` type containing the AppleTalk information from the network-overview section of the System Profile tab. Here is a sample return value:

```
{AppleTalk installed:true, AppleTalk state:true, AppleTalk
version:"60", default AppleTalk zone:"Not available", active
network ports:"Ethernet built-in LocalTalk (printer) built-in",
AppleTalk network:"0", AppleTalk node:"123", AppleTalk
address:"08.00.07.00.00.00", AppleTalk router:"<not available>",
AppleTalk info:true}
```

`AppleTalk installed` *(boolean)(report class)*

This property returns a subset of the AppleTalk info property value. See
`AppleTalk info` for a sample return value.

`AppleTalk state` *(boolean)(report class)*

This property returns a subset of the AppleTalk info property value. See
`AppleTalk info` for a sample return value.

`Apple Talk version` *(string)(report class)*

This property returns a subset of the AppleTalk info property value. See
`AppleTalk info` for a sample return value.

`file sharing` *(boolean)(report class)*

This is a `true/false` value indicating whether file sharing is started in
the File Sharing control panel.

`default AppleTalk zone` *(string)(report class)*

This property returns a subset of the AppleTalk info property value. See
`AppleTalk info` for a sample return value.

`active network ports` *(string)(report class)*

This property returns a subset of the AppleTalk info property value. See
`AppleTalk info` for a sample return value.

`AppleTalk network` *(string)(report class)*

This property returns a subset of the AppleTalk info property value. See
`AppleTalk info` for a sample return value.

`AppleTalk node` *(string)(report class)*

This property returns a subset of the AppleTalk info property value. See
`AppleTalk info` for a sample return value.

`AppleTalk address` *(string)(report class)*

This property returns a subset of the AppleTalk info property value. See
`AppleTalk info` for a sample return value.

`AppleTalk router` *(string)(report class)*

This property returns a subset of the AppleTalk info property value. See
`AppleTalk info` for a sample return value.

`TCPIP info` *(record)(report class)*

This property returns a `record` type containing the TCP/IP data for the
machine, such as TCP/IP address, version, and subnet mask. The return
value looks like:

```
{TCPIP installed:true, TCPIP status:true, TCPIP version:"2.6.1",
web sharing:false, multihoming:false, TCPIP netmask:"255.255.0.
0", TCPIP address:"192.168.0.3", TCPIP gateway:"192.168.0.1",
TCPIP domain:"", TCPIP nameserver:"192.168.0.1", TCPIP
info:true}
```

The data is derived from the network overview section of the System profile tab.

TCPIP installed *(boolean)(report class)*

This property returns a subset of the TCPIP info property value. If TCP/IP is not installed then this property returns **false**.

TCPIP status *(boolean)(report class)*, **TCPIP version** *(string)(report class)*, **multihoming** *(boolean)(report class)*

These properties return a subset of the TCPIP info property value. See **TCPIP info**.

web sharing *(boolean)(report class)*

This property returns a subset of the TCPIP info property value. It is **true** if web sharing has been started in the Web Sharing control panel.

TCPIP netmask *(string)(report class)*

This property returns a subset of the TCPIP info property value. It returns a **string** such as "255.255.255.0." See **TCPIP info**.

TCPIP address *(string)(report class)*

This property returns a subset of the TCPIP info property value. It returns a **string** such as "172.128.0.1." See **TCPIP info**.

TCPIP gateway *(string)(report class)*, **TCPIP domain** *(string)(report class)*, **TCPIP nameserver** *(string)(report class)*

These properties return a subset of the TCPIP info property value. You can also find this information in the TCPIP control panel. See **TCPIP info**.

production info *(record)(report class)*

This property returns a record type that contains any production information on the machine, such as it serial number. A sample return value is:

```
{ROM revision:"$77D.28F1", boot ROM version:"Not available",
boot ROM file version:"Not available", serial number:"Not
applicable", software bundle number:"Not applicable", sales
order number:"Not applicable", production info:true}
```

The following six properties are subsets of the production info value:

ROM revision (string)(report class)
boot ROM version (string)(report class)
boot ROM file version (string)(report class)
serial number (string)(report class)
software bundle number (string)(report class)
sales order number (string)(report class)
not applicable (string)(report class)

This returns the **string** "not applicable" if the machine is using a U.S. version of ASP. Otherwise it returns the translated version of "not applicable."

not available *(string)(report class)*

This returns the **string** "not available" if the machine is using a U.S. version of ASP. Otherwise it returns the translated version of "not available."

`monitors` (string)(*report class*)

This property returns the number of monitors that are connected to the machine.

`report`

This class represents an Apple System Profiler report. These `reports` assemble all or a subset of system information as either an ASP document or text file. Most of the `report` object's properties (it has no elements) are shared with the `application` object; those that are not shared are defined in the upcoming section. See the `application` class discussion for the definitions of most of the `report` class's properties. The following are `report` properties:

`name` (international text; *read-only*)

This property returns the report name as a `string`.

`id` (integer; *read-only*)

Every report has a unique id that looks like 182306468. You can get the ID of the frontmost report with code such as:

```
tell app "Apple System Profiler" to get id of report 1
```

If you set this value to a variable you can then refer to the report by its ID:

```
report ID 182306468
```

`index` (integer; *read-only*)

Open ASP reports can be identified with a 1-based index: report 1 for the first report that is created, report 2 for the second, etc. You can initially get the ID of a report with the code:

```
set myid to id of report 1
```

`report contents` (list *of constants*)

`report contents` is a `list` containing any of the following constants:

```
all                      network overview
applications             printing overview
control panels           production information
devices and volumes      software overview
extensions               system folders
hardware overview        system profile
memory overview
```

This is a `list` of the type of data that the report contains. You can also use this property when you make a new ASP report; see the *make* command description in this chapter. The system profile category constitutes the software overview, memory overview, hardware overview, network overview, printing overview, and production information categories.

`report text` (string; *read-only*)

This property returns a large `string` of tab-delimited values if the report is extensive in its coverage. Its return value might be useful if you wanted to save the `string` to a file and then import it into a database file.

window *class*

This is an ASP window object that has the typical properties of a Mac window.

bounds *(bounding rectangle)*

This returns the boundary rectangle for the window as a list of integers, such as {50, 50, 594, 764}.

closeable (boolean; *read-only)*

This returns true or false depending on whether the window has a close box.

titled (boolean; *read-only)*

This is a true/false value depending on whether the window has a title bar.

name (international text; *read-only)*

This property returns the window's title, which could be useful when you try to identify a particular ASP report.

modal (boolean; *read-only)*

This returns a true/false value indicating whether the window is modal or not. Since most ASP windows are document windows (you can move them around and access other windows behind the document window), this property often returns false.

resizable (boolean; *read-only)*

This returns a true/false value indicating whether the window can be resized by dragging its corners.

zoomable (boolean; *read-only)*

This returns a true/false value indicating whether the window has a zoom box in its upper right-hand corner.

zoomed (boolean)

You can use this property to increase or decrease an ASP-report window size:

```
set zoomed of window 1 to true.
```

Examples

This script gathers important system information on the local machine and displays the dialog shown in Figure 11-2:

```
try -- trap any errors caused by running ASP
    tell application "Apple System Profiler"
        launch -- run the app but don't bring it to the front
        set sys to system version -- a string like "9.04"
        set startdisk to StartupDiskName
        set ram to physical RAM size -- how much RAM does the machine have?
        set megh to rated speed -- how fast the machine is in megahertz
        set cpu to processor type -- an example is "PowerPC G3 400"
        (* Assemble a message to the user in the sysmessage variable *)
        set sysmessage to return & "The system version is : " & sys & ¬
        return
        set sysmessage to sysmessage & "Startup disk name: " & startdisk ¬
```

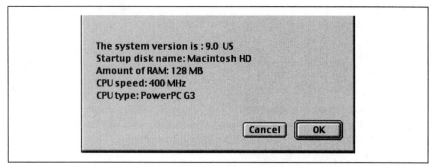

Figure 11-2: The Apple System Profiler Example dialog box

```
          & return
          set sysmessage to sysmessage & "Amount of RAM: " & ram & return
          set sysmessage to sysmessage & "CPU speed: " & megh & return
          set sysmessage to sysmessage & "CPU type: " & cpu & return
          display dialog sysmessage
     end tell
on error errMessage
     display dialog "Opening ASP caused this error: " & errMessage
end try
```

CHAPTER 12

Keychain Scripting and Apple Verifier

Mac OS 9 ships with a number of applications and files that help users protect their files, folders, and passwords from intruders. Apple Computer groups these technologies under the Apple Data Security umbrella term. These software tools include:

- The Apple Verifier program, which verifies files that have been digitally signed

- Apple File Signer software for applying digital signatures to files (this is only available in the Security Software Developers Kit)

- Apple File Security, which you can use to encrypt and decrypt files

- The Keychain Access control panel and Keychain Scripting, which involve the storage of passwords in a secure repository or database called a *keychain* file

- Several extension files in the *startup disk:System Folder:Extensions* folder, including *Security Cert Module, Security Library, Security Manager, Security Policy Module, Security Storage Module*

Look in the *startup disk:Applications:Security* folder and you will find the Apple File Security and Apple Verifier programs. Apple File Security allows you to encrypt and decrypt files using a passphrase of five or more characters that you create. You *must* remember this password unless you have used Keychain Access with the file encryption, which is explained later in this chapter. Encryption mathematically scrambles the file data into a hodge-podge of nonsensical ASCII characters that look like Example 12-1, which is part of this paragraph after it was encrypted. It is extremely difficult, if not impossible (if they do not have your passphrases), for unintended or malicious recipients to break the code and decipher encrypted files.

Example 12-1: A Sample Portion of an Encrypted File

```
_!Âm¿__-#8_ÁÎ>'CªE_$ ë"Bj,/Z_.·,©._fnB,"† VS'íu,>...£ıË-_éΣI_{_ÇR ôY] *oe}g_
Z2<Ú⁻e)Eií3&bEa_Ü__E,â#@aí'ÌÌ•k_m_].¿__'__AQHuè·Ë...e>>é>¤>/ø_>⁻>Ø>_>>=_>ØØS>
N-
```

Just open a file from Apple File Security's File menu, and it will prompt you for a password before encrypting it. You can also encrypt a file from the Finder's File menu in Mac OS 9. Finally, just drag the file over the Apple File Security icon and it displays the dialog window that Figure 12-1 shows. If you checked the "Add to Keychain" checkbox when you encrypted the file (see Figure 12-1), then you can just double-click the file later to decrypt it (return it to its readable and insecure state). If you did not add the passphrase to a keychain then you have to recall the password to decrypt it. Otherwise, no one (including Apple's engineers) will be able to help you decrypt the file. So do not encrypt that email exonerating you and your company from abusing a software monopoly unless you plan to remember the passphrase.

Figure 12-1: Apple File Security adds an encrypted file passphrase to a keychain

Apple File Security is not scriptable with Mac OS 9, but another security program that works closely with Apple's encryption method can be used with AppleScript—Keychain Access. This is a control panel, but its scripting functions are accessible through the Keychain Scripting software tucked away with the scripting additions in the *startup disk:System Folder:Scripting Additions* folder. Figure 12-1 shows the checkbox that allows you to add a passphrase for an encrypted file to a keychain. Again, in Mac OS 9, a keychain is a password file or database that is stored in encrypted form in *startup disk:System Folder:Preferences:Keychains*. You can have one or more keychains as long as you give them unique names. The keychain is designed to provide automatic passwords for:

- Logging on to an AppleTalk or AppleShare IP server (i.e., a computer that you are connected to via Ethernet)
- Decrypting a file that has been encrypted using Apple File Security
- Logging in to a remote web site
- Usage by a software program
- Accessing a digital certificate that you have added to a keychain

---

Not all of this functionality (e.g., using Keychain Access with web sites) was widely available by Winter 2001, but keychains are very useful with files and AppleShare servers. For example, once you have added an AppleShare key to a keychain, then you can mount the specified volume simply by clicking a button (it says "go there") in Keychain Access's Get Info window for that AppleShare key. Again, Keychain Access is a control panel that is located in *startup disk:System Folder:Control Panels.*

Apple Verifier is the other scriptable security application that this chapter describes. Another part of Apple Data Security services is Apple Code Signing. Apple Code Signing is a new Mac OS 9 technology that allows developers to digitally sign applications, plug-ins, and content. Digital certificates are unique IDs that you can apply to software (such as a program that you have coded) so that the software's recipients can be sure that it came from you (and so that you cannot *deny* that it came from you!). Apple Code Signer is another security program that is only distributed with the Apple Security Software Development Kit. Software security and crytography are very interesting but large subjects, so I recommend that you try external information sources to learn more about them.

 Pretty Good Privacy is freeware software for strong encryption (there is a commercial version also). There is a Macintosh version that will work with your email program to encrypt email. The PGP international site has some good documentation on software encryption at *http://www.pgpi.org/doc/.* Apple Computer's security site is *http://developer.apple.com/macos/security.html.* You can obtain the Apple Security SDK at *ftp://ftp.apple.com/developer/Development_Kits/Security_SDK.sit.hqx.* The following sites describe and tell you how to obtain digital certificates: *http://www.thawte.com* and *http://www.verisign.com.*

This chapter will describe AppleScripting with Keychain Scripting and Apple Verifier, which is Apple Computer's program for checking the digital signatures of files or programs that you download from some potentially insecure source such as the Web.

Keychain Scripting

As I mentioned before, a keychain is a password file or database that is stored in encrypted form in *startup disk:System Folder:Preferences:Keychains.* The scripting of keychains, which store important passwords for entry to systems such as local networks, is accomplished through the Keychain Scripting software that is included with the scripting additions in the *startup disk:System Folder:Scripting Additions* folder. Figure 12-1 shows the checkbox that allows you to add a passphrase for an encrypted file to a keychain. You script the Keychain Scripting application just as you would target any other program, such as by enclosing Keychain Scripting commands in `tell` statements.

Syntax

```
tell app "Keychain Scripting"
   get current keychain -- get default keychain
end tell
```

Dictionary commands

count keychains or keys

This command counts the number of keychains the computer system has or the number of keys in a keychain. You can have more than one keychain; for example, I have a separate keychain just for linking with other Macs on my Ethernet. One keychain is always the default or active one and receives any new keys you create (see the current keychain property of the keychain application class). If you want to count just the number of keychains, use this code:

```
tell app "Keychain Scripting" to count keychains
```

This code gets a count of keys within a keychain and returns an integer:

```
tell application "Keychain Scripting"
   tell keychain "MyPasses" to count keys
end tell
```

each class

You can use the *each* labeled parameter to specify the counting of keys or keychains:

```
count each key
```

delete keychain or key

You can remove a key from a keychain or delete a keychain altogether with this command. The next example deletes a certain key that involves connecting to another computer over a TCP/IP network. The script does not delete the key if the keychain is locked, which is why it is a good idea to lock the keychains whenever you are not adding or removing keys from them! This is particularly true because a malicious script can just make an index reference to a key (e.g., Internet key 1) and delete the key without knowing its actual name.

```
tell application "Keychain Scripting"
   delete Internet key 1 of keychain "MyPasses"
end tell
```

exists reference to keychain or key

This command is designed to find out whether a key or keychain exists:

```
set thebool to (exists keychain "BogusHacker")
```

Unfortunately, this command does not yet work with my version of Mac OS 9 (as of 9.0.4).

lock reference to keychain

This command locks a keychain so it cannot be accessed (for instance, by a script). If you use *lock* without a keychain reference, then all the keychains

---

are locked. This code locks a particular keychain, but first finds out whether it is locked at all:

```
tell application "Keychain Scripting"
    if (not locked of keychain "MyPasses") then
        lock keychain "MyPasses"
    end if
end tell
```

You could use similar code in a utility script that makes sure all keychains are locked:

```
tell application "Keychain Scripting" to lock
```

make

Use this command to automate the generation of new keys or keychains. The *new* and *at* labeled parameters are required (unless you are making a new keychain, in which case *at* is not required); the rest are optional. This example makes a new **Internet key** in a keychain called "MyPasses":

```
tell application "Keychain Scripting"
    try
        make new Internet key at current keychain with properties ¬
        {server:"my.yahoo.com", comment:
        "General login id for yahoo services",
        name:"yahoo_login", account:"login_anon",
        password:"X$50*LiL"}
        on error errmessage
        display dialog "There was an error: " & errmessage
    end try
end tell
```

new class

If you are making a new key, then the class can be "Internet key" (for a web login service), "AppleShare key" (for automating the username and password for a file server), or "generic key" (other key types such as passphrases for encrypted files). If you are making a new keychain, then the syntax is:

```
make new keychain with properties {name:"test_key",
locked:false}
```

at location

If you are making a new key, use the *at* labeled parameter to specify the keychain location:

```
make new Internet key at current keychain...
```

This parameter is not necessary if you are making a new keychain rather than a new key.

with data anything

It is not necessary to use this **with data** parameter with the *make* command, since you provide the new key's or keychain's properties with the *with properties* parameter.

```
with properties record
```
This labeled parameter fills in the properties of the new key or keychain. This example provides the properties for linking to a file server over TCP/IP:

```
tell application "Keychain Scripting"
    try -- catch any errors and report the message
        make new AppleShare key at keychain "program_link" ¬
        with properties {server:"iMac", zone:"192.168.10.15", ¬
        volume:"Macintosh HD", comment:"Login for iMac", ¬
        name:"iMac_ login", account:"powerpc", password:"Xi$ap%"}
        on error errmessage
        display dialog "There was an error: " & errmessage
    end try
end tell
```

quit

You can quit the Keychain Scripting app with this command:

```
tell app "Keychain Scripting" to quit
```

unlock reference to keychain

Unlock a keychain with this command and optionally provide a password if you do not want the Keychain Access program to display the dialog that is necessary for the user to enter the keychain's password. The example code is:

```
unlock keychain "prog_link" with password "Xi$ap%"
```

Dictionary classes

```
application
```
This class represents the Keychain Scripting program. For example, you can get the current keychain (otherwise known as the default keychain) with code such as:

```
tell app "Keychain Scripting" to get current keychain
```

`name string` *(read-only)*

This property returns the string "Keychain Scripting."

`current keychain` *reference to keychain*

This property returns the name of the current or default keychain, such as "MyPasses."

`version version` *(read-only)*

This property returns a `string` specifying the Keychain Scripting software version, such as "2.0."

```
keychain
```
This class represents a keychain that you can create with either the Keychain Access control panel or AppleScript and the Keychain Scripting program. For example, you can make a new keychain with code such as:

```
make new keychain with properties {name:"test_key", locked:false}
```

Or you can find out whether a certain keychain is locked or not with the code phrase:

```
get locked of current keychain
```

name string *(read-only)*

This property returns the name of the Keychain as a **string**, such as "MyPasses."

locked boolean *(read-only)*

The true/false locked property is **true** if the keychain is locked. The following code locks all keychains:

```
tell app "Keychain Scripting" to lock
```

key

This is the "super" class for all types of specific keys (e.g., **AppleShare key**) and the return value for code such as:

```
tell app "Keychain Scripting" to get keys of current keychain
```

This code returns a **list** of all the key objects contained by the default keychain. The return value looks something like this:

```
{Internet key 1 of keychain "MyPasses" of application "Keychain
Scripting", generic key 1 of keychain "MyPasses" of application
"Keychain Scripting", generic key 2 of keychain "MyPasses" of
application "Keychain Scripting", generic key 3 of keychain
"MyPasses" of application "Keychain Scripting"}. In other words, this
is a reference to four different keys in the keychain "MyPasses."
```

name string

This property returns the key's name as it appears in the Keychain Access control panel window.

account string

If the key involves a password (for example, a key that has an Apple-Share password), then this password is returned as a **string**, such as "_$0iX6."

creation date date *(read-only)*

This **creation date** property returns an AppleScript **date** object representing the date when the key was created. The **creation date** appears when you click the Get Info button in the Keychain Access control panel, with a specific key selected. See the **Date** type information in Chapter 3, *Data Types.*

modification date date *(read-only)*

This **modification date** property returns an AppleScript **date** object representing the date when the key was modified. The **modification date** appears when you click the Get Info button in the Keychain Access control panel, with a specific key selected. See the **Date** type information in Chapter 3.

description string

If there is any description involved with the key, such as if you included a **description** property in scripting the creation of the key, then this property holds this description as a **string**. The return value may be an empty **string**.

comment string

This value appears in the Comments text field in the Keychain Access control panel's Get Info window. This return value can also be an empty string if there are no comments associated with the key.

creator code class

This returns the Mac creator code for the icon associated with the key (i.e., as it is displayed in the Keychain Access control panel). Using code such as:

```
get creator code of generic key 1 of keychain "MyPasses"
```

I get a return value in raw data:

```
«class ppcx»
```

file type class

This returns the key's Mac file type, which is used to match the key with a specific icon. Using code such as:

```
get file type of generic key 1 of keychain "MyPasses"
```

I get a return value in raw data:

```
«class genp»
```

Chapter 3 describes the Data data type.

custom icon boolean

This returns true if the key uses a custom icon:

```
get custom icon of generic key 1 of keychain "MyPasses"
```

invisible boolean

This property returns false if the key is visible to the user.

negative boolean

This property returns true if the key prevents the keychain from being used.

password string

If the key is associated with a password (as most are), this property contains the password string. Get all passwords associated with an *unlocked* keychain as a list type with the following code (if your keychain is called "MyPasses"):

```
get password of (keys of keychain "MyPasses")
```

AppleShare key

This class is a subclass of the key class, so it has the same properties as the key class in addition to the following specialized properties. For example, if you use the Chooser to connect to another computer or file server via TCP/IP, and check the Add to Keychain checkbox, then an Appleshare key is automatically created for that file server and added to the default keychain.

zone string

This string property identifies the AppleTalk zone or the IP address (as in "192.168.0.5") if the AppleShare key connects to a computer via the TCP/IP protocol.

---

server string

> This property returns the name of the file server associated with the key, as in "iMacHome."

volume string:

> This string identifies the volume that is mounted on the desktop when you use this AppleShare key to connect to another computer.

Internet key

This class represents a type of key that is designed to automatically log you on to a server. As a subclass of the key class, it also inherits the properties of that class. In other words, an Internet key also has creation-date and modification-date properties, along with its five custom props.

server string

> This string returns the server address or hostname of the key to a web server, as in *my.yahoo.com* for a (hypothetical) login key to *Yahoo.com's* servers.

path string

> *This property* returns a string to a file or directory, such as *finance/get_stock.cgi* if *my.yahoo.com/finance/get_stock.cgi* existed. If there is no URL path after the hostname (*my.yahoo.com*) then this property is an empty string.

security domain string

> This string is empty if there is no specified security-domain property for the Internet key.

port integer

> This represents the TCP/IP port number, as in 80 for a typical web server.

protocol constant

> The protocol can be any of the following constants: FTP/HTTP/IRC/NNTP/POP3/SMTP/SOCKS/IMAP/LDAP/AppleTalk/AFP/Telnet. For example, if the hypothetical Internet key was used for gaining access to an File Transfer Protocol server, then FTP would be the protocol.

authentication constant

> This property can be any one of the following constants: NTLM/MSN/DPA/RPA/HTTP digest/default.

generic key

The key class is considered generic if it is not an Appleshare or an Internet key, such as an Apple File Security password. For example, if you encrypt a file and opt to store the encryption passphrase or password for that file in a keychain, this would be considered a generic key. You could reference the key in code by its index:

```
tell app "Keychain Scripting" to get service of generic key 1 of
keychain "MyPasses"
```

service string

> This is a string that usually contains the name of the key, such as the filename for a file that has been encrypted by Apple File Security and added to a keychain.

Apple Verifier

Apple Verifier is a program that verifies whether or not the files you open with it have been digitally signed. In Mac OS 9, you can find it in the *startup disk:Applications:Security* folder. Apple Code Signing is a security measure that gives the recipient of your code a way to verify if the code came from a certain software developer. Apple Code Signer (used to apply digital certificates to programs) is another security program that is only distributed with the Apple Security Software Development Kit (see the note earlier in this chapter for how to download this kit).

Syntax

```
tell app "Apple Verifier"
    open alias_to_signedFile
end tell
```

Dictionary commands

open alias *or* list *of aliases*

Apple Verifier has two commands, *open* and *verify*. Both commands apparently attempt to verify any digital signatures applied to the file, since the *open* command can result in the dialog window of Figure 12-2. The parameter for the *open* command is an **alias** or a **list** of aliases:

```
open alias "A2gig:fm db: pbwp.fm"
```

Figure 12-2: Apple Verifier open command can display this result

verify alias *or* list *of aliases*

The *verify* command could be used to verify the digital signatures of a folder full of files by using a **list** of aliases with *verify*, as in this example:

```
set folPath to ((path to desktop as text) & "today") (* get path to
folder of files to verify *)
set folList to (list folder folPath) (* get the contents of that
folder into a list type *)
tell application "Apple Verifier"
    activate
    repeat with f in folList
        verify (alias (folPath &  ":" & f))
    end repeat
end tell
```

CHAPTER 13

Desktop Printer Manager

Desktop Printer Manager (DPM), shown in Figure 13-1, is an application that was introduced in Mac OS 8.5. Located in the *startup disk:System Folder:Scripting Additions* directory, it is controlled entirely by Apple events and scripts. It does not have a graphical user interface or an Application Switcher icon. As an Apple-Scripter you have the privilege to control these applications that others rarely know exist, as long as they are scriptable.

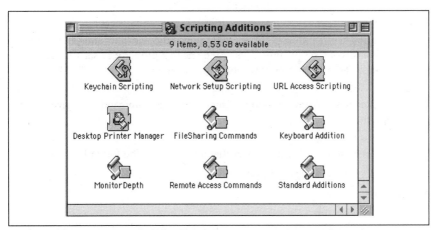

Figure 13-1: Desktop Printer Manager application in the Scripting Additions folder

As you have probably figured out by its name, DPM lets you write powerful scripts that create and set several properties of desktop printers. These are desktop icons (they can be located in folders other than the Desktop folder) that can be used for printing or otherwise processing documents and files. You just drag and drop the document on to the icon, as you would when manually placing a file in a folder. Desktop printers can be created for PostScript printers, not, alas, with the trusty

Hewlett-Packard DeskJet that is connected to my Mac. PostScript is an Adobe Systems graphics programming language that has become an industry printing standard. For instance, if you have a LaserWriter, which uses the LaserWriter 8 driver, then you can control desktop printers with DPM. You can also create desktop printers with the Desktop Printer Utility in the *startup disk:Apple Extras:Apple LaserWriter folder.*

Desktop Print Manager

Syntax

```
tell app "Desktop Printer Manager"
    (* Find out which installed drivers can work with desktop printers; a
    list of these drivers is stored in the drivers variable, if your
    computer has any supported drivers *)
    set drivers to supported drivers
end tell
```

The following dictionary commands and classes are based on the Desktop Printer Manager Version 1.0. The DPM has been scriptable since Mac OS 8.5 (in fact, it was introduced with that OS version).

Dictionary commands

run

This command sends DPM a *run* Apple event to open it (this is not usually necessary since a `tell` statement targeting DPM will implicitly launch the application if it's not already open).

quit

This quits the DPM app. The DPM quits automatically after it is finished processing your script, unless its `quit delay` property is set to `never`. See the `quit delay` section elsewhere in this chapter.

make

You can make a new desktop printer with this command and give it some properties:

new desktop printer object

A required labeled parameter that always takes the form of:

```
make new desktop printer ...
```

not:

```
make new file
```

or some other object. See the `desktop printer` class description for a review of this object's properties.

`at alias`

This is a labeled parameter that lets you decide where to create the desktop printer icon. If you do not include this optional parameter then the desktop printer (DTP) is created on the desktop. An example is:

```
make new desktop printer at (alias "macintosh hd:desktop
folder:printers:") with properties {name: "Laser",is default: true,
driver name: "LaserWriter 8", address: addSpec } (* addSpec is a
variable holding an address specification object *)
```

See the **address specification** class description elsewhere in this
chapter.

with properties record

This is a **record** type that holds the properties of the new desktop
printer. **with properties** is a required labeled parameter with the *make*
command; the **address** and **driver name** properties have to be identified in this **record**. See the *at* parameter description preceding this
segment for an example of the *with properties* parameter. Chapter 3, *Data
Types,* describes what a **record** data type is.

count

This command returns an **integer** representing the number of desktop
printers:

```
count desktop printers or count each desktop printer.
```

each desktop printer

The *each* labeled parameter is optional. You do not have to use **each** if
your code has the syntax:

```
count desktop printers
```

Otherwise use:

```
count each desktop printer
```

delete reference to desktop printer

You can delete a desktop printer with code such as:

```
tell app "Desktop Printer Manager" to delete desktop printer "Laser"
```

You can also identify the desktop printer to delete by its index:

```
delete desktop printer 1
```

If there is only one DTP then:

```
desktop printer 1
```

refers to it. If there is more than one DTP, your script has to be more specific
in identifying them:

```
every desktop printer whose protocol is "AppleTalk"
```

Dictionary classes

application

The **application** class represents the Desktop Printer Manager program
itself. This class has one or more **desktop printer** elements and four properties. The following is an **application** element:

desktop printer

This element represents one or more desktop printers. You can find out
how many desktop printers there are with code such as:

```
tell app "Desktop Printer Manager" to count desktop printers
```

Or you can get a handle on a desktop-printer object by storing it in a variable:

```
tell app "Desktop Printer Manager" to set dtp to ¬
    desktop printer 1
```

The following are `application` properties:

default printer (desktop printer *object*)

This is a settable property that allows a script to decide which desktop printer the computer sends its jobs to. If you are connected to more than one PostScript printer, then DPM scripting lets you dynamically choose which printer will do your printing at the moment.

supported drivers (*list of strings; read-only*)

This property returns a value like

```
{"LaserWriter 8"}
```

which is a list of drivers installed on the computer that support desktop printers.

quit delay (default/never *or* integer)

This property can be set to a constant, such as **never** or **default**, or to a certain number of seconds (e.g., 15). DPM will then quit after the last script command is processed and the specified number of quit-delay seconds has passed (or it will not quit automatically if you set this property to **never**). You could set this property to **never** if you expect to run DPM scripts several times during a computing session.

credits (string; *read-only*)

This is a self-congratulatory list of the Desktop Printer Manager programmers.

desktop printer

This class represents a **desktop printer** object. These objects are returned by the application's **default printer** property, as well as by the command desktop printers or every desktop printer, which will return a **list** of printers or an empty **list** if you do not have or cannot support desktop printers.

properties (record)

This desktop printer property returns a **record** type containing name/value pairs for various desktop-printer properties. The return value looks something like this:

```
{name:"Graphics printer", container:alias "Macintosh HD:Desktop
Folder:", is default:true, PPD file:generic, queue size:0, queue
status:idle, queue stopped:false, shows manual feed alert:true,
address:{class:address specification, AppleTalk machine:"
LaserWriter 16/600 PS", AppleTalk zone:"Graphics_1", theme
desktop pattern:"LaserWriter", protocol:AppleTalk}, driver
name:"LaserWriter 8"}
```

name (string)

This is the name of the desktop printer as it appears on the desktop.

`container` (alias)

This property lets the script set the folder that contains the desktop printer:

```
set container of desktop printer 1 to alias "macintosh
hd:desktop folder:today"
```

`is default` (boolean)

You can use `is default` to find out if a `desktop printer` object is the default printer:

```
if desktop printer 2 is default then set default printer to
desktop printer 1
```

`PPD file` (generic *constant or* alias *file path*)

The PostScript Printer Description file property can be either the constant `generic` or an `alias` file path such as:

```
"macintosh hd:System Folder:Extensions:Printer Descriptions:
LaserWriter 8500 PPD v1.2" as alias
```

`queue size` (integer; *read-only*)

The `queue size` is the number of print jobs that the desktop printer has at the moment.

`queue stopped` (boolean)

This is a `true`/`false` value reflecting whether the print queue is stopped or not starting any print jobs.

`queue status` (*constants* idle/stopped/printing/alert; *read-only*)

The `queue status` value is one of these four constants. For example, if

```
tell app "Desktop Printer Manager" to get queue status of
default printer
```

returns `printing`, then the default printer is printing at the moment.

`shows manual feed alert` (boolean)

A `true`/`false` value that turns this printer property on or off with the `desktop printer` object:

```
set default printer's shows manual feed alert to false
```

`address` (address specification *object; read-only*)

This represents the `address` or protocol/port configuration that the desktop printer is using. See the `address specification` class.

`driver name` (string; *read-only*)

This is the driver name as a `string` for this printer, as in `"LaserWriter 8."`

`protocol` (*constants* serial/AppleTalk/IP/SCSI/USB/custom/spool file/ translator/unknown; *read-only*)

This is a constant representing the protocol used by the printer's `address` property.

`address specification`

This class, an instance of which is returned by the `desktop printer` object's `address` property, represents a device specification such as a Universal Serial Bus (USB) printer. The `conduit` property involves how the printer is connected to the computer, and the `protocol` determines how the machine communicates with its printer, such as over a TCP/IP network (an IP protocol).

properties *(record)*

> This is a settable record of the address spec's properties (see the Examples section at the end of this chapter).

conduit *(constants* `printer port, modem port, SCSI, USB, infrared)`

> This property is set to one of five constants. The `conduit` is the port by which printing data is sent.

protocol *(constants* `serial, AppleTalk, IP, SCSI, USB, custom, spool file, translator unknown)`

> The `protocol` is the communication method between the desktop computer and the printing device or software. It can be set to one of nine constants, including `custom`.

AppleTalk address

This class designates the connection properties of a device that uses the AppleTalk networking protocol. See the Examples section at the end of this chapter. It inherits some properties from the **address specification** class, such as `protocol`.

AppleTalk machine *(string)*

> This is the printer's name on the AppleTalk network.

AppleTalk zone *(string)*

> This is the AppleTalk zone returned as a `string`, such as "Graphics_1."

AppleTalk type *(string)*

> This is an AppleTalk type, such as "LaserWriter."

IP address

This class designates the connection properties of a device that uses the TCP/IP networking protocol.

This class inherits some properties from the **address specification** class, such as `protocol`.

ID *(string)*

> This property is the IP address of the device as a `string`, such as "209.172.15.5."

queue name *(string)*

> This is the queue name for this address as a `string`. It is not a required property if you are making a new desktop printer with the *make* command.

SCSI address

`SCSI address` designates the connection properties of a SCSI device.

This class inherits some properties from the **address specification** class, such as `protocol`.

ID *(integer)*

> This is a SCSI ID number such as 5 (SCSI devices have unique ID numbers).

USB address

This class designates the connection properties of a USB device such as a USB printer.

USB address inherits some properties from the address specification class, such as protocol.

name (string)

This is the USB device's name as a string.

translator address

Your desktop printer might actually be software that translates PostScript code (a PostScript file is usually identified with a *.ps* suffix). The desktop printer object's protocol would be translator. This class represents a PostScript translator output folder.

translator address inherits some properties from the address specification class, such as protocol.

destination folder (alias)

This is the alias file path for the folder that will contain the translated output.

custom Printer address

This class represents the configuration of a custom printer, which is not described by the other address specification types.

custom Printer address inherits some properties from the address specification class, such as protocol.

target application (alias)

This is the alias file path for an application that will process the printer data.

Examples

```
set err to "" --this will hold any error messages
tell app "Desktop Printer Manager"
    set addSpec to {class: address specification, AppleTalk machine: ¬
    "LaserWriter 16/600 PS", AppleTalk zone: "Graphics_1", ¬
    AppleTalk type: "LaserWriter", protocol: AppleTalk }
    try -- check for errors in making a new desktop printer
        make new desktop printer with properties { name: "Graphics¬
printer",driver name: "LaserWriter 8", address:  addSpec, is default: ¬
        true }
        on error errMesg
        set err to errMesg
    end try
end tell
if length of err > 0 then display dialog "An error occurred when making ¬
the desktop printer; it was:" & err
```

CHAPTER 14

Mac OS 9 Finder Commands

If automation honchos want to do anything with their computer, it's command and control the operating system itself. You want to be able to back up, create, delete, or otherwise manage files, but only of certain types or modification dates, for example. A programmer wants a script to be able to return information about all of the volumes on the desktop, including the bytes of free or occupied space and the contents of these disks. A scripter desires to find out about a machine's largest free block of memory space, then shut the machine down or put it to sleep. These tasks and much more can be accomplished by scripting the Finder. This is the venerable Mac application that handles the graphical interface between the user and the machine's operating and file systems. Finder objects like icons, folders, windows, and menus are what you see on your computer screen. The much hallowed Finder is the alternative to working solely within a featureless window typing phrases on a single command line. The Finder provides the visual nature of the Macintosh that has largely made this computer brand famous.

The Finder has a very large dictionary (as indicated by this chapter's extensive reference!), which exposes objects like folders, files, disks, and the Finder application itself for scripters to do (almost) whatever they want with. Figure 14-1 shows the Finder's application icon, which in Mac OS 9 is located in *startup disk:System Folder*.

Finder

Figure 14-1: The Finder icon

You can open the Finder's dictionary by choosing *File → Open Dictionary...* from the Script Editor's menu, then choosing the Finder in the resulting dialog window.

Figure 14-2 shows the Finder's dictionary window. Chapter 2, *Using Script Editor with OS 9 and OS X,* describes the Script Editor and dictionaries.

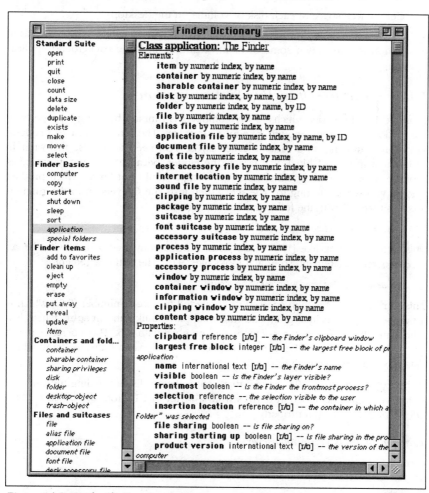

Figure 14-2: Finder dictionary window

Example Finder Scripts

Before we begin our long but intriguing hike through the Finder commands and classes, we will first get our feet wet with five short Finder scripts. These are scripts that I use *all* the time, so often that I frequently cut and paste them into larger scripts. Together, they help demonstrate the power and ease of Finder scripting. These scripts are designed to accomplish the following tasks:

- Get the Operating System version that is running on the machine that hosts the script

- Display the file type and creator type of files that are dragged to this "droplet"

- Go into specified directories and delete the notorious "Word Work Files" that Microsoft Word 98 creates

- Get the free space of each disk or volume on the desktop

- Display all running processes or programs on your machine and give you the option to shut down some of them, including invisible background applications

Finding Out the Operating System Version

Example 14-1 finds out which OS the computer is running by using a property of the Finder called, aptly enough, product version. The script first saves product version, a string, to a variable called myOS. You need to enclose this variable assignment in a tell block that targets the Finder, because product version is a property of the Finder. Otherwise, AppleScript would not know which product version you were referring to. The script then tests the OS version to determine if it is less than 8.5 with the following code statement:

```
characters 1 thru 3 of myOS
```

This returns a list like {"9", ".","0"}. This list is converted to text with the as text coercion statement, so now it looks like "9.0." The entire statement is:

```
(characters 1 thru 3 of myOS as text)
```

This string ("9.0") is then coerced or converted to a real number (9.0), which is a number with a decimal point and fractional part (unlike an integer, which is a whole number), so we can compare this number with 8.5. This coercion is not strictly necessary, but I like to make explicit conversions so I always know which data type I am working with.

If the myOS value (e.g., 9.0) is less than 8.5, a dialog displays telling the user the script will quit. This function derives from a script that I wrote depended on Mac OS 8.5 or greater to run properly.

Example 14-1: OS Version Retriever

```
getOS()
(* function definition *)
on getOS()
   tell application "Finder"
      set myOS to (product version)
      if ((characters 1 thru 3 of myOS as text) as real) < 8.5 then
         display dialog "You cannot run this applet unless the computer" & ¬
         " has Mac OS 8.5. or later." & return & return & ¬
         "Applet is quitting."
         giving up after 45
         return -- quit applet
      else
         display dialog "Good, your OS is: " & myOS
      end if
   end tell
end getOS
```

Displaying the File and Creator Types of Files

It is often important to get the file type and creator type of files. These are actually two properties of the `file` object, which is a class that the Finder application makes available to AppleScripters. The `file type` is specifically a four-character name for the kind of file, such as `'TEXT'` for a simple text file or `'APPL'` for an application file that will execute a program if you double-click it.

> The Mac OS X file system supports "file types," but their use is optional and some files may not have a file type. Some files will instead be identified by their extension, as in *textfile.txt* or *myapplication.app*. Apple Computer suggests that scripts which rely on file types for identifying certain files should be augmented to include a check for certain extensions. For example, if the script is looking for all files that are pict, gif, or jpeg image files, then it should check for file types (e.g., `'PICT'`, `'GIFf'`, or `'JPEG'`) *and* certain extensions (e.g., *.pct*, *.gif,* or *.jpg*).

The `creator type` is a four-character name for the program that will try to open the file if you double-click the file. For example, if the file has a `creator type` of `'ttxt'` then SimpleText tries to handle it; a `creator type` of `'R*ch'` opens BBEdit if you double-click the file. The following script is a droplet that will display the `file type` and `creator type` of any `file` you drag and drop on the droplet's icon. Figure 14-3 shows what this dialog box looks like.

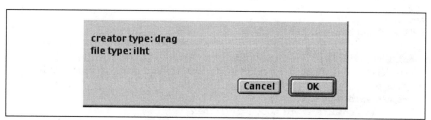

Figure 14-3: The gettype droplet's dialog window

You can save a script as a droplet by enclosing its statements in an `on open` handler (see Chapter 2 for more details on saving droplets). Once again, this script targets the Finder `app "Finder"` because the `file` object is an element of the Finder class. In the following example, only the Finder knows what a "file" and "creator and file types" are:

```
on open (list_of_aliases)
    tell application "Finder"
        set myfile to item 1 of list_of_aliases
        if kind of myfile is not "folder" then display dialog ¬
        "creator type: " & (the creator type of myfile) & return & ¬
        "file type: " & (the file type of myfile)
    end tell
end open
```

Finding and Deleting Only Certain File Types

Microsoft Word creates a lot of extra files on your hard disk when you are working on a word-processing document. Sometimes Word never disposes of these files (say, if the computer happens to crash). The following script helps trash these leftover files to make sure that your disk is not cluttered up with them. The next example will delete any file in a folder the user chooses that has the following characteristics:

- The filename contains "Word Work File."
- The file type is "PDBN."
- The creator type is "MSWD."

The creator type and file type were exposed for these files by using the script in the previous example. The script in Example 14-2 first uses the *choose folder* scripting addition to get the user to select a folder. It then calls the *list folder* osax to get a list of the contents of the selected folder (this list is stored in the flist variable). Appendix A, *Standard Scripting Additions*, covers the scripting additions (otherwise known as osax, or osaxen in plural form). With each of the folder's files, the script finds out whether its name contains "Word Work File" and whether it has a creator type of "MSWD" and file type of "PDBN." These are the only kinds of files we want to delete. The Finder's *delete* command puts these files in the trash. We keep track of how many files got deleted and display this number to the user. I call this script in Example 14-2 unceremoniously "TrashWord."

Example 14-2: The TrashWord Script

```
set fol to choose folder
set counter to 0
tell application "Finder"
    set folpath to (fol as text) (* the folder path as a string, such as
"macintosh hd:desktop folder:MyFolder:" *)
    set flist to list folder fol (* returns a list of strings representing
    file paths *)
    repeat with n in flist
        if (n contains "Word Work File") then
            set f to (file (folpath & n)) (* creates file references out of
the strings *)
            if (creator type of f is "MSWD") and (file type of f is "PDBN") ¬
                then
                delete f
                set counter to counter + 1
            end if
        end if
    end repeat
    display dialog ("We trashed " & counter & " files")
end tell
```

Displaying the Free Space of Each Disk

Like other Mac users, I have a bunch of different volumes, which the Finder treats as separate disks, on my desktop. It is nice to be able to monitor how much space each one of these disks has left, since each of them inevitably fills up with files and new apps. The Finder provides some simple tools to display this data to the user. These include the `disk` object, which has a **free space** property. This property returns the amount of space that is left on the disk as `integer` bytes. So if disk "MyDisk" only had 1024 bytes left on it, then:

```
free space of disk "MyDisk"
```

would return 1024. You would have to enclose the latter code fragment in a `tell` statement that targets the Finder, because the Finder application knows about `disk` objects and **free space** properties. This script, which I call "GetFreeSpace," gets a `list` of all the disks and stores the `list` in a `dskList` variable. Since the Finder application class has `disk` elements, you can get a `list` of all disks simply by sending the *disks* command to the Finder. This script gets each disk's **free space** in megabytes with the following code phrase:

```
((d's free space) / 1024 / 1024)
```

It adds this information to a `mesg string` variable that is finally displayed to the user when all of the free space and total space is computed. The result is a dialog window that looks like Figure 14-4.

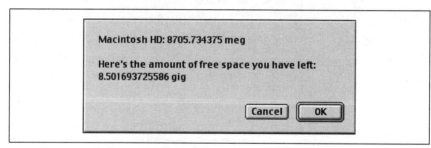

Figure 14-4: GetFreeSpace script's dialog window

You could do something else with this `disk` data, like store it in a database:

```
tell application "Finder"
    set total_space to 0
    set mesg to ""
    set dskList to disks -- get a list of disks
    repeat with d in dskList
        (* get each disk's free space as megabytes*)
        set mesg to mesg & (name of d) & ": " & ((d's free space) / ¬
        1024 / 1024) & " meg" & return
        set total_space to total_space + (free space of d)
    end repeat
    (* get the total_space as gigabytes *)
    set total_space to (total_space / 1024 / 1024 / 1024)
    set mesg to mesg & return & "Here's the amount of free space you" & ¬
    "have left: " & total_space & " gig"
    display dialog mesg
end tell
```

Displaying the Running Processes in a list Box and Optionally Closing Some of Them

The "CloseApps" script of the next example displays a list in a dialog window that the user may choose from. The list contains the names of all of the application processes that are running on the computer. These include the programs that have a user interface (e.g., windows and menus that you can interact with) and *faceless background applications* (FBAs) such as Time Synchronizer or File Sharing Extension. FBAs are programs that work invisibly in the background without interacting with the user. CloseApps is similar to one of the functions of the Windows NT Task Manager utility, which lets you select and shut down a process. Figure 14-5 shows the dialog window displayed by this script. Users may choose one or more processes, and the script will quit the selected programs.

Figure 14-5: A dialog window displays running processes

The script shown in Example 14-3 uses the *choose from list* scripting addition and a list of application processes. An application process is an element of the Finder's application class. You can get a list of all of the currently running app processes simply by requesting all of the Finder's *application processes*, as in:

```
tell app "Finder" to application processes
```

This phrase does not sound syntactically pleasing, but it does the job. The script gets a list of all application processes with the code:

```
set applist to application processes
```

It then creates a list of all of the process names by getting the name property of each member of applist (which contains the application process objects) and adding the name to the list (stored in the namelist variable). An example of the name property of process "Application Switcher" is naturally enough "Application Switcher." The *choose from list* scripting addition populates the window with the list of process names in namelist. The user can select one or more of the list names and click the Close Em button, and the script will send a quit Apple event withto each of the selected processes.

Example 14-3: The choose from list Script

```
set applist to {} -- will contain list of process objects
set namelist to {} -- will contain list of process names
set closelist to {} (* will contain list of process names that the user wants
to shut down *)
tell application "Finder"
    set applist to application processes
    repeat with proc in applist
        set namelist to namelist & (name of proc) (* get names of each running
process *)
    end repeat
end tell
Choose from list namelist with prompt "Which open applications do you " & ¬
"want to close ?" OK button name "Close Em" cancel button name "Outta Here" ¬
with multiple selections allowed
set closelist to the result
try
    set closelist_len to (length of closelist)
    if closelist_len is greater than 0 then
        repeat with proc in closelist
            try -- trap any errors caused by quitting the program
                tell application proc (* send a quit command to each of the
selected programs *)
                    quit
                end tell
            on error number errNum
                activate
                display dialog (proc & "reported error number " & errNum & ¬
                " when trying to respond to the quit Apple event.")
            end try
        end repeat
    end if
on error number errNum (* this error triggered when the user cancels the
program *)
    if errNum is equal to -1728 then
        set theMessage to
        "No programs will close because the app was cancelled."
        display dialog theMessage
    else
        display dialog
        "An unknown error occurred while processing this command."
    end if
end try
```

Finder Commands

The following commands can be used by enclosing them in a `tell` statement that targets the Finder, as in:

```
tell app "Finder" to sleep
```

Dictionary commands

add to favorites reference

The Apple Menu in the upper left corner of the Mac OS 9 screen has a Favorites menu item that includes folders and programs that are displayed or executed if you select them. You can use this command to add to the Favorites list:

```
tell application "Finder" to add to favorites (folder "today" of
desktop)
```

This adds a folder called *today* on the desktop to the Favorites menu.

clean up reference

This command neatly arranges buttons or icons in an open window or on the desktop:

```
tell application "Finder" to clean up window "HFSA2gig"
```

(See the Finder's View menu, which determines how Finder items like folders are aligned on the desktop.) If you use `clean up all`, this command has the same effect as clean up desktop by name.

by property

This labeled parameter determines how items are arranged; e.g., by comment, modification date, name, size, or version. An example is:

```
clean up desktop by name
```

This Finder command arranges the desktop items by their name in alphabetical order.

close reference

Use the *close* command followed by a reference to one or more windows. An example is:

```
tell application "Finder" to close window "HFSA2gig"
```

You can also close multiple objects:

```
tell app "Finder" to close every window
```

This command closes every Finder window on the desktop, such as folder or disk windows.

computer constant *or* string

The *computer* command provides information about the machine running the script. The following example displays how much memory is available in megabytes, including virtual memory. This command is the AppleScript equivalent of the Gestalt function that is part of the Macintosh Application Programming Interface (API). You can find out more about this function at *http://developer.apple.com/techpubs/mac/OSUtilities/OSUtilities-11.html.*

You can use the following constants with the computer command: CPU, FPU, hardware, memory available, memory installed, MMU, operating system, and sound system. There are also numerous other selectors that you can use instead of these constants, as long as you know the four-character string and what its return value means (an integer). For example, the command computer "scr#" tells you how many active scripting systems the computer has, and computer "sysa" indicates whether the computer is a PowerPC (result value of 2 means yes).

```
tell application "Finder"
    set mem to (computer memory available)
    display dialog (mem / 1024 / 1024)
end tell
```

has integer

The *computer* command returns a boolean value if you use this labeled parameter:

```
tell app "Finder" to computer "sysa" has 2
```

This code phrase returns true if the computer is a PowerPC.

In Mac OS X, the *computer* command has been removed from the Finder dictionary and placed in the Standard Additions osax as the command *system attribute*. You do not have to enclose *system attribute* in a Finder tell block (as you have to with *computer*), because *system attribute* is not a Finder command.

---

copy

This command copies selected objects to the clipboard, as long as the Finder is the frontmost program (use the *activate* command first). The following example copies *today* to the clipboard:

```
tell application "Finder"
    activate
    select (folder "today" of desktop)
    copy
end tell
```

count reference to object

You can count the number of objects within another object, such as count files of folder *MyFolder*. The command returns the number of counted objects as an integer. You can also use the form:

```
tell folder "MyFolder" to count files
```

or:

```
count each file of folder "MyFolder", or count every file of folder ¬
"MyFolder"
```

each class

Use the each keyword to specify the class of the object you are counting:

```
tell app "Finder" to count each item of apple menu items folder
```

or:

```
Count items of apple menu items folder
```

data size reference to object(s)

> *data size* returns the size in bytes of the object reference that would be returned from a *get* command. In other words, if you used the phrase:

```
data size of (file "Boston" of desktop)
```

the return value would not be the size of the file on disk; it would be the byte size of the actual reference:

```
file "Boston" of application "Finder"
```

Yes, I agree, it is difficult to find a purpose for this command. Except that you can get the byte size of an icon family with code such as:

```
data size of icon of (file "Boston" of desktop)
```

as class

> If we were to use this labeled parameter with one of the aforementioned examples, the code would look like:

```
data size of (file "Boston" of desktop) as reference.
```

In other words, **data size** is computing the size of a **reference** class type (e.g., file "Boston" of desktop), not the file size.

delete reference to object(s)

> You can delete more than one object with this command:

```
delete every item of folder "actions"
```

This code deletes all folders and files in the "actions" folder on the desktop. Or, you can use syntax such as:

```
delete {file "test", folder "saved template"} of folder "actions"
```

This is a handy method when the items that will be trashed are dynamically assembled in a **list** variable:

```
delete deleteList of folder "actions"
```

> If you refer to files or folders in a Finder command and do not specify their container, AppleScript assumes they are on the desktop.

---

duplicate reference to object

> Duplicate an object like a file or folder with code such as:

```
tell application "Finder" to duplicate folder "today" to folder ¬
    "actions" of folder "desktop" with replacing
```

This code will take the "today" folder on the desktop and duplicate it (reproduce it and its contents) to a desktop folder called "actions." This code will also replace any "today" folders that are contained by the "actions" folder. This is a good command to use when you are backing up files from one volume or disk to another.

to *location reference*
> You can copy or duplicate the objects to another location on your machine by using this labeled parameter. You have to specify a valid location such as:
>
> ```
> duplicate folder "today" to folder "2000archive" of disk
> "BackUp"
> ```
>
> The location reference would be to `folder "2000archive" of disk "BackUp"`. If you do not use this *to* labeled parameter, the objects are duplicated in the same container as the original and given the original name with "copy" appended to it.

`replacing boolean`
> If you use `replacing true` then any objects with the same name located in the same container where you are copying an object are replaced by the new object.

`routing suppressed boolean`
> This command only applies to objects that are being duplicated to the System Folder. The Finder automatically routes certain objects that are dropped on the System Folder like the Calculator accessory (it is routed to the Apple Menu Items folder). If you set this labeled parameter to `false` then a file or folder that is duplicated to the System Folder is not automatically routed to a certain location.

eject `reference`
> If you just use *eject* alone, then every ejectable disk is ejected. For example, the following code causes the computer to eject a zip disk from a disk drive and a floppy disk at the same time:
>
> ```
> tell app "Finder" to eject
> ```
>
> You can specify the disk to eject, as in `eject disk "backupZip"`. Using *eject* with a non-ejectable disk such as an internal or external hard disk raises a script error.

empty or empty trash
> The following code empties the trash:
>
> ```
> tell app "Finder" to empty
> ```

Using this command when the trash is already empty just returns a reference to the trash, as in:

```
trash of application "Finder"
```

erase reference to disk
> This command erases a disk and thereby wipes it clean of all of its data; it is the equivalent of using the Finder's *Special → Erase Disk...* menu command. You cannot erase a disk that has File Sharing turned on for it (which means it is being shared over a network). You should use this command with care (in other words, back up any disk data that you want to preserve).

exists reference to object
> You can find out whether a file or folder exists with code such as:
>
> ```
> set itExists to (exists folder "today")
> ```

If the "today" folder does not exist on the desktop then the itExists variable will be false. You have to provide the *exists* command with a complete object reference or the Finder will not be able to verify the object's existence. Another example is:

```
exists (file "Web Sharing Extension" of Extensions Folder)
```

The parentheses are optional but make the code easier to understand.

make

You can make a new element of the Finder (like a folder or text or image file) with this powerful command. This is a useful command for such tasks as creating a log file and a folder to contain that log. This example creates a new BBEdit text file called "theLog" on the desktop:

```
tell app "Finder" to make file at desktop with properties {name: ¬
"theLog", creator type: "R*ch", file type: "TEXT"}
```

If you leave out the at location part when making a new file or folder, then the Finder will by default make the new file or folder on the desktop. The return value of the *make* command is the object that you created. The "Finder" code sample beneath the "with properties record" section stores the new folder in a variable and then makes a new file in that folder in the next line, using the folder variable as the new file location.

The Finder has a quirk that requires you to not use the new keyword when making a new file, as in make file... instead of make new file.... You have to use the new keyword in most other circumstances when making a new object. You can, however, use the syntax "make new..." with the Finder and AppleScript 1.6 in Mac OS 9.1 and Mac OS X.

---

new class

What kind of object do you want to make? Use this labeled parameter to declare whether you are making a folder, or some other object:

```
make new folder with properties {name: "backup"}.
```

at *location reference*

In most cases you have to specify where you are making the new object (except for the Finder's default behavior to make new files or folders on the desktop if you leave the at labeled parameter out of your *make* statement). Be sure to specify a complete location reference as in the example under "with properties record."

to reference

If you are making an alias file type, refer to the alias file's original or parent file with the to labeled parameter. This code phrase tells the Finder to make a new alias file to the Word application on the desktop:

```
tell app "Finder" to make alias file to application file ¬
((name of startup disk) & ":Microsoft Office 98:Microsoft Word")
```

with properties record

You use this labeled parameter to give the new file or folder its properties. The properties are specified as one or more name/value pairs enclosed by curly braces (for example, a record data type). You can find out the properties that you can provide values for by examining the object in the Finder's dictionary. For example, before I created the following example, I found out that the Finder's folder object inherits some properties from the container object, including the icon size property. So I included icon size in the with properties record, with a value of large (a constant). A lot of property values, like the names of files and folders, are strings. with properties is not a required parameter when making files or folders. If you do not use it, then the folder is given the name "untitled folder" and the file is named "untitled":

```
tell application "Finder"
    activate
    set lfol to (make new folder with properties ¬
    {name:"LogFolder", icon size:large})
    make file at lfol with properties ¬
    {name:"Log file", creator    type:"ttxt", file type:"TEXT"}
    open lfol
end tell
```

move reference to object

You can move files and folders around to new locations using this command. Unlike *duplicate*, this command does not create a copy of the object and leave one copy in the original place; it moves it to the new location. This script moves a folder from the desktop to inside another desktop folder called "actions." The script also positions the folder to a spot 10 pixels from the left edge of the parent folder and 10 pixels down from the "actions" folder's top border. The exception is moving files or folders from one disk or volume to another; this copies the original items to the new locations and leaves the originals intact:

```
tell application "Finder"
    activate
    move folder "LogFolder" to folder "actions" positioned at {10, 10}
end tell
```

to *location reference*

This is a required parameter specifying where you want to move the object. Unless the location is on the desktop, you have to make a complete location reference, in the form of folder "HFSA2gig:1wordfiles" or (folder "1wordfiles" of disk "HFSA2gig").

replacing boolean

If the replacing parameter is true then any items with the same name as the items you moved are replaced in the new location. In other words, if the "actions" folder already has a LogFolder folder, then the folder you moved replaces it if replacing is true. replacing is false by default.

`positioned at list`
>You can position the item you moved in the new location by passing the *move* command a `point` object. This is a `list` of coordinates specifying the upper left corner of the item's icon.

`routing suppressed boolean`
>This command only applies to objects that are being moved to the System Folder. The Finder automatically routes certain objects that are dropped on the System Folder icon, such as the Calculator accessory (it is routed to the Apple Menu Items folder). If you set this labeled parameter to `false` then a file or folder that is moved to the System Folder is not automatically routed to a certain location.

open reference to object(s)
>You can open one or more files or folders using the Finder's *open* command. You can also have the Finder create an object and then instruct another application (the object's or file's creator) to open it. Open several objects at once by passing the Finder *open* command a `list`:

>```
>open {folder "today",folder "actions"}
>```

This command opens two desktop folders, since the Finder assumes that incomplete folder references are on the desktop. If you refer to files or folders without complete file or folder paths (unless they are located on the desktop) then your code will raise an error. Since the following are hypothetically complete path references, the Finder will open each of the folders without an error:

>```
>open {folder "Macintosh HD:Logs:JuneLogs",folder "Macintosh ¬
>HD:Logs:JulyLogs"}
>```

`using` *reference to* `application file`
>You can specify the application to open the file with this labeled parameter:

>```
>open file "Bfile" using ¬
>    application file "Macintosh hd:BBEdit 5.0:BBEdit 5.0:" & ¬
>    "BBEdit 5.1"
>```

This code uses the BBEdit 5.0 text editor to open the file. With most files, the *open* command issued from the Finder results in the file displayed by the proper software program. In other words, if you use the code `open file "bigpic.gif"` and this is a Photoshop file, then the file will most likely open up in Photoshop. In this case, the Finder's *open* command is the equivalent of double-clicking the file.

`with properties record`
>This command is designed to pass some object properties along to the application when you are specifying another program to open the file or folder:

>```
>using application file "MyProgram" with properties ¬
>{name:"Newfile"}
>```

But I assume that few programs support this syntax with the Finder's *open* command, since I have had difficulty finding any:

```
tell application "Finder"
   activate
   set bpath to "macintosh hd:BBEdit 5.0:BBEdit 5.0:BBEdit 5.1"
   set tf to (make file at desktop with properties ¬
{name:"sfile2", creator type:"R*ch", file type:"TEXT"})
   open tf using application file bpath
end tell
```

print reference to object(s)

This does what you would expect it to do—prints a file with code such as `print file "myfile"`. Selecting a printer in the Chooser before using this command helps avoid errors with it.

with properties record

This command is designed to pass some object properties along to the application that will print the file, but the program must support this extension to the *print* command (which makes it is difficult to find an effective use for this parameter).

put away reference to object

put away serves two main purposes: to eject disks and to return files and folders from the desktop to the disk or folder where they came from. The example below puts two files that were placed on the desktop back into the folders where they were saved. As you can see, you can pass a list as a parameter to the *put away* command to put away multiple objects. Or you can just use a single object like a disk as the parameter. If disk "flop" was a floppy disk, then using the code

```
put away disk "Flop"
```

would eject the disk. The code is the equivalent of selecting the disk icon and typing *Command-Y*:

```
tell application "Finder"
   activate
   put away {file "finderclasslist", file "findercomlist"}
end tell
```

quit

This command quits the Finder. If you want to close the Finder, essentially shutting down the computer's operation, you might as well use the more intuitive *restart* and *shutdown* Finder commands.

restart

This command is the equivalent of choosing the Restart menu item in the Finder's Special menu. It closes all open programs and restarts the computer.

reveal reference to object

When used with a running program, *reveal* makes that program the frontmost one in the Finder. You would normally use the *activate* command to initiate this behavior. You can also use *reveal* to open a folder in a disk:

```
reveal folder "Macintosh HD:MyFolder"
```

This code opens the "MyFolder" folder and makes it the frontmost item on the desktop. Using *reveal* with other desktop items like document files selects those items but does not open them into a window (use *open* to do that).

select reference to object(s)

> You can select one or more objects on the desktop with this command. For instance, if you record a Finder operation in which you click on and open various objects, the recorded script usually contains a lot of *select* commands. Once you have selected the objects, you can use the term "open selection," as shown in the following example:
>
> ```
> tell application "Finder"
>     activate
>     select {disk "HFSB2gig", disk "HFSA2gig"}
>     open selection (* opens two Finder windows showing the contents of
> each disk *)
>     end tell
> ```

shut down

> This command closes open applications and shuts down the computer; it is equivalent to choosing Shut Down in the Finder's Special menu.

sleep

> This command powers down the computer but does not shut down open applications. The Finder is restored to its initial state once the computer "wakes up" after a key is tapped. The command is equivalent to choosing Sleep in the Finder's Special menu.

sort list *of references*

> You can sort files or folders by various properties such as creation date, modification date, name, or size. The by part of the command is required. *sort*'s return value is the sorted list of objects. If you sort files by date, the sort will be in the order of newest files first; if you sort by name, then the sort will be in alphabetical order. The following example sorts the files in a certain folder by their creation date:
>
> ```
> tell application "Finder"
>     activate
>     sort files of folder "HFSA2gig:1wordfiles:fol1" by creation date
>     end tell
> ```

by property

> This required labeled parameter specifies how to sort the objects. You can use all kinds of properties with the *sort by* command; it depends which object(s) you are sorting. For example, you can use the following properties, among others, to sort files: creation date, creator type, file type, kind, modification date, name, and size.

update reference to object

> This command updates the display of objects like windows and disks to match their representation on disk. This task is usually done automatically by the operating system. The effect of this command is to force the update of, for instance, a disk on which a script has made a lot of changes.

CHAPTER 15

Mac OS 9 Finder Classes

The best way to script the Finder under Mac OS 9 is to get up close and personal with its object model. What is an object model? An object model is an abstract depiction of a software program (such as the Finder). This model, similar to an architectural model of a house or landscape design, conveys the program's behavior or what it is designed to do in the form of functions and commands, for example:

    shut down

or:

    get size of folder "giantFolder"

The object model also depicts the software units that comprise the software, along with the elements or properties that distinguish the Finder from other Mac software programs. The values of elements and properties differentiate one version of the Finder from another. You might recall from the brief Chapter 1, *AppleScript: An Introduction*, object discussion that an object has exactly one of its properties (e.g., the Finder has one name property and that is, as you might have guessed, "Finder"). A person object might have an age property. They can only have one age value at any given time, except for those of us in our forties who are fond of trying to recapture our twenties (we can have two ages at any given time, chronological and imagined). On the other hand, an object can have zero or more elements. For instance, the Finder has an item element, because the Finder usually works with numerous items during its computing session, such as disks, folders, and files. Figure 15-1 shows the Finder's object model, including its elements and properties.

If you have ever dealt with object-oriented software and design before, then you might have guessed that Finder elements and properties are associated with classes and objects too. An inheritance structure defines Finder elements. This structure is summarized in Figure 15-2.

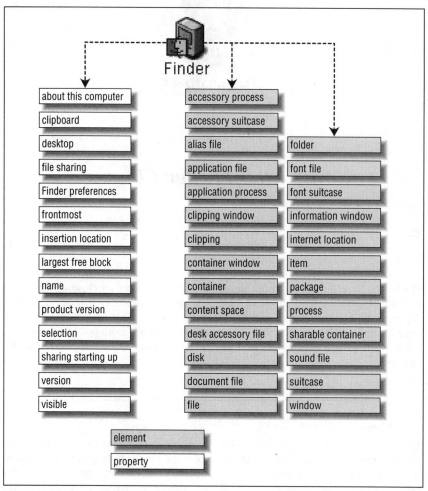

Figure 15-1: Finder's object model

 The Finder objects, and their elements and/or properties, are listed in the Finder's dictionary window. You can display this window by choosing *File:Open Dictionary...* when you are in Script Editor, then selecting the Finder in the resulting dialog window.

The inheritance structure is like a family tree. At the top of this structure is the item. Most things that you refer to in scripts inherit from the item class and are therefore item objects, such as disks, files, and folders. An item has properties such as folder (the folder that contains the item), name (a string like "Myfolder"), size (the logical size in bytes of the item), and creation date (the date the item was first saved to the hard disk). Figure 15-2 shows a subset of the properties for each object beneath the object's name. Some of these objects, such as document file, a specialized subclass of file, do not have separate properties compared with their parent class.

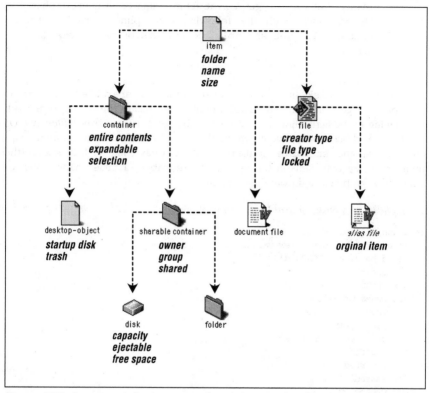

Figure 15-2: Summary inheritance tree for various Finder objects

If an object, such as a file, inherits from or is a child object of the item class, then it also has name, folder, size, and creation date properties. The container object also inherits from the item class; sharable container in turn inherits from the container class and adds some of its own file-sharing related properties such as owner and shared (a true/false value). Finally, the disk and folder objects are child objects of sharable container. They also inherit from the super class (container) of their own parent (sharable container), so they have the properties of the container class, such as entire contents. If you work your way up the inheritance tree, then you find that disks, files, and folders are also items, and in this case inherit all of the item's properties.

When using the Finder's *make* command to create new objects, you have to stick to specific, non-abstract classes such as files and folders. You cannot "make" a new sharable container or item, for instance. But you can get a `list` return value of all items or sharable containers with the following code phrases: `tell app "Finder" to get sharable containers` or `get items`. See Example 15-1.

For example, a `disk` has all of the properties of `sharable container`. Example 15-1 gets all of the `sharable container`–related properties of a `disk` for viewing in the Script Editor's Event Log (Chapter 2, *Using Script Editor with OS 9 and OS X,* describes the Event Log window). But a `disk` also has its own properties that another `sharable container` does not have, like such as `space` (the number of free bytes left on the disk) and `ejectable` (a `true/false` value for whether it can be ejected from the computer).

Example 15-1: A Disk's sharable-container Properties

```
tell application "Finder"
    (* use Event Log to view values *)
    set d to disk "HFSA2gig"
    d's owner
    d's group
    d's owner privileges
    d's group privileges
    d's guest privileges
    d's privileges inherited
    d's mounted
    d's exported
    d's shared
    d's protected
end tell
```

Finder Classes

In summary, getting to know Finder objects such as the `application` and `item` classes is a tremendous benefit to scripters. The following section describes the 36 classes that are part of the Finder dictionary in Mac OS 9. Remember that an object can have more than one of its elements, such as the Finder application's container windows, but only one value for each of its properties. If you want to get a `list` of all of an object's values for a certain element, enclose the element in plural form in a `tell` statement targeting the object, as in the following (which returns all open container windows in a `list`):

```
tell app "Finder" to container windows
```

It only sounds weird because I've left out the unnecessary `get` part of `get container windows`. Forthwith are all of our Finder classes.

Dictionary classes

`alias file`

> This class represents an `alias`, which is a `file` that points to another `file`. For example, if you select a file called *myfile* and type *Command-M*, then this action creates an `alias file` in the same folder with the name "myfile alias" in italics. The following is an `alias file` property:
>
> `original item reference`
>
> > This property returns the original item that the `alias` points to. For instance, if you make an `alias file` that opens Photoshop 5.5 when you double-click it, then this alias file's `original item` property returns:
> >
> > ```
> > file "Adobe Photoshop 5.5" of folder "Adobe Photoshop 5.5" of ¬
> > startup disk of application "Finder"
> > ```

`alias list`

> This is a class that represents a `list` of aliases (surprise, surprise). It can be handy to use this class with the `as` keyword to convert a bunch of `file` or `folder` references to aliases. Why would you want a `list` of aliases instead of `file` object references? One reason is that it is very easy to get the path of an `alias` in a readable form; you just coerce the `alias` to a `text` type, as in:
>
> ```
> set thePath to myalias as text
> ```
>
> This code returns a `string` that gives you the full path on the computer to the file. Overall, the reference `alias "HFSA2gig:1wordfiles:fol1:file.1"` is more intuitive to me than the reference:
>
> ```
> file "file.1" of folder "fol1" of folder "1wordfiles" of disk ¬
> "HFSA2gig"
> ```
>
> To coerce a `list` of `file` references to an `alias list`, you would use code such as:
>
> ```
> set myAlls to fileList as alias list
> ```

`application`

> This class represents the Finder itself. See Figure 15-1 for a visual depiction of the Finder `application` object and its elements and properties. You can grab a `list` of references to any of the elements by using the plural version of the element as a command:
>
> ```
> tell app "Finder" to application processes
> ```
>
> This code returns a `list` of all the programs that are running on the computer at the moment.
>
> The following are `application` elements:
>
> `accessory process`
>
> > An `accessory process` is an `application` such as Calculator or Note Pad that is installed with the Mac system. Use the code `every accessory process` to get a `list` of the running accessory processes. See the `accessory process` class description.
>
> `accessory suitcase`
>
> > This is a type of `suitcase` that can only hold `desk accessory` files. See the `suitcase` and `accessory suitcase` class descriptions.

alias file

The command **every alias file** returns all the alias files that currently reside on the desktop. See the **alias file** class description.

application file

These are files that launch an application, including an AppleScript applet, when double-clicked. The command **application files**, when sent to the Finder, returns all of the app files that reside on the desktop (**application** processes will return all the running programs, on the other hand). See the **application file** and **application process** class descriptions.

application process

These elements are the software programs, including some of the invisible system programs, that are running on the computer at the moment. See the **application process** class description.

clipping window

These are the windows that the Finder displays when you double-click on a clipping file. See the **clipping window** class description.

clipping

A **clipping** is a (usually) small file that can be dragged into programs that support drag-and-drop behavior. Get every clipping on the desktop with code such as:

```
tell app "Finder" to clippings
```

See the **clipping** class description.

container window

This is a more specialized type of **window** that inherits from the **window** class. If you send the Finder a command that looks like **container windows**, the return value is a list of windows. An example return value is:

```
{container window of folder "chap15Scripts" of application
"Finder"}
```

See the **container window** class description.

container

A **container** is a super class for other objects such as disks, folders, and sharable containers. You can encompass all of the desktop objects that can contain something with code such as:

```
tell app "Finder" to get containers
```

content space

This is a broad abstraction of the **window** class that includes all open windows and the desktop. If you use code such as **items of content spaces**, then you will get a possibly large **list** of references to every **folder** and **file** on the desktop and in any open windows. If you have a **disk** window open, this will be a very large list.

desk accessory file

> `desk accessory files` are the files that you would double-click to open programs such as Calculator or the Chooser. See the `desk accessory file` class description.

disk

> A `disk` is a type of `sharable container`. You can get all of the disks mounted on the desktop, including the computer's own disks and network volumes, using code such as:
>
> ```
> tell app "Finder" to get disks
> ```
>
> This returns a `list` of `disk` references that looks like:
>
> ```
> {disk "B2gig", disk "scratch_disk", startup disk, disk "Z2gig"}
> ```

document file

> Getting the Finder's `document file` elements only returns text, word-processing, and image files, not `alias`, `clipping`, and other file types. Use code such as:
>
> ```
> tell app "Finder" to get document files
> ```
>
> This can be a more efficient way to pull word-processing files out of a very large folder, rather than getting all files first into a giant `list` then sifting through them. See the `document file` class description.

file

> `file` is an element that encompasses all types of files, from application and alias files to document files. If you want to distinguish the files from the folders in a directory, then you can use code such as:
>
> ```
> tell app "Finder" to get files of folder "today"
> ```
>
> See the `file` class description.

folder

> If you send the Finder a *get folders* or *get every folder*, command then AppleScript returns references to all folders and disks on the desktop. In this case, a `disk` is considered a specialized kind of folder, even though its dictionary definition indicates that disk inherits from the `sharable container` class (just as `folder` objects inherit from the `sharable container` class).

font file

> This `file` is usually located in a `font suitcase`, but you can pull it out of the suitcase if you want and take a look at it. An example of a `font file` is *Verdana (bold, italic)* inside the *Verdana* suitcase. See the `font file` class description.

font suitcase

> These are `suitcases` that can only contain `font files`. See the `font suitcase` class description. This code gets the Finder's hundreds of `font suitcases` from inside the *Fonts* folder in the *System Folder*:
>
> ```
> get font suitcases of fonts folder
> ```

information window

This is the specialized window type that opens up when you select a file, folder, or disk and type *Command-I*. See the information window class description.

internet location

This element is a file that contains an Internet location. See the internet location file class description.

item

An item is a super class for several child objects such as aliases, clippings, disks, files, and folders. If you want an indiscriminate (and large) list of all the stuff on the desktop, use code such as:

```
tell app "Finder" to get items
```

See the item class description.

package

A package is a special kind of folder that is designed to contain an application, an alias to the program, and perhaps support files such as help files and libraries. The following web site describes packages: *http://developer.apple.com/technotes/tn/tn1188.html*. See the package class description.

process

This class is the parent class for other types of processes, such as application processes and accessory processes. The following code fetches a list of the currently running processes on the machine:

```
tell app "Finder" to get processes
```

A sample return value is:

```
{process "BBEdit 5.1" of application "Finder"}
```

(although the actual return value contains a dozen or more process objects). See the process class description.

sharable container

This is the parent class for a folder or disk, for instance, that has file-sharing related properties such as an owner and a shared true/false value. The code phrase tell app "Finder" to sharable containers returns a list of these desktop objects. See the sharable container class description.

sound file

This element represents files that contain sound data. An example Finder reference to a sound file is:

```
item "ChuToy" of suitcase "System" of folder "System Folder" ¬
of startup disk of application "Finder"
```

You can get the sound files that provide your system's sound effects with code such as:

```
get sound files of suitcase "system" of system folder.
```

See the sound file class description.

suitcase

A suitcase is the parent class for accessory suitcases and font suitcases.

window

This class is what you expect it to be: a window that opens when you double-click a folder or disk. It is also the super class to specialized window types such as information windows, preferences windows, and clipping windows (which inherit the properties of the window class). Using code such as:

```
tell app "Finder" to get windows
```

only returns Finder windows, however, not application windows such as Script Editor's or BBEdit's. Therefore, you can have a desktop full of open application windows, and get windows can still return an empty list. See the window class description.

The following are application properties:

about this computer list *of processes (read-only)*

This property returns a list of running processes on the computer. It is associated with the About This Computer dialog window from the Mac OS 9 Apple menu. You then can get memory-use information by querying each of the returned process objects. See the process class description.

clipboard reference *(read-only)*

This property returns the Finder's clipboard window. You can open this window by telling the Finder to open clipboard. The clipboard contains the contents of anything that the Finder or another application has selected and copied.

desktop *(read-only)*

desktop returns a desktop object value that represents your desktop. See the desktop object class description. One easy way to get the text path to a computer's desktop is to use this code phrase inside of a Finder tell block: (path to desktop as text). This returns a string such as "Macintosh HD:Desktop Folder:."

execution state constant

The execution state property returns on eof the following six constants: restarting, starting up, running, rebuilding desktop, copying, or quitting. This property is only available on the systems that are running OS 9.1 or later. Execution state allows the script to determine whether it has been called as part of a computer shutdown or restart, for instance.

file sharing boolean

This is a true/false value indicating whether file sharing is turned on. You can turn file sharing off or vice versa with code such as:

```
set file sharing to false
```

Finder preferences preferences *(read-only)*

This property returns a preferences object, from which you can get all kinds of information about the preferences you are using for viewing files and folders (see the **preferences** class description). For example, if you want to find out whether a file-list view in a folder includes the file's comments, use code such as: **shows comments of Finder preferences** (a **true/false** value).

This is the equivalent of going to the Finder's *View: View Options...* menu.

frontmost boolean
If the Finder is the frontmost application then this property returns **true**. You can make the Finder the frontmost application by telling the Finder to **activate** or by using syntax such as:

```
tell app "Finder" to set frontmost to true
```

insertion location reference *(read-only)*
This property returns a reference to the folder in which a new untitled folder would appear if you typed *Command-N* on the keyboard. It is an indication of which Finder window (i.e., the desktop itself or an open window on a disk) is active at the moment.

largest free block integer *(read-only)*
This handy property returns the number of bytes that represents the largest free block of RAM that can be used to open an application. This information is also available from the Apple menu's About This Computer window. You can get the largest free block in megabytes by dividing this property twice by 1024, as in:

```
(largest free block / 1024 /1024)
```

name international text *(read-only)*
This property returns the Finder's text name, "Finder."

product version international text *(read-only)*
This property returns the following **string** on my machine: **"9.0.4 PowerPC Enabler 9.0.4"**. See "Finding out the Operating System Version" in Chapter 14.

selection reference
Anything that happens to be selected at the time (such as a file or folder on the desktop) is returned as a **reference** by the **selection** property. Code such as:

```
tell app "Finder" to get selection
```

provides a "list of references" return type such as {**file "Internet Explorer" of application "Finder"**}.

sharing starting up boolean *(read-only)*
If file sharing is in the process of starting up then this property returns **true**.

version international text *(read-only)*
This returns the version of the Finder, such as "9.0."

visible boolean
If the Finder layer, your desktop, is visible, then this property returns **true**. Setting it to **true** when you have a bunch of application windows (such as Photoshop palettes or word-processing windows) covering up

the Finder has no effect, however. In other words, setting `visible` to `true` will not reveal the Finder and push the other windows out of the way.

application file

An `application file` is a child class of `file` that adds a few more properties. In other words, it inherits some `file` properties such as `file type` and `creator type`. This is a file that you double-click to open a software program.

The following are `application file` properties:

`accepts high level events boolean` *(read-only)*

If the program accepts high-level events such as Apple events, then this property returns true.

`has scripting terminology boolean` *(read-only)*

If the application has a dictionary that you can view in Script Editor, for example, then this property is `true`. Version 1.4.3 of Script Editor, however, returns `false` for this property.

`minimum size integer`

This property is derived from the Memory section of the Get Info window (select an application and type *Command-I*). Its return value represents the minimum memory size in bytes that can be used to run the program.

`preferred size integer`

This property is derived from the Memory section of the Get Info window (select an application and type *Command-I*). Its return value represents the preferred memory size in bytes that can be used to run the program. If there is enough memory when the software program is executed, then this is the amount of RAM in Mac OS 9 reserved for the application.

`suggested size integer` *(read-only)*

This property is derived from the Memory section of the Get Info window (select an application and type *Command-I*). Suggested size is provided by the application file's programmer; you cannot change it. Its return value represents the suggested memory size in bytes that should be used to run the program.

application process

When an `application file` is executed and runs on your machine, it becomes one of the application processes. This is a child object of the `process` class and thus inherits `process` properties, such as `name`, `file type`, and `creator type`. The following example gets the `name` and `creator type` of all the current application processes in two separate lists. The bottom of the example shows a sample return value. The first `list` is all the names, and the second is the creator types:

```
tell application "Finder"
    {name, creator type} of application processes
end tell
(* return value sample *)
```

```
{{"Control Strip Extension", "DAVE Sharing Extension", "Folder
Actions", "HP Background", "OSA Menu Lite", "Time Synchronizer", "Web
Sharing Extension", "ShareWay IP Personal Bgnd", "Outlook Express",
"Adobe® Photoshop® 5.5", "BBEdit 5.1", "FileMaker Pro", "StuffIt
Deluxe™", "Microsoft Word", "Script Editor"}, {«class sdev», «class
TSSS», «class ssrv», «class HPBG», «class osaL», «class tims», «class
wbsh», «class aIPG», «class MSNM», «class 8BIM», «class R*ch», «class
FMP3», «class SIT!», «class MSWD», «class ToyS»}}
```

application file

This returns the file that is associated with the application process as an
application file object. See the application file class description.

clipping

A clipping is a file that is created automatically when you drag text from a
document window, for instance, to the desktop. You can then drag the
clipping from the desktop to another document window to reproduce the
text. For example, you can drag an address from a word-processing document on to the desktop and create a clipping, which can then be dropped
onto an email message window. Figure 15-3 shows the clipping file icon. A
clipping is a subclass of the file class, so it has some file properties such
as creator type and file type.

Figure 15-3: A clipping file

clipping window

This class represents a Finder window that is produced when you double-
click on a clipping. It is a subclass of window, and thus has some window
properties such as bounds (which is a list of coordinates such as {525, 47,
825, 247} that represent the screen positions of the upper left and lower right
window corners). See the window class description.

container

A container is a folder or a disk (an item that contains other items).
container is a subclass of item, so it inherits all of item's properties. It also
has its own properties, which are specified in the following list. container is
the super class of folder and disk. You can get all the desktop containers
with code such as:

```
tell app "Finder" to get containers
```

All of the elements described here can be contained by a container (i.e., a
container can contain accessory suitcases and alias files). The
following container elements are described in their corresponding class
description in this chapter:

```
accessory suitcase
alias file
application file
clipping
```

```
container
desk accessory file
document file
file
folder
font file
font suitcase
internet location
item
package
sharable container
sound file
suitcase
```

The following are container properties:

`completely expanded boolean`

You can completely expand a container such as a folder in "list" view by using the command:

```
set completely expanded of folder "today" to true
```

This command opens up the disclosure triangles in the folder's list view to show the contents of all folders and nested folders.

`entire contents reference`

This very handy property returns the entire contents, nested folders and everything, of a container. However, this property can be very unreliable, according to an AppleScript veteran who reviewed this book, particularly when dealing with a relatively large number of items in a container. In some of these cases, depending on unknown factors, the entire contents property returns incomplete results but does not raise an error.

`expandable boolean` *(read-only)*

If the container can be expanded as an outline, then this property is true.

`expanded boolean`

If the container, like a folder, is expanded so that the contents of folders are listed, then this property is true. It is settable if the container is in "list" view (i.e., *View:as List* in the Finder menu).

`icon size integer or mini/small/large`

You can specify the size of icons in the container as either an integer or one of the constants mini, small, or large. The integer values are large (0), small (1), and mini (2).

`selection reference`

The items that are selected in the container, if any, are returned as a list of references when this property is invoked. For example:

```
get selection of container "today"
```

A return value might be:

```
{file "find_objmodel.psd" of folder "chap15Scripts" of
application "Finder"}
```

container window

This is a kind of Finder window that contains items, such as a folder that is double-clicked to produce a window. It has all of the window class's properties, depending on whether the container window is set as a pop-up window or a standard Finder window in Finder's View menu. It also has some of its own special properties, which can be obtained with syntax such as:

```
calculates folder sizes of container window "today"
```

The following are container window properties:

button view arrangement constant

This property returns one of the following constants: not arranged, snap to grid, arranged by name, arranged by modification date, arranged by creation date, arranged by size, arranged by kind, arranged by label.

calculates folder sizes boolean

If the size of contained folders are displayed in the container window, this property is true. You can set it for the applicable container windows (in other words, not for suitcase windows).

container reference *(read-only)*

This property returns a reference to the container associated with this window.

has custom view settings boolean

If this container window uses the default view settings from the Finder preferences window then this property is false.

item reference *(read-only)*

This property returns a reference to the item associated with this window.

previous list view constant *(read-only)*

This property returns one of the column names from a folder in list view, such as Name, Date Modified, or Size.

shows creation date boolean

This is a true/false value indicating whether the creation-date column is showing in the folder or disk window. The property is settable when the container window is in list view.

shows kind boolean

This is a true/false value indicating whether the kind column is showing in the folder or disk window. The property is settable when the container window is in list view.

shows label boolean

This is a true/false value indicating whether the label column is showing in the folder or disk window. The property is settable when the container window is in list view.

`shows modification date boolean`

This is a `true`/`false` value indicating whether the Date Modified column is showing in the folder or disk window. The property is settable when the `container window` is in list view.

`shows size boolean`

This is a `true`/`false` value indicating whether the size column is showing in the folder or disk window. The property is settable when the `container window` is in list view.

`shows version boolean`

This is a `true`/`false` value indicating whether the version column is showing in the folder or disk window. The property is settable when the `container window` is in list view.

`sort direction normal/reversed`

If you set the `sort direction` to reversed, then the name column for instance lists filenames in reverse alphabetical order, and the Date-Modified column lists the most recently modified files last.

`spatial view arrangement constant`

This property determines how icons are arranged in a `container window`. It can be set to one of the following constants: `not arranged`, `snap to grid`, `arranged by name`, `arranged by modification date`, `arranged by creation date`, `arranged by size`, `arranged by kind`/`arranged by label`.

`uses relative dates boolean`

If this is set to `true` then the Date Modified column uses relative dates like `today` and `yesterday`.

`view constant`

This property returns the currently selected column, such as Name or Date Modified.

`content space`

The following code returns all open Finder windows and the desktop:

```
tell app "Finder" to get content spaces
```

There are easier ways to get a reference to the desktop, such as through the Finder's `desktop` property. Use the phrase (`path to desktop as text`) to get any Mac's file path to the desktop (as long as that machine has the *path to* scripting addition installed).

`desk accessory file`

The files that launch the Calculator and the Chooser are considered `desk accessory files`. See the `desk accessory process` description.

`desk accessory process`

If you launch the Calculator `process` class or the Chooser, they are considered `desk accessory processes` and inherit some of their properties. For example, if the Chooser is running then the code:

```
tell app "Finder" to get desk accessory processes
```

returns a value that looks like:

```
{process "Chooser" of application "Finder"}
```

The following are desk accessory properties:

`desk accessory file reference` *(read-only)*

This property returns the `desk accessory file` that is associated with the `process`.

`desk accessory suitcase`

This is a special kind of `suitcase` for `desk accessory files`. A `suitcase` is like a folder (even though it is a `file` subclass!), but it can only contain certain types of files like font files. You will get an icon on the desktop that looks like Figure 15-4 if you tell the Finder to `make new desk accessory suitcase` (it is created on the desktop by default because the latter code phrase did not specify a location with the *make* command).

untitled DA suitcase

Figure 15-4: A new desk accessory suitcase

The following is a `desk accessory` elements:

`item`

If you want to get the contents of a `desk accessory` (DA) suitcase stored in a *da_suit* variable, for example, then `items` of `da_suit` returns a `list` of items or an empty `list` if the `suitcase` is empty.

`desktop object`

This is the object that is returned when you get the Finder application's `desktop` property. Actually, the `desktop` is the Finder's default property, so you can use syntax such as in the following example to get all the alias files on the desktop, without even referring to the `desktop` property:

```
tell application "Finder"
    (* returns all the alias files on the desktop in a list *)
    alias files
end tell
```

The definitions of the following `desktop object` elements are the same as their class descriptions in this chapter:

```
accessory suitcase
alias file
application file
clipping
container
desk accessory file
disk
document file
```

```
file
folder
font file
font suitcase
internet location
item
package
sharable container
sound file
suitcase
```

The following is a desktop object property:

```
startup disk disk
```

    Since the desktop is the Finder's default property and does not have to be explicitly invoked, every time you refer to startup disk in a Finder tell statement you get this disk object as a return value. You can then find out valuable things about the startup disk, such as how much free space is left on it: free space of startup disk. See the disk class description.

The Scriptable Startup Disk in Mac OS 9.1

The Startup Disk control panel is scriptable in Mac OS 9.1. For example, the startup disk alias property returns an alias to the disk that contains the System Folder from which the computer started up. You can also get the value of the System Folder from which the computer started up with the startup system folder alias property. Startup Disk's dictionary also has two boolean properties: netboot and localboot (a true/false value indicting whether the computer will boot from a local disk). Localboot did not return any value in my testing. NetBoot is a service provided by Mac OS X server that allows Power Mac computers and PowerBooks to login and boot directly from a server rather than a local hard disk. See the technical note at *http://developer.apple.com/technotes/tn/tn1151.html*. In Script Editor, choose File → Open Dictionary to see the Startup Disk's dictionary. Chapter 1 and Chapter 2 of this book describe an application's or control panel's dictionary.

```
trash trash-object
```

    This is the class for that trusty drum that sits on your desktop. It is a container for items that are deleted when you "empty" the trash (by sending the Finder an *empty* command). You can get the contents of the trash by querying the items of trash. The trash object class only has one distinct property called warns before emptying. This is the equivalent of checking the "Warn before emptying" checkbox in the trash's Information Window (select the trash icon and type *Command-I*).

disk

A disk is a specialized container or sharable container, and thus inherits the properties of these parent classes along with embodying a few attributes of its own. Important properties for managing disks in AppleScript are capacity and free space. The following code finds all the alias files on a disk, including those buried in any nested folders:

```
tell application "Finder"
    alias files of (entire contents of disk "HFSA2gig")
end tell
```

The descriptions of the following disk elements are the same as their class descriptions:

accessory suitcase
alias file
application file
clipping
container
desk accessory file
document file
file
folder
font file
font suitcase
internet location
item
package
sharable container
sound file
suitcase

The following are disk properties:

capacity integer *(read-only)*
> This property returns the total number of bytes on the disk, including the used and free space. You can get this figure in kilobytes by using (capacity / 1024) and in megabytes by using (capacity / 1024 / 1024). The parentheses are not required but make equations easier to read and perhaps comprehend.

ejectable boolean *(read-only)*
> If the disk is ejectable like a floppy or zip disk, then this property returns true.

free space integer *(read-only)*
> This property represents the number of bytes of free space on the disk. To get the free space in kilobytes use:
>
> (free space / 1024); in megabytes (free space / 1024 /1024)

local volume boolean *(read-only)*
> You can determine whether the disk is a local or network disk with this true/false property (if it's true then it is local, like one of your hard disks).

startup boolean *(read-only)*

> If the `disk` is the startup or boot disk, then this property is `true`. An easy way to get a reference to the startup disk is by using the following code (or something similar to it):
>
> ```
> tell app "Finder" to get name of startup disk
> ```

document file

> A `document file` is a subtype of the `file` class that has a different `file` type than other kinds of files. A `document file` might have a file type of `'TEXT'` while an `application file` has a `file type` of `'APPL'`. If you want to just get references to the text and word-processing files on the desktop, for example, use code such as:
>
> ```
> tell app "Finder" to get document files
> ```

The `document file` class inherits all of the `file` class's properties.

file

> `file` is the super class for the other `file` subtypes, such as `document file`, `alias file`, and `application file`. It is also a subclass of `item` so it has an item's properties. There are generally two ways to refer to files. The Finder's terminology is the inside-out method of file referral, as in:
>
> ```
> file "chap15" of folder "today" of desktop
> ```

You can also use the keyword `file` followed by the full path to the `file`, as in:

```
file "macintosh hd:desktop folder:today:chap15"
```

One easy way to get a `file` reference is to hit the record button on Script Editor then select the `file` in the Finder. Or, select the `file` and paste the reference inside of a Finder `tell` statement by using Script Editor's *Edit:Paste Reference* menu item.

The following are `file` properties:

file type *class type*

> This property is the four-character code for the file's `file type`. An example is `'APPL'` for an `application file`.

creator type *class type*

> This property is the four-character code for the file's `creator type`.

locked boolean

> If the `file` is locked (by checking the locked checkbox in the file's Get Info window, which is displayed by selecting the file and typing *Command-I*), then you cannot save any changes to it. You can set a file's `locked` property with syntax such as:
>
> ```
> set locked of file "chap15" to true
> ```

stationery boolean

> If the `file` is a "stationery pad" or a template for making new files, then this property is `true`.

product version international text

This is the product version in the file's Get Info window. This can be an empty string ("") if there is no valid product version number for the file.

version international text

This is the version at the bottom of the file's Get Info window. This can be an empty string ("") if there is no valid version.

folder

This is a class for a typical Finder folder. It is also a subclass of sharable container and, further up the inheritance tree, container and item. Therefore, it also shares the relevant properties of those classes. You can get all of the folders in a directory tree with the following simple AppleScript command in Mac OS 9:

```
tell app "Finder" to get folders of (entire contents of folder ¬
"bigDeepFolder")
```

All of the following folder elements, the things that you can place and store in a folder, are the same as their class descriptions in this chapter. Refer to them in the manner of document files of folder "today". Or, more generally, items of folder "today". The following are folder elements:

accessory suitcase
alias file
application file
clipping
container
desk accessory file
document file
file
folder
font file
font suitcase
internet location
item
package
sharable container
sound file
suitcase

font file

A font file is a special subclass of file that usually lives in the *startup disk:System Folder:Fonts* folder. It has all of the relevant properties of a file and, by extension, an item.

font suitcase

This is a special kind of suitcase or container that can only contain font files. Figure 15-5 shows a font suitcase. A font suitcase inherits from suitcase and file; it has a file type of 'FFIL' The following are font suitcase elements..

Arial

Figure 15-5: A font suitcase file

`item`

You can get a `list` of a `font suitcase`'s contents with syntax such as:

```
items of suitcase "Adobe Sans MM" of fonts folder.
```

`icon family`

This class is the return value for the icon property of an `item`. Items like files and applications on the desktop have icons that visually identify them. You can get the data for these images by querying their icon properties. The following example stores in a variable the icon property of a desktop file, then gets the icon's small eight bit icon property. The return value for the small eight bit icon property is of type `raw data` (see Chapter 3, *Data Types* for the raw-data description). The following code shows an example raw-data value for this `icon family` member. The `raw data` value mostly consists of a long series of hexadecimal numbers (e.g., AFFF). The return value in the dictionary entry for `icon family` (e. g., "ics8") is a four-character code that represents a particular icon type. A sample abbreviated version of this return value is «data ics8000000...». Broken down into its components, this is the left double-arrow or guillemet character ("«"), followed by the word "data" and a space, then the four-character identifier for the icon (e.g., "ics8"), a long series of hexadecimal numbers, and finally the closing guillemet ("»").

```
tell application "Finder"
    set ic to icon of file "auto_insure_info"
    small eight bit icon of ic
end tell
(* sample return value for 'small eight bit icon' *)
«data
ics8000000FFFFFFFFFFFFFFFFFFFF000000000000FFF5F5F5F5F5F5F5FFFF
0000000000FFF5FFF5F5F5F5F5F5FF2BFF00000000FFFF2AFFF5F5FDFDF5FFFF
FFFF000000FF2A2A2AFFF5F5F5F5F5F5FF0000FF2AFF2A2A2AFFF5F5FDFDF5
F5FF00FF2A2AFF2A2A2A2AFFF5F5F5F5FFFF2A2A2AFFFFFF2A2A2AFFF5FDFD
F5FFFF2A2A2AFF2A2AFF2A2AFFF5F5F5FF00FF2A2AFF2A2AFF2AFFF5F5FDFD
F5FF0000FF2AFFFFFF2AFFF5F5F5F5F5FF000000FF2A2A2AFFF5F5FDFDFDF5
F5FF000000FFFF2AFFF5F5F5F5F5F5F5FF000000FFF5FFF5F5FDFDFDFDFDFD
F5FF000000FFF5F5F5F5F5F5F5F5F5FF000000FFFFFFFFFFFFFFFFFFFFFFFF
FFFF»
```

`large 32 bit icon 'il32'`

The large 32-bit color icon for the file

`large 4 bit icon 'icl4'`

The large 4-bit color icon

`large 8 bit icon 'icl8'`

The large 8-bit color icon

large 8 bit mask '*l8mk*'
>   The large 8-bit mask for large 32-bit icons

large monochrome icon and mask '*ICN#*'
>   The large black-and-white icon and the mask for large icons

small 32 bit icon '*is32*'
>   The small 32-bit color icon

small 4 bit icon '*ics4*'
>   The small 4-bit color icon

small 8 bit icon '*ics8*'
>   The small 8-bit color icon

small 8 bit mask '*s8mk*'
>   The small 8-bit mask for small 32-bit icons

small monochrome icon and mask '*ics#*':
>   The small black-and-white icon and the mask for small icons

information window

>   This is the window subclass for the Get Info window. This window is
>   displayed when you select a file and type *Command-I* or choose Get Info
>   from the Finder's File menu. Its properties are derived from the information
>   that is displayed in this window. You get an information-window object by
>   querying an item's information window property, as in information window
>   of item "today" (if item "today" was a folder called "today"). The following
>   are information window properties:

comment international text
>   This is the text from the comment area of the Get Info window. This is a
>   settable property, as in:
>
>    ```
>    set comment of (information window of item "today") to "A ¬
>    folder for today"
>    ```

creation date date *(read-only)*
>   This is the date when the item associated with this window was created.

current panel constant
>   This property can be any one of the following constants, depending on
>   which part of the information window is showing: General
>   Information panel, Sharing panel, Memory panel, Status and
>   Configuration panel, Fonts panel.

icon icon family
>   This is the icon family of the icon property for the item associated
>   with this window.

item reference *(read-only)*
>   This is the item associated with this information window. See the
>   item class description.

locked boolean
>   If the file associated with this information window is locked then this
>   property is true.

`minimum size integer`

This property is derived from the Memory section of the Get Info window (select an application and type *Command-I*). Its return value represents the minimum memory size in bytes that can be used to run the program.

`modification date date`

The date when the item associated with this window was last modified. You can arbitrarily change the modification date of an item as displayed in its information window with code such as the following, which alters the modification date of the item to the day before the current day. See the date object description in Chapter 3.

```
tell application "Finder"
    set modification date of (information window of (item ¬
    "today")) to ((current date) - (1 * days))
end tell
```

`physical size integer` *(read-only)*

This is the physical size in bytes of the information window's item, which is the total amount of space the item takes up on disk. See the size property description for the information window object.

`preferred size integer`

The integer that corresponds to the Preferred Size: field in the information window. This property is derived from the Memory section of the Get Info window (select an application and type *Command-I*). Its return value represents the preferred memory size in bytes that can be used to run the program. If there is enough memory when the software program is executed, then this is the amount of RAM in Mac OS 9 reserved for the application.

`product version international text` *(read-only)*

This property represents the product version identified at the top of the Get Info window.

`size integer` *(read-only)*

This is the logical size in bytes of the item associated with the information window. This size is the actual number of bytes represented by the file and is usually smaller than the physical size number, which represents the total space taken up on the hard disk by the item. The following example shows the Script Editor's Event Log for querying these properties:

```
tell application "Finder"
    get size of information window of item "today"
    --> 3.85481E+5
    get physical size of information window of item "today"
    --> 4.39296E+5
end tell
```

`stationery boolean`

This property is true if the item associated with the information window is a stationery pad or file template.

`suggested size integer` *(read-only)*

> The application's author suggested at least this much memory for standard performance, in bytes. This property is derived from the Memory section of the Get Info window (select an application and type *Command-I*). Suggested size is provided by the application file's programmer; you cannot change it. Its return value represents the suggested memory size in bytes that should be used to run the program.

`version international text` *(read-only)*

> This property represents the version of the file that is displayed at the bottom of the Get Info window.

`warns before emptying boolean`

> This `true`/`false` value is only applicable to the trash's Get Info window. If `true`, a dialog window is displayed before items are deleted from the trash.

`internet location file`

> This class represents a `file` that, when double-clicked, opens up your default browser and loads the web page identified in its `location` property. Figure 15-6 shows an internet location file.

apple home

Figure 15-6: An internet location file

The following is an `internet location file` property:

`location international text` *(read-only)*

> This property returns the web page location or Uniform Resource Locator (URL), as in *http://www.apple.com*:
>
> ```
> tell application "Finder"
>     (* sample return value: {"http://www.apple.com"} *)
>     location of (internet location files of folder "favorites" ¬
>     of system folder)
>     -- will return a list type since the code gets several files
> end tell
> ```

`item`

> `item` is the super class for the non–Window Finder objects. Disks, files, folders, and other objects that can be manipulated in the Finder are all items, and therefore have the following `item` properties. To get the names of all the objects in a `folder`, you can use syntax such as:
>
> ```
> name of (items of folder "today")
> ```

The following are `item` properties:

`bounds bounding rectangle`

> The `bounds` returns all four coordinates for the `icon` of an `item` in its container. This is a settable property, as in:
>
> ```
> set bounds of item "today" to {22, 62, 38, 78}
> ```

comment international text

This property is the comment section from the item's Get Info window. It can be an empty string if the user has not provided a comment for the item.

container reference

This is a reference to the container, such as a folder, of the item. You can find out which object contains an item with syntax such as:

```
get container of item "myfile"
```

content space reference

This property returns the window that would open if the item were opened.

creation date date *(read-only)*

This property represents the date on which the item was created. The return value is a date object so you can get date-related properties of creation date, as in time string of theDate. See the date description in Chapter 3.

description international text

The description property is a long string about the item along the lines of:

```
"BBEdit 5.1 document" & return & "You can open and modify this
document using the BBEdit 5.1 application program."
```

disk reference

This property represents the disk that is currently storing an item. If you reference the disk of desktop item, the return value might look like:

```
startup disk of application "Finder"
To get more information about this disk, you can use code such
as name of (disk of file "auto_insure" of folder "today")
```

folder reference

This property represents the folder in which the item resides. It returns a reference to that folder as in:

```
folder "today" of application "Finder"
```

icon icon family

This property represents the icon associated with the item. See the icon family class description.

index integer

This property represents the item's 1-based numerical position in its container. Using the index is a good way to iterate over the elements of a container using a repeat loop.

information window reference

This property returns an information window object representing this item's Get Info window. The Finder displays these windows when you select the item and type *Command-I* or choose Get Info from the Finder's File menu. See the information window class description.

`id integer`

Items on the desktop have unique `id` numbers. The `id` numbers don't change, even if the item is renamed and moved into a new folder. Therefore, you can use the `id` to track an `item` accurately, as in `item whose id is 386397`. For instance, the code `ids of files` returns a `list` that looks like {387321, 386397, 374477, 378392, 386776}.

`kind international text`

This `string` is the "kind" value (found under the kind column in a folder list view) of the `item`. This is a descriptive phrase about the item like "BBEdit text file."

`label index integer`

This property returns a number associated with a particular colored label. You can assign these labels in the label section of the item's `information window`. The number reflects the position of the label in the label pop-up menu button. For example, the label "Hot" could be associated with the number 2.

`modification date date`

This property represents the `date` on which the `item` was last modified. The return value is a `date` object so you can get `date`-related properties of `modification date`, as in `time string of theDate`. This property is settable, unlike `creation date`. See the `date` description in Chapter 3.

`name international text`

This is the item's `name` in the Finder, as in "today" for a folder called "today."

`physical size integer` *(read-only)*

This `integer` represents the total number of bytes an `item` is taking up on its disk.

`position`

`position` returns the pixel coordinates of the upper left corner of the `item` in its container. The return value looks like {82,75}; in other words, a `list` of integers. If the container is not in button or icon view (i.e., it's in list view in the Finder's View menu) then this property returns {-1,-1}.

`selected boolean`

If the `item` is selected in its `container`, such as selecting a file or folder on the desktop, then this property is `true`.

`size integer` *(read-only)*

This is the logical size in bytes of an `item` on the hard disk, as in a 2,048 byte file in a 16,384 segment of the disk. In this case, `size` would return 2048.

`window reference`

`Window` returns the `window` object for the window that would open if the `item` were opened. See the `window` class description in this chapter.

label

A `label` object is associated with the various `label` colors that you can assign to files and folders. You cannot make a new `label` with the Finder's *make* command, however. `label` is not a property of an `item` or other object (`item` does have a `label index` property), so it is difficult to find a use for this object. The following are `label` properties:

color RGB color

This returns the label color as an `RGB color`, which is a `list` of integers like {204,255,204}. See the `RGB Color` class description in Chapter 3.

index integer

This is the number of the label in the `label` pop-up menu (which is displayed on Get Info windows).

name international text

This is the name of the `label` as a `string`.

package

A package is a specialized `item`, like a folder, which contains an application file and its support files such as libraries and help files. A package must have an alias file at its top level. This alias file points to the application file in the package. The following web site describes packages: *http://developer.apple. com/technotes/tn/tn1188.html*. The purpose of packages is for software developers to include an application and all of its dependent files in a neat "package," as opposed to depositing more files into the Preferences folder and other System Folder directories.

preferences

This class represents the object that is returned by the Finder `application` class's `Finder preferences` property. As you might have guessed, these properties allow the getting and setting of various Finder attributes. These preferences are also available from the Finder's *Edit:Preferences...* menu. For example, if you set the `preferences` property `uses wide grid` to `true` (it's a `boolean` value), then this action has the same effect as going to *Edit:Preferences...* and choosing the Wide radio button under Grid Spacing in the General Tab. This is illustrated in Figure 15-7.

The following are `preference` properties:

button view arrangement constant

This property returns one of the following constants, which determine how buttons are arranged in containers that have a button view: `not arranged`, `snap to grid`, `arranged by name`, `arranged by modification date`, `arranged by creation date`, `arranged by size`/`arranged by kind`, `arranged by label`.

button view icon size integer

This property returns or sets the icon size of buttons in a Finder button view (i.e., the contents in a folder are displayed as buttons). The same preference can be set from the View tab in the Finder Preferences window.

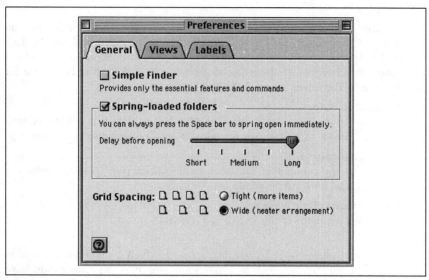

Figure 15-7: You can choose grid spacing from Finder's Preferences window

calculates folder sizes boolean

This **true/false** value determines whether folder sizes are displayed in list-view windows (select a folder and choose *View:as List* from the Finder menu). This is a settable property, as in **set calculates folder sizes to true.**

delay before springing integer

You can use this property to set the ticks (60 per second) before a container like a folder springs open. The shortest delay is 12; 60 is the longest. Setting this property is the equivalent of setting the "Delay before opening" control in the Finder Preferences General tab.

list view icon size integer

This settable property represents the size of icons in Finder list views (for example, files are listed in the folders rather than appearing as buttons).

shows comments boolean

If **shows comments** is **true**, then any comments associated with a file are displayed in Finder list views. This property can also be set in the appropriate checkbox in the Views tab of the Finder Preferences window.

shows creation date boolean

If **shows creation date** is **true**, then the **creation date** of files are displayed in Finder list views. This property can also be set in the appropriate checkbox in the Views tab of the Finder Preferences window.

shows kind boolean

If **shows kind** is **true**, then the **kind** of a **file** is displayed in Finder list views. An example of a **kind** property is "application program." This property can also be set in the appropriate checkbox in the Views tab of the Finder Preferences window.

shows label boolean

If shows label is true, then any labels associated with a file are displayed in Finder list views. This property can also be set in the appropriate checkbox in the Views tab of the Finder Preferences window.

shows modification date boolean

If shows modification date is true, then a file's modification date is displayed in Finder list views. This property can also be set in the appropriate checkbox in the Views tab of the Finder Preferences window.

shows size boolean

If shows size is true, then the space that the file is taking up on the hard disk is displayed in Finder list views. This property can also be set in the appropriate checkbox in the Views tab of the Finder Preferences window.

shows version boolean

If shows version is true, then any file versions are displayed in Finder list views. This property can also be set in the appropriate checkbox in the Views tab of the Finder Preferences window. Most ordinary text files do not have a version so this file property returns the string "n/a".

spatial view arrangement contstant

This property can be one of the following constants: not arranged, snap to grid, arranged by name, arranged by modification date, arranged by creation date, arranged by size, arranged by kind, arranged by label. If the files in a folder are in "icon view," for instance, then these constants determine how the icons are sorted (e. g., arranged by name).

spatial view icon size integer

This number is designed to determine the size of the icons when the files are in icon view, for instance. However, setting the icon size to various integer values does not appear to effect how icons are displayed under Mac OS 9.

spring open folders boolean

This true/false property determines whether folders automatically open ("spring open") when the cursor is positioned on them (and they are closed) for a specified short delay. You can use code such as:

```
set spring open folders to false
```

uses relative dates boolean

This true/false property can also be set from the Views tab of the Finder Preferences window. It determines whether a list-view folder shows a recent date as "Today" or "Yesterday" or in standard date format (e.g., "Fri, Jul 07, 2000 6:15 PM").

uses simple menus boolean

Setting this property to **true** is the same as checking "Simple Finder" in the General tab window of the Finder Preferences window.

uses wide grid boolean

Setting this property to **false** is the same as choose the Tight radio button under Grid Spacing in the Finder Preference's General tab.

view font integer

This number represents the ID number of the font that the machine is using to display text in the Finder. An example is:

```
set view font of Finder preferences to 2001
```

view font size integer

Set the size of the Finder font display using this property, as in:

```
set view font size of Finder preferences to 12.
```

window preferences window *(read-only):*

This property returns the **preferences window** object associated with the window that is displayed when you choose *EditPreferences...* from the Finder menu. See the **preferences window** class description.

preferences window

The **preferences window** is a **window** subclass that has one property: **current panel**. You can thus set the panel in the Finder Preferences to any of those **current panel** constants, as in:

```
set current panel of (window of Finder preferences) to ¬
Button View Preferences panel.
```

The following is a **preferences window** property:

current panel constant

This property can be one of the following constants: **General Preferences panel**, **Label Preferences panel**, **Icon View Preferences panel**, **Button View Preferences panel**, **List View Preferences panel**.

process

The **process** class is the super class for the **application process** and **desk accessory process** classes. An **application process** represents a software program that is running on your computer. For example, the code

```
tell app "Finder" to get processes
```

returns a **list** of **process** objects, one of which might look like:

```
process "Adobe® Photoshop® 5.5" of application "Finder"
```

You can then get various properties for each running process, such as its **partition space used**. This property gives you the number of bytes of RAM that the process is using (which for Photoshop will probably be quite large!).

The difference between an application process and an application file is that a process object is not created unless a process is actually running on the computer (i.e., you have double-clicked an application and the operating system loads the software into memory and displays its windows/menus). You get can the properties of any application file that is stored on disk, however, whether or not it is open on the computer. For example, if Photoshop is not running at the time but is on your computer, then getting all of the Finder's application processes will not reveal an "Adobe® Photoshop® 5.5" process.

The following are process properties:

accepts high level events boolean (read-only)
This property is true if the process object responds to high-level events like Apple events.

accepts remote events boolean (read-only)
This property returns true if the process can accept a remote event (originating from other than the local computer). This example shows the return value of a get accepts remove events command targeting the Finder:

```
tell application "Finder"
    name of processes
    accepts remote events of processes
end tell
(* return values, first process names *)
{"Control Strip Extension", "DAVE Sharing Extension", "Folder
Actions", "HP Background", "OSA Menu Lite", "Time Synchronizer",
"Web Sharing Extension", "Outlook Express", "Microsoft Word",
"Script Editor", "BBEdit 5.1", "Internet Explorer", "Adobe®
Photoshop® 5.5", "FileMaker Pro", "Contract Timer"}
(* boolean values reflecting whether each process accepts remote
events *)
{false, true, false, true, true, false, false, false, true,
true, true, true, true, true, true}
```

creator type (read-only)
This is the creator type for the process, as in "R*ch" for BBEdit, "8BIM" for Photoshop, and "FMP3" for FileMaker Pro. The types of return values actually look like «class FMP3».

file reference (read-only)
This property returns the file object from which the program was launched. If you use the code:

```
tell app "Finder" to get file of processes
```

then you will get a large list of file references that look like:

```
file "FileMaker Pro" of folder "FileMaker Pro 4.1 Folder" of
disk "HFSA2gig"
```

file type class *(read-only)*

This property returns the four-character file type of the process, which is often 'APPL' for application. The return value is a class object in raw data form, as in «class APPL».

frontmost boolean

frontmost returns true if the process is the frontmost or active application (i.e., if you select a window on the desktop to make it active, then its associated application is the frontmost one).

has scripting terminology boolean *(read-only)*

If the application is scriptable (can be controlled by AppleScript), then this value is true.

name international text *(read-only)*

This property returns the process's name as text. Get all the names of the processes with the intuitive phrase:

```
tell app "Finder" to get name of processes
```

partition space used integer *(read-only)*

This property returns in bytes the amount of RAM the process is actually using, as opposed to how much RAM has been reserved for the program (see total partition size). The return value of this property may be altered, compared with what it looks like in the About This Computer window (accessed from the upper left corner of the Mac screen), if the machine is using virtual memory.

total partition size integer *(read-only)*

This number represents the number of bytes of memory with which the program was launched. You can convert this value into megabytes with code such as:

```
(total partition size of process "FileMaker pro" /1024 / 1024)
```

visible boolean

If you use code such as the following (in a Finder tell block) then the only processes that the Finder returns are those whose windows and/or menus are visible on the desktop:

```
get every process whose visible is true
```

This code phrase doesn't return any invisible background processes or programs whose windows are no longer displayed (i.e., you Option-clicked the desktop with the program active, making its visible layer vanish).

sharable container

A sharable container is a subclass of container with special file-sharing related properties. A disk or folder that is being shared is considered a subclass of sharable container. The descriptions of the sharable container's elements are all the same as their class descriptions in this chapter. In terms of a Finder containment hierarchy, a sharable container (like a shared folder) can "contain" other folders. The following are sharable container elements:

accessory suitcase
alias file

```
application file
clipping
container
desk accessory file
document file
file
folder
font file
font suitcase
internet location
item
package
sharable container
sound file
suitcase
```

The following are `sharable container` properties:

`exported boolean` *(read-only)*
This is `true` if the `container` can be shared (for instance, mounted on another desktop networked via TCP/IP). File sharing must be on to use this property.

`group international text`
This property gets or sets the file-sharing group or user for the `container`. For example, if the disk "MYDisk" has a user named "iMac," then the code phrase `group of disk "MYDisk"` will return "iMac."

`group privileges sharing privileges`
This settable property returns a `sharing privileges` object for the `container`. You can also set the `group privileges` for a `sharable container`. See the `sharing privileges` class.

`guest privileges sharing privileges`
This settable property returns a `sharing privileges` object for the `container`. You can also set the `guest privileges` for a `sharable container`. See the `sharing privileges` class.

`mounted boolean` *(read-only)*
This property returns `true` only if file sharing is turned on and the `sharable container` is mounted on another machine's desktop.

`owner international text`
This property returns the owner name as text, but only if file sharing is turned on. Another way to find out a container's file-sharing owner is by selecting the container, typing *Command-I*, then choosing the sharing pop-up menu option in the displayed Get Info window.

`owner privileges sharing privileges`
This settable property returns a `sharing privileges` object for the `container`. See the `sharing privileges` class.

privileges inherited boolean

If this property is true, then the container has inherited its sharing properties from its own container or parent (as in a folder inheriting its sharing properties from its disk). File sharing has to be turned on to get this property, or the script will raise an error.

protected boolean

The sharing segment of a container's Get Info window has a checkbox labeled "Can't move, rename, or delete this item (locked)." If that item is checked, then this property is true. This property is settable too. If you try to use this property in a script when file sharing is not on, the script will raise an error.

shared boolean

If the container is being shared, then this property is true. If you try to use this property in a script when file sharing is not on, the script will raise an error.

sharing privileges

This class represents the privileges that a scripter can get or set for a container's group, guest, or owner privileges. It has three properties, all returning true/false values. The following are **sharing privileges** properties:

make changes boolean

If this property is true then the group or guest can make changes to the shared object, like a folder or file. You can refer to this property in the following manner (inside a tell statement targeting the Finder):

```
set make changes of folder "today"'s group privileges to false
```

see files boolean

If the **sharable container** contains files (such as files inside of a folder), then the scripter can use this property to make the files visible or invisible to the users who are sharing the folder. Here is some sample code:

```
set see files of folder "today"'s group privileges to false
```

You cannot set or get this property unless file sharing has been turned on.

see folders boolean

If the **sharable container** contains folders (such as folders inside of a folder), then the scripter can use this property to make the folders visible or invisible to the users sharing the folder. Here is some sample code:

```
set see folders of folder "today"'s group privileges to false
```

You cannot set or get this property unless file sharing has been turned on:

```
tell application "Finder"
set see files of group privileges of folder "today" to true
set see folders of group privileges of folder "today" to true
set make changes of group privileges of folder "today" to false
end tell
```

sound file

> This class represents the kind of sound files that are stored in the *System* suitcase file in the *System Folder*. They have names such as "Chu Toy," "Laugh," and "Uh oh." They are used for purposes such as the alert sounds that you can set in the Sounds control panel in Mac OS 9. As a subclass of the `file` object, sound files have some file-related properties like `name`. Figure 15-8 shows a sound file icon.

Figure 15-8: A sound file icon in the Finder

The following is a `sound file` property:

sound data

> This property is designed to return the `sound data` for a `sound file`. You have to pull the `sound file` or copy it out of the *System* suitcase to retrieve its `sound data`, however. The return value of the `sound data`, which is in raw-data format, is a giant series of hexadecimal numbers that partially look like this:
>
> ```
> «data snd
> 000100010005000000C0000180510000000000140000000000000000002AC44...»
> ```
>
> Chapter 3 describes `raw data` value types, which are delimited by guillemet characters (« »).

special folders

> The Finder can directly reference every one of the folders that are formally properties of the `special folders` class. In other words, you can use the following syntax to get an `alias` to the *Extensions* folder:
>
> ```
> tell app "Finder" to get extensions folder as alias
> ```
>
> This returns a value that looks like `alias "Macintosh HD:System Folder:Extensions:"`. You have to make sure to include the word "folder" in the reference, as in `extensions folder`. But you do not have to capitalize these folders, even though their names are capitalized in the Finder. Or, you can get the file path to the *startup disk:System Folder:Preferences* directory as a `string` by coercing the `file` reference to a `string` or `text`, as in `get preferences folder as text`. This return value looks like "Macintosh HD:System Folder:Preferences:". These special-folder references are very handy for navigating around an unfamiliar directory structure since you can use them as point of references. This example uses the `system folder reference` to see if the scripting addition *Jon's Commands* exists in the *System Folder's Scripting Additions* folder:
>
> ```
> tell application "Finder"
>     set sa to folder "scripting additions" of system folder
>     set hasJons to exists (file "Jon's Commands" of sa)
> end tell
> ```

The following are **special folder** properties:

`system folder reference`

> The property returns a **reference** to the startup disk's *System Folder.* You can get the **reference** with the syntax:
>
> ```
> tell app "Finder" to get system folder.
> ```

`apple menu items folder reference`

> This property returns a **reference** to the *Apple menu Items* folder in the *System Folder.* You can get the **reference** with the syntax:
>
> ```
> tell app "Finder" to get apple menu items folder.
> ```

`control panels folder reference`

> This property returns a **reference** to the System Folder's *Control Panels* folder. You can get the **reference** with the syntax:
>
> ```
> tell app "Finder" to get control panels folder.
> ```

`extensions folder reference`

> The property returns a **reference** to the System Folder's *Extensions* folder. You can get the **reference** with the syntax:
>
> ```
> tell app "Finder" to get extensions folder
> ```

`fonts folder reference`

> The property returns a **reference** to the System Folder's *Fonts* folder. You can get the **reference** with the syntax:
>
> ```
> tell app "Finder" to get fonts folder
> ```

`preferences folder reference`

> The property returns a **reference** to the System Folder's *Preferences* folder. You can get the **reference** with the syntax:
>
> ```
> tell app "Finder" to get preferences folder
> ```

`shutdown items folder reference`

> The property returns a **reference** to the System Folder's *Shutdown Items* folder. You can get the **reference** with the syntax:
>
> ```
> tell app "Finder" to get shutdown items folder
> ```

You can then use this **reference** to store an `alias` to an application or applet that you want to run before the computer shuts down, for instance.

`startup items folder reference`

> The property returns a **reference** to the System Folder's *Startup Items* folder. You can get the **reference** with the syntax:
>
> ```
> tell app "Finder" to get startup items folder
> ```

You can then use this **reference** to store an `alias` to an application or applet that you want to run when the computer starts up.

`temporary items folder reference`

> The **temporary items** folder is an invisible folder on the startup disk where the operating system and applications store temporary files.

However, you can find out what is being stored in this folder with code such as:

```
tell app "Finder" to get entire contents of temporary items
folder
```

This code returns a `list` of `file` references.

suitcase

A `suitcase` is a special kind of file that is designed to hold font files or desk-accessory files. `suitcase` is a subclass of `file` (even though it seems like a container) and the super class of the `font suitcase` and `desk accessory suitcase` classes. Therefore, suitcases have the relevant properties of their parent class `file`. See Figure 15-4 for a look at a `desk accessory suitcase` icon (for what it's worth, the icons look like suitcases). The following is a `suitcase` element:

item

A `suitcase` contains stuff like font files, which are by extension `items`. You can find out the contents of a `suitcase` with the syntax: `items of suitcase "DA suitcase"`.

trash-object

This is the class of the `trash` object, which is really a property of the Finder's `desktop` object. But the Finder can refer to the `trash` object directly, without first using a `desktop` reference, as in:

```
tell application "Finder" to get warns before emptying of trash
```

This code gets a `true`/`false` value that determines whether a dialog box is displayed before trashed items are finally deleted. The Trash is a little barrel icon that is displayed by default in the lower right corner of the computer screen. The `trash-object` can contain anything that can be thrown away or deleted. The descriptions of these elements are the same as their class descriptions elsewhere in this chapter. The following are `trash-object` elements:

accessory suitcase
alias file
application file
clipping
container
desk accessory file
document file
file
folder
font file
font suitcase
internet location
item
package
sharable container
sound file
suitcase

The following is a `trash-object` property:

warns before emptying boolean
> The `trash-object` inherits some relevant properties from its `container` parent class, such as `entire contents,` which gives you a `list` of references to whatever is in the trash. The `trash-object` has one of its own properties. You can suppress the dialog box that displays before an item is deleted from the trash with this syntax:

```
set warns before emptying of trash to false
```

window
> A Finder `window` is the `window` that opens up when you double-click a `folder` or `disk` to reveal their contents. Another example is the Get Info windows that open up when you select a file and choose Get Info from the Finder's *File* menu or type *Command-I.* These windows should not be confused with the application windows, such as the word-processing window I am typing in now, or the tool-palette windows that are displayed by Photoshop. The following code will only return its own windows, not the application windows that you have open on your desktop:

```
tell app "Finder" to get windows
```

A Finder window is not a `container` class, so you cannot use code such as `entire contents of window 1` to get a window's contents. The following example shows a better way to get the contents of a window. It gets the `container` property of each `container` window that is open in the Finder. `container window` is a subclass of `window`. Therefore, the *windows* command returns all `container` windows (i.e., any open windows attached to a container like a `folder`), each of which has a `container` property that identifies the window's `disk` or `folder`.

```
tell application "Finder"
    (* the equivalent of asking the Finder for 'all folders and disks
    that have open Finder windows' *)
        container of windows
    end tell
    (* Sample return value *)
    {folder "actions" of application "Finder", disk "HFSgig" of
    application "Finder", startup disk of application "Finder"}
```

The following are `window` properties:

bounds bounding rectangle
> This settable property represents the screen coordinates for the upper right and lower left corners of the window. The return value looks like {10,50,210,250}. A `bounding rectangle` class is really a `list` of four integers.

closeable boolean *(read-only)*
> This property is `true` if you can close the `window` by clicking the box in its upper left corner.

---

collapsed boolean

This is true if the window is "collapsed" or pulled up like a window shade. In Mac OS 9, you can collapse a window by double-clicking its title bar (the bar along the top window border that contains the window's title). This property does not apply to pop-up windows (in Mac OS 9, windows that are anchored to the bottom part of the screen and "pop up" when you click them).

floating boolean *(read-only)*

This value is false if the window is not a floating window (i.e., it always floats in front of other windows, whether or not you highlight it by clicking on the window). Rest assured this value will be false since no Finder windows are floating ones.

index integer

Finder windows are indexed, beginning with 1, from front to back. window 1, for example, inhabits the layer in front of window 2 and therefore covers window 2 if their regions overlap. The code fragment window index 1 is the same as the shorthand window 1. If no windows are open then trying to get window 1 will raise a script error, however.

modal boolean *(read-only)*

This will be false if the window is not modal. A modal window sits in front of other windows in the Finder and has to be dismissed (with a Cancel button, say) before you can click on other windows or menus.

name international text *(read-only)*

The name of the window is displayed in its title bar, if it has a title bar. You can refer to a window by its name without using the keyword name, as in get window "MyFolder".

popup boolean

This property is false if the window is not a pop-up window.

position point

This point property represents the upper left coordinate of the window, as in {10,50}.

pulled open boolean

This property returns true if the window is a pop-up window and it is open. If the window is not a pop-up, and you refer to its pulled open property, then you will raise a script error.

resizable boolean *(read-only)*

If you can change the size of the window by dragging the cursor along the lower right corner, as you can with a lot of Finder windows, then the window's resizable is true.

titled boolean *(read-only)*

If the window has a title bar, then this property is true.

visible boolean *(read-only)*

If the window is open, its visible property returns true.

zoomable boolean *(read-only)*

If the window can be zoomed, or increased or decreased in size by clicking a button on the title bar, then this property returns true.

zoomed boolean

This property is false if the window is not zoomed to its full size (by clicking the title bar button adjacent to the button in the upper right order).

zoomed full size boolean

This true/false property can only be set (as in set zoomed full size of window 1 to true), and only applies to non–pop-up windows. If the script sets a window's zoomed full size to true then the Finder will try to expand the window to fill the screen space.

CHAPTER 16

Network Setup Scripting

Open Transport is the Apple technology under Mac OS 9 that allows program-mers and users to send and receive bytes across networks using TCP/IP, AppleTalk, Infrared, or Remote Access methods. When you can mount network volumes on your desktop over an Ethernet network, you are using Open Trans-port. When you log on to the Web using an analog modem, cable modem, digital subscriber line (DSL), or some other method, you are also calling on various Open Transport protocols. You specifically use Remote Access and TCP/IP to make most connections to the Web using a Mac. For example, I connect to the Web using a Local Area Network (LAN) connection to a proxy server and cable modem, and thus rely on my Mac's TCP/IP configuration to access the Internet. My father, on the other hand, uses a 56K modem and dial-up connection in a remote part of Maine. His Mac system uses Remote Access and TCP/IP configurations to connect over a phone line to his Internet Service Provider (ISP).

 Network Setup Scripting Version 1.1.1 and Open Transport Version 2.6.1 are used for the examples in this chapter.

Configurations are collections of settings for various network methods, like Apple-Talk, TCP/IP, or Remote Access. Open Transport stores these settings in a database system called the Open Transport configurations database. AppleScripts can access this database and all the various network configurations that you may want to script via the Network Setup Scripting application. Figure 16-1 shows this application icon. This program is located in the *startup disk:System Folder:Scripting Additions* folder. Therefore, all of your Network Setup Scripting AppleScripts have to target this application, as in:

```
tell app "Network Setup Scripting..."
```

You can look at the Network Setup Scripting dictionary by choosing this application in Script Editor's *File → Open Dictionary...* menu.

Network Setup Scripting

Figure 16-1: Network Setup Scripting icon

Example 16-1 opens the Open Transport database then cycles through all of its configurations, looking for the TCP/IP configuration. Once it finds the TCP/IP configuration, it attempts to get the IP address of the machine. The code encloses the Network Setup commands in a `try` statement, so that if an error occurs it is caught and the Open Transport configurations database is closed. When you are accessing data in this database, you should close the database when you finish so that Open Transport continues to function properly. The script example shows the return values of these code statements, as they appear in Script Editor's Event Log window. Chapter 2, *Using Script Editor with OS 9 and OS X,* describes the Event Log. In this case, the machine is using the DHCP protocol (its IP address is allocated by a proxy server when the client machine boots up), and Open Transport returns a series of zeros (0.0.0.0) in lieu of the actual IP address.

Another way to get the machine's actual IP address (not 0.0.0.0) is to send a *get IP address* Apple event to the Apple System Profiler:

```
tell app "Apple System Profiler" to get IP address
```

This will return a `string` like "172.158.73.1" for the machine's IP address, if it has one. See Chapter 11, *Apple System Profiler.*

Notice that the script uses the *open database* and *close database* commands of the Network Scripting application. You have to use these commands to get any data from the Network Setup Scripting application.

Example 16-1: Opening the Open Transport Configuration Database

```
tell application "Network Setup Scripting"
    try
        open database
        set con_set to current configuration set
        set con_list to con_set's configurations (* gets list of all the
        current open transport configurations *)
        repeat with con in con_list -- look for a TCPIP config in this list
            if (class of con is TCPIP v4 configuration) then
                IP address of con
            end if
        end repeat
        close database
        (*make sure the open transport database is closed if the script is
        interrupted by an error *)
```

```
on error
    close database
end try
end tell
(* sample return value in Event Log window*)
get current configuration set
--> configuration set "My Network Settings"
get every configuration of configuration set "My Network Settings"
--> {AppleTalk configuration "printer_config", Modem configuration "Default",
Remote Access configuration "Default", TCPIP v4 configuration "sygate"}
-- some return values snipped here ...
get IP address of TCPIP v4 configuration "sygate"
--> "0.0.0.0"
```

The rest of this chapter explains the Network Setup Scripting commands and classes in their own reference sections. The first section describes the commands that you can use to script the Open Transport network system, such as *open database* and *close database*. The classes are the blueprints for the *objects* that your scripts will target, such as the Network Setup Scripting application itself and Remote Access configurations (which are commonly used to connect modems with the Web).

Network Setup Scripting

Commands are the action verbs that you use to script Network Setup Scripting, such as *open database, close database,* and *connect* (which you use to automate a modem's connection to the Internet). The *make* command, for instance, allows a script to make a new network configuration, such as a TCP/IP configuration, "on the fly." See the example under the *make* command section.

Dictionary commands

abort transaction

> This command terminates a transaction. None of the changes that the script initiated within a *begin/end transaction* block will be completed. See *begin transaction* later in this chapter.

add reference

> You can use this command to add a configuration such as a TCP/IP setting to Open Transport's configuration sets. Configuration sets are, as they sound, a group of configurations.

> *to* configuration set

>> This identifies the configuration set to add the configuration to, as in:

>>> configuration set "My Network Settings" or current configuration set

Example

```
tell application "Network Setup Scripting"
    set tId to "" -- this var will hold the transaction ID
```

Network
Setup

```
try
    open database
    (*use this when the script is changing the open transport database;
the var tId will hold the transaction id integer *)
    set tId to begin transaction
    add TCPIP v4 configuration "newMacIP" to ¬
    configuration set "My Network Settings"
    end transaction
    close database
on error (* make sure transaction is aborted and database gets closed
if there is an error *)
    if tId is not equal to "" then
        abort transaction
    end if
    close database
end try
end tell
```

authenticate reference

Use this command to determine if a user has permission to access an Open Transport configuration:

```
set bool to authenticate AppleTalk configuration "my_config" with ¬
password "wIsT$"
```

The command returns a boolean value, true or false.

with password string

This required labeled parameter is the password string.

begin transaction

This command begins a transaction and returns a transaction ID as an integer. An example is:

```
set transID to begin transaction
```

begin transaction prevents the database from being changed by any other scripts or applications while the transaction is still active. The transaction is finished or rendered inactive with the command *end transaction*. See the example in the *add* reference section.

close database

This command closes the Open Transport configuration database to the reading or writing of data. It is used to close the database following the command *open database*. See Example 16-1 and the example in the *add* reference section.

connect Remote Access configuration *object*

connect makes a connection with a Remote Access configuration, such as one that will access the Web with a dial-up modem. The parameter for the *connect* command is a Remote Access configuration object, such as connect RAconfig (if Raconfig were a variable holding a Remote Access configuration). See the following example and the Remote Access configuration class description (this command is used with the *disconnect* command, which is described later in this section):

```
set err to "" (* this var will hold any error messages to be ¬
displayed to the user *)
```

```
tell application "Network Setup Scripting"
    try
        open database
        set ra to Remote Access configuration "Default"
        (* connect to a remote network, in this case the Web over a
dial-up connection *)
        connect ra
        delay 60 (* wait 60 seconds before disconnecting, for demo
purposes *)
        disconnect ra
        close database
    on error errmesg
        set err to errmesg -- save any error messages
        close database
    end try
end tell
if length of err > 0 then display dialog err (* display any error
messages *)
```

count reference

This command returns a count of objects, such as Open Transport configurations or configuration sets, as an `integer`. You can use the `count configurations`, `count` each `configuration`, or `count` every `configuration` syntax.

each class:

You can optionally use the *each* keyword, as in `tell app "Network Setup Scripting"` to count each configuration:

```
tell application "Network Setup Scripting"
    open database
    set configC to count configurations
    close database
    return configC
end tell
```

delete reference

You can delete an Open Transport object such as an Open Transport configuration with this command. An example is:

```
delete TCPIP v4 configuration "local_Lan"
```

This code would delete one of the configurations that is viewable from the TCP/IP control panel's *File* menu. You have to open the Open Transport configurations database, issue the *delete* command, and then close the database for the *delete* command to work properly. This is because AppleScript has to explicitly open this database before making any changes to it.

disconnect Remote Access configuration

This command disconnects a Remote Access connection such as a dial-up connection to a remote network (e.g., the Internet). It is usually used in scripts that open the connection with the *connect* command. You follow the *disconnect* command with the `Remote Access configuration` object that you are disconnecting, as in `disconnect Raobject` (if the variable `Raobject` held a reference to a `Remote Access configuration` object).

duplicate reference

You can duplicate a configuration with this command:

```
duplicate AppleTalk configuration "printer_config" with properties ¬
{name:"Test config"}
```

You have to open and close the Open Transport configurations database to make these changes. You also have to use the *begin transaction* and *end transaction* commands to make sure that the new configuration is added to the database.

with properties record

You provide the properties for the new configuration with this labeled parameter, as in with properties{name:"newTCPIP", connecting via:Ethernet}. With *duplicate*, the new configuration inherits the properties of the original configuration (the one that was duplicated), unless you change those properties with this parameter:

```
tell application "Network Setup Scripting"
    set tId to "" -- this var will hold the transaction ID
    try -- catch and deal with any errors
        open database
        set tId to begin transaction
        duplicate TCPIP v4 configuration ¬
            "newMacIP" with properties {name:"newconfig2"}
        (* test a property to confirm that the config copy
inherits the original configuration's properties *)
        configuration method of TCPIP v4 configuration ¬
        "newconfig2"
        (*see if the new config was added to all of the database's
configurations *)
        set cs to configurations
        end transaction
        close database
    on error (* abort transaction and close database if there is
an error *)
        if tId is not "" then
            abort transaction
            close database
        end if
    end try
    return cs -- view the list of configurations
end tell
```

end transaction

This command is used to complete a transaction that was initiated with the *begin transaction* command. A transaction constitutes one or more database actions that are executed as a group and rolled back if any of the changes causes an error. *begin transaction* prevents the database from being changed by any other scripts or applications while the transaction is still alive. The transaction is finished or rendered inactive with the command *end transaction*. See also the *abort transaction* command.

exists reference

exists tests whether a certain AppleScript object exists and returns a true/false (boolean) value. An example is:

```
set bool to ( exists TCPIP v4 configuration "newconfig2" )
```

This code statement returns true if the specified configuration exists. Then the AppleScript might do something based on the *exists* return value, such as delete the configuration (if it exists) or make a new one (if it does not exist).

 Make sure to open the Open Transport configurations database first, check if the configuration exists or not, then close the database.

If you do not use the *open database* and *close database* commands, then the *exists* command will not raise an error but returns false, even if the configuration you are searching for actually does exist.

get protection property reference

You can find out whether a property of a configuration is locked or unlocked by using the *get protection* command. For example, the TCP/IP control panel allows you set the user mode (from its *Edit→User Mode...*menu) to basic, advanced, or administration. In administration mode, the control panel user can enter a password then lock or prevent the TCP/IP properties in the TCP/IP control panel from being changed by users who do not know the password. *get protection* returns either of two constants: locked or unlocked. See the following example and the *set protection* command description later in this chapter:

```
tell application "Network Setup Scripting"
    open database
    (* return value is locked or unlocked *)
    get protection of ¬
    (configuration method of TCPIP v4 configuration "sygate")
    close database
end tell
```

make

The *make* command is used to make a new object, such as a Remote Access or TCPIP v4 configuration. Use the labeled parameters that go with this command (e.g., with data, with properties) to specify the new configuration's elements and properties. with data is used to make new elements; you use with properties to specify the new object's property values.

new class

The script uses this labeled parameter to specify the kind of object that it will create, as in:

```
make new Remote Access configuration...
```

or:

```
make new TCPIP v4 configuration...
```

at location reference

This parameter is not necessary when making new Open Transport configurations with AppleScript and the *make* command.

with data anything

You can use the optional *with data* parameter to make a new element (as opposed to a property) for a configuration that the script has created. An anything object can hold a string, constant, or other class type. Chapter 3, *Data Types,* describes the anything data type.

with properties record

Use this command to specify the properties of the new configuration object that the script is creating with the *make* command. with properties takes a record data type, which is one or more name/ value pairs enclosed in curly brackets ({ }). See the following example for how to use *with properties:*

```
tell application "Network Setup Scripting"
    set tid to "" -- var tid will hold transaction id
    try
        open database
        set tid to begin transaction (* holds an integer like
25909 *)
        (* make the new TCP/IP config *)
        make new TCPIP v4 configuration ¬
            "MYNewIP" with properties ¬
            {connecting via:Ethernet, configuration method:DHCP, ¬
            subnet mask:"255.255.255.0", uses IEEE8023:false, ¬
            user mode:advanced}
        (* make new elements for the TCP/IP configuration *)
        tell TCPIP v4 configuration "MYNewIP"
            make new router address 1 with data "192.168.153.1"
            make new name server address 1 with data "192.168. ¬
            153. 1"
        end tell
        end transaction
        close database
        on error (* make sure the transaction is aborted and
database closed if there's an error *)
        if tid is not "" then
            abort transaction
            close database
        end if
    end try
end tell
```

open database

This command opens the Open Transport configuration database for reading and writing. Once the script does whatever it has to do with the database, the database is closed with the *close database* command. You cannot get any data from the Open Transport configuration database without using the *open database* command first. Most of this chapter's code examples demonstrate how to use *open database.*

quit

This command quits the Network Setup Scripting application. This application is a "faceless background application," meaning it has no standard user interface (menus and windows) and is controlled by Apple events and script code. It usually quits automatically after the AppleScript statements have finished executing, but you can explicitly quit Network Setup by using *quit*.

remove reference

This command removes an object such as a configuration from a configuration set, as in:

```
remove TCPIP v4 configuration "local_TCP" from configuration set "My
Network Settings"
```

A configuration set is a group of network settings that usually includes TCP/IP, Remote Access, Modem, and AppleTalk configurations. Removing a configuration from a configuration set does not delete the configuration object from the Open Transport configurations database.

from configuration set

Use this labeled parameter to specify the configuration or transport options to remove from a configuration set. Removing a configuration or transport options from a configuration set does not delete the configuration object from the Open Transport configurations database. See the following example and the transport options class description later in this chapter:

```
tell application "Network Setup Scripting"
    try
        set tid to "" -- this will hold the transaction id
        open database
        set tid to begin transaction
        set cs to (current configuration set)
        remove Modem configuration "Default" from cs (* remove a
Modem config *)
        from the current config set
        set lc to cs's configurations (* var lc will show that the
config has been removed *)
        end transaction
        close database
        lc (* view the var's value in Script Editor to confirm
that the Modem config is gone *)
        on error (* if there's an error make sure the transaction
is aborted and Open Transport database is closed *)
            if tid is not "" then
                abort transaction
                close database
            end if
    end try
end tell
```

run

> This command executes the Network Setup Scripting application. It is not necessary to use *run* because targeting Network Setup with a `tell` statement starts up the program:
>
> ```
> tell app "Network Setup Scripting"...
> ```

set protection property reference

> A script may lock or unlock a configuration's property with this command. When the property is locked in administration mode (with an administration password provided), the property cannot be changed by a script unless the script uses the *authenticate* command with the proper password. The example below shows how to use the *set protection* command. Also see the *authenticate* command description elsewhere in this chapter.

`to locked/unlocked:`

> This required labeled parameter sets the property to either of two constants, `locked` or `unlocked`. Locking the property requires password authentication to make any changes to it. See the following example:
>
> ```
> tell application "Network Setup Scripting"
>     set tid to "" -- this will hold the transaction id
>     try -- catch any errors
>         open database
>         set tid to begin transaction
>         set ipConfig to TCPIP v4 configuration "sygate"
>         (* create administration password *)
>         set user mode of ipConfig to administration
>         set administration password of ipConfig to "x$1957"
>         (* lock the TCP/IP configuration method *)
>         set cleared to (authenticate ipConfig with password ¬
>         "x$1957")
>         if cleared then
>             set protection (configuration method of ipConfig) to ¬
>         locked
>         end if
>         end transaction
>         close database
>         on error (* make sure that transaction is aborted and the
>     database is closed if an error occurs *)
>         if tid is not "" then
>             abort transaction
>             close database
>         end if
>     end try
> end tell
> ```

Dictionary classes

The Network Setup Scripting classes represent the network-related items that a script targets, mainly network configurations such as a Macintosh's AppleTalk or TCP/IP setup. You can find out a lot of information about a machine's networking configurations by querying the properties of the Network Setup Scripting application class, for instance (not to mention looking at the return values for other Network Setup Scripting objects such as the Remote Access configuration, which is used in part to control dial-up access to the Internet). Here is a list of the classes:

AppleTalk configuration

This class represents an AppleTalk network configuration (group of settings) that can be created or altered with an AppleScript. As a type or subclass of configuration, AppleTalk configuration also has the properties of the parent class (name, active, valid). The following example gets the properties of an AppleTalk configuration for viewing in Script Editor's Event Log (Chapter 2 describes the Script Editor's Event Log window):

```
tell application "Network Setup Scripting"
    set tId to ""
    try
        open database
        set tId to begin transaction
        set cc to current configuration set
        (* set the conAt var to the AppleTalk configuration that is
part of
         the current configuration set *)
        set conAt to item 1 of AppleTalk configurations of cc
        (* get properties of this config; example return values follow
each property *)
        conAt's addressing -- dynamic
        conAt's AppleTalk zone -- ""
        conAt's connecting via -- "Printer Port"
        conAt's network ID -- 0
        conAt's node ID -- 123
        conAt's protocol -- AppleTalk
        conAt's user mode -- basic
        conAt's name -- "printer_config"
        conAt's valid -- true
        conAt's active -- true
        end transaction
        close database
    on error
        if tId is not "" then
            abort transaction
            close database
        end if
    end try
end tell
```

The following are AppleTalk configuration properties:

addressing dynamic/static

This property returns either one of the two constants.

AppleTalk zone string

This property returns the AppleTalk zone as a string (e.g., "Graphics_ dep") or an empty string ("") if the configuration is not associated with a zone.

connecting via modem port/printer port/modem printer port/
Ethernet *or* string
> connecting via returns one of the port-related constants (e.g.,
> Ethernet) or a string data type. The return value for the AppleTalk
> configuration that is part of the current configuration set will
> be the same value as the "Connecting via" pop-up menu in the Apple-
> Talk control panel window. See Figure 16-2.

network ID integer
> This property returns a unique ID number such as 0.

node ID linteger
> node ID returns an integer such as 123. A node is an outward branch
> of a network system, if the system is viewed conceptually as a tree-like
> structure.

protocol AppleTalk *(read-only)*
> This property returns just the constant AppleTalk.

administration password string *(write-only)*
> You can only set, not get the value of, an administration password.
> Once a password is established, a script has to use the *authenticate*
> command to obtain administration permission to change a
> configuration property. See the *authenticate* command.

user mode basic/advanced/administration
> This property returns one of the three Open Transport configuration user
> modes (e.g., advanced).

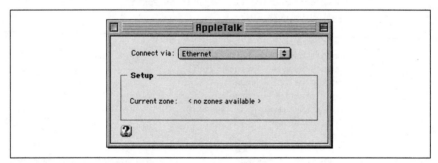

Figure 16-2: The AppleTalk control panel window

AppleTalk options

> This is a subclass of the transport options class, so it also has the proper-
> ties of its parent class (i.e., name, active, consequence, valid). The
> following example shows all of the available transport options, which
> provide global values for the various network protocols:

```
tell application "Network Setup Scripting"
    try
        open database
        repeat with c from 1 to (count of transport options)
            transport options c (* view each transport option in Event
Log *)
```

```
                end repeat
                close database
                on error
                close database
            end try
        end tell
        (* example Event Log output *)
        open database
        count every transport options of current application
        --> 4
        get transport options 1
        --> AppleTalk options "AppleTalk Globals"
        get transport options 2
        --> transport options "Remote Access Globals"
        get transport options 3
        --> TCPIP v4 options "TCP/IP Globals"
        get transport options 4
        --> transport options "Modem Globals"
        close database
```

AppleTalk active boolean

The code phrase AppleTalk active of AppleTalk options returns true or false, depending on whether AppleTalk is active or being used on the machine.

application

This class represents the Network Setup Scripting application itself. The application has three elements: configurations, configuration sets, and transport options objects. The upcoming code example views the return values of these elements in Script Editor's Event Log. See the class descriptions of these elements elsewhere in this chapter.

The following are application elements:

configuration

This is an Open Transport configuration that you would use to connect to a network, as in a Remote Access configuration. See the configuration class description.

configuration set

This object represents a named group of configurations, such as:

```
        configuration set "My Network Settings"
```

See the configuration set class.

transport options

Each one of the configuration types—AppleTalk, Modem, Remote Access, TCPIP v4—has some global properties that are stored in a transport options object. See the TCPIP v4 options, for instance. You can access one of a configuration set's transport options by its index, as in:

```
        tell app "Network Setup Scripting" to get transport options 2 ¬
        of current configuration set
        tell application "Network Setup Scripting"
            try
```

```
            open database
            configuration sets -- get list of configuration sets
            transport options 1 (* view return value for first
    transport options object *)
            configurations -- get list of configurations
            close database
            on error
            close database
        end try
    end tell
    (* Example return values in Event Log *)
    get every configuration set
    --> {configuration set "My Network Settings"}
    get transport options 1
    --> AppleTalk options "AppleTalk Globals"
    get every configuration
    --> {TCPIP v4 configuration "localt", TCPIP v4 configuration
    "mediaone", Remote Access configuration "Default", TCPIP v4
    configuration "NTNET", AppleTalk configuration "Default",
    AppleTalk configuration "printer_config", TCPIP v4 configuration
    "sygate, Modem configuration "Default"}
```

The following are **application** properties:

current configuration set *(read-only)*

> This property returns as a **configuration set** object the group of Open Transport configurations that the computer is using at the moment. For instance, to get a reference to the TCP/IP configuration, you could use the code in the next example. To get any elements or property values of the **current configuration set**, you have to set it to a variable first:

```
    set cs to (current configuration set)
```

> See the **configuration set** class description.

```
    tell application "Network Setup Scripting"
        try
            open database
            set cs to (current configuration set)
            set tcp to (every TCPIP v4 configuration of cs)
            close database
            on error
            close database
        end try
    end tell
```

name string *(read-only)*

> The **name** property returns "Network Setup Scripting." It is primarily used to target the app in a **tell** statement, as in:

```
    application "Network Setup Scripting"
```

version version *(read-only)*

> This property returns a **string** (the **version** object is implemented as a string) representing the version of the software program, as in "1.1.1."

---

configuration

This class is the parent class for all the other configuration types, such as Remote Access and TCPIP v4 configurations. You cannot make a new configuration (as in make new configuration), but you can make the subclass types. An example is:

```
make new Remote Access configuration with properties{...}
```

See the *make* command. The configuration child classes inherit these three properties. In other words, a TCPIP v4 configuration has active, name, and valid properties.

name string

This property returns the name of the configuration, such as the "newIP" part of TCPIP v4 configuration "newIP."

active boolean

If the configuration is part of the computer's current Open Transport settings, then its active property is true.

valid boolean *(read-only)*

If the configuration is a usable, valid Open Transport configuration that the machine can probably make a connection with then this property returns true. You can get the property with code such as:

```
get valid of TCPIP v4 configuration "newMacIP"
```

configuration set

This class represents a group of configurations and is implemented as a list type, as in the following return value:

```
{TCPIP v4 configuration "localt", TCPIP v4 configuration "mediaone",
Remote Access configuration "Default", AppleTalk configuration
"Default", Modem configuration "Default"}
```

In other words, configuration set is a list of configuration objects. This is the object that is returned by the application's current configuration set property. The following are configuration set elements:

configuration

Each configuration set contains one or more configurations. See the example return value in the configuration set description.

transport options

A configuration set may contain one or more transport options. See the transport options class description elsewhere in this chapter.

The following are configuration set properties:

name string

Every configuration set has a name, as in

```
configuration set "My Network Settings"
```

active boolean

This property returns true if the configuration set is currently being used for Open Transport network services on the machine. A configuration set can exist but not be active (its active is false).

`modem configuration`

A `modem configuration` can be created either with AppleScript or with the Modem control panel. The Open Transport configurations database usually stores at least one `modem configuration` (called `modem configuration "Default"`). Most of the `modem configuration` properties can also be set in the control panel.

These are `modem configuration` properties:

`connecting via modem port/printer port/modem printer port` *or* `string`

This property returns either one of these constants (e.g., `modem port`) or a `string` like "Internal Modem."

`dialing method tone/pulse`

This property is the script version of the Tone or Pulse radio buttons on the Modem control panel. You set this property to either of the two constants.

`ignores dial tone boolean`

This `true/false` value is the script equivalent of the "Ignore dial tone" checkbox on the Modem control panel. You can set this property using code such as the following:

```
set ignores dial tone to true
```

`modem script name string`

If the `modem configuration` is associated with a Modem script in the *startup disk:System Folder:Extensions:Modem Scripts* folder, then this property returns the filename as a `string`. An example return value is "Global Village 28.8-K56."

`modem speaker enabled boolean`

If you want to enable the modem's speaker during a connect or disconnect, then set the `modem speaker enabled` property of the configuration, which controls that modem to `true`.

`administration password string` *(write-only)*

You can protect a `modem configuration` by creating an administration password and locking the various properties, just as you can with other Open Transport configurations. You can only set this property, not get its value with a script (it is write-only). See the *authenticate* command description in this chapter for how to lock or unlock a property with password protection.

`user mode basic/advanced/administration`

User mode returns one of the three Open Transport configuration user modes (e.g., `advanced`) as constants. This property is the script equivalent to setting the User Mode with the Modem control panel (shown in Figure 16-3). For example, you can password-protect a `modem configuration`'s properties by using administration mode as shown.

`Remote Access configuration`

This class represents a `configuration` that you can create with the Remote Access control panel. This Open Transport technology lets you to make a

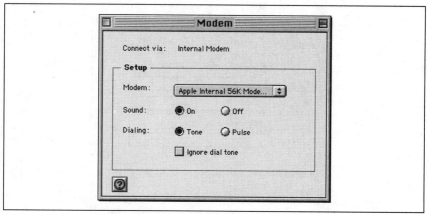

Figure 16-3: The Modem control panel

dial-up connection with the Web via an ISP, as well as allow other computers to dial in to your machine and use it as a file server. A `Remote Access configuration` is identified with its `string` name:

```
Remote Access configuration "Default"
```

Most of its properties are the script equivalents of creating and maintaining Remote Access settings with the Remote Access control panel. See Figure 16-4.

The following are `Remote Access configuration` properties:

`user name string`

This property is the username that the `configuration` must provide to connect to a remote network. It is the script equivalent of the "Name" field in the Remote Access control panel. An example is:

```
set user name of Remote Access configuration "Default" to ¬
"bruce19"
```

`password string`

This property is the script equivalent of the "Password" field in the Remote Access control panel (see Figure 16-4). It is the password that would be required to connect with a remote network.

`saves password boolean`

`saves password` is the script equivalent of the "Saves password" checkbox in the Remote Access control panel. It is a `boolean` value, as in:

```
set saves password of Remote Access configuration "Default" to ¬
true
```

If `false`, the connection will request a password every time the script attempts to log in. This value is ignored if the `guest access` property is `true`.

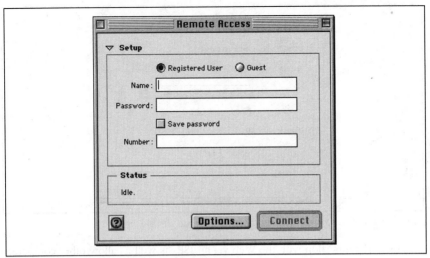

Figure 16-4: The Remote Access control panel

guest access boolean

If this property is **true**, then the script will try to log in to the remote network as a guest rather than as a specific authenticated user. If **guest access** is true then the **user name, password,** and **saves password** properties of this **configuration** are ignored. This property is the script equivalent to the Guest radio button on the Remote Access control panel.

status Remote access status *(read-only)*

status returns as a **Remote Access status** object the status information for a connection (Is it idle? Connecting? Disconnecting?). See the **Remote Access status** class description elsewhere in this chapter.

phone number string

This **string** is the phone number that the **modem configuration** uses to dial in to a remote connection, as in "978 352-3522". It is the property-equivalent to the "Number" field in the Remote Access control panel.

alternate number string

The **alternate number** property represents the alternate phone number to use when redialing in to a remote connection. This number is used if the **redialing** property is set to **main and alternate**.

uses DialAssist boolean

This **true/false** value is the equivalent of the *RemoteAccess* → *DialAssist...* menu command in the Remote Access control panel. DialAssist is a control panel that provides detailed settings for dialing outside of local regions.

area code string

You can provide an area code for the **modem configuration**, as in:

```
set area code of Modem configuration "Default" to "978"
```

This property applies only if **uses DialAssist** is **true**.

---

country string

The country property for the configuration can be set to a string, as in "Switzerland." This property corresponds to a pop-up menu choice in the DialAssist control panel. The country property applies only if uses DialAssist is true.

redialing off/main only/main and alternate

You can set redialing for the configuration to any of the three constants. This property corresponds to the Redial pop-up menu in the Remote Access control panel. See Figure 16-5.

times to redial integer

This property specifies how many times to redial while making a remote connection with this modem configuration before the connect attempt quits. An example is:

```
set times to redial of Remote Access configuration "Default" ¬
to 3
```

The property corresponds to the "Redial" edit field in the Remote Access control panel. See Figure 16-5.

time between redials integer

This property corresponds to the "Time between retries" edit field in the Remote Access control panel. Use it to specify the time in seconds that the configuration should wait before redialing in to the remote network, as in:

```
set time between redials of Remote Access configuration ¬
"Default" to 5
```

verbose logging boolean

This true/false value is equivalent to checking the "use verbose logging" checkbox in the Remote Access control panel (i.e., the "Connection" tab in the "Options..." window). An example is:

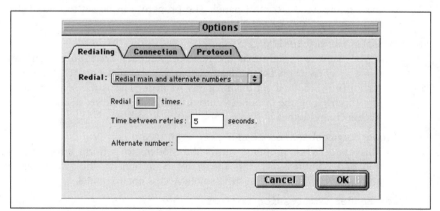

Figure 16-5: Tabbed panels in the Remote Access control panel's Options section

```
tell Remote Access configuration "Default" to ¬
    set verbose logging to true
```

flashes icon boolean

If this property is true and you make a connection using this configuration, then an icon flashes in the computer's menu bar. The property is the script equivalent to the "Flash icon..." checkbox in the Remote Access control panel.

prompts to stay connected boolean

A script can set this property in the following manner:

```
tell Remote Access configuration "Default" to ¬
    set prompts to stay connected to false
```

The latter code fragment unchecks the "Prompt every 5 minutes checkbox..." in the Remote Access control panel.

time between prompts integer

If prompts to stay connected is true, then you can specify the number of minutes between prompts with this property.

disconnects if idle boolean

A script can disconnect a connection after a specified number of minutes, if there is no activity (such as no bytes transferred across the network connection). To disconnect an idle connection automatically, set this property to true then specify the number of minutes with the idle time allowed property.

idle time allowed integer

This property specifies the number of minutes that the connection can remain idle before it is automatically disconnected, if disconnects if idle is true.

protocol PPP/ARAP

This property is the script equivalent of the Use protocol pop-up menu in the Remote Access control panel. The property can be set to one of the two constants, PPP or ARAP.

connects automatically boolean

If you want to specify that the Remote Access configuration will make its connection automatically whenever you make an HTTP request with a browser, then set this property to true. This is the script equivalent to checking the "Connect automatically..." checkbox in the Remote Access control panel.

allows compression boolean

This true/false property allows the Modem to perform error correction and compression. It is the script equivalent to the "Allow error correction..." checkbox on the Remote Access control panel.

uses header compression boolean

This true/false property allows the compression of packet headers during network communications. It is the script equivalent to the "Use TCP header compression" checkbox on the Remote Access control panel.

connects using command line boolean

If this property is set to `true`, then the configuration specifies the display of a command-line shell when a connection is initiated. It is the script equivalent to the "Connect to a command-line host" checkbox on the Remote Access control panel.

command line type terminal window/connection script

This property specifies the command-line type as either of the two constants. It is the equivalent of the "Use terminal window" and "Use connect script" radio buttons on the Remote Access control panel.

connection script file alias

With some Remote Access connections, it is convenient to specify a script that automatically provides text entries to a command-line window. You can specify this script as a `configuration` property. An example is:

```
set connection script file of Remote Access configuration ¬
    "Default" to alias "macintosh hd:con scripts:connector"
```

administration password string *(write-only)*

If you want to lock some of these Remote Access properties and thus prevent them from being changed by other users, then set a password with this property (it cannot be read by a script, only set). This is the equivalent of using the administration user mode under the Remote Access control panel's Edit menu.

user mode basic/advanced/administration

This property returns or sets one of the three constants that represent the Open Transport configuration user modes.

Remote Access status

This class represents the object that is returned by the Remote Access configuration's `status` property. This object's properties give scripts a certain amount of information about the status of a remote connection, such as how long the machine has been connected (`time connected`) to the remote network. For example, you would use the following code to find out the name (i.e., IP address) of the remote server the machine is connected to:

```
get server name of (status of Remote Access configuration "Default")
```

The following are `Remote Access status` properties:

activity idle/connecting/connected/disconnecting/unknown *(read-only)*

Get the `activity` property to find out what the connection is doing at the moment, as in:

```
get activity of (status of Remote Access configuration ¬
    "Default")
```

This returns one of the constants, such as `connected` or `disconnecting`.

time connected integer *(read-only)*

The `time connected` property returns a number of seconds:

```
time connected of (status of Remote Access configuration ¬
    "Default")
```

An example return value is 486 (if the connection had been established for eight minutes and six seconds).

time remaining integer *(read-only)*

This property returns a number of seconds or -1 if the connection has an unlimited amount of time left (i.e., the value for "Time remaining:" in the control panel's Status area is "Unlimited").

user name string *(read-only)*

This **string** property is the user name associated with the connection. This is the name that the user or script logged on to the remote network with.

server name string *(read-only)*

You can get the server name of the remote network by reading the **server name** property. The return value for this property can be "<Unknown>". The return value can also be the server's IP address, as in "204.167.109.3." An example is:

```
get server name of (status of Remote Access configuration ¬
"Default")
```

message string *(read-only)*

This property contains the most recent message received for this connection. These are the messages that appear in the Remote Access control panel's Status area (see Figure 16-4). An example return value for this property is "Connection: 27400 bps."

speed string *(read-only)*

This property returns the baud rate for the connection as a **string**. An example return value is "26400."

bytes received integer *(read-only)*

This property returns the number of bytes received by the computer or client, such as if it received a web page from the remote network over the connection. An example return value is 197374.

bytes sent integer *(read-only)*

The bytes sent is an **integer** like 200374. It represents bytes sent from the client machine to the remote network, such as if the connection was established and you opened a browser and made an HTTP request over the connection.

router address

This class represents a **router address** as a **string**, such as "192.168.0.1." You can make new router addresses and associate them with a new TCP/IP configuration.

search domain

This class represents a search domain as a **string**. This is the information that can be entered into the domain name and "Additional Search domains" fields in the TCP/IP control panel. See Figure 16-6. The following Apple Computer tech info library (TIL) article has more information on configuring TCP/IP and search domains: *http://til.info.apple.com/techinfo.nsf/artnum/ n75085*.

TCPIP v4 configuration

This class represents a network configuration that is used to connect to a TCP/IP network, such as the Internet or an Ethernet. A TCPIP v4 configuration object can have zero or more of its elements (e.g., router address). Its properties, such as IP address and configuration method, can also be set manually in the TCP/IP control panel (see Figure 16-6). You can access this object by its name:

```
set tcp to TCPIP v4 configuration "Default"
```

This type of configuration also has the three properties of its parent class configuration (i.e., name, active, and valid).

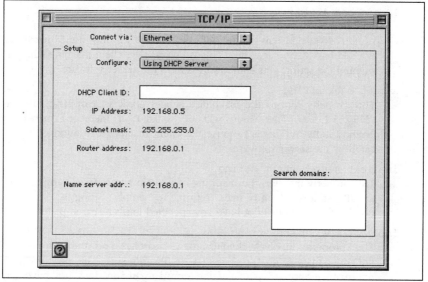

Figure 16-6: TCP/IP control panel

The following are TCPIP v4 configuration elements:

router address

This is the IP address of the router in string form. One way to access the router address is by its index:

```
get router address 1 of TCPIP v4 configuration "Default"
```

See the router address class description.

name server address

This is the IP address of the name server in string form. One way to try to access the name server address is by its index:

```
get name server address 1 of TCPIP v4 configuration "Default"
```

See the name server class description.

search domain

This is the string value returned for the search domain field, which involves advanced TCP/IP configuration.

The following are `TCPIP v4 configuration` properties:

`connecting via Ethernet/MacIP/PPP` *or* `string`
> The return value of this property is either a `string` or one of the three constants (e.g., `Ethernet`):
>
> > `get connecting via of TCPIP v4 configuration "sygate"`

`configuration method BootP/DHCP/MacIP manual/MacIP server/ manual/RARP/PPP server`
> The `configuration method` is one of the seven constants, as in:
>
> > `set configuration method of TCPIP v4 configuration "sygate" to ¬ DHCP`

`IP address string`
> This property returns the machine's active IP address as a `string`, such as "192.168.0.5." This value will be "0.0.0.0" if the `configuration method` is `DHCP`, for instance. This is because the client machine (the one running the script) gets its IP address from the server software.

`subnet mask string`
> This property returns the machine's subnet mask as a `string`, such as "255.255.255.0." This value will be "0.0.0.0" if the `configuration method` is `DHCP`. This is because the client machine's IP address is allocated by the server software.

`implicit search start string`
> This property involves the mapping of domain names (e.g., "apple.com") to IP addresses and may return an empty string ("") if the `configuration` does not have any specified implicit search paths.

`implicit search end string`
> This property involves domain name searches and the mapping of domain names (e.g., "apple.com") to IP addresses. The property may return an empty string ("") if the `configuration` does not have any implicit search paths.

`DHCP client ID string`
> This property applies only if the configuration's `configuration method` is `DHCP`.

`MacIP server zone string`
> An example return value for the `MacIP server` zone (from my active `TCPIP v4 configuration`) is "*".

`uses IEEE8023 boolean`
> This `true`/`false` value is the script equivalent to the "Use 802.3" checkbox on the TCP/IP control panel. If the checkbox control is checked, then this property is `true`. This checkbox only appears if the configuration connects via Ethernet.

`protocol TCPIP v4` *(read-only)*
> This property returns the constant `TCPIP v4`.

`administration password string` *(write-only)*
> This is a settable-only property (you cannot read it with script) for the configurations with which you want to lock or prevent any unauthorized

changes to properties. When a `TCPIP v4 configuration` has locked properties, little padlock icons appear next to the properties (e.g., "Connect via") on the TCP/IP control panel. See the *authenticate* command description elsewhere in this chapter for working with passwords and locked/unlocked properties.

user mode basic/advanced/administration

This property returns one of the three Open Transport configuration user modes for TCP/IP (e.g., **advanced**). You can also change the user mode from the TCP/IP control panel's *Edit:User Mode...* menu.

TCPIP v4 options

This class represents the options that apply to all `TCPIP v4 configurations` that are part of an Open Transport configurations database. `TCPIP v4 options` also has the properties of its `transport options` parent class: name, `active`, `consequence`, and `valid`. See the upcoming example.

TCPIP active boolean

Test this `true/false` property to find out if TCP/IP is an active networking protocol on the computer. The next example finds out whether TCP/IP is active and, if so, gets the value of all of its options (e.g., `consequence`). `consequence` means, what happens if you change these option's settings (i.e., do you have to restart the computer for the network protocol to work properly?).

```
tell application "Network Setup Scripting"
    open database
    set tpt to TCPIP v4 options 1 (* get TCPIP v4 options object
by its index *)
    if (active of tpt) then (* if its active property is true
then get vals for other properties *)
        tpt's name
        tpt's TCPIP active
        tpt's valid
        tpt's consequence
    end if
    close database
end tell
(* Sample return values viewed in Script Editor's Event Log *)
open database
get TCPIP v4 options 1
--> TCPIP v4 options "TCP/IP Globals"
get active of TCPIP v4 options "TCP/IP Globals"
--> true
get name of TCPIP v4 options "TCP/IP Globals"
--> "TCP/IP Globals"
get TCPIP active of TCPIP v4 options "TCP/IP Globals"
--> true
get valid of TCPIP v4 options "TCP/IP Globals"
--> true
get consequence of TCPIP v4 options "TCP/IP Globals"
--> benign
```

transport options

This is the parent class for the AppleTalk and TCPIP v4 options. Thus, those two classes inherit the four transport options' properties. The transport options apply to all of the configurations of the same class. So if you set the TCPIP v4 options, they apply to each instance or copy of a TCPIP v4 configuration (see the TCPIP v4 options class description elsewhere in this chapter). You can gain access to the various transport options by name or by index:

```
tell app "Network Setup Scripting" to get transport options 3
```

The following are transport options properties:

name string

Each transport option object has a name, as in:

```
TCPIP v4 options "TCP/IP Globals"
```

The name is "TCP/IP Globals."

active boolean

If the transport options object is active or associated with a network protocol (like TCP/IP) that is used on the computer, then this value is true.

consequence benign/may affect services/must restart configuration/must restart protocol/must restart computer *(read-only)*

This property returns one of the five constants (e.g., benign). The constant return value reflects the consequences of any changes to the option's settings. You get the return value with code such as the following:

```
consequence of (TCPIP v4 options "TCP/IP Globals")
```

valid boolean *(read-only)*

If the options are usable and valid on the computer then this boolean value returns true.

CHAPTER 17

Scripting Sherlock 2

Sherlock 2 is the Apple Computer program that allows you to search the Web or your local file system for any files or web pages that meet the criteria you specify in the search text field. Figure 17-1 shows the Sherlock 2 window. The program is the Find application from pre–Mac OS 8 lineage, but it is significantly renovated for web searching (the second Sherlock version, Sherlock 2, installed with Mac OS 9).

Figure 17-1: Sherlock 2 window

The software is modeled in part on Internet search-engine methods. For example, Sherlock 2 presents its web search results as a list of hyperlinks ranked by relevance. If you click on the hyperlink, Sherlock 2 opens the default browser and attempts to load the page found by the search. Your machine has to be online, however, for Sherlock 2 to search the Web. For example, if you wanted to find a web page that describes the Berkeley Software Distribution (BSD) commands (so that you can test the use of these commands in Mac OS X's command shell), then initiate these steps with the Sherlock 2 window:

1. Choose the Internet channel icon (the planet Earth) at the top of the Sherlock 2 window.

2. Type "BSD commands" in Sherlock 2's search text field.

3. Click the magnifying glass icon at the right of the text field to start the search.

You can also use Sherlock 2 to initiate finely grained file searches on your local volumes, but only if you have indexed these volumes with Sherlock's indexing feature. Figure 17-2 shows the application's Index Volumes window. Indexing speeds up searching by creating a catalog of important and/or frequently used terms in the document, similar to an index in the back of a book. Indexing a large disk with Sherlock 2 can take an hour or more, but the resultant search speed and results are impressive. You cannot index web sites in this manner, just disks, folders, and files. You can also update or create a new index on folders and files (not just volumes) by selecting the folder or file and choosing *Index selection...* from the contextual menu. If you want to search just a folder, not any volumes, you can drag the folder into the Sherlock 2 window then initiate a search (as long as the folder was previously indexed).

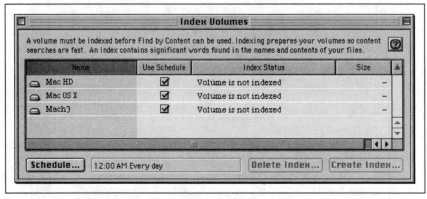

Figure 17-2: Sherlock 2's Index Volumes window

Of course, all of these tasks—searching the Web or a giant local hard disk, or indexing files, folders, and volumes—can be accomplished using an AppleScript. To get you started, Example 17-1 tells Sherlock 2 to search the Web for web pages that are relevant to the command "BSD commands." It uses the *search Internet* command, which has an optional labeled parameter *display* that specifies whether to show the search results in a Sherlock 2 window:

```
search Internet for "BSD commands" display true
```

In this case we want to see the search results. The *search Internet* command returns a list of URL strings that resulted from the search (see the *search Internet* command description elsewhere in this chapter).

Example 17-1: Simple Script for Searching with Sherlock 2

```
tell application "Sherlock 2"
    activate -- make Sherlock the active window
    set query to "BSD commands"
    (* make sure that you catch any network errors and display the error to
the user *)
    try
        search Internet for query with display
        on error errmesg
        display dialog errmesg
    end try
end tell
```

Sherlock 2

The following sections describe the commands and classes included with the Sherlock 2 dictionary. Chapter 2, *Using Script Editor with OS 9 and OS X,* describes application dictionaries if you are not familiar with them.

Dictionary commands

count reference *to object*

This command counts the number of objects that are specified in its parameter:

```
tell app "Sherlock 2" to count channels
```

If you added the code count result to the end of Example 17-1 (just before end tell), then this code would return the number of web sites that the search returned. The return value is an integer.

exists reference *to object*

If your Sherlock 2 script is running on a different machine than your own, you will have to find out whether a certain channel exists before you specify it in a scripted search. The following example initiates a search only if the "Apple" channel exists on the machine running the script. This command returns a boolean value, true or false:

```
tell application "Sherlock 2"
    if exists channel "Apple" then
        activate
        (* make sure that you catch any network errors and display the
error to the user *)
        try
            search Internet in channel "Apple" for "Mac OS X" with ¬
            display
            on error errmesg
            display dialog errmesg
        end try
    else
```

```
            display dialog "The Apple channel is not installed."
        end if
    end tell
```

get reference *to object*

This is the common AppleScript *get* command, which can be omitted in most cases when you are getting references to Sherlock objects. For example, you can use the code:

```
tell app "Sherlock 2" to channels
```

instead of the code:

```
tell app "Sherlock 2" to get channels
```

(although the latter phrase is more grammatically correct). Both of these statements return a list of channel objects. An example return value is:

```
{channel "Files" of application "Sherlock 2", channel "Apple" of
application "Sherlock 2", channel "Internet" of application "Sherlock
2", channel "My Channel" of application "Sherlock 2", channel "News"
of application "Sherlock 2", channel "People" of application
"Sherlock 2", channel "Reference" of application "Sherlock 2",
channel "Shopping" of application "Sherlock 2"}.
```

index containers list *of aliases*

This command indexes or updates the index of the specified files, folders, or volumes. Using *index containers* is the equivalent of choosing Sherlock 2's *Find:Index Volumes...* menu command (just for indexing disks or volumes) or control-clicking a folder or file and choosing *Index selection...* from the contextual menu. The following example asks the user to choose a folder, using the *choose folder* osax, then tells Sherlock 2 to index or update the index on that folder. If you want to index several files, folders, or volumes, then use this command with a list of aliases to these indexable objects:

```
index containers {alias "Macintosh HD:Desktop Folder:today:", alias
"Macintosh HD:Desktop Folder:scripts:"}.

tell application "Sherlock 2"
    set theFol to (choose folder with prompt ¬
        "Choose a folder for Sherlock to index.")
    index containers theFol
end tell
```

open list *of aliases*

By passing a file alias to the *open* command, you can have Sherlock launch another search with search criteria that you previously saved in a file. For example, you can specify detailed search criteria in Sherlock 2's Find File mode or tab, then save this criteria in a file for future searches. To save the search criteria to a file, you use Sherlock 2's *File→Save Search Criteria...* command. The resulting file has a magnifying glass icon that looks like Figure 17-3. If you double-click this icon, then Sherlock 2 will either launch (if it is not open already) or spawn a new search window and re-do the search based on the search file's criteria. You can also launch the search by using the *open* command, as in the following example (again, if Sherlock 2 already has a window open, then the *open* command spawns a new window):

search_crit

Figure 17-3: A Sherlock 2 search criteria file

```
tell application "Sherlock 2"
   activate
      open alias "Macintosh HD:Desktop Folder:htm_sher"
end tell
```

quit

This command quits the Sherlock 2 application:

```
tell app Sherlock 2 to quit.
```

run

In most cases it is not necessary to use the *run* command to execute this program, since targeting Sherlock 2 in a `tell` statement block executes the program if it is not already open.

search `list` *of aliases*

You can use the *search* command on folders or volumes to find files that contain a specified `string`, that have content that is similar to other files, or that are returned as the results of an executed search criteria file. The *search* command has four optional labeled parameters that are described in the following section. You can only use one of the first three parameters. For instance, you cannot use the `similar` to parameter if you have already specified a search `string` with the `for` parameter. If you try to use more than one of the first three parameters, your script will raise an error. This command returns a `list` of aliases to the files that the search found.

Sherlock 2 searches any folders nested in the folder that is specified by the *search* command, a handy feature that only requires the script to identify the top-level folder. If the volume containing the folder specified by the *search* command has not been indexed, then this command will raise an error.

`for string`

Use this labeled parameter to specify one or more words to search for in the files:

```
search alias "HFSA2gig:nutshell book:chapters:" for ¬
   "AppleScript"
```

If you want to search for more than one word, separate the different words with a space. You cannot use this parameter if you also use the `similar` to or `using` parameter.

`similar to list` *of aliases*

As opposed to searching with a `string` of words, you can search for files that contain similar content to the files that you specify in "list of aliases." For example, the following code finds files that are similar to the *home.html* and *search.html* files (but these two files have to be previously indexed):

```
search alias "HFSA2gig:nutshell book:chapters:" similar to ¬
{alias "macintosh hd:desktop folder:home.html", alias ¬
"macintosh  hd:desktop folder:search.html"} with  display.
```

using alias

You can use a saved file that contains search criteria (see Figure 17-2) instead of specifying a search **string** to initiate your Sherlock 2 search. For example:

```
search alias "HFSA2gig:nutshell book:chapters:" using alias ¬
"macintosh hd:desktop folder: htm_sher" with display
```

To save search criteria to a file you use Sherlock 2's *File:Save Search Criteria...* command (see the *open* command description). If you use the using parameter, you cannot use the other two labeled parameters: for and similar to.

display boolean

This is a **true/false** value indicating whether you want the search results to be displayed in a Sherlock 2 window. Usually you will want to display this window, unless you are going to further process the search return value, which is a **list** of aliases to the files that Sherlock returns as a result.

```
tell application "Sherlock 2"
    activate
    (* make sure that you catch any network errors and display
the error to the user *)
    try
        search alias "HFSA2gig:nutshell book:chapters:" for ¬
        "AppleScript" with display
        on error errmesg
        display dialog errmesg
    end try
end tell
```

search Internet list *of strings*

A script can search the Web using a **string** of one or more search words or a saved search criteria file (see the *open* command description). The following example searches HotBot.com for the Vertech altimeter watch. The **"list of strings"** parameter is optional, but if you use it, Sherlock 2 limits the search to only the web site(s) identified in the parameter. This parameter is not case-sensitive so you can use "HotBot" or "hotbot." The *search-Internet* return value is a **list** of URLs that comprise the search result. Since Sherlock 2 can save search criteria in a file but not the search results itself, this return value allows scripters to extend the application by having the script save the resulting sites to a file or database:

```
tell application "Sherlock 2"
```

```
        activate -- make Sherlock the active window
        (* make sure that you catch any network errors and display
    the error to the user *)
        try
            search Internet "hotbot" for "vertech altimeter" with ¬
            display
            on error errmesg
            display dialog errmesg
        end try
    end tell
```

in channel string

By default, *search Internet* searches the Internet channel, but you can switch the search to another channel by using this optional labeled parameter.

for string

This optional parameter identifies the words that you are searching for, as in "Vertech altimeter watch." You have to use either the *for* or *using* parameters with *search Internet*, but not both.

using alias

This parameter identifies a search criteria file to use in the search. This is a search query that has been saved in a file (see Figure 17-2 and the *open* command description).

display boolean

By default, *search Internet* does not display the Sherlock 2 window or show any results. The web pages that are returned by the search (if any) are returned by *search Internet* as a list of strings. You can, however, display the search results in a Sherlock 2 window by using `display true` or `with display`, as in:

```
    search Internet for "global warming" with display
```

select search sites list *of strings*

This command pre-selects a bunch of web-search sites (in the Internet channel by default):

```
    select search sites {"HotBot", "AltaVista"}
```

The Internet sites that are identified in the "list of strings" parameter are case-sensitive, so `{"HotBot", "AltaVista"}` puts checkmarks next to only those sites in the Internet channel, but `{"hotbot", "altavista"}` does not select those sites.

in channel string

You can optionally specify the channel in which to select the search sites. The following example first selects the Apple Tech Info Library site in the "Apple" channel then searches only that site:

```
    tell application "Sherlock 2"
        activate
        select search sites {"Apple Tech Info Library"} in channel ¬
        "Apple"
        (* make sure that you catch any network errors and display
    the error to the user *)
```

```
try
    search Internet in channel "Apple" for ¬
    "Mac OS X public beta" with display
    on error errmesg
    display dialog errmesg
end try
end tell
```

set reference

A script can set one of Sherlock 2's properties with this command:

```
set current tab to Find by Content Tab
```

See the `application` class description.

to anything

Use this labeled parameter to specify the value of a property:

```
tell app "Sherlock 2" to set current channel to "Apple"
```

Provide the keyword `to` followed by the property value, which in the example is the string "Apple." `anything` is an AppleScript data type that can be, well, anything. In other words, it can contain a `string` or a `number` or a `constant`, among other value types.

Dictionary classes

application

This class represents the Sherlock 2 application. It has several `channel` elements, which a script can obtain as a `list` value with the code:

```
tell app "Sherlock 2" to set allch to channels
```

In this sample code, the `allch` variable holds the `list` of `channel` objects. The Sherlock 2 app has three properties, two of which are settable:

```
set current channel to channel "People"
```

The following are `application` elements:

channel

The Sherlock 2 app has several `channel` elements, which are returned as a `list` value by code such as:

```
tell app "Sherlock 2" to get channels
```

An example return value is:

```
{channel "Files" of application "Sherlock 2", channel "Apple" of
application "Sherlock 2", channel "Internet" of application
"Sherlock 2", channel "My Channel" of application "Sherlock 2",
channel "News" of application "Sherlock 2", channel "People" of
application "Sherlock 2", channel "Reference" of application
"Sherlock 2", channel "Shopping" of application "Sherlock 2"}
```

Each member of this `list` is a `channel` object; see the `channel` class description.

The following are `application` properties:

current channel reference

A script can find out and optionally change the currently active channel with this settable property. An example is:

```
set current channel to channel "People"
```

all search sites reference *(read-only)*

This property returns the Internet search sites as a `list`. An example return value is:

```
{"Aladdin Systems", "Aladdin Systems: Frequently Asked
Questions", "AltaVista", "Apple iReview", "Best Site First",
"CNET", "CNET Download.com", "Direct Hit", "Excite", "GoTo.com",
"HotBot", "Infoseek", "LookSmart", "Lycos", "Rolling Stone"}.
```

current tab Find File Tab/Find by Content Tab/Search Internet Tab

You can set the current tab or focus of the Sherlock 2 window with code such as:

```
set current tab to Search Internet Tab
```

However, Sherlock 2 in Mac OS 9 tends to return `Find File Tab` from the `current tab` property, no matter which of the window elements (Search Internet or Find File) currently has the focus.

channel

This class represents a `channel` object, which is a representation of the various areas of the Web or your filesystem that Sherlock will search. The channels are depicted in the Sherlock 2 window as icons along the top of the frame (see Figure 17-1). When you select one of the icons (e.g., "Internet," "People," "Shopping"), Sherlock 2 displays the web sites, disks, or folders that it will search. `channel` objects are returned by the Sherlock 2 application object's `current channel` property, for instance. A `channel` object is identified by using the keyword `channel` followed by its `string` name:

```
channel "People"
```

The following are `channel` properties:

all search sites reference *(read-only)*

A script can obtain all the search sites attached to a `channel` by getting the channel's `all search sites` property value:

```
get all search sites of channel "Apple"
```

An example return value from this code is:

```
{"Apple iReview", "Apple Macintosh Products Guide", "Apple ¬
Tech Info Library", "Apple.com"}
```

name international text *(read-only)*

The `name` of a channel is a `string`:

```
channel "Internet"
```

CHAPTER 18

URL Access Scripting

The URL Access Scripting application provides an easy method for scripts to download files from and upload them to a remote directory. This application is located in the *startup disk:System Folder:Scripting Additions* folder. It provides two intuitive commands that can be used with the File Transfer Protocol (FTP) and HyperText Transfer Protocol (HTTP), *download* and *upload*. You can use these commands anywhere in your script, including within a `tell` block that targets another application, as long as the two commands do not conflict with that application's own commands. In other words, if a hypothetical program called ScriptableWebApp already has a *download* command in its dictionary, then the usage of *download* within the `tell` block `tell app "ScriptableWebApp"` will invoke *that* application's *download* command, not the URL Access *download* command.

URL Access can use HTTP to download the source code of a web page to a file of your choice or FTP files and whole directories back and forth from a web server. You have to have the cooperation of a web server, however, before your scripts undertake any directory/file uploads or directory downloads. With URL Access and FTP, you can have your script display a dialog window to allow the user to enter a username and password and thus be authenticated by the web server (see Figure 18-4 later in the chapter). Figure 18-1 shows the URL Access Scripting icon in the *Scripting Additions* folder.

URL Access Scripting

Figure 18-1: URL Access Scripting icon

URL Access Scripting

The following descriptions detail the available URL Access commands (*download* and *upload*) available for scripting.

Dictionary commands

download

The *download* command downloads a file using either FTP or HTTP to the disk of the machine running the script. The web file can then be viewed with a browser locally. Any images, however, are not downloaded with the web page using HTTP, so you would have to download the images separately using the *download* command. *download* takes two required parameters: a string URL (as in *http://www.parkerriver.com*) and a `file specification` object to which the script downloads the file. A `file specification` is an AppleScript data type that represents the name and location of a file before it is actually saved to the hard disk. In other words, you can create a new file with the *new file* scripting addition, which will have the operating system reserve a unique path for the new file. The *new file* osax displays a dialog box requesting that the user choose a location and name for the new file. Figure 18-2 shows this *new file* dialog window.

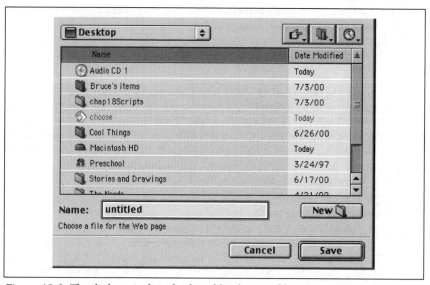

Figure 18-2: The dialog window displayed by the new file osax

The return value for *new file* is a `file specification` object. You can then download a file to this reserved file path and an actual file is saved to the hard disk with the prior specified location and name. You have to enclose the *download* command in a `tell` block targeting the URL Access Scripting application, as in:

```
tell app "URL Access Scripting" to download ¬
"http://129.69.59.34/index.html" to filespec
```

The rest of the *download* command's parameters are optional. The return value of the *download* command is a reference to the file after it is downloaded:

```
file "Macintosh HD:Desktop Folder:parkerriver.com"
```

The following example encloses the *download* script in a `try/on error/end try` block to catch any errors that are associated with the download, including the user clicking the Cancel button on the *new file* dialog window. The script also uses a `with timeout` statement to give the *download* command two minutes to complete its task, before AppleScript raises an "Apple event timed out" error. By default, AppleScript gives an application 60 seconds to respond to an Apple event before the script times out. See Chapter 7, *Flow-Control Statements*, for more details on `with timeout`.

The following are `download` properties:

`to file specification`

This property is a required labeled parameter that identifies the `file specification` object to which the web page will be downloaded. For example:

```
download "ftp://www.parkerriver.com/resources.html" to filespec
```

`replacing yes/no`

If a file already exists at this location, then `replacing yes` replaces that file with the new one, as in:

```
download "http://my.yahoo.com" to filespec with progress ¬
replacing yes
```

`unpacking boolean`

If you are downloading a BinHexed and/or stuffed file, then this labeled parameter (e.g., `unpacking true`) attempts to decode and/or decompress the file. AppleScript uses the Stuffit Engine extension, which is inside the *System Folder's Extensions* folder, to decode and decompress files. An example of a file that would have to be decoded and unstuffed would be a file that has been encoded using the BinHex protocol and compressed using Aladdin Stuffit. These files sometimes have suffixes such as "afile.sit.hqx."

`progress boolean`

We all know that downloading web files with FTP or HTTP, particularly those that involve some server-side processing, can be a tricky and lengthy process. This parameter requests the display of a progress bar during the web-file download, which is a good idea. A progress bar is a horizontal cylinder shape that gradually fills with solid color as a task is executed. Figure 18-3 shows the progress bar. Just add a `with progress` to your download command:

```
download "http://www.highendDesign.com/index.html" to filespec ¬
with progress
```

The progress bar includes a Stop button that causes AppleScript to quit the script (with error number –128) containing the *download* command if the user clicks the button.

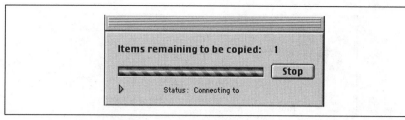

Figure 18-3: The download command's progress bar

form data string

You can post some data to a Common Gateway Interface script on the Web with the optional parameter form data. This would be the equivalent of a web user filling out a form and submitting it to a CGI script on a web server. A CGI script intercepts web data on a server and processes it in some way (such as storing the user data in a database) before sending back a response page to the user. The following is an example use of the *download* command with the with data parameter:

```
tell application "URL Access Scripting" to download URLstr to ¬
filespec form data "username=adminenter&password=mypass#$" ¬
with progress
```

The with data parameter is a URL-encoded string, in other words, one or more name/value pairs (e.g., firstname=Bruce) separated by a "&" character.

directory listing boolean

This true/false value is designed to download a directory listing using FTP. The result is a text file in which each line is of the form "-rw-rw-rw- 1 owner group 17 Oct 29 1998 myfile.txt." An example of using this labeled parameter is:

```
download "ftp://www.parkerriver.com" to filespec with ¬
directory listing, authentication and progress
```

download directory boolean

This true/false value is designed to download a directory of files using FTP. With this parameter, the script should download the files to a folder alias:

```
alias "Macintosh HD:Desktop Folder:WebFiles"
```

An example of using this labeled parameter is:

```
download "ftp://www.parkerriver.com" to folder_alias with ¬
download directory, authentication and progress
```

authentication boolean

This optional parameter displays a dialog box asking for a username and password, if the web server requires authentication for FTP and HTTP requests. Figure 18-4 shows this authentication window. An example of using this parameter is:

```
tell app "URL Access Scripting" to download ¬
"ftp://my.yahoo.com" to filespec with authentication
```

Figure 18-4: An authentication window

```
try -- catch any errors caused during the download
    (* get a file specification first, and optionally give the
new file a default name *)
    set filespec to new file with prompt ¬
        "Choose a location for the Web file" default name ¬
        "resources.html"
    with timeout of 120  seconds (* give the download command two
minutes before the Apple Event times out *)
        tell application "URL Access Scripting" to download ¬
            "ftp://www.parkerriver.com/resources.html" to ¬
            filespec with progress and authentication
    end timeout
on error errmesg number errNum
    if errNum is -128 then (* if the user cancels the file dialog
or the progress dialog *)
        display dialog
            "You quit before downloading a file: the applet " & ¬
            "will quit now."
    else
        display dialog (errNum as text) & ": " & errmesg & ¬
        return & return & "An error occurred during the " & ¬
         "download. Try running the applet again."
    end if
end try
```

upload

Use this command if you want your script to upload a file or a directory of files with FTP. Like the *download* command, you can optionally provide a username and password for authentication (usually required for FTP uploads) and display a progress-bar window. If your script is uploading an entire directory of files, you can use the *choose folder* scripting addition to allow the script user to choose the directory to upload. *choose folder* returns an `alias` to the folder that the user chooses. You can then use this `alias` as a parameter to the *upload* command:

```
tell app "URL Access Scripting" to upload folder_alias to ¬
"ftp:// www. mysite.org" with authentication
```

You have to enclose the *upload* command in a `tell` statement targeting the URL Access Scripting application. Chapter 7 describes the `tell` statement.

to string

Provide the receiving server with this URL string, as in "ftp://www.parkerriver.com". You have to include the protocol ("ftp://") part of the URL. An example is:

```
upload myfile to "ftp://www.mysite.org"
```

replacing yes/no

If a version of the uploaded file already exists on the server, then the upload-command default is `replacing no`. If you want to replace any existing files, use:

```
upload myfile to "ftp://www.mysite.org" replacing yes
```

progress boolean

Display a progress bar for longer tasks such as uploading a directory of files. For example:

```
upload myfolder to "ftp://www.mysite.org/newfiles/" with ¬
authentication and progress
```

The default value for this parameter is `false`.

binhexing boolean

The default value for the *binhexing* parameter is `true`. This encodes the uploaded files for safer transfer across the network. If you do not want to binhex the files, use `binhexing false` in your *upload* command:

```
upload myfile to "ftp://www.mysite.org" replacing yes ¬
binhexing false
```

upload directory boolean

This `true`/`false` parameter uploads an entire directory of files. An example of using the upload directory parameter is:

```
tell application "URL Access Scripting" to (upload fol_alias ¬
to "ftp://www.parkerriver.com/" with progress, ¬
upload directory and authentication)
```

This parameter is `false` by default.

authentication boolean

Many FTP sites require the user to be authenticated with the username and password before they are allowed to upload any files or directories. If you use `authentication true` or `with authentication` with your *upload* command, then the script will display an authentication dialog window that looks like Figure 18-4. This parameter is `false` by default. For example:

```
tell application "URL Access Scripting"
    try -- catch any upload errors
        set fil to (choose file with prompt ¬
        "Choose a file to upload")
        set bool to (upload fil to ¬
        "ftp://www.parkerriver.com/" with authentication  and ¬
        progress)
```

```
        on error errmesg number errnum
        if errnum is not -128 then
            display dialog (errnum as text) & ": " & errmesg & ¬
            return & return & "Applet quitting."
            return
        end if
    end try
end tell
```

PART IV

Scripting Mac OS 9 Control Panels and Extensions

CHAPTER 19

Appearance Control Panel

The Appearance control panel, shown in Figure 19-1, lets the user customize the look and behavior of their desktop, such as its background color, the font for desktop text, the sounds that play when you manipulate window controls, and how window title bars and scroll bars work. These settings can be encapsulated into *themes* that you can name and load using AppleScript and the control panel itself. The Appearance control panel is located in *startup disk:System Folder:Control Panels*.

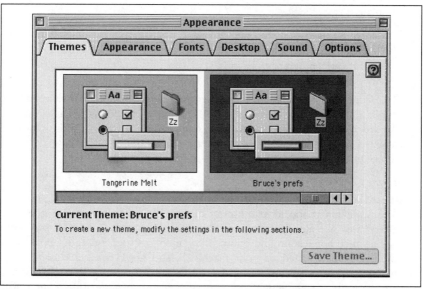

Figure 19-1: Appearance control panel

You can change the current Appearance theme with a bit of AppleScript, such as:

```
tell app "Appearance" to set current theme to theme "Golden Poppy"
```

Then you might want to change it back to your favorite theme once you get a look at "Golden Poppy"!

Appearance Control Panel

Syntax

```
tell app "Appearance" to get picture file of monitor 1 (* returns "no
picture" if the desktop has a color but not a picture *)
```

Dictionary commands

count

This command returns an integer representing a count of certain Appearance objects, such as:

```
count of monitors
```

or:

```
count of themes
```

You can also use the syntax count each theme or count each monitor.

exists

This indicates whether an object exists and returns a boolean value, as in:

```
exists monitor 2
```

This command returns false if the machine is hooked up to only one monitor.

quit

This quits the Appearance application:

```
tell app "Appearance" to quit
```

run

This command sends a *run* Apple event to Appearance, which opens the application if it is not already open. Using this command is not necessary as AppleScript sends an implicit *run* command to the applications that are targeted in a tell statement. Chapter 7, *Flow-Control Statements*, describes the tell statement.

Dictionary classes

Application

The Appearance Application class has two elements: theme and monitor. There are in reality about two dozen theme objects associated with each Appearance application and one or more monitors (depending on how many monitors are attached to your machine). The Application class has the following properties (appearing here in their Dictionary order), all of which are accessible by targeting the Appearance app in a tell statement. The properties are accompanied by their data type in parentheses:

name (string)

> This represents the application's name, as in "Appearance."

frontmost (boolean)

> This returns true if Appearance is the active application on the desktop (i.e., its window is highlighted).

version (version *type, like a* string)

> Use this property, as in

```
tell app "Appearance" to get version
```

> to find out the control panel's version on the machine. You'll have to coerce the **version** property to a **string** to pass it to the *display dialog* osax:

```
version as string
```

current theme (reference)

> This is a **reference** to the selected theme under the Theme tab of the control panel. You can use this property to get information on the current theme:

```
name of current theme
```

appearance (string)

> This property corresponds to the Appearance pop-up menu under the control panel's Appearance tab. This is the name for the overall look of icons, menus, and other desktop elements, as in "Apple platinum."

appearance variant (string)

> This property corresponds to the Variation pop-up menu under the control panel's Appearance tab. It returns a **string** such as "Lavender," representing another variation on the desktop appearance (the dictionary entry of an **integer** return value is wrong).

background pattern (international text)

> This property corresponds to the Patterns list box under the control panel's Desktop tab. It returns the pattern name like "Azul Dark."

highlight color (string)

> This property represents the Highlight Color pop-up menu under the control panel's Appearance tab. You can dynamically change the computer's highlight color for text with code such as set highlight color to "Azul".

highlight color (RGB color)

> You can also pass an RGB Color value to this property to alter the color to a custom hue. RGB Color values are list types with three numbers ranging from 0 to 65535; the integers represent the red, green, and blue components for the custom color. For example, get highlight color as RGB color would return {39321,52428,65535}, which represents the color Azul. Chapter 3, *Data Types,* discusses AppleScript's value types like list.

`minimum font smoothing size` (`integer`)

This corresponds to the "Smooth all fonts on screen" checkbox in the Fonts tab of the control panel. It returns an `integer` representing the minimum-sized font for which the computer will turn on anti-aliasing, a graphics term for smoothing the jagged look of some fonts on the computer screen.

`system font` (`international text`)

This property returns the name of the font your system is using, such as "Charcoal." It corresponds to the Large System Font pop-up menu choice in the control panel's Fonts tab.

`small system font` (`international text`)

This property returns the name of the font your system is using for displaying small text items. It corresponds to the Small System Font pop-up menu in the control panel's Fonts tab.

`views font` (`string`)

This property contains the name of the font the machine is using for views, such as folder listings. An example `views font` value is "Geneva." It corresponds to the Views Font pop-up menu choice in the control panel's Fonts tab.

`views font size` (`integer`)

This is the property for the size of the views font, which is an `integer` (e.g., 10).

`font smoothing` (`boolean`)

This is a `true` or `false` value indicating whether font smoothing is on.

`scroll box style` (`fixed/proportional`)

This property corresponds to the Smart Scrolling checkbox in the Options tab. Unchecked enables `fixed`, and checked is `proportional`. To find out what kind of scroll box setting you have, use code such as:

```
get scroll box style
```

which returns either `fixed` or `proportional`.

`scroll bar arrow style` (`single/both at one end`).

Checking Smart Scrolling in the control panel's Options tab gives your windows both up and down arrows at the bottom of each window scroll bar. Control this with AppleScript code such as the following:

```
set scroll bar arrow style to single
```

`Single`

This produces a single arrow at the top and bottom of the scroll bar. If Smart Scrolling is checked then this value is `both at one end`.

`collapsible via title bar` (`boolean`)

This property, a `true` or `false` value, determines whether clicking on a window's title bar makes the window itself disappear or collapse, except for the title bar. The property corresponds to the "Double-click title bar to collapse windows" checkbox in the Options tab.

sound track (*no sound track/string*)

Checking this property returns either the constant **no sound track** or a string like "Platinum Sounds." This property corresponds to the pop-up menu in the control panel's Sounds tab.

sound effects (*list of constants:* **menu sounds/control sounds/ window sounds/finder sounds**)

You can control which desktop elements (e.g., menus, windows) play sounds when you manipulate them by setting the **sound effects** property to a **list** of constants such as:

> {menu sounds, control sounds}

If **sound track** is set to **no sound track**, then setting the **sound effects** property does not have a practical effect (you still won't have any sounds).

theme

This class encapsulates an individual theme in your Appearance settings. The Appearance application's **current theme** property returns a **reference** to an enabled **theme** object. The **theme** class has zero elements and the following nine properties. All of these properties are the same as the **Application** properties, except that they are read-only; you cannot change their values.

name (**string**; read-only)
appearance (**string**; read-only)
appearance variant (**string**; read-only)
background pattern (**international text**; read-only)
highlight color (**RGB color**; read-only)
system font (**international text**; read-only)
small system font (**international text**; read-only)
views font (**international text**; read-only)
views font size (**integer**; read-only)

Monitor

This class represents the monitor(s) attached to the computer. It has zero elements and the following two properties:

picture file (*no picture/alias*)

This either returns the value **no picture** (a **constant** type, not a **string**) or an **alias** to the picture (which can be coerced to a **string**, as in "Macintosh HD:pics:sunset.jpg").

picture positioning (*automatic/tiled/centered/scaled/filling*)

This is a **constant** value specifying how to display the picture file on the desktop.

Examples

```
global theMessage
tell application "Appearance"
   (* boolean variables *)
   set MyCollapsible to false
   set ScrollBoth to false
   (* test 'collapsible via title bar' property *)
```

```
    if collapsible via title bar then set MyCollapsible to true
    (* check 'scroll bar arrow style' property: can be either 'single' or
'both at one end' *)
    if scroll bar arrow style is both at one end then
        set ScrollBoth to true
    end if
    set theMessage to ¬
    "You can double-click the title bar to collapse the windows: " & ¬
    MyCollapsible & return
    set theMessage to theMessage & ¬
    "The scroll bars have the arrows at one end: " & ScrollBoth & ¬
    return & return
    set theMessage to theMessage & "The current theme is: " & ¬
    (name of current theme)
    set theMessage to theMessage & return & "The appearance prop is: " & ¬
    (appearance of current theme)
end tell
(* use display dialog osax to display the values of these Appearance
properties *)
display dialog theMessage
```

CHAPTER 20

Apple Data Detectors Extension

Apple Data Detectors (ADD) is a technology that Apple Computer introduced during the late 1990s. It allows a scripter to specify an AppleScript for the processing of certain types of information that users encounter in desktop windows, such as web site addresses or geographic locations. Apple Data Detectors are designed to identify these important snippets of data, including email and Newsgroup addresses, in almost any application window you might be working in. Figure 20-1 shows the Apple Data Detectors 1.02 control panel.

On	Name	Kind
▷ ✓	**Email Address**	Category
▷ ✓	**FTP**	Category
▷ ✓	**Host**	Category
▷ ✓	**HTTP**	Category
▷ ✓	**Newsgroup**	Category

Apple Data Detectors

Configure the items that Apple Data Detectors look for and what actions to take for each category:

Item Information:

For item information, select an item in the list.

Apple Data Detectors Status:

Apple Data Detectors is ready for use.

Figure 20-1: Apple Data Detectors control panel

For example, you might be in AppleWorks, WordPerfect, or Microsoft Word and come upon a Uniform Resource Locator (URL) that you want to open up in your browser and visit. Or you find an email address of someone to whom you would like to send an instant email message. Rather than manually cut and paste the URL or email address into another application (which might not even be running at the time), ADD allows you to select the text or paragraph that contains the text and then *Control-click* the selection. Up pops a contextual menu in the canvas space of the window. The menu contains a list of actions that you can perform with the selected data—even if you just selected a whole paragraph surrounding the text. ADD is designed to look for and pull out evidence of the specified data in the chunk of selected text, such as protocol strings (e.g., "http," "ftp") or Newsgroup prefixes such as "comp."

These menu actions might include the text "Open URL in Netscape Communicator" or "New OutLook Express Message Recipient." Once you choose the action in the contextual menu, an AppleScript is executed to process just the snippet of text that you are targeting! ADD does not always work as intended, however; you have to experiment, test, and debug.

ADD has to be installed on your system before you can use it. As of the spring of 2001, you can download and install ADD 1.02 from the following address:

http://www.apple.com/applescript/data_detectors/updates.00.html

The ADD installation puts dozens of Apple's "actions" or scripts inside of *startup disk:System Folder:Apple Data Detectors:Actions*, along with the Internet Address Detectors (IAD) software. IAD detects web URLs, email addresses, FTP sites, Internet hostnames (*www.apple.com*), and USENET newsgroups in window text. With separate downloads, you can also install U.S. Geographic Detectors, which can recognize city or state references such as "San Francisco, CA." One of the associated geographic actions looks up a map for the selected city at the Yahoo! map web site. Apple has also promised to release a Currency Detectors package that will work with currency formats (e.g., $1,200) in various languages.

This is powerful functionality, yet the technology gets even more inspiring when you imagine all of the AppleScripts you can *write yourself* and use with ADD. While the ADD control panel itself is minimally scriptable with Mac OS 9 (you can send it basic Apple events such as *activate*), the types of scripts that you can develop and trigger by using the *Apple Data Detectors Scripting* osax offer greater possibilities. (Appendix A, *Standard Scripting Additions*, goes into detail about scripting additions or osax.) The script in the Examples section creates a new Outlook Express email message from any email addresses that Internet Address Detectors detect.

Apple Data Detectors

Syntax

```
(*
Identify detector in Script Editor Description window with the
package::detector-name syntax as in Apple::Email Address  for the Email
Address Internet Address Detector.
*)
```

```
Apple::Email Address  -- Name of detector to handle
New OutLook Express Message Recipient  (* string that will appear in
contextual menu *)
(*
end of Script Editor Description Window phrases
*)
(*
define the handle detection routine ; it has a parameter of data type
record that contains the detected text
*)
on handle detection theDetector
    --actual script with 'handle detection' handler, statements, and code
...
end handle detection
```

Dictionary commands

handle detection (from the Apple Data Detectors Scripting osax)

This event is fired when the user chooses the action containing this routine in the contextual menu. For example, the user might select and *Control-click* the text "user@hersite.com." The resulting contextual menu may have a submenu displaying the title "New OutLook Express Message Recipient." If the user chooses this title in the contextual menu, then the script action associated with that title is executed and it calls its *handle detection* routine. This routine stores the `detector instance`, an object of type `record`, in the handle-detection routine's parameter. An example code snippet is: on `handle detection theDetector...end handle detection` (`theDetector` is the parameter or `detector instance`). For example, an email-related script could find out the selected email address with the code:

```
detected text of theDetector
```

(which might evaluate to a `string` such as "user@hersite.com"). The functionality you want this action script to have is defined in the *handle detection* routine, including calling other functions.

Dictionary classes

`detector instance` *(from the Apple Data Detectors Scripting osax)*

This class represents a `record` type sent as a parameter to the *handle detection* routine of your action scripts. The `detector instance record` has the following properties:

name *(string)*

This is the name of the detector that detected the text, as in "Apple::Email Address."

detected text *(string)*

This is the `string` that was detected by the detector identified in the `name` property, as in "theuser@hersite.com."

sub detections *(list)*

`sub detections` is a property of type `list`; each `item` of this `list` is data of type `record`. Not very many detectors return anything but an empty `list` for this property. Some detectors return a list of `record` objects. Consider, for example, the Apple US Geographic::USCityState detector. If you wrote an action script for this detector, then you could obtain the detected city/state string (e.g., "San Francisco, CA") by using the code (if the variable theDetector was the parameter for the *handle detections* routine):

```
detected text of theDetector
```

Let's say the string the user had selected was "San Francisco, CA." The property

```
sub detections of theDetector
```

would contain a list of records that looks like this: { {name: "theCity",detected text:"San Francisco"}, {name: "theSeparator", detected text: ","}, {name: "theState", detected text: "CA"} }. Each of the three records in this sub detections list contains two properties—name and detected text—with strings for the property values. A list of records is certainly difficult to look at. Another way to conceive of sub detections is as an array that contains associative arrays as array elements.

Examples

```
on handle detection theDetector
    try
        set emailAdd to detected text of theDetector    (* store the
detected text in a variable *)
        set theSubject to the text returned of ¬
        (display dialog "Please enter the email subject:" ¬
        default answer "" buttons {"Okay", "Cancel"} ¬
            default button 1)
          set theContent to the text returned of ¬
          (display dialog "Please ¬
    enter the message content:" default answer  "" buttons {"Okay",  ¬
            "Cancel"} default button 1)
        tell application "Outlook Express"
            activate
            make new draft window with properties {subject:theSubject, ¬
            content:theContent, to recipients:emailAdd} (* make a new
            email-message window *)
        end tell
        on error errMessage
        display dialog "You could not create a new email message" & ¬
        " due to the following  error:" & errMessage
    end try
end handle detection
```

You have to install any new detectors that you download by using the Apple Data Detectors control panel. Use the File → Install Detector File… command from the control panel's window. Use the File → Install Action File… command to install the AppleScripts or actions that you write for Apple Data Detectors. Once installed, the actions are kept in the directory *startup disk:System Folder:Apple Data Detectors:Actions.*

When you write an ADD action, you have to include certain information in the Script Editor Description field, or the ADD control panel will not install the action.

The Description field is a text area at the top of the Script Editor window (*Chapter 2* is devoted to Script Editor). This information includes the detector that is used to handle the action, as in Apple::HTTP for the HTTP detector, and the action title that the contextual menu will display. The contextual menu displays when the user Control-clicks some selected text that contains data which ADD looks for, such as a web site address. The next example shows the text that you must add to the Script Editor Description field for a script that opens a web site in Internet Explorer:

```
(* the first two lines go in the Script Editor Description field *)
Apple::HTTP  -- Name of detector to handle
Get website in IE4.5  -- Contextual menu string
on handle detection decRecord
    set theURL to detected text of decRecord
    tell application "Internet Explorer 4.5"
      Activate
      OpenURL theURL
    end tell
end handle detection
```

Table 20-1 shows the detector names that scripters use with their action scripts. The first four detector names identify the detectors that are a part of the Internet Address Detectors package; the last two are part of the U.S. Geographic Detectors package.

Table 20-1: Detector Packages and Names

Detector Name	Package
Apple::FTP	Internet Address Detectors
Apple::Host	Internet Address Detectors
Apple::HTTP	Internet Address Detectors
Apple::Newsgroup	Internet Address Detectors
Apple US Geographic::USCityState	U.S. Geographic Detectors
Apple US Geographic::USState	U.S. Geographic Detectors

The AppleScript statements that you include outside of the *handle detection* subroutine do not run when the action script executes, unless you include them in another routine that *handle detection* calls. For example, the statement:

```
display dialog "I am called in handle detection"
```

executes because it is part of a *doDisplay* function that is called by *handle detection*:

```
On handle detection decRecord
    Set theSel to detected text of decRecord
    Display dialog "here's what you selected: " & theSel ¬
    doDisplay()
End handle detection

On doDisplay()
    display dialog "I am called in handle detection"
End doDisplay
```

CHAPTER 21

Apple Menu Options Control Panel

Apple Menu Options is a scriptable control panel that configures the Apple menu. This is the sticky menu that drops down from the little apple icon at the upper left corner of your screen. The Apple menu shows what's inside the directory *startup disk:System Folder:Apple Menu Items* as a hierarchical menu. This is where the user can gain quick access to Chooser, Apple System Profiler, Network Browser, as well as the control panels and the contents of any folder (or alias to that folder) that you place in this location. For example, placing an alias in the Apple Menu Items folder will display the contents of that aliased folder from the Apple menu, as well as submenus showing what is in any nested folders. Handy!

Figure 21-1 shows the grand total of five elements that you can configure from this control panel. Recent applications, documents, and servers are menu items under the Apple menu that provide links via submenus to, for instance, the recent documents you have had open on your computer. You can script these features using this control panel's application object (Chapter 1, *AppleScript: An Introduction,* describes Apple event object models and application objects).

Apple Menu Options

Syntax

```
tell app "Apple Menu Options"
    activate
    set recentStuff to recent items enabled (* this is an Apple Menu
    Options property *)
end tell
```

Dictionary commands

quit

This command quits the control panel (i.e., it is no longer running and loaded into memory).

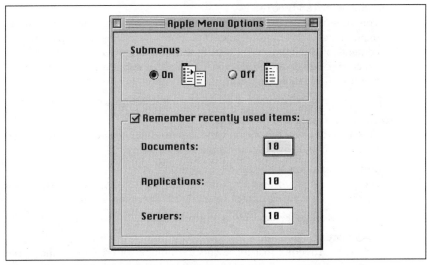

Figure 21-1: Apple Menu Options control panel

run

Sending the *run* command is the same as double-clicking the control panel or choosing it from the Apple menu Control Panels submenu.

get (reference to an object)

Use this command to get the value of a property, such as:

```
tell app "Apple Menu Options" to get submenus enabled
```

get returns the value of the property.

as (class)

You can use the optional labeled parameter **as**, followed by data of type **class**, to specify the type of data to return (rather than the default, which is a **boolean** or **integer** for this control panel's properties).

set (reference to an object)

Change how the Apple menu behaves by setting a value, such as:

```
tell app "Apple Menu Options" to set maximum recent documents to 12
```

This code stores up to 12 aliases to the documents that you had open recently.

to

The **to** labeled parameter is required; otherwise the app would not know what value the script wants to set the property to.

Dictionary classes

application

This class represents the Apple Menu Options control panel. It has the following five properties. To obtain the values of these properties, use code such as:

```
tell app "Apple Menu Options" to get maximum recent documents
```

submenus enabled (*boolean*)

This returns `true` if passing the mouse over a folder item in the Apple menu, such as Control Panels, produces a submenu displaying the contents of that folder. You usually want this feature enabled in order to execute control panels. But you can remove submenus from the Apple menu with code such as:

```
tell app "Apple Menu Options" to set submenus enabled to false.
```

recent items enabled (*boolean*)

This is a `true`/`false` value indicating whether the Apple menu keeps track of recent items, such as applications, documents, or servers.

maximum recent applications (*integer*)

Scripters can get or set the number of apps the Apple menu creates aliases for by viewing or changing this `integer` property value:

```
set maxApps to maximum recent applications.
```

maximum recent documents (*integer*)

This is an `integer` that represents the number of documents the Apple menu displays in its *Recent Documents* folder.

maximum recent servers (*integer*)

This command represents the number of recent servers that the Apple menu displays, as in:

```
set maximum recent servers to 4
```

Examples

```
tell app "Apple Menu Options"
    (* Set your preferences for the Apple menu *)
    set submenus enabled to true
    set recent items enabled to true
    set maximum recent applications to 6
    set maximum recent documents to 12
    set maximum recent  servers to 1
end tell
```

CHAPTER 22

Application Switcher Extension

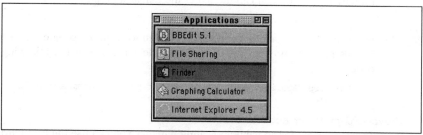

Rest your gaze upon the upper right hand corner of the Mac screen and you find the subtle but handy Application menu. It displays the icons and names of the programs that are currently running, including the Finder. By simply selecting this portion of your screen and dragging the mouse, you can tear off the menu and convert it to a floating palette. This small window is called the Application Switcher, shown in Figure 22-1. You can also cycle through the running apps by using the keyboard combination *Command-Tab* or a different combination that can be controlled with AppleScript.

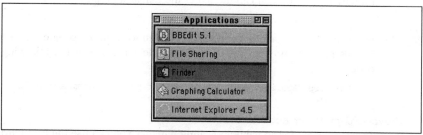

Figure 22-1: Application Switcher palette

With AppleScript, you set the size, orientation (vertical or horizontal), and position of the floating palette by altering the properties of Application Switcher's **window** class. You can also recreate the keyboard combination you use to cycle through the open programs and the order in which the programs are displayed in the palette (e.g., ordered by when they were launched). The following description of commands and classes applies to Application Switcher Version 1.0, which is installed with Mac OS 9.

Application Switcher

Syntax

```
tell app "Application Switcher"
    set palette's orientation to vertical -- programs are displayed top to
bottom
end tell
```

Dictionary commands

run

This launches the application if it isn't running and is the same as double-clicking its icon.

quit

This command quits Application Switcher, releasing its memory resources.

Dictionary classes

application

This class represents the Application Switcher application. It has the following five properties, which can be accessed simply by referring to them within a:

```
tell app "Application Switcher"
```

block, as in:

```
tell app "Application Switcher" to set palette's button ordering to ¬
alphabetical
```

palette (window *object*)

This property returns as a **window** object the palette that displays all the running programs. You can then alter the palette's properties, as in:

```
set palette's position to upper left
```

For example, you can show only the program icons in the palette (so that it does not take up very much room on the screen) with the following code:

```
tell app "Application Switcher" to set palette's names visible ¬
to false
```

keyboard cycling active (boolean)

This is a **true**/**false** value indicating whether you can use the keyboard combination, *Command-Tab* or otherwise, to switch from one open program to another. See "cycling keystroke" for how to set your own keyboard combination for this cycling behavior.

cycling keystroke (keystroke *object*)

You can set the keyboard combination for cycling through open programs (each program will become the highlighted program on the desktop in sequence as you press this key combo). This example changes this cycling keystroke to *Control-F1*:

```
tell application "Application Switcher"
    set stroke to {key:F1 key, modifiers:{control down}}
    set cycling keystroke to stroke
end tell
```

The `keystroke` object takes the form of a `record` type, a series of property/value pairs separated by commas and contained within curly braces ({ }). You can set its `key` property to either a `string` (e.g., "p") or a constant like `tab key`, `up arrow key`, or `F1 key`. Its `modifiers` property is also set to a constant such as `control down`. So the value of the cycling keystroke property can be set to a `record` such as the following:

    {key:F1 key, modifiers:{control down}}

quit delay *(constants* default/never *or* integer*)*

Accessing this property will return the constants `default`, `never`, or an `integer` representing the number of seconds, approximately, of delay before the application quits. By changing this property, I did not see any change in the Switcher's behavior when it was quit or its window was hidden. Anyway, even if you quit Application Switcher, say by using its *quit* command, you can quickly reproduce the palette by dragging with the mouse from the upper corner.

credits *(*string*)*

This is a self-congratulatory message from the Application Switcher programmers.

keystroke

The keystroke object is returned by the Application Switcher's `cycling keystroke` property (see its description in this chapter). This class has `key` and `modifiers` properties.

key *(*string *or constant)*

This property can be set to either an alphanumeric keyboard character such as "h" or one of the following constants:

clear key	F8 key
delete key	F9 key
down arrow key	forward del key
end key	help key
enter key	home key
escape key	left arrow key
F1 key	page down key
F2 key	page up key
F3 key	return key
F4 key	right arrow key
F5 key	tab key
F6 key	up arrow key
F7 key	

See the next example and the "cycling keystroke" description for more details.

modifiers *(list of constants)*

`modifiers` can be a `list` of any of the following constants: `option down`/ `command down`/`control down`/`caps lock down`. If you want to cycle through your open apps with the F1 key pressed together with the control key, the value of the keystroke object is:

    {key:F1 key, modifiers:{control down}}

window
: This class represents the Switcher's floating palette. The application class' `palette` property returns a `window` object; you can then control its display and behavior with the following properties.

properties *(record)*
: The value of this `record` type is all of the open palette's properties. Here's an example:

```
{position:{943, 288}, bounds:{943, 288, 1039, 432}, anchor
point:upper left, button ordering:launch order, constraint:none,
frame visible:true, icon size:small, name width:72, names
visible:true, orientation:vertical, visible:true}
```

You can create a custom Switcher palette by setting the application's palette to your own `record` value, as in the following (add a `record` value like the preceding example):

```
tell app "Application Switcher" to set palette's properties to ...
```

visible *(boolean)*
: A `true`/`false` value determining whether the palette is visible.

orientation *(horizontal/vertical)*
: The palette in Figure 14-1, for example, is in the `vertical` orientation.

position *(point object or constants* upper left/upper right/lower left/ lower right.)
: You can set the palette position with one of the four constants (e.g., upper right) or a point in the top left corner of the window, as in:

```
set palette's position to {50, 150}
```

This code moves the palette to the position 50 pixels from the left border of the screen and 150 pixels down.

bounds *(bounding rectangle)*
: You can also establish the palette's position as a list of four coordinates, such as {943, 288, 1039, 432}. See the Examples section at the end of this chapter.

anchor point *(constants* upper left *or* lower right)
: Get or set the anchor point of the palette to either of the two constants. This prop does not affect the way a vertical palette can be dragged in size, however. You can only drag the window horizontally to the point where the longest program name is fully displayed.

button ordering *(constant)*
: This property can be set to one of the following constants: alphabetical/ launch order/reverse alphabetical/reverse launch order.

constraint *(constants* none, all monitors, *or* one monitor)
: You can display the palette on one or more monitors connected to the computer.

frame visible *(boolean)*
: You can remove the title bar of the Application Switcher's palette with a phrase such as:

```
set palette's frame visible to false
```

The palette can still be moved around the screen by Command-clicking it.

icon size *(small or large)*

Use this property to control the size of icons in the palette.

names visible *(boolean)*

This property is a true/false value that determines whether the palette will display only icons or icons and program names.

name width *(integer)*

Set the amount of space that Switcher devotes to the program names to the pixel width of your choice. If it cannot fit in the palette, the program name will be truncated with an ellipses (...) added to the end of it.

Example

```
(* This script sets the bounds of Switcher based on the bounds of a Word
window *)

(* Find out how many programs are running that are displayed in Switcher
so that we can set the height of the palette; 24 pixels per program
including the Finder. The script uses the Finder's application processes
property, then does not count the background processes that do not
display in the Switcher *)

tell application "Finder"
    set noDisplay to
    {"Control Strip Extension", "DAVE Sharing Extension", ¬
    "HP Background", "Time Synchronizer", "File Sharing Extension", ¬
    "ShareWay IP Personal Bgnd", "Application Switcher", ¬
    "Time  Synchronizer"}
    set procs to application processes -- list of running processes
    set counter to 0 -- count of processes that are displayed
    repeat with p in procs
        set n to (name of p) -- name of app like "Script Editor"
        (* count the app if it is not in the list of programs that don't
display in Switcher *)
        if noDisplay does not contain n then set counter to counter + 1
    end repeat
end tell
set counter to counter + 1 (* include the Finder in apps that are
displayed in Switcher *)
tell application "Microsoft Word"
    activate
    (* Get the bounds of this window *)
    set wdbounds to bounds of window 1
end tell
tell application "Application Switcher"
    (* set X coordinate of palette's upper left corner to 5 pixels to the
right of the Word window.  If Word window bounds are {52, 99, 983, 720}
then item 3 of the bounds is 983 *)
    set rightpoint to (item 3 of wdbounds) + 5
    (* we want the palette height to be the number of displayed apps times
24 pixels *)
    set height to counter * 24
```

(* set palette bounds to 5 pixels to the right of Word win, one and a
half inches from the top of the screen (about 108 pixels), a width of 127
pixels, and a height of 108 plus (the number of programs * 24 pixels).
The Switcher will dynamically accommodate all the displayed programs in
the palette height anyway *)

    set palette's bounds to {rightpoint, 108, (rightpoint + 127), (108 + ¬
    height)}

    log palette's bounds -- check out the new bounds in Event Log window
end tell

CHAPTER 23

ColorSync Extension

The scriptable ColorSync extension is used to synchronize the color inputs and outputs of monitors, scanners, printers, and other devices to help ensure that the graphics the devices produce have consistent color. ColorSync uses embedded International Color Consortium (ICC) profiles in images. The profiles contain information about the color capabilities of the device that produced the image. For example, if you save an image as a jpeg with an embedded ICC profile, then ColorSync compares this profile with the printer's color profile in order to reproduce the image's colors in the printed document as well as it can. An Apple Computer ColorSync site is *http://www.apple.com/colorsync.*

In AppleScript, you can create droplets that manage the embedded profiles of the images that you drag onto the droplet.

A droplet is a type of script file that will process the files whose icons you drag onto the droplet's icon. See Chapter 2, *Using Script Editor with OS 9 and OS X,* for details.

Only certain image-file types, such as JPEG, PICT, and TIFF, can have embedded ICC profiles. The directory *startup disk:AppleScript Extras:ColorSync Extras:AppleScript Files* contains a number of ColorSync droplets you can use with these files. Dozens of ICC profile files are located in *startup disk:System Folder: ColorSync Profiles.*

If you try to extract a profile from an image type that does not support embedded profiles (TIFF, JPEG, and PICT *do* support ICC profiles), then ColorSync Extension will not return any value from the script command. In general, check the image's file type before you open it with ColorSync Extension (e.g., a jpeg image's file type is JPEG).

ColorSync

Syntax

```
tell app "Colorsync Extension"
  (* embed ICC profile referred to by the variable profFile in the image
file represented by variable jpegImage *)
  embed jpegImage with source profFile
end tell
```

The following commands and classes derive from ColorSync Extension Version 3.0, which is installed with Mac OS 9.

Dictionary commands

run

> This opens the ColorSync application as an invisible or faceless background application (i.e., one that doesn't have a graphical user interface).

quit

> This quits the ColorSync Extension application.

open object reference

> This opens an image to inspect its profile (see the Examples section). This command returns a reference to the opened image.

save object reference

> This command saves an image file with a new ICC profile, for instance.

> ### in alias
>
> > This provides an `alias` file path for saving the image file.

close object reference

> This closes an image file, as in:
>
> ```
> close imgFile saving in alias "Macintosh HD:Desktop ¬
> Folder:cowgirl2.jpg"
> ```
>
> ### saving yes/no
>
> > If you have embedded a new ICC profile in an image file, you probably would want to:
> >
> > ```
> > close imgFile saving yes
> > ```
> >
> > As you might have guessed, this code saves the image file before the script closes it; you can close the file without a save with the `saving no` parameter.
>
> ### saving in alias
>
> > This saves an open object in an `alias` file before closing it:
> >
> > ```
> > close imgFile saving in ¬
> > (alias "macintosh hd:desktop folder:cowgirl.jpg")
> > ```

embed alias

> This command embeds an image with an ICC profile from the *System Folder:ColorSync Profiles* folder, as in:
>
> ```
> embed imgFile with source profile "Apple Studio Display"
> ```

with source profile *object*

This required labeled parameter identifies the ICC `profile` object you want to embed in the file. You can either use a specific profile, as in:

```
profile "Apple Studio Display"
```

or a variable that refers to a `profile` object. See the `profile` class in this chapter.

matching with *constant*

Follow the `matching with` optional labeled parameter with one of these constants: `perceptual intent`/`relative colorimetric intent`/`saturation intent`/`absolute colorimetric intent`. These terms specify the "rendering intent," which affects how the colors of the image with its embedded profile are rendered on the destination device, such as a monitor.

using quality `normal`/`draft`/`best`

Optionally specify another parameter for rendering the image with one of the three constants.

saving into *file specification*

If you include this optional labeled parameter with a folder name, then a new file is created in that folder with the same name as the original file. The original file is modified if this labeled parameter is not used. This example asks the user for a file in which to embed the "Apple Studio Display" ICC profile, then saves it in the folder of the user's choice:

```
set nfile to (choose file of type {"JPEG", "TIFF", "PICT"})
set folSpec to (choose folder)
tell application "ColorSync Extension"
    embed nfile with source profile "Apple Studio Display" ¬
    saving into folSpec
end tell
```

replacing *boolean*

This is an optional `true`/`false` value that specifies the replacement of an existing file with the newly embedded file.

unembed *alias*

This command removes any embedded ICC profiles from an image specified in the `alias` parameter.

saving into *file specification*

You can save the file, now with its ICC profiles removed, to a different file than the original. The user may choose the new destination file with the *choose file* scripting addition. Or, if the user chooses a folder instead in response to the *choose folder* osax, then an image file with the same name as the original file will be saved into the folder (but this new file is sans ICC profiles). This is demonstrated in the prior example, which uses the *embed* command that also has a `saving into` labeled parameter.

replacing *boolean*

This is a `true`/`false` value that specifies the replacement of an existing file with the newly unembedded file.

match alias

Use this command to match an image with a destination profile, such as a profile for a certain printer. You can let the user choose a file for this command with the *choose file* scripting addition. See the Examples section to learn how to choose both the image file and the ICC profile before initiating the *match* command.

from source profile *object*

This includes an optional source profile for the match, as in:

```
from source theProf (* theProf is a variable containing a
profile object *)
```

to destination profile *object*

This specifies the destination profile or the profile associated with the device on which the image will be displayed. See the Examples section for a demonstration of this labeled parameter's usage.

matching with *constant*

This labeled parameter takes one of the "rendering intent" constants: perceptual intent/relative colorimetric intent/saturation intent/absolute colorimetric intent. This setting affects how the colors of the image are rendered on the destination devices, such as monitors or printers.

using quality normal/draft/best

Specify the optional match quality with one of these three constants, as in:

```
using quality best
```

saving into file specification

You can use the *choose folder* or *choose file* scripting additions to provide this labeled parameter with a file spec. If you use *choose folder*, then the matched image file is saved with the original file's name to the folder the user specifies.

replacing boolean

This is an optional true/false value indicating whether to replace the existing image file. For example:

```
set nfile to (choose file of type {"JPEG", "TIFF", "PICT"})
(* get the list of profiles from ColorSync Profiles folder *)
set pfol to list folder ¬
"macintosh hd:system folder:colorsync profiles"
set prof to choose from list pfol ¬
without multiple selections allowed
tell application "ColorSync Extension"
    set theProf to (profile (item 1 of prof))
    match nfile to destination theProf
end tell
```

proof alias

This command allows you to proof an image or preview the printed results of an image on the system's display without outputting the image to the printer.

from source profile *object*

> Specify an optional source profile for the match. See the profile class in this chapter.

to destination profile *object*

> This is a required labeled parameter specifying the destination profile, such as a printer's ICC profile. See the profile class.

matching with *constant*

> This optional labeled parameter takes one of the rendering intent constants: perceptual intent/relative colorimetric intent/ saturation intent/absolute colorimetric intent. *matching with* specifies the rendering intent for matching between the source and destination profiles. This setting affects how the colors of the image are rendered on the destination devices, such as monitors or printers.

onto proof profile *object*

> This is a required parameter that references the proof profile for the color match. See the profile class description in this chapter for more information on profile objects.

proofing with *constant*

> This optional labeled parameter takes one of the rendering intent constants. *proofing with* specifies the rendering intent for matching colors between the destination and proof profiles. The rendering-intent setting affects how the colors of the image are rendered on the destination devices, such as monitors or printers.

using quality normal/draft/best

> This is an optional parameter corresponding to the match quality, as in:
>
>   using quality normal

replacing boolean

> This is an optional true/false value indicating whether to replace the existing image file.

match link **alias**

Match a file with a "device link profile," a series of profiles corresponding to a specific configuration of devices.

through link profile *object*

> Use this required labeled parameter to identify the device link profile with a reference to a profile object, such as:
>
>   match link imgFile through link theProf (* theProf contains the
>   profile object *)

matching with constant

> This optional labeled parameter takes one of the rendering intent constants. This setting affects how the colors of the image are rendered on the destination device.

using quality normal/draft/best

> This is an optional labeled parameter you follow with one of the three constants.

`saving into file specification`

If you include this optional labeled parameter with a folder name, then a new file is created in that folder with the same name as the original file. The original file is modified if this labeled parameter is not used.

`replacing boolean`

This is an optional `true`/`false` value indicating whether to replace the existing image file.

Dictionary classes

`application`

The `application` class represents the ColorSync Extension app. It has numerous properties and contains three elements: `profile`, `image`, and `display` (each of these classes is described elsewhere in this chapter). For example, you can get a reference to the monitor's default ICC profile with code such as the following:

```
tell app "ColorSync Extension" to set monProf to (display profile ¬
of  display 1)
```

This code first gets a reference to one of the ColorSync application's `display` elements (i.e., display 1), which will be `display 1` if you are deprived like me and have only one monitor connected to your computer. It then sets a `monProf` variable to the `display profile` property of the `display` object. This property is itself a `profile` object. The value of `monProf` could be:

```
profile "Generic RGB Profile"
```

Every one of the properties is settable (not read-only) except for the `profile folder`.

The following are `application` elements:

`profile`

This is a `profile` type. You can get a reference or set a variable to one of the application class' profiles by using a numerical index:

```
tell application "ColorSync Extension" to get profile 1
```

See the `profile` class description.

`image`

ColorSync Extension has image elements if a script uses the *open* command to open a JPG, PICT, or TIFF file, for instance. These open images can be identified by their index, as in:

```
get image 1
```

This code in turn might return a value such as:

```
image "kayak.JPG" of application "ColorSync Extension"
```

See the `image` class description.

`display`

The application's `display` objects represent the monitor(s) you have connected to your computer. See the `display` class description.

The following are `application` properties:

`system profile location` (alias)

This property returns an `alias` reference to the file that contains the system profile, as in:

```
file "Macintosh HD:System Folder:ColorSync Profiles:Generic ¬
RGB Profile"
```

The profiles all live in the *System Folder:ColorSync Profiles* folder.

`default RGB profile location` (alias)

The return value for this property is the file that contains the default RGB profile. Use code such as:

```
tell application "ColorSync Extension" to set defRGBpath to ¬
    default RGB profile location
```

`default CMYK profile location` (alias)

The return value for this property is the file that contains the default CMYK profile. All of these profiles live in the *System Folder:ColorSync Profiles* folder.

`default Lab profile location` (alias)

The return value for this property is the file that contains the default Lab profile. The return value might look like

```
file "Macintosh HD:System Folder:ColorSync Profiles:" & ¬
"Generic Lab Profile"
```

`default XYZ profile location` (alias)

The return value for this property is the file that contains the default XYZ profile.

`default Gray profile location` (alias)

The return value for this property is the file that contains the default Gray profile. Like all other profile files, it is located in the *System Folder:ColorSync Profiles* folder.

`system profile` (profile *object*)

Unlike the "location" properties, which return `alias` types involving file pathnames, these properties return the various ICC profiles as `profile` objects. See the `profile` class description.

`default RGB profile` (profile *object*)

This property returns the default RGB profile as a `profile` object. See the `profile` class description for information on the `profile` object's properties. Use code such as:

```
tell app "ColorSync Extension" to set defRGB to ¬
default RGB profile
```

`default CMYK profile` (profile *object*)

This property returns the default CMYK profile as a `profile` object. See the `profile` class description.

`default Lab profile` (profile *object*)

This property returns the default Lab profile as a `profile` object. See the `profile` class description.

default XYZ profile (profile *object)*

This property returns the default XYZ profile as a profile object. See the profile class description.

default Gray profile (profile *object)*

This property returns the default Gray profile as a profile object. See the profile class description.

preferred CMM (automatic *constant or other type)*

You can get or set this property; it returns the constant automatic or another Color Match Method like Apple CMM or Heidelberg CMM (this method can also be set in the ColorSync control panel).

profile folder (alias, *read-only)*

This property returns a reference to the *System folder:ColorSync Profiles* folder.

quit delay (immediate/default/never *or* integer*)*

This property specifies how long the application will idle (await another command) before quitting. It can be either one of the three constants or an integer representing the number of seconds before the idling app will quit. For example, if you:

```
set quit delay to 60
```

the application will idle for 60 seconds and, if you do not send it any Apple events, it will then quit.

profile

This class represents a ColorSync ICC profile object. Once you have stored a profile object in a variable, then you can access its properties and/or set some of them. The Example section at the end of this chapter gets and displays a bunch of the props for a JPEG image's embedded profile.

size (integer*; read-only)*

This is the size of the profile in bytes.

preferred CMM *(type class)*

This is the profile's Color Match Method (e.g., Apple CMM).

version (international text*)*

This property returns the version as a **string** of the profile.

device class (constant*; read-only)*

This property returns any of the following constants: monitor/input/ output/link/abstract/colorspace/named.

color space *(constant; read-only)*

color space, an indication of whether the profile represents the RGB, CMYK, or gray color space, returns any of the following constants: RGB/ CMYK/Lab/XYZ/Gray/Five channel/Six channel/Seven channel/ Eight channel/Five color/Six color/Seven color/Eight color/ Named.

connection space (Lab/XYZ*; read-only)*

If it has a connection-space value, this property returns one of two constants.

creation date (date)

This returns the profile's creation date as a date object, such as:

date "Tuesday, February 18, 1997 10:56:57 AM"

platform (property type)

This property is returned as a four-character type such as 'APPL'.

quality (normal/draft/best)

A profile's quality is one of these three constants.

device manufacturer (property type)

If the profile does not represent a device such as a printer or monitor then this returns none. Otherwise, a profile such as "HP ScanJet IICX/T" returns a value such as "HP."

device model (integer)

This property returns an integer such as a serial number.

rendering intent (constant)

This returns one of the following constants: perceptual intent/ relative colorimetric intent/saturation intent/absolute colorimetric intent.

creator (property type)

This property returns a creator type or code such as "KODA" for the profile "3M Matchprint Euroscale."

name (international text)

This returns the text name of the profile.

location (alias)

This property returns an alias or file path to the profile.

image

The image object has one or more embedded profile objects and three different properties, all of them read-only (not settable). You can extract property values from images after they have been opened by ColorSync Extension.

The following are image elements:

profile (profile object)

This is an object representing an embedded ICC profile. See the profile class.

The following are image properties:

color space (constant; read-only)

This returns one of the following constants: RGB/CMYK/Lab/XYZ/Gray/ Five channel/Six channel/Seven channel/Eight channel/Five color/Six color/Seven color/Eight color/Named.

name (international text; read-only)

This property is the text name of the image.

location (alias; read-only)

This property returns the image's file path location on the computer:

```
set img to (choose file of type {"JPEG", "TIFF", "PICT"})
tell application "ColorSync Extension"
```

```
                    set imgfile to (open img)
                    set imginfo to imgfile's name & " : " & ¬
                    imgfile's color space & return & imgfile's location
                end tell
                display dialog imginfo
```

display

This object represents a monitor connected to the computer. For example, if you have one monitor, you can access this object with code such as:

```
        tell app "ColorSync Extension" to get display 1
```

number (integer)

This returns the index number of the display as in:

```
        display 1
```

name (international text)

This property returns the text name of the monitor.

display profile (profile *object*)

This returns the ICC profile associated with the display as a profile object.

Examples

```
    tell application "ColorSync Extension"
        (* open a jpeg image and display a bunch of the properties for its
    embedded ICC profile *)
        set img to (open alias "Macintosh HD:Desktop Folder:cowgirl.jpg")
        set theProf to profile 1 of img (* theProf refers to one embedded
    profile *)
        (* gather some profile object properties on this profile in a string
        variable called mesg; display them in a dialog box with the display
        dialog scripting addition *)
        set mesg to "Profile name: " & name of theProf & return
        set mesg to mesg & "preferred CMM: " & preferred CMM of theProf & ¬
        return
        set mesg to mesg & "device class: " & device class of theProf & return
        set mesg to mesg & "color space: " & color space of theProf & return
        set mesg to mesg & "creation date: " & creation date of theProf & ¬
        return
        set mesg to mesg & "platform: " & platform of theProf & return
        set mesg to mesg & "device namufacturer: " & device manufacturer of ¬
        theProf & return
        set mesg to mesg & "device model: " & device model of theProf & return
        set mesg to mesg & "quality: " & quality of theProf & return
    end tell
    display dialog mesg
```

CHAPTER 24

File Exchange Control Panel

At some time or another, every Mac user has dealt with files that they inherited over a network from a PC or Unix OS and then cannot open in any of their applications. A simple example is the familiar *.html* files that a web developer grabs over a network to work on (basically, text files that can be viewed in a browser). They appear on the desktop as a featureless icon and cannot be opened from the browser's File menu. This is because these files have no Mac file type or creator type that the Mac OS can identify them with. The File Exchange control panel was designed to deal with these frustrating situations. You can do two things with this application:

- Map a file extension like *.htm* or *.html* to a particular Mac OS creator type and file type, so that whenever files with these extensions are downloaded the Mac OS knows what to do with them. In File Exchange parlance this process is called "extension mapping." This is handled in the PC Exchange panel of the File Exchange control panel.

- Map a file type to an application (or more than one) that will be used to handle those files. For instance, you might choose BBEdit 5.0 to deal with the file whenever you want to handle files of type "TEXT." This is called "translation mapping." The File Exchange File Translation tabbed panel handles these mappings.

Of course, all of these elements are AppleScriptable, or we would not be wandering this path. You can create new extension mappings with the scriptable File Exchange control panel. This capability virtually cries out for a droplet that, for example, creates a new extension mapping based on a file that you drag to the droplet. This is accomplished in the Example section at the end of the chapter, which covers Version 3.0.3 of File Exchange. You can find out the version of your File Exchange simply by checking its **version** property, as in the upcoming syntax example. Figure 24-1 shows the PC Exchange tabbed panel of the File Exchange app in OS 9.

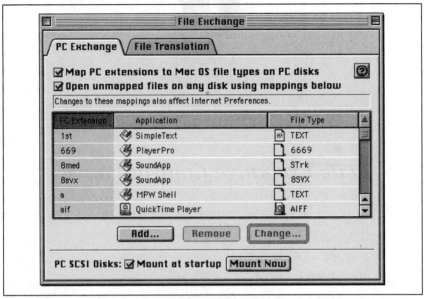

Figure 24-1: Create extension mappings with AppleScript or File Exchange

File Exchange

Syntax

```
tell app "File Exchange"
    get version -- returns something like "3.0.3"
end tell
```

Dictionary commands

run

Sending File Exchange this command is the same as double-clicking it in the *System Folder:Control Panels* folder, but *run* will have no effect if the control panel is already open. Just including:

```
app "File Exchange"
```

in a `tell` statement sends the app an implicit *run* command if it is not already open.

reopen

This command has no discernible effect on the application when it is already open.

quit

This command quits the File Exchange application.

make

Use this command to make a new extension mapping by passing it a record containing the properties for the new mapping.

---

new extension mapping
> This identifies the new object you are creating with script, as in:

```
make new extension mapping
```

with properties record
> with properties provides the properties for the new extension mapping. This code example makes sure that BBEdit opens the PC files with *.htm* extensions on my machine:

```
tell application "File Exchange"

make new extension mapping with properties {PC extension: ¬
"htm",  creator type:"R*ch", file type:"TEXT"}

end tell
```

delete
> This deletes a certain extension mapping or translation mapping. The following example searches the first 10 extension mappings for the PC extension "8med"; if this is found, the extension mapping is deleted and the applet lets the user know about it with the *display dialog* osax. Appendix A, *Standard Scripting Additions*, covers the scripting additions. Chapter 7, *Flow-Control Statements*, covers the repeat statement.

```
tell application "File Exchange"
    repeat with m from 1 to 10
        if (PC extension of extension mapping m) is equal to ¬
"8med" then
            delete extension mapping m
            display dialog "Deleted 8med"
            exit repeat
        end if
    end repeat
end tell
```

mount now
> This command immediately mounts on the desktop any available PC SCSI volumes, or returns zero if your computer is not networked to any PC disks.

Dictionary classes

application
> This class represents the File Exchange application, as in:

```
tell app "File Exchange" to get version
```

> The two elements, extension and translation mapping, represent what the user can accomplish with the two tabbed panels of the File Exchange control panel: PC Exchange and File Translation.

> The following are application elements:

extension mapping
> This represents the mapping of a PC extension like *.doc* to an application on the computer. You can identify the various extension mappings by their index, as in:

```
extension mapping 1
```

The prior multi-line example iterates through the first 10 extension mappings with a `repeat` statement, looking for a mapping that uses the extension "8med." This mapping is then summarily deleted. See the `extension mapping` class for a description of its properties.

translation mapping

File Exchange also has numerous translation mappings, which represent the mapping of a file type like `'TEXT'` to an application, like Apple-Works 6. You can identify these mappings by their index as in `translation mapping` 5. See the `translation mapping` class description.

The following are `application` properties:

name (`international text`; *read-only*)

The application name is "File Exchange."

frontmost (`boolean`; *read-only*)

This is a `true/false` value indicating whether the application is the active program on the desktop.

version (`version` *object; read-only*)

This returns the File-Exchange program version as the version number surrounded by double quotes, as in "3.0.3." You can display the control panel version in the Script Editor results window with the following code:

```
tell app "File Exchange" to get version
```

Chapter 2, *Using Script Editor with OS 9 and OS X,* is devoted to Script Editor.

current panel (`PC exchange` *or* `file translation`)

This command will return or set either of these constants depending on which of the File Exchange tabbed panels is active at the time.

mapping PC extensions (`boolean`)

You can automatically turn on or off the mapping of PC extensions like *.doc* or *.htm* to Mac creator and file types by setting this property. This is equivalent to the "Map PC extensions to Mac OS file types on PC disks" checkbox in the PC Exchange section of the File Exchange control panel.

mapping on opening files (`boolean`)

If set to `true`, Mac applications will open files based on their extension (i.e., the *.htm* part of *index.htm*), regardless of whether the file has a valid Mac file type or creator type.

PC disks mount at startup (`boolean`)

This is a `true/false` value that sets or unchecks the related checkbox at the bottom of File Exchange's PC Exchange panel.

automatic translation (`boolean`)

If set to `true` then any file you double-click in the Finder or select from a dialog box is automatically translated based on its mapping in the File Translation portion of the File Exchange control panel. This choice is the equivalent of checking or removing the check from the "Translate documents automatically" checkbox.

---

always shows choices (boolean)

Set this **true**/**false** value to give (or deny) the user a choice of file-translation applications when she encounters a file that is mapped to application(s) in the File Exchange control panel. For example, if this property is **true**, then the user is presented with a dialog box giving her a choice of opening a file with any applications that are mapped in File Exchange to that file's file type.

dialog suppress if only one (boolean)

If this property is **true**, then File Exchange automatically maps a file to its corresponding translator (i.e., application) as long as there is only one application mapped to the file type. In other words, it won't display the dialog of program choices to the user. This property corresponds to the "Don't show choices if there's only one" checkbox on the File Translation panel of File Exchange.

includes servers

Setting this property has the same effect as checking or unchecking its corresponding checkbox in the File Translation panel of File Exchange. Setting **includes servers** to **true** includes in any translation-choice dialog windows any relevant applications that are installed on connected servers.

PC file system enabled

The computer can read and write PC disks if this property is **true**.

extension mapping

This class represents the mapping of a file extension like *.jpg* to a Mac file type and creator type in File Exchange. This object has the following three properties:

PC extension (string)

A file extension **string**, as in the *.jpg* part of *sunshine.jpg*.

file type (string)

A four-character **string** for the file type, as in **'APPL'**.

creator type (string)

A four-character **string** for the creator type, as in **'ToyS'**. The creator type represents the program that created or owns the file; **'ToyS'** is the Script Editor's creator type.

translation mapping

This class or object results from the mapping in File Exchange of a file and creator type to a particular application. You cannot "make" a new translation mapping using File Exchange's *make* command (as you can with extension mappings), however.

file type *(string)*

> A four-character string for the file type, as in 'TEXT'

creator type *(string)*

> A four-character string for the creator type, as in 'ToyS'

translator application *(string)*

> A four-character string ID for the application, as in "8BIM" (Photo-shop's application signature)

translator type *(string)*

> A four-character identifier for the translator that is used to translate the file (usually "bltn" for "built-in")

Examples

```
on open (alias_list)
    (*
    alias_list is a list of aliases corresponding to the file(s) that were
    dragged to the droplet
    *)
    set err_occurred to false (* this will be set to true if an error
happens, then a dialog will be displayed *)
    set dropped to item 1 of alias_list (* alias of the file dropped on
to the droplet *)
    (*
    find out whether the file has a period in it; if it doesn't then it
does not have a discernable extension, so return from the droplet empty
handed.
    *)
    tell application "Finder"
        if (offset of "." in (dropped as string)) = 0 then
            display dialog "The dropped file has no extension!"
            return
        end if
        (*
    get the last three characters of the file name. If there are only
two extension characters as in ".pl" then the extension mapping will only
use the two non-period characters anyway
        *)
        set ext to (characters -1 thru -3 of (dropped as text)) as string
        (*
    get the file type and creator type of the dropped file and use ¬
    them to make the new extension mapping
        *)
        set dropped_typ to the file type of dropped
        set dropped_cr to the creator type of dropped
    end tell
    try
        tell application "File Exchange"
            make new extension mapping with properties  {PC extension:ext, ¬
            file type:dropped_typ, creator type:dropped_cr}
        end tell
```

```
on error errmesg
    display dialog "The extension mapping failed with error " & ¬
    "message: " errmesg
    set err_occurred to true
end try
if not err_occurred then display dialog "extension mapping succeeded!"
end open
```

CHAPTER 25

File Sharing Control Panel

The Mac OS allows the owners of disks and folders to set the access privileges for other users that may connect to their computer over a TCP/IP, AppleTalk, or other type of network. For example, you can configure one of your hard disks to allow read-only privileges for a named group of users (they will not be able to add new files to the disk or alter and save existing files). This is usually accomplished with the File Sharing control panel, which is also scriptable (see Figure 25-1). The Mac OS allows the user to set privileges for disks and directories with File Sharing but not for individual files, which can otherwise be locked or encrypted under Mac OS 9.

The owner name, password, and computer name can be set in File Sharing's Start/ Stop tab (See Figure 25-1) in Mac OS 9. You can create new users and groups in the Users & Groups tab. The owner can establish disk and folder permissions for logical groups of users, depending on what type of users might have access to your computer. When you add a user to a group they inherit the group's permissions when they log on to your machine. You can also turn Program Linking on or off with File Sharing. This is a powerful feature that allows users to execute your applications on their connected computer, including AppleScript applets. But they cannot use your applications while you are using them.

With AppleScript, you can create, alter, or remove File Sharing users and groups, and find out information about any connected users. For example, you can create a log file of all the connected users who were disconnected from your machine when it was automatically shut down. This applet is demonstrated in the Example section at the end of the chapter. The following dictionary commands and classes are associated with *Version 9.0* of the File Sharing control panel.

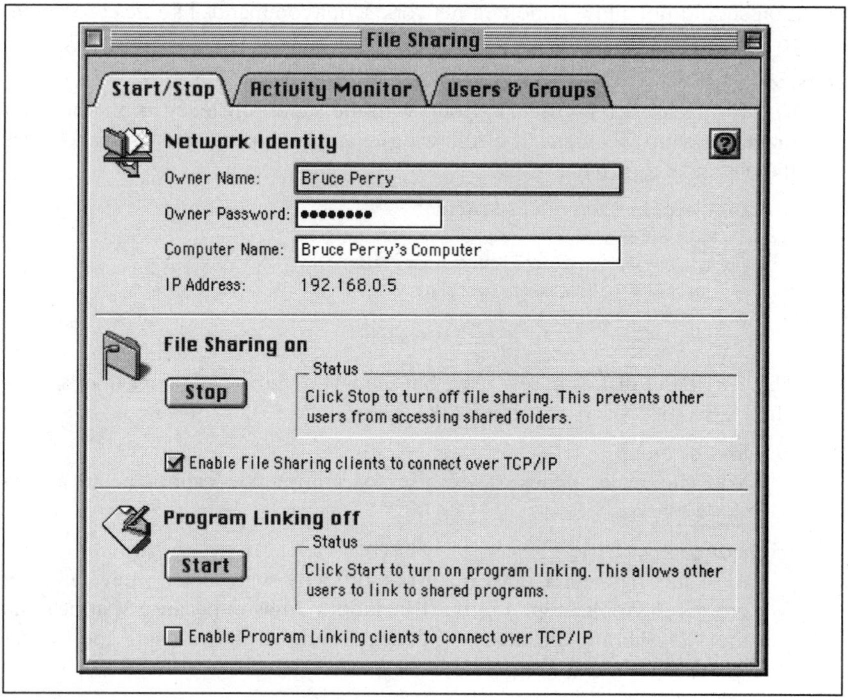

Figure 25-1: File Sharing control panel

File Sharing

Syntax

```
tell app "File Sharing"
    (* find out about the first user connected to your machine *)
    name of connected user 1
end tell
```

Dictionary commands

close reference to object

You can close a File Sharing window used to set or alter the privileges for a user or group:

```
close user "Guest"
```

This window can be opened from the Users & Groups tab by selecting the username and clicking the Open button (AppleScript cannot open this window, however).

delete reference to object

You can delete a user or group:

```
delete user "temp"
```

You should not allow important network script commands like *delete* or *make* to fall into the wrong hands.

duplicate list

You can create a new user or group with the same privileges as another user or group with *duplicate*. The following example duplicates a user and gives the new user a name:

```
tell application "File Sharing"
    activate
    set nw_user to duplicate user "iMarc"
    set name of nw_user to "iMarc2"
end tell
```

make

This command makes a new user, but the **with data** parameter that is identified in its dictionary does not work.

new *user or group*

You can make either a new user or group; you cannot make a new shared item.

with data anything

Alas, this parameter does not work properly with making new users or groups in AppleScript 1.4, but I include it anyway because it appears in the File Sharing dictionary. The next example shows user- and group-creating code that *does* work:

```
tell application "File Sharing"
    activate
    set group_name to "graphics"
    set user_name to "Van Gogh"
    (* make the group first *)
    set n_group to make new group
    set name of n_group to group_name
    (* make the user *)
    set n_user to make new user
    set name of n_user to user_name
    set can connect of user user_name to true
    set can change password of user user_name to true
    set can do program linking of user user_name to false
    (* add the new user to the new group *)
    add user user_name to group group_name
end tell
```

disconnect list *of connected users*

You should be able to use this command to disconnect a specified user, but under Mac OS 9 none of the following commands have worked properly:

```
disconnect {connected user 1}, disconnect connected user 1,
disconnect  connected user "iMac," disconnect (connected user whose
id = 131082}
```

Well, you get the picture. I am in search of a workaround or solution to the *disconnect* command.

show privileges of list *of* shared item *objects*
> On my computer, the File Sharing control panel exposes just two shared items to AppleScript; both are disks. Neither shared item responds without an error to the *show privileges of* command, as in:
>
> ```
> show privileges of (shared item 1)
> ```

add reference to object
> You can add a user to a group with this command:

> . to *reference to object*
> > This labeled parameter involves the keyword to followed by a reference to a group:
> >
> > ```
> > add user "new_user" to group "new_group"
> > ```

remove reference to object
> You can remove a user from a group with this command:
>
> ```
> remove user "defunct" from group "graphics"
> ```

> from *reference to object*
> > Follow the from label with a reference to a group:
> >
> > ```
> > remove user "defunct" from group "graphics"
> > ```

Dictionary classes

application
> This class represents the File Sharing control panel. It has two elements that represent the users who are connected to your computer and the shared items on the machine, such as hard disks. You get access to File Sharing by targeting the app in the tell statement, as in:
>
> ```
> tell app "File Sharing" to get connected users
> ```
>
> The following are application elements:

connected user
> The connected user object represents a user who is connected to your machine via File Sharing. See the connected user class later in this chapter for a description of its properties.

shared item
> A shared item is an element such as a disk that can be shared via File Sharing. The only property that can be accessed with your script is its name. For example:
>
> ```
> tell app "File Sharing" to get name of shared item 2
> ```
>
> The following are application properties:

frontmost (boolean; *read-only*)
> This is true/false value indicating whether File Sharing is the desktop's active application (i.e., its windows are highlighted):
>
> ```
> tell app "File Sharing" to get frontmost
> ```

name (international text; *read-only*)
> The name property returns "File Sharing."

version (international text; *read-only*)

The **version** property returns a value such as "9.0."

file sharing (boolean)

If File Sharing is turned off on your computer (i.e., network users cannot get access to your disks and folders), then this property returns **false**; otherwise **true**.

sharing starting up (boolean; *read-only*)

When you turn File Sharing on, the app can take several seconds to complete the task. If File Sharing is not undergoing its startup routine, then this property is **false**.

program linking (boolean)

If a user has program-linking privileges (which are set in the Users & Groups tabbed panel of File Sharing), then she can execute applications that reside on your machine. The program is actually executed on her connected machine, even though its binary executable code resides on your machine. The program-linking user cannot open applications that are already open on your machine, however. For example, if user "Gill" does not have Photoshop 5 on her machine but you do, Gill can access this program on her machine if that privilege is configured for her and program linking is on. You can stop program linking from the File Sharing control panel, as well as determine whether the users connected over TCP/IP can use program linking. For instance, you can stop program linking with script by setting this property to **false**:

```
tell app "File Sharing" to set program linking to false
```

owner name (international text)

This property returns the text from the Network Identity section of File Sharing's Start/Stop tab. If the owner of File Sharing privileges on your computer is called Admin, this property returns "Admin."

owner has password (boolean; *read-only*)

If the owner name identified in the File Sharing control panel has a password then this property returns **true**.

computer name (international text)

This property returns the computer name from the Network Identity section of File Sharing's Start/Stop tab.

connected user

This class represents a user that is connected to your machine via File Sharing. The available properties are its **name**, as in:

```
connected user "G4Power"
```

and its ID number. The code:

```
tell app "File Sharing" to get connected users
```

will return a **list** type, as in:

```
{connected user "G4Power" of application "File Sharing"}
```

name (international text; *read-only*)

This property returns the user's name as text, such as "graphicsUser1."

id (integer; *read-only*)

Every user has an id number of the form 65546.

shared item

This class represents a item than can be shared via File Sharing, such as a disk. Use the code:

```
shared items
```

to get a `list` of these resources, which looks like:

```
{shared item "my2gig" of application "File Sharing", shared item
"Macintosh HD" of application "File Sharing"}
```

name (international text; *read-only*)

This command returns a shared-item name as text, such as "my2gig."

group

The `group` class represents a group-sharing entity that can be created with File Sharing. The permissions can then be configured for each group from the shared element's Get Info window. For example, you might give the "Graphics" group read-only privileges on the disk "my2gig." File Sharing groups can be referred to in AppleScript by their name, as in group "Graphics." The code

```
tell app "File Sharing" to get groups
```

returns a `list` type with each one of the groups as a member of the list. The multi-line code example earlier in this chapter shows how you can make a new group.

name (international text; *read-only*)

This property returns the name of the group as text.

id (integer; *read-only*)

Every group is distinguished by an id number like 17.

user

`user` objects represent the users that are configured in your File Sharing control panel. They are distinguished from connected-user objects, which are only created when a user has actually connected to your computer. Users have names, IDs, and a few other properties that can also be set in the File Sharing control panel.

name (international text; *read-only*)

This is the name of the user as text, as in "graphicsUser1."

id (integer; *read-only*)

Every user has an id number of the form 18.

can connect (boolean)

If you do not want to allow a user to connect to your machine, set this property to `false`:

```
set can connect of user "virusMan" to false
```

can change password (boolean)

Set this property to true if you want to allow users to dynamically change their passwords (they have to know the original password to create a new one).

can do program linking (boolean)

This property can be set to false if you do not want to allow users to execute your applications.

see entire disk (boolean; *read-only*)

Only the local File Sharing owner, who is also a user, can have this property set to true. You can find out whether they have this privilege with the following code:

```
set sed to see entire disk of user owner name
```

The **owner name** property returns the local owner's name as text, so they can be identified in script code:

```
user owner name
```

Examples

```
(* make sure this variable can be accessed from anywhere in the script *)
global cu
tell application "File Sharing"
    set cu to connected users -- returns a list of connected users
end tell
(* this subroutine writes user names to a file if there is at least one
connected user *)
writeUsers()
on writeUsers() -- subroutine definition
    set ulength to (length of cu) -- number of connected users
    if ulength is greater than 0 then
        tell application "Finder"
            activate
            set tf to (make file with properties {name:"connected users", ¬
            file type:"TEXT", container:desktop}) -- make this log file
            set tf to tf as alias
        end tell
        open for access tf with write permission (* use osax from Standard
Additions *)
        write ("Here are the connected users:" & return) to tf
        repeat with n from 1 to ulength
            write ((name of item n of cu) & return) to tf
        end repeat
        close access tf
    else
        display dialog "There are no connected users!"
    end if
end writeUsers
```

CHAPTER 26

Folder Actions Extension

Folder actions allow the scripter to trigger specified AppleScripts when certain folder behaviors take place, such as the adding or removing of files from the directory. You can attach or associate more than one script or folder action with a folder. There are a lot of practical uses for folder actions, such as logging activity in a certain directory or doing automatic backups of files that are added to a particular folder. You can attach a script to a folder in one of two ways:

• Control-click the folder and select the "Attach a folder item…" contextual-menu item

• Use AppleScript to attach an action or script code to a folder

When a folder has an attached action, its folder icon changes to include a little script icon, as in Figure 26-1.

today

Figure 26-1: A folder with an attached script

The commands that you use in your script (see the "Dictionary commands" section later in this chapter) derive from the Folder Actions suite of five commands. You can find these command definitions in the *startup disk:System Folder:Scripting Additions:Standard Additions* set of scripting additions. So before we become completely confused, let's go over this one more time:

• Folder actions are AppleScripts that execute when certain actions take place with the folder, like adding items to it or moving it.

- Folder action commands constitute the Folder Actions suite of the Standard Additions osax and the dictionary commands that derive from the Folder Actions extension. Both sets of commands are described in this chapter.

- You have to attach folder actions to the folders that you want these actions to control. You can attach a script with AppleScript code or a contextual menu command. Contextual menus are produced by selecting the folder and holding down the Control key.

- You can attach more than one folder action to a folder by either including more than one command or handler (e.g., on opening folder theFolder...end) in an attached script or by attaching multiple scripts to a folder. Before it is attached to a folder, the script has to be saved as a compiled script, not an applet (see Chapter 2, *Using Script Editor with OS 9 and OS X*).

- You can group all of your folder action scripts in the *System Folder:Scripts: Folder Action Scripts* folder.

 In Folder Actions 1.5.5, an extension that installs with Mac OS 9.1, the "Icon\n" file is only created inside a folder if a script is actually attached to the folder. In Folder Actions 1.4.3 and earlier, Folder Actions would create an invisible "Icon\n" file in any folder that you control-clicked, whether or not an action was attached to that folder.

Folder Actions

Syntax

```
(*
display a dialog whenever a certain folder is opened. The f variable
contains an alias to the folder that was opened.
 *)
on opening folder f
    tell application "Finder"
        activate
        display dialog ("You opened " & (name of f)) giving up after 10
    end tell
end opening folder
```

Dictionary commands for Folder Actions Suite

opening folder alias

This command is used as a subroutine or handler, in the form of:

```
on opening folder theFolder...end opening folder
```

The theFolder variable contains an alias to the folder. The subroutine definition

```
on opening folder...
```

can then access elements of the folder by using Finder commands.

closing folder window for `alias`

Use this command as part of a subroutine definition for handlers that trigger when attached folder windows are closed:

```
on closing folder window for theFolder...end closing folder window
for
```

The `theFolder` variable contains an `alias` to the attached folder. This code example backs up all files in a folder to a backup disk when the folder window is closed:

```
on closing folder window for theFolder
    tell application "Finder"
        try
            activate
            (* make the backup folder if it doesn't exist *)
            if not (exists (folder "mybackup" of disk "backup")) then
                set backupFolder to (make new folder at disk "backup" ¬
                with properties {name:"mybackup"})
            else
                set backupFolder to (folder "mybackup" of disk "backup")
            end if
            (* get a list of the files of the attached folder *)
            set f to (files of theFolder)
            (* only do this if the folder is not empty *)
            if (count of f) > 0 then
                repeat with fl from 1 to (length of f) (* duplicate each
file to the backup folder *)
                    duplicate (item fl of f) to backupFolder replacing yes
                end repeat
            end if
        on error errmesg
            display dialog "An error: " & errmesg
            return -- return empty-handed if there was an error
        end try
        display dialog "backup complete!"
    end tell
end closing folder window for
```

moving folder window for `alias`

You can have a script execute when a folder is moved using this command. The syntax would be:

```
on moving folder window for theFolder from rec...end moving folder
window for
```

The variable `theFolder` (or whatever name you give it) receives an `alias` to the folder. The variable `rec` receives a `list` of coordinates that represent the top left and top right corners of the screen space the window occupied before it was moved. The next code example gets and displays the coordinates of the window (in the form of "10 : 50 : 370 : 500") stored in `rec`. The windows that have the attached scripts have to be open in the Finder for the "moving folder window for" and "adding folder items to" folder actions to execute properly.

from bounding rectangle

The from labeled parameter gives whatever variable you supply with it a rectangle value, as in {10,50,370,500} (basically a list of integers). For example:

```
on moving folder window for tf from rec
    set old_delim to text item delimiters
    set text item delimiters to " : "
    display dialog (rec as text)
    (* set text item delimiters back to empty string default *)
    set text item delimiters to old_delim
end moving folder window for
```

adding folder items to alias

This command is triggered when items are added to an open window that has one of these folder-action types attached to it (this folder action only works when the attached folder window is open). The following example displays a count of the number of folder items every time a new one is added to the directory. This is just a folder-action functionality example; you might want to log similar folder activity, but you normally would not want to display a dialog every time something happened with a folder, unless you want to antagonize users:

```
on adding folder items to f
    tell application "Finder"
        activate
        set fcount to (count files of f)
        display dialog ("there are now " & fcount & ¬
            " files in the folder " & (name of f)) giving up after 10
    end tell
end adding folder items to
```

removing folder items from alias

This subroutine is executed when items are removed from an attached folder. You use it in the form of:

```
on removing folder items from theFolder after losing alias_list...end
removing folder items from
```

The theFolder variable (or whatever name you give it) contains an **alias** of the folder. The **alias_list** variable contains a list of aliases referring to the items that were removed from the folder. This next example admonishes the user after an item is removed from the folder.

after losing list of aliases

This labeled parameter contains a list of aliases representing the items that were removed from the folder. This code demonstrates this parameter:

```
on removing folder items from theFolder after losing alias_list
    tell application "Finder"
        display dialog "Removing " & ((item 1 of alias_list) as & ¬
            text) & " from " & (name of theFolder) & ¬
            " is strictly forbidden!"
    end tell
end removing folder items from
```

Dictionary commands for Folder Actions extension

run

This command runs the Folder Actions server. See *quit.*

attach action to folder alias

Attach a folder action to a folder using this command:

```
attach action to fol_alias using script alias
```

The `fol_alias` variable contains an `alias` to a folder. The `script_alias` variable is an `alias` to the AppleScript that will be attached to the folder. The Example section lets the user choose a folder to attach actions to.

`using alias`

Use this labeled parameter to specify the script that will be attached to the folder. The script itself is stored in an `alias` variable or in a literal `alias`:

```
using script (alias "macintosh hd:desktop folder:moveApplet")
```

remove action from alias

You can script the removal of a folder action from a folder with this command. You have to identify the folder with an `alias` variable or a literal `alias`.

`action number integer`

This labeled parameter specifies by index number which action to remove from the folder (if there is more than one attached action). For example, if you want to remove the second folder action, then use:

```
action number 2
```

 In Folder Actions 1.5.5, an extension that installs with Mac OS 9.1, the action number parameter has been changed to "using action number."

`action name string`

As an alternative, you can specify the name of the script to remove, as in: `action name "moveScript"`. The name of the attached script also shows up in the contextual menu (attained by Control-clicking the folder) under the menu item "Remove a folder action."

```
set f_alias to ¬
(choose folder with prompt ¬
"choose a folder, cleanse its action")
tell application "Folder Actions"
    remove action from f_alias action number 2
end tell
```

edit action of alias

You can open up an attached script in Script Editor by using code such as:

```
edit action of theFolder action name "moveScript"
```

Chapter 2 is devoted to Script Editor.

```
action number integer
```
Use this labeled parameter to specify the index number of the attached action:
```
action number 2
```
```
action name string
```
You can specify the name of the action to edit with this labeled parameter:
```
action name "myAction"
```

attached scripts `alias`

You can find out if a folder has any attached scripts by passing the folder as an `alias` to this command:
```
tell app "Folder Actions" to attached scripts folder_alias
```
The `folder_alias` variable (or whatever you name it) contains an `alias` to the folder you are examining for attached scripts. This command returns a `list`. Each member of the `list` is a `list` containing a file `alias` for the attached script. The return value looks like:
```
{{alias "Macintosh HD:Desktop Folder:moverScript"}}
```
Yes, for some reason this command returns a `list` inside of another `list`.

quit

This command quits the Folder Actions server. See *run* and the following example.

Examples

```
set fol to choose folder with prompt ¬
"Choose the folder to attach the action to"
set theAction to alias "Macintosh HD:Desktop Folder:moverScript" (* this
script will be attached to the folder the user chooses *)
tell application "Folder Actions"
    (*start the Folder Actions server; it is not strictly necessary to use
run or quit *)
    run
    attach action to fol using theAction
    quit
end tell
```

CHAPTER 27

FontSync Control Panel and Extension

Apple computer provides the FontSync control panel and its related FontSync extension file to allow users to create a profile for all the fonts on their computer. This is for users who may be creating a document on one computer but printing it on another. They want to make sure the printing computer's fonts are synchronized with the production machine's (i.e., the computer where the document was created). Figure 27-1 shows the FontSync profile icon. This profile is then taken to the machine that will print the document. The user compares the fonts on the machine that created the document (these fonts are described in the profile) with the computer that will print the document by using a provided AppleScript called "Match FontSync Profile." Along with another script called "Create FontSync Profile," the Match script is stored in *startup disk:Apple Extras:Font Extras*. You can also find the FontSync control panel in this folder. This control panel (shown in Figure 27-2) lets you choose the font characteristics that will be used when the sets of fonts are compared or matched. If you use this control panel a lot with Mac OS 9, you might as well move it to the *startup disk:System Folder:Control Panels* folder.

Figure 27-1: Icon for FontSync profile file

This chapter describes the dictionaries for the FontSync control panel and extension.

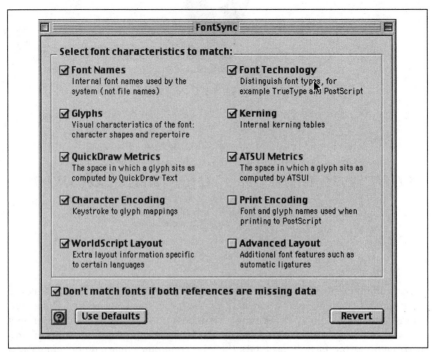

Figure 27-2: FontSync control panel

FontSync Control Panel

Syntax

```
tell app "FontSync"
    properties -- get the control panel's properties
end tell
```

Dictionary commands

get

This command gets data for an object, optionally as a certain data type (see the *as* parameter description and the accompanying code example).

as class

You can have the script return the data for, say, the FontSync control panel's `default matching options` in the specified data type. This code example gets the "on options" (e.g., font names, font types, encoding) for the control panel's font specifications as `text` values separated by a semi-colon:

```
(* save the old text item delimiter which is the empty string ""
*)
set old_delim to text item delimiters
set text item delimiters to ": " (* separate values with colon
and space *)
tell application "FontSync"
```

```
        set dmo to default match options
        set on_opt to on options of dmo as text
    end tell
    set text item delimiters to old_delim
    on_opt -- take a look at the on options
    (*
    on options values:
    "font names: font types: glyphs: encodings: QuickDraw metrics:
    ATSUI metrics: kerning: WorldScript layout: advanced layout:
    print encoding: missing data mismatches"
    *)
```

quit

> This command quits the FontSync control panel.

run

> This sends a *run* Apple event to the FontSync control panel, which launches
> the program if it is not already open.

set

> Use this command to set a property, as in the following code example:

```
tell application "FontSync"
    set default match options to {class:match options, on options: ¬
        {font names, font types, glyphs, encodings, QuickDraw ¬
            metrics, ATSUI metrics, kerning, WorldScript layout, ¬
            missing data mismatches}, off options:{advanced layout, ¬
            print encoding}}
end tell
```

Dictionary classes

application

> This class represents the FontSync control panel. You can open it with:

```
tell app "FontSync" to run
```

Get its properties with:

```
tell app "Fontsync" to get properties
```

properties record

> This property returns a record type that looks like:
> {name:"FontSync", frontmost:false, version:"1.0", default
> match options:{class:match options, on options:{font names,
> font types, glyphs, encodings, QuickDraw metrics, ATSUI
> metrics, kerning, WorldScript layout, missing data
> mismatches}, off options:{advanced layout, print
> encoding}}}. A record type constitutes one or more name/value pairs
> that are separated by commas and enclosed in curly braces. Chapter 3,
> *Data Types*, describes the record data type.

name international text *(read-only)*

> This property returns the text "FontSync."

frontmost boolean *(read-only)*

> If the FontSync control panel is the active window on the desktop then
> this property is true.

version version *(read-only)*
> This property returns the version number as a string, as in "1.0."

default match options match options
> All of the options that are checked or unchecked in the FontSync control panel window are represented by this *default match options* record data type. The *default match options* looks like this: {class:match options, on options:{font names, font types, glyphs, encodings, QuickDraw metrics, ATSUI metrics, kerning, WorldScript layout, missing data mismatches}, off options:{advanced layout, print encoding}}. See the *match options* class.

match options
> This class represents the FontSync reference matching options that are checked (or unchecked) in the FontSync control panel. The FontSync application's *default matching options* property returns this object.

on options list *of constants (read-only)*
> This property returns a list of any or none of the following constants:

advanced layout	Kerning
ATSUI metrics	missing data mismatches
encodings	print encoding
font names	QuickDraw metrics
font types	WorldScript layout
glyphs	

> In other words, if font names is checked in the FontSync control panel, then the *on options* list includes this constant.

off options list *of constants*
> This property returns a list of any or none of the following constants:

advanced layout	Kerning
ATSUI metrics	missing data mismatches
encodings	print encoding
font names	QuickDraw metrics
font types	WorldScript layout
glyphs	

> If font names is unchecked in the FontSync control panel, then the off options list includes this constant.

FontSync Extension

Syntax

```
(* 'tell app "FontSync"' targets the FontSync control panel. Make sure to
specify "FontSync Extension" if you are using the extension's commands
not the control panel's. They are different applications! *)
tell app "FontSync Extension"
```

```
set theProfile to (new file with prompt "Save the profile as: " ¬
default name "FontSync profile")
end tell
```

Dictionary commands

create font profile `alias`

This command creates a FontSync profile of the computer's active fonts and stores it in the file represented by the `alias` parameter. You can use the *new file* scripting addition (which returns an `alias` type) to prompt the user to create a new file for the profile. This example creates a FontSync profile in the `alias` represented by the `theProfile` variable:

```
create font profile (new file with prompt ¬
"Pick the FontSync profile file location" ¬
default name "FontSync profile" )
```

`with creator class`

This property specifies the four-character creator type for the FontSync profile file. The default type is "'fns'." If you try to set this property to other creator types such as "R*ch," then you will raise a script error.

`version integer`

As of FontSync 1.0, you cannot use this parameter without raising an error.

get reference to object

Use this command to get some FontSync Extension data such as:

```
tell app "FontSync Extension" to get version
```

match against `alias`

Use this command to match the font information in one computer system with another computer's font sets. The `alias` parameter must point to a Fontsync profile file. An example of *match against* is:

```
tell application "FontSync Extension" to match against (alias ¬
"Macintosh HD:Desktop Folder:font profile")
```

The "font profile" file could have been created with the *create font profile* command. *match against* then returns a `list` of `match result` objects, which are `record` types that report any problems with certain fonts. The `match results` look like this:

```
{class:match result, problem reported:mismatch, name:"Arial Narrow",
font:2000, style:3}
```

See the `match result` class.

`using fonts from` `alias`

When you use `match against` without the `using fonts from` parameter, then the command compares the computer system's active fonts against the specified FontSync profile. If you want to compare two FontSync profile files, then use code such as the following:

```
tell application "FontSync Extension" to match against (alias ¬
"Macintosh HD:Desktop Folder:font profile") using fonts from ¬
(alias "Macintosh HD:Desktop Folder:FontSync profile")
```

This code phrase compares the two files "font profile" and "FontSync profile" and returns any mismatch information. This is an optional parameter.

with match options match options

You can use a different set of match options than those specified in the FontSync control panel by specifying a `match options` object with the `with match options` labeled parameter. An example is:

```
tell application "FontSync Extension"
    set matchOpts to ¬
    {class:match options, on options:{font names, font types,
    glyphs, encodings, QuickDraw metrics, ATSUI metrics, kerning,
    WorldScript layout, missing data mismatches}, off options:
    {advanced layout, print encoding}}
    match against ¬
    (alias "Macintosh HD:Desktop Folder:applescriptcode_Appen.txt") ¬
    with match options matchOpts
end tell
```

See the `match options` class.

quit

This command quits the FontSync Extension application.

run

If it is not already open, this command runs the Fontsync Extension application. In other words, it will be added to the list of running applications on your computer, even though it is a faceless background application. It does not have a graphical appearance on the computer, such as windows and menus, for interacting with the user (FontSync Extension *can* be controlled with AppleScript, however).

set

Use this command to set some FontSync Extension data, as in:

```
tell app "FontSync Extension" to set quit delay to 30
```

This application's `quit delay` is 60 by default. See the `application` class' `quit delay` property.

Dictionary classes

application

This class represents the FontSync Extension program. It is the target of the `tell` statement in the code:

```
tell app "FontSync Extension" to set quit delay to 30
```

name international text

This **name** property evaluates to the value "FontSync Extension."

version version

version returns a `string` for the program's version number, which on Mac OS 9.0.4 is "1.0."

quit delay *the constants* immediate/default/never *or an* integer

Fontsync Extension is a faceless background application that opens, hopefully does its job, and then quits after a default of 60 seconds. You can change this delay time to suit your purpose, such as to never, so that Fontsync Extension stays open until it is sent a *quit* Apple event, or to a number of seconds, such as 30.

match options

This class is a `record` type that looks like {class:match options, on options:{font names, font types, glyphs, encodings, QuickDraw metrics, ATSUI metrics, kerning, WorldScript layout, missing data mismatches}, off options:{advanced layout, print encoding}}. A `record` is one or more name/value pairs separated by commas and enclosed by curly braces ({}). In this case, some of the values are `lists`, such as all of the font characteristics that are "on" and therefore will be matched for each font in a profile or computer system, such as:

```
on options:{font names, font types, glyphs, encodings, QuickDraw
metrics, ATSUI metrics, kerning, WorldScript layout, missing data
mismatches})
```

A `match options` object is used with the `with match options` labeled parameter for the *match against* command. An example is:

```
tell application "FontSync Extension"
    set matchOpts to ¬
    {class:match options, on options:{font names, font types,
    glyphs, encodings, QuickDraw metrics, ATSUI metrics, kerning,
    WorldScript layout, missing data mismatches}, off options:
    {advanced layout, print encoding}}
    match against ¬
    (alias "Macintosh HD:Desktop Folder:applescriptcode_Appen.txt") ¬
    with match options matchOpts
end tell
```

on options list *of constants (read-only)*

This on `options` property is a `list` of one or more of the following:

advanced layout	Kerning
ATSUI metrics	missing data mismatches
encodings	print encoding
font names	QuickDraw metrics
font types	WorldScript layout
glyphs	

off options list *of constants (read-only)*

This off `options` property is a `list` of one or more of the following:

advanced layout	Kerning
ATSUI metrics	missing data mismatches
encodings	print encoding
font names	QuickDraw metrics
font types	WorldScript layout
glyphs	

`match result`

This object is returned from the *match against* command, which matches a system's font sets to a FontSync profile or matches two FontSync profiles. `match result` is a `record` type that looks like {`class:match result`, `problem reported:mismatch`, `name:"Arial Narrow"`, `font:2000`, `style:3`}. In this case, a FontSync match reported a problem with the "Arial Narrow" font. A `record` is one or more name/value pairs separated by commas and enclosed by curly braces ({}). Chapter 3 describes the `record` type.

`problem reported` mismatch *or* noRef *(read-only)*

This property evaluates to the constants `mismatch` or `noRef`.

`name international text`

This property returns the font name, such as "Arial."

`ID integer`

This ID number represents the font family of the problem font; if the font does not belong to a font family, this value may be −1.

`style integer`

This property is a number such as 3 or −1 if the property does not apply to the font.

Examples

```
(*
This script can be found in startup disk:Apple Extras:Font Extras
*)
on run
    if OKToProceed() then
        set theProfile to new file with prompt "Save the profile as: " ¬
        default name "FontSync profile"
        try
            -- This can take a while...
            tell application "FontSync Extension" to create font profile ¬
            theProfile
            display dialog "Created FontSync profile named \"" & name of ¬
            (info for theProfile) & "\"" with icon note buttons {"OK"} ¬
            default button 1
            on error err
            display dialog "Encountered an error (" & err & ") while ¬
            creating \"" & name of (info for theProfile) & "\"" with icon ¬
            stop buttons {"OK"} default button 1
        end try
    end if
end run

on OKToProceed()
    set theButton to button returned of (display dialog "This can take a ¬
    long time if you have many fonts. Do you wish to proceed?" with icon ¬
    caution giving up after 30)
    return (theButton = "OK")
end OKToProceed
```

CHAPTER 28

Location Manager Control Panel

Location Manager is a control panel that allows the user to establish and switch between various named computer and networking configurations. The (minimally) scriptable control panel is located in *startup disk:System Folder:Control Panels*. Figure 28-1 shows the Location Manager window. You can use it to set up and name a configuration or location that controls several characteristics of your system, including:

- AppleTalk and TCP/IP settings

- The default printer

- File sharing (whether it is on or off)

- The set of Extension files that loads when the computer boots up

- Internet settings (such as the default browser, FTP, and telnet apps)

- Remote Access

- The time zone for the computer's internal clock

You can switch between settings using an AppleScript, but not much more. The Examples section at the end of the chapter checks the `current location` (a property of the Location Manager program), and then changes the location to a different one.

Location Manager

Syntax

```
tell app "Location Manager"
    set curApp to current location (* set a variable to location returned
    by "current location" property *)
end tell
```

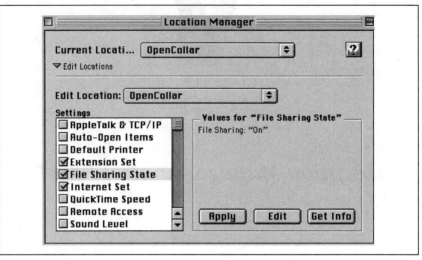

Figure 28-1: Location Manager window

Dictionary classes

`application`

This class represents the Location Manager program:

```
tell app "Location Manager" to launch
```

The `application` has one or more `location` objects as elements. To examine one of these objects, use code such as:

```
tell app "Location Manager" to get location 1
```

See the `location` class later in this chapter. The Location Manager `application` also has one property, `current location`.

The following are `application` elements:

`location`

If you use Location Manager to set several different configurations (which is what it is designed for), then each configuration or location is accessible as a `location` element. This code example gets the name of each location and displays the names in a dialog window:

```
set locs to "The location names are: " & return
    tell application "Location Manager"
    repeat with ct from 1 to (count location)
        set locs to locs & (name of location ct) & return
    end repeat
    display dialog locs
end tell
```

The following are `application` properties:

`current location location`

This `current location` property returns the currently active location. It is a settable property; see the Examples section at the end of this chapter.

`location`

This class represents a `location` you can create with Location Manager. A `location` is a set of system configurations such as file sharing, TCP/IP, and Extension sets, among other settings. The `application` class for Location Manager has `location` objects as elements:

```
tell app "Location Manager" to get current location -- returns the
active location
```

`name international text` *(read-only)*

This is the name the location has in the Location Manager window. For example:

```
tell app "Location Manager" to get location "cable_tcpip"
```

The return value for this code phrase (if you had a location called **"cable_tcpip"**) looks, naturally enough, like:

```
location "cable_tcp" of application "Location Manager"
```

Examples

```
tell application "Location Manager"
    set loc to current location
    if (name of loc) is "cable_tcpip" then
        set current location to location "dialup"
    end if
end tell
```

CHAPTER 29

Memory and Mouse Control Panels

If you are a programmer who likes to tinker with various memory settings, such as turning virtual memory on and off or adjusting the disk-cache size, then the scriptable Memory control panel is right up your alley. This control panel (see Figure 29-1) controls three aspects of computer memory usage, all of which are scriptable:

Disk cache

> The operating system reserves a certain amount of Random Access Memory (RAM) for the storage of frequently used bits of data. This repository is called a disk cache. By default, your disk cache is set to 32 KB times the amount of megabytes of physical RAM you have. My disk cache is set to 6656 KB, or 32 KB times 208 MB. This size is adjustable via AppleScript (see the **application** class description later in this chapter).

Virtual memory

> A portion of your hard disk the operating system uses as if it were RAM is called virtual memory (VM). This increases the computer system's available memory; however, VM slows down the use of some programs and uses up space that could be used to store files. AppleScript can turn on and off or adjust the size of VM.

RAM disk

> A RAM disk is a part of memory that can be used like a disk for storing files. It is the opposite of virtual memory, which uses a disk to act like memory. An icon for the RAM disk shows up on your desktop, and you can drag folders and files onto it. A RAM disk persists through a computer restart, but its contents are erased on some Mac systems if the computer is shut down or loses power abruptly. See the **RAM disk settings** class description in this chapter.

The end of this chapter describes how to alter the behavior of the mouse via AppleScript.

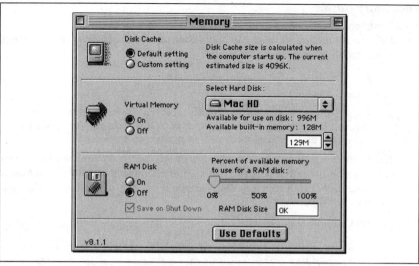

Figure 29-1: The Memory control panel

Memory Control Panel

Dictionary commands

close

This command closes the Memory control panel, as in:

```
tell app "Memory" to close
```

count reference

Use this property to count the elements of a class:

```
tell app "Memory" to count available disks
```

This code fragment returns the number of disks the computer could use for virtual memory. *count* returns an **integer** value. See the **available disk** class.

each type class

You can also use the syntax:

```
count each available disk
```

This usage returns the same value as:

```
count available disks
```

use default settings

If you use the following code, the control panel will set Disk cache, virtual memory, and RAM disk to default values (e.g., the default value for a RAM disk is "off"):

```
tell app "Memory" to use default settings
```

Dictionary classes

application

This class represents the Memory control panel. It has one element, available disk, as in:

```
get available disks
```

This returns a value that looks like:

```
{Disk Volume "Macintosh HD" of application "Memory", Disk Volume
"H2gig" of application "Memory", Disk Volume "HB2gig" of application
"Memory", Disk Volume "scratch" of application "Memory"}
```

The Memory application can also get or set various features of disk caches, virtual memory, and RAM disks. This code example finds out the state of virtual memory (active if VM is enabled on one of the local disks) and the size of VM:

```
tell application "Memory"
    set VMOn to state of virtual memory
    set VMsize to size of virtual memory
    display dialog "The state of VM on this machine is: " & VMOn & ¬
    return  & "The size of VM is: " & (VMsize / 1024 / 1024)
end tell
```

The following are application elements:

available disk

This class represents a disk that can be used for virtual memory. Get a list type containing references to the computer's available disks with this code:

```
tell app "Memory" to get available disks
```

See the available disk class.

The following are application properties:

disk cache disk cache settings

This is a property of the Memory application, but a script cannot get a return value for disk cache in the usual manner. In other words, you cannot use the syntax:

```
get disk cache
```

You have to use the code (an example return value is active):

```
get state of disk cache
```

or the following code (which returns the number of bytes in the system's disk cache):

```
get size of disk cache
```

These are settable attributes, so a script can change the state of a disk cache:

```
set state of disk cache to inactive after restart
```

or, a script could set the size of the disk cache to a new value:

```
set size of disk cache to ((size of disk cache) + (1024 * 1024))
```

This code adds a megabyte to the `size` of the `disk` cache. See the `disk cache settings` class.

`frontmost boolean` *(read-only)*
> If `frontmost` is `true`, then the Memory control panel is the active application on the desktop.

`name international text` *(read-only)*
> This property returns the `name` of the `application` as a `string` ("Memory").

`RAM disk RAM disk settings`
> The `RAM disk` property returns a `RAM disk settings` object, which cannot be referenced directly in your script. In other words, the following syntax raises a script error:
>
> ```
> tell app "Memory" to get RAM disk
> ```
>
> The script has to use syntax such as:
>
> ```
> get state of RAM disk or get persistence of RAM disk
> ```
>
> The latter code gets a `boolean` value referring to whether the contents of the RAM disk will be saved if the computer is shut down. See the `RAM disk` class description.

`version version` *(read-only)*
> This property returns a `string` (the `version` object return value is implemented as a `string`) that represents the Memory application version, as in "8.1.1."

`virtual memory virtual memory settings`
> `virtual memory` returns the VM settings for the computer. You can reference these settings in the following manner:
>
> ```
> tell app "Memory" to get size of virtual memory (* or get
> configured volume of virtual memory *)
> ```
>
> If you try to access the VM settings directly, as in the following, the script raises an error:
>
> ```
> get virtual memory
> ```
>
> See the `virtual memory settings` class description.

`available disk`
> This class represents a disk that can be used for storing virtual memory. For example, the Memory `application` object has `available disk` elements. You can access the disks that the machine can use for virtual memory with code such as:
>
> ```
> tell app "Memory" to get available disks
> ```

The example at the end of the property definitions gets all the properties of the `available disk` that the machine is currently using for virtual memory. The script first tests whether `virtual memory` is `active` (turned on). If it is, then the `available disk` that is holding `virtual memory` storage is accessed with the following code:

```
set vmdisk to configured volume of virtual memory
```

One way to view the property values of the `available disk` is in Script Editor's Event Log window. See Chapter 2, *Using Script Editor with OS 9 and OS X,* for details on the Event Log, and see the `virtual memory settings` class description.

The following are `available disk` properties:

`capacity double integer` *(read-only)*
> This property returns the maximum number of bytes that can be stored on the disk. The Memory dictionary identifies the return-value data type as "double integer," but AppleScripters will recognize it as a `real` type, such as 2.121269248E+9.

`creation date date` *(read-only)*
> This property returns the `creation date` of the disk volume or partition as a `date` type that looks like:
> > date "Friday, July 16, 1999 1:59:29 PM"

`free space double integer` *(read-only)*
> The `free space` of the disk holding virtual memory is the number of bytes not being used. An example return value is 1.494134784E+9. Apple Computer recommends that the disk used for VM have a free space equal to the total amount of VM you want to use plus the amount of physical RAM installed on the machine. You should always have a little bit more VM than physical RAM, so if your machine has 150 MB of memory, then the VM amount could be 151 MB, which requires a total of 301 MB of free space. Find out whether you have optimum `free space` on a VM disk with code, such as:
> > get free space of virtual memory's configured volume
>
> This code has to be enclosed in a `tell` statement targeting the Memory application.

`ID integer` *(read-only)*
> The `ID` property is a unique `integer` that identifies each disk, such as –3.

`modification date date` *(read-only)*
> This property returns the `modification date` of the disk volume or partition as a `date` type that looks like:
> > date "Friday, July 16, 2000 2:59:29 PM"

`name international text` *(read-only)*
> You can get the name of the disk with the following code fragment:
> > get name of (configured volume of virtual memory)
>
> The `name` is returned as a `string`, such as "MyDisk."

`startup boolean` *(read-only)*
> If the `available disk` object is the machine's startup disk, or the disk the machine was booted up from, then this property returns `true`. A script can access this property with code such as:
> > (* this example gets a lot of virtual-memory property values *)
> > tell application "Memory"

```
        set isStartup to (startup of (configured volume of virtual
    memory))
        if state of virtual memory is active then -- find out whether
    VM is on
            (* if VM is on, get a reference to the disk storing the VM
    *)
            set vmdisk to configured volume of virtual memory
            set proplist to {vmdisk's name, vmdisk's ID, vmdisk's ¬
            creation  date, vmdisk's modification date, vmdisk's ¬
            capacity, vmdisk's free space, vmdisk's startup}
        else
            display dialog "Virtual memory is not active right now!"
        end if
    end tell
    (* Sample return value *)
    {"HFSB2gig", -3, date "Friday, July 16, 1999 1:59:29 PM", date
    "Monday, July 17, 2000 4:56:57 PM", 2.121269248E+9, 1.
    494134784E+9, false}
```

disk cache settings

This class is the return value for the Memory application's disk cache property. Since this is a subclass of memory settings, you can find out about the computer's disk cache with code such as the following (state and size are properties of the memory settings super class):

```
    state of disk cache or size of disk cache
```

If you are like me, you might want to try to look at the disk cache settings object with code, such as:

```
    tell app "Memory" to get disk cache
```

But this syntax raises a script error. You have to get or set only the size or state properties.

memory settings

This is the super class for disk cache, RAM disk, and virtual memory settings classes. Therefore, each of these classes have the state and size properties, too (because AppleScript subclasses, in most circumstances, inherit their parent class's properties).

state constant

This property specifies whether or not the memory setting, such as virtual memory, is active. It can be one of the following constants: active, inactive, active after restart, or inactive after restart. For example, if virtual memory is "off" in the control panel, then

```
    state of virtual memory
```

returns the constant inactive (or inactive after restart if you just switched VM off in the Memory control panel).

size integer (or minimum, maximum, default)

This is the amount of memory or disk space allocated in bytes to the disk cache, RAM disk, or virtual memory. You can set the amount in bytes:

```
    set size of disk cache to (size of disk cache + (1024 * 1024))
```

Or use one of these constants: `minimum`, `maximum`, or `default`. If you use an AppleScript to:

```
set size of disk cache to maximum
```

then the Memory control panel will show a new custom setting in its disk cache area. The new setting takes effect when the computer is restarted.

RAM disk settings

This class is returned by getting the Memory application's `RAM disk` property:

```
tell app "Memory" to get persistence of RAM disk
```

The script raises an error if it tries to use syntax, such as:

```
tell app "Memory" to get RAM disk
```

You have to get the `size`, `state`, or `persistence` properties in code that references the `RAM disk settings`.

persistence boolean

If the `RAM disk` will keep its contents after a computer has been shut down and restarted, then this property is `true`. A RAM disk is a segment of RAM set aside and used as if it were a disk on the desktop. You can drag folders and files into it, but the disk contents on some systems are lost if the computer is shut down or loses power.

virtual memory settings

This class is returned by getting the Memory application's `virtual memory` property, as in:

```
tell app "Memory" to get configured volume of virtual memory
```

This code fragment returns the disk used to hold virtual memory. The script will raise an error if it tries to use syntax, such as:

```
tell app "Memory" to get virtual memory
```

You have to get the `size`, `state`, or `configured volume` of this object; `virtual memory` itself is not directly accessible. Even if `virtual memory` is currently "off" in the Memory control panel, getting its `size` property will still return the number of bytes that would be reserved for it if VM were on. Find out whether it is on by getting the state of virtual memory. See the `memory settings` class description.

configured volume available disk

The `configured volume` property returns the disk as an `available disk` object that stores virtual memory. See the `available disk` class.

Mouse Control Panel

Dictionary commands

application

This class represents the Mouse control panel. Figure 29-2 shows what this control panel looks like in Mac OS 9. You can get or set the four properties of the Mouse `application` class if you are compelled to use AppleScript to control your mouse input device:

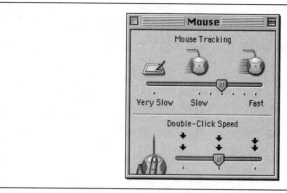

Figure 29-2: The scriptable Mouse control panel

```
tell application "Mouse"
    (* get all these properties and view in Event Log *)
    tracking speed
    double click speed
    mouse tracks
    thick ibeam
end tell

(* Sample view in Script Editor Event Log *)
get tracking speed
--> 6
get double click speed
--> 2
get mouse tracks
--> 0
get thick ibeam
--> false
```

tracking speed integer

This settable number determines how fast the mouse cursor follows the user's mouse movement. The higher the number, the faster the tracking speed, as in the following (this is a high-speed mouse):

```
tell app "Mouse" to set tracking speed to 6
```

double click speed integer

This number determines how fast you have to double-click for the computer to determine that two clicks equal a double-click (as opposed to a single click followed by another single click). The higher the number, the faster the speed at which the user has to double-click.

mouse tracks integer

Setting this property to something other than 0 causes the mouse to leave visible "tracks" or mouse cursor images as it moves about the screen. This may make the cursor easier to find on the screen with bright small screens like those of the PowerBook or iBook.

`thick ibeam boolean`

If this property is `true`, the mouse will be a thick ibeam shape:

```
tell app "Mouse" to set thick ibeam to true.
```

CHAPTER 30

Speech Listener and SpeakableItems Extension

Mac OS 9 offers three different ways to use AppleScript to control how the computer responds to verbal commands and "speaks" back to the computer user. Using combinations of these methods, you can create complex and useful speech-related scripts:

- The *listen for* AppleScript command, which controls the computer's response to spoken commands. The options that control how the computer listens for commands, such as the key on your keyboard that will toggle this technology on and off, can be controlled with the Speech control panel (see Figure 30-1).

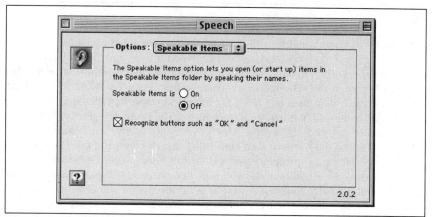

Figure 30-1: The Speech control panel

- The SpeakableItems technology allows the user to execute a script inside the SpeakableItems folder (which is located in the *startup disk:System Folder:Apple Menu Items* folder) just by speaking the script's filename into the computer's microphone.

- The *say* command, a scripting addition that has been part of the Standard Additions osax since Mac OS 8.5 (See Appendix A, *Standard Scripting Additions*). As long as the Speech Manager extension is enabled, the computer will speak any text or string that you specify in an AppleScript with *say*, as in:

```
say "It's nice to hear text rather than read it sometimes."
```

Figure 30-2 shows the three extensions that have to be installed with Mac OS 9 to use the three speech-related technologies with AppleScript.

SpeakableItems	Speech Manager	Speech Recognition

Figure 30-2: Speech extension files

Speech Listener Application

Dictionary commands

listen for

> *listen for* is the only command in the Speech Listener application's dictionary. The Speech Listener app is located in the *startup disk:System Folder:Scripting Additions* folder. Figure 30-3 shows the Speech Listener icon.

Speech Listener

Figure 30-3: Speech Listener app icon

> *listen for* allows a script to "listen for" any text provided in a `list` of strings (or numbers), then respond accordingly when it hears one of the listed words or numbers. The return value of the *listen for* command is the text or number that is recognized. The following example first sets a `fam` variable to a `list` of names. It then uses the *listen for* command to prompt the user to say one of the names. If the name is recognized (let's say it's "Emily") then the computer responds by saying "Hey guys, Emily is my family member too!" The `[[emph - ]]` syntax is an embedded speech command that (in this case) de-emphasizes the pronunciation of the following word. Embedded speech commands are explained elsewhere in this chapter. If the script listens but does not hear any spoken commands in 60 seconds, it will time out and raise error number -1712. The example script catches this error, says "bye-bye," and exits the `repeat` loop (effectively terminating the script). *Listen for* also raises an error when text is heard but does not match any of the specified text options.

```
(* repeat the prompt until a family name is identified or the script
times out *)
repeat
    try
```

```
        tell application "Speech Listener"
            set fam to {"Stacy", "Bruce", "Rachel", "Emily", "Anne", ¬
            "Dean", "Bob"}
            (* listen for returns the recognized text, which the fam_
    member variable is set to *)
            set fam_member to (listen for fam with prompt "Say a ¬
            family [[emph - ]] member")
        end tell
        say "Hey guys, " & fam_member & " is my family [[emph - ]] ¬
        member too!"
        exit repeat
    on error number errnum
        If errnum is -1712 then
            say "Bye-Bye"
            exit repeat
        else
            say "I'm sorry, try again."
        end if
    end try
end repeat
```

listen for list *of* strings *or numbers*

The *listen for* command has to be nested in a `tell` block targeting the Speech Listener application, as in `tell application "Speech Listener"`...`end tell`. Chapter 7, *Flow-Control Statements*, describes the `tell` statement. *Listen for*'s required parameter is a `list` of strings or numbers comprising the text that the machine listens for. The example below listens for certain numbers and, if it hears one, will speak that number squared. In other words, if it hears "5," then the script will speak the result of 5 * 5. This example uses embedded speech commands, such as `[[ slnc 500 ]]` (which produces half a second of silence). These commands are explained elsewhere in this chapter. The three *listen for* labeled parameters are optional.

with prompt string

The machine says this prompt before listening for the designated text, as in `with prompt "say your name"`.

giving up after integer

You can designate a number of seconds for the Speech Listener app to wait before it returns a timeout error (error number -1712) and quits listening. If you do not specify an `integer` for `giving up after`, then the default timeout will occur in 60 seconds.

filtering boolean

If filtering is `true`, the Speech Listener app skips phrases that contain special characters:

```
    tell application "Speech Listener"
        set numList to {1, 2, 3, 4, 5, 6, 7, 8, 9, 10, "cancel"}
        repeat (* keep repeating the prompt until a number from 1-10
    or "cancel" is *)
        heard
            try
```

```
                  set n to (listen for numList with prompt "say a ¬
                  number, between  1 and [[ emph - ]] 10, and I will ¬
                  square [[ ¬ emph - ]]it." giving  up after 15)
                  if n is equal to "cancel" then
                      say "bye bye"
                      return -- exit the applet
                  end if
                  say "The answer is [[ slnc 1000 ]]  [[ emph - ]]" & ¬
                  ((n  * n) as  text)
                  on error number errnum
                  if errnum is -1712 then
                      return
                  else
                      say "Sorry, please try again."
                  end if
              end try
          end repeat
      end tell
```

SpeakableItems Extension

You can make your scripts executable by spoken command as long as you have
the SpeakableItems extension file loaded on your machine, and you have turned
SpeakableItems on in the Speech control panel (see Figure 30-1). This speech
technique is as simple as this: create a script that does whatever you want then
give it a filename that you will use to verbally execute the script. For instance, you
can save the script as an applet with the filename *go*. As long as the script has
been saved in the *startup disk:System Folder:Apple Menu Items:SpeakableItems*
folder and SpeakableItems is turned on, all the user has to do is say "go" into the
computer's microphone and the script is executed. The following example uses a
web browser to open up the my.yahoo.com page upon spoken command, which
in this case is "go to yahoo" (i.e., the filename of the script must be *go to yahoo*,
and the script must be saved to the SpeakableItems folder):

```
tell application "Internet Explorer"
    Activate
    GetURL "http://my.yahoo.com"
end tell
```

say scripting addition

The *say* command is an osax that you can use to have the computer speak text to
the script user. It is extremely easy to use; simply follow the keyword *say* with the
string text that you want the computer to say. This command requires the
Speech Manager extension (see Figure 30-2), which enables the computer to read
text to the user. You can use the *say* command alongside other speech technologies, such as the Speech Listener application. The following example tells the user
what time it is. It gets the current time from the *current date* scripting addition.
The time string property returns just the time portion of the date, as in
"10:52:26 AM." Appendix A also describes the *say* command. A description of *say*
and its parameters follows this example. The example also uses embedded speech
commands (which are explained at the end of this chapter):

```
set t to (time string of (current date)) (* returns something like
"11:17:00 AM" *)
set t1 to "" (* t1 var will hold just the time part as in "11:17:00",
without the "AM" *)
set t2 to ((characters -1 thru -2 of t) as text) -- holds "AM" or "PM"
set t3 to "" -- will hold the lower case "am" or "pm"
(* remove the " AM" part of "11:17:00 AM," for instance, and store the
result in a variable *)
repeat with chr from 1 to (t's length)
    if (character chr of t) is space then exit repeat
    set t1 to t1 & (character chr of t)
end repeat
(* create a lower case version of "AM" or "PM" so that the speech
software reads the time of day as "ay-em" or "pee-em" using the [[ char
LTRL ]] embedded speech command *)
repeat with chr from 1 to 2
    set n to (ASCII number (t2's character chr)) + 32 (* converts from
upper to lower case using ASCII number osax *)
    set t3 to t3 & (ASCII character n) -- uses ASCII character osax
end repeat
say "It is [[ emph - ]] [[ slnc 500 ]]" & t1 & " [[ char LTRL ]]" & t3
```

say anything

This command speaks the text parameter to the *say* osax in the voice that is configured in the Speech control panel. You can use this command for debugging purposes by saying the value of certain variables.

displaying string

This parameter displays text in the SpeakableItems feedback window, if you have the SpeakableItems extension installed.

using string

You can specify the voice you want to use, such as "Deranged" or "Hysterical":

```
say "This project is disintegrating!" using "Hysterical"
```

waiting until completion boolean

The default is **waiting until completion** true, which does not return from the call to *say* until the speech has been uttered. This is important when you are using *say* in a **repeat** loop, as you do not want to move on to the next loop of **repeat** until the speaking voice has finished its speech. Chapter 7 describes the **repeat** loop.

Embedded Speech Commands

The earlier examples used embedded speech commands like "[[emph -]]," which de-emphasizes the pronunciation of the word following the command. These embedded commands give the scripter more control over how the voice sounds when it reads text, such as the volume and emphasis of syllables. The commands are delimited by two pairs of opening and closing brackets ("[[ ]]"). Most of the commands have parameters. For instance, the emphasis command ("emph") has a plus (+) or minus (-) parameter that either gives greater or less emphasis to the

---

word following the command. The following web site contains more information on embedded speech commands: *http://developer.apple.com/techpubs/mac/Sound/Sound-200.html.*

[[char LTRL]]

If you use the LTRL parameter, then the speech synthesizer will read every letter, number, and space separately rather than the words themselves. It reads the words normally if you use NORM as the parameter.

[[cmnt here is a comment]]

Use this syntax to enter comments in the speech code. The speech synthesizer will not read the comments text.

[[emph -]]

This command de-emphasizes or emphasizes (e.g., [[emph +]]) the word that follows the command.

[[inpt PHON]]

This command determines whether the speech synthesizer speaks the text in normal text mode or phoneme mode. Phonemic mode spells words as they sound, as in "Maykael" rather than "Michael." If you use [[inpt PHON]] then the speech synthesizer will use phonemic mode. The command [[inpt TEXT]] is the default.

[[nmbr LTRL]]

This command determines the number-speaking mode of the speech synthesizer. The syntax example would read the code say [[nmbr NORM]] 500 as "five hundred"; whereas the code say [[nmbr LTRL]] 500 would be read as "five zero zero."

[[pbas +1]]

The baseline pitch command makes the voice higher or lower. If you use a + or - symbol with the **real** number parameter (in a range from 1.0 to 127.0), the pitch is adjusted relative to its current value.

[[pmod +1]]

The pitch modulation command also changes the sound attributes of the computer voice. If you use a + or - symbol with the **real** number parameter (in a range from 0.0 to 127.0), the modulation is adjusted relative to its current value.

[[rate +50]]

The speech rate determines how fast the text is read. For example, [[rate +50]] speeds up the speech synthesizer's reading of text. The rate number parameter falls between 0.0 and 65535.999, a range that equates to 50 to 500 words per minute.

[[rset]]

Use the reset command to reset the voice attributes back to their default values.

[[slnc 500]]

The silence command causes a speech delay for parameter number of milliseconds (there are 1,000 milliseconds in a second). So if you want two

seconds of silence followed by the word "heaven," you could use the code
`say "[[ slnc 2000 ]] heaven"`.

[[volm +0.5]]

The speech volume command adjusts the voice's volume (how loud it is) in a range from 0.0 to 1.0. If you precede the parameter with a + or – symbol, the volume is adjusted based on its current value.

CHAPTER 31

Web Sharing Control Panel

Personal Web Sharing is a powerful (but potentially hazardous) technology that was introduced with Mac OS 8.5. Using the Web Sharing control panel and extension, you can turn your computer into a web server over an intranet or the Internet. As long as they know your IP address and/or domain name, people can connect to a home page that you designate in the Web Sharing control panel just by entering your address in their web browsers. Domain names are the plain English versions of numerical IP addresses, such as *www.nateweb.net.*

 You know you have Web Sharing installed if you have a Web Sharing control panel and a *Web Pages* folder on your hard drive. Web Sharing is installed by default with Mac OS 9.

For example, if your IP address on the Web happened to be 207.169.50.110 and you have started up Web Sharing on your machine, then another person on the Web would just have to enter *http://207.169.50.110* in their web browser and up pops your designated home page or a directory listing of your web folder. This also applies to people who have dial-up connections to the Web and are dynamically assigned IP addresses by their Internet Service Providers. When they are online, they can use the TCP/IP control panel to find out their IP address at the moment, and as long as they have started up Web Sharing on their machines, a web user can connect to their designated web page by using that IP address as the URL. You can even run Common Gateway Interface (CGI) programs written in AppleScript using Personal Web Sharing. I'll demonstrate AppleScript and Web Sharing CGIs in this chapter. If you just need to serve some files and directories and run CGI scripts over an Appleshare TCP/IP network, for instance, then who needs to install an expensive and time-consuming server suite?

However, all of this nifty technology comes with a large security caveat. Offering remote access to your computer over the Web should never be done without carefully restricting the users' access to directories. The Web Sharing control panel (see Figure 31-1) gives you the option to use File Sharing to control user access to files and folders.

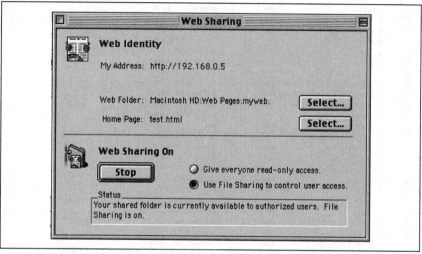

Figure 31-1: Web Sharing control panel

It is a good idea to use properly generated usernames and passwords to restrict web access to your files. Make sure that you do not blithely leave on Web Sharing when you don't really need it. Figure 31-2 shows what a directory listing looks like in a browser accessing a Web Sharing computer. This careless user has offered web access to their System Folder!

The Web Sharing control panel has a dictionary, but the program's developers have not yet exposed Web Sharing's object model to scripters. In other words, you can use basic commands such as:

```
tell app "Web Sharing" to run
```

However, you cannot do things like designate Web Sharing home pages, open the log file, or start and stop Web Sharing with a script. For that reason, I am not going to use this space to describe Web Sharing's dictionary, which is depicted in Figure 31-3. Chapter 1, *AppleScript: An Introduction,* has more information on how an object model relates to AppleScript.

A program's dictionary describes in barebones fashion the AppleScript commands you can use to control the software. Open an application's dictionary by choosing the program in Script Editor's *File → Open Dictionary...* menu. See Chapter 2, *Using Script Editor with OS 9 and OS X,* for more information on Script Editor and dictionaries. This chapter will describe two CGI scripts that you can use with Personal Web Sharing.

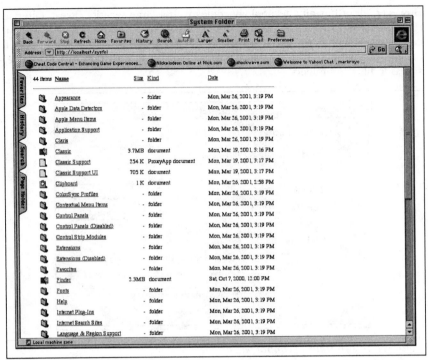

Figure 31-2: A directory listing of someone's System Folder displayed in a browser

What are CGI programs? A CGI program is software that executes and processes web information in response to an HTTP request. Instead of delivering a static HyperText Markup Language (HTML) file to a web user, a server can launch a CGI program in response to the request and then dynamically generate some data for the user, such as delivering product information from a database. A popular use of CGI programs on the Web has been to process form data that a user submits (usually by filling out a form and clicking the Submit button). The CGI program processes the form entries (by storing the submitted data in a database, for example), and then generates an acknowledgement in the form of a web page for the submitting user. CGI programs can be written in AppleScript for Macintosh servers. This chapter uses CGIs running under Personal Web Sharing server software, but these scripts could be used with a full-fledged web server such as StarNine's WebStar.

When you save an AppleScript web server script you should remember a few important tips:

- Make sure to save the script with a suffix of *.cgi* or *.acgi* or else Personal Web Sharing will not run it properly. "Myscript.acgi" is an example. The "a" in "acgi" stands for asynchronous. This suffix instructs the server that the script can simultaneously initiate its processing while the computer is busy with other tasks. Using this suffix usually helps the script execute more efficiently.

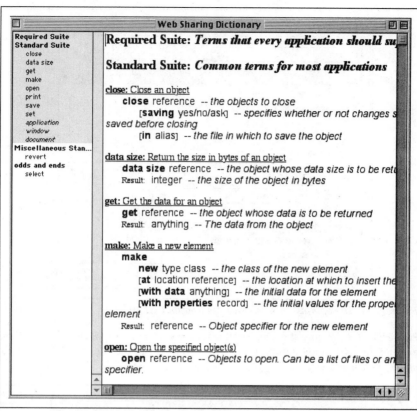

Figure 31-3: Web Sharing control panel's dictionary

- Make sure that the checkboxes "Never Show Startup Screen" and "Stay Open" are checked when you save the script in Script Editor (Figure 31-4 shows this *Save script as...* window). These are checked so that the first time the script is executed, it stays open on the server, processing new requests more quickly. Also, when the script is executed, you do not want the startup screen to display on the server, waiting for someone to click a Run or Quit button. Checking "Never Show Startup Screen" ensures that the applet starts up without this interruption.

The CGI program in Example 31-1 uses the *handle CGI request* scripting addition. This is a handler or function (as in on `handle CGI request...`) that fills in several built-in `string` variables, giving you, as the server, scripter information about the request. This information includes the client IP address and the data that follows the "?" character in the URL (e.g., the "first=Bruce&last=Perry" part of "http://www.parkerriver.com?first=Bruce&last=Perry"). The *handle CGI request* function returns an HTML page, so you should generate an HTTP response header and page as the function's return value.

To use this script with Web Sharing, you have to add it to the server's list of actions by using the Web Sharing control panel's Preferences window (see

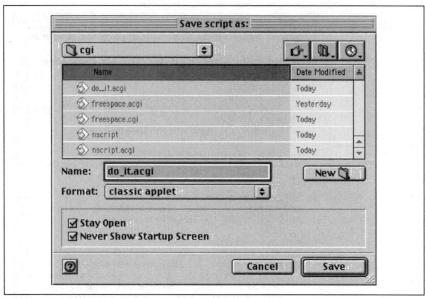

Figure 31-4: The options for saving an AppleScript CGI program

Figure 31-5). Configure the script in this window as a Filter-type action. Users can execute the CGI by requesting it in their browser, as in the *http://207.169.50.110/ cgi/do_it.acgi* address.

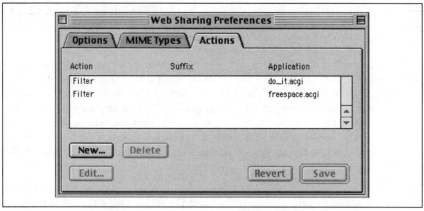

Figure 31-5: Configure CGI actions in Web Sharing's Preferences window

Example 31-1 stores the submitted query string ("first=Bruce&last=Perry") in the theString variable. It also tries to get the URL from which the user linked to the CGI program. The web server stores this data in the referred by labeled parameter (if there is an identifiable referer) for the *handle CGI request* function.

Example 31-1: A Simple CGI Script for Web Sharing

```
on handle CGI request searching for theString referred by referer
    set crlf to (ASCII character 13) & (ASCII character 10)
    set theHTML to "HTTP/ 1.1 200 OK" & crlf & "Content-type: text/html" & ¬
    crlf & crfl
    set theHTML to theHTML & "<html><head><title>First page</title> ¬
    </head><body bgcolor=#ffffff>" & "You were referred by: " & referer & ¬
    "<p>" & ¬
    "The search string is: " & theString & "</body></html>"
    return theHTML
end handle CGI request
```

Notice that Example 31-1 returns a web page (`return theHTML`) as the return
value for *handle CGI request*. The `theHTML` variable is a string that contains the
source code for the HTTP response. Example 31-2 shows the power and the
danger of Web Sharing. It executes a CGI that delivers sensitive information about
the server computer, such as how much free space is left on all of its disks. The
handle CGI request function calls the *getfreespace* method, which then scripts the
Finder. This shows that a CGI program is not limited in what it can script, which is
exciting in your hands but perhaps malicious in another's. A CGI script could just
as well exhibit behavior like the "I Love You" virus by grabbing all the contacts in
OutLook Express's contact list and sending thousands of unwanted emails to these
contacts. OutLook Express is a scriptable program, and it is easy to grab email
addresses from its contact list.

Example 31-2: Scripting the Finder from a CGI Script

```
on handle CGI request
    set crlf to (ASCII character 13) & (ASCII character 10)
    set theHTML to "HTTP/ 1.1 200 OK" & crlf & "Content-type: text/html" & ¬
    crlf & crlf
    set theHTML to theHTML & "<html><head><title> ¬
    Freespace CGI</title></head><body bgcolor=#ffffff>" & "The total free ¬
    space on this computer is: " & getfreespace() & "</body></html>"
    on this computer is: " & getfreespace() & "</body></html>"
    return theHTML
end handle CGI request
on getfreespace()
    tell application "Finder"
        set total_space to 0
        set dsk to (items of desktop whose kind is "disk")
        repeat with d in dsk
            set total_space to total_space + (free space of d) (* returns free
space of each disk in bytes *)
        end repeat
        set total_space to (total_space / 1024 / 1024) (* get free space as
megabytes *)
        return total_space
    end tell
end getfreespace
```

If you want to test Personal Web Sharing on your own machine, turn it on in the Web Sharing control panel. Then enter the following IP address into your browser: *http://127.0.0.1*. This address connects with your local web server (and loads up your designated web page or web folder if they are configured properly).

You can include aliases to folders in your Web Sharing folder, as in my cautionary example of serving up your System Folder over the Web (Don't try this at home!). A user can request the `alias` file in their browser, and they then see a directory listing of that folder. Let's say you have a folder full of MP3 files, and you create an `alias` to this folder called `MP3fol`. Place that `alias` in your designated web folder. The web user can then request a directory listing of the `alias` with a URL similar to *http://169.210.110.40/MP3fol*. To use aliases in your Web Sharing folder, you have to enable the checkbox with the following label in Web Sharing Preferences: "Allow aliases to open files outside the Web folder."

PART V

Scripting the Mac OS X System

CHAPTER 32

Scripting the OS X Desktop

This chapter describes how to script the Finder application with Mac OS X, which is Apple's dramatically redesigned operating system (see Figure 32-1). While the Finder has undergone a major visual face-lift in OS X, scripting the Finder is not very different from scripting the OS 9.0.4 and 9.1 Finder, as you'll see from the examples in the rest of this chapter (see Chapter 14, *Mac OS 9 Finder Commands*, and Chapter 15, *Mac OS 9 Finder Classes*, on the OS 9 Finder's commands and classes).

What is the Finder? The Finder manages the user's interaction with the OS X desktop and Aqua graphical user interface, which includes the Dock, translucent windows, tear-dropped shaped button controls, and the computer disks or partitions that are displayed on the OS X desktop. The Finder application can be found in the following directory in OS X: */System/Library/CoreServices*. The icons displayed along the bottom of the screen are part of the Dock, which can contain applications, documents, image files, aliases, and other file types. The window is a Finder window, which is described elsewhere in this chapter.

Figure 32-2 shows a Finder window in column view. You can display a Finder window by using the Finder's Go menu from the menubar along the top of the computer screen, as well as by typing *Command-N*. You can also make a new Finder window programmatically in AppleScript (See the upcoming section "Working with Finder and Inspector Windows"). Inspector windows, as defined in the Finder dictionary, are OS X's next-generation version of OS 8's and 9's Get Info windows.

Figure 32-1: Mac OS X Desktop

Figure 32-2: Finder window in column view

The Finder application defines the `inspector window` class to manipulate Info windows in the Mac OS X desktop. Info windows are specified by the Aqua Human Interface Guidelines. These can be downloaded from *http://developer.apple.com/techpubs/macosx/ SystemOverview/AquaHIGuidelines/AquaHIGuidelines.pdf.*

The user displays these windows in OS X by selecting a Finder item like a file and typing *Command-I* or choosing Show Info from the Finder menu bar. Figure 32-3 shows an inspector window that targets a folder.

As with any other scriptable application, you can examine the Finder's dictionary by opening up Script Editor, choosing "Open Dictionary..." from its File menu, and then selecting the Finder from this dialog window. See Chapter 2, *Using Script Editor with OS 9 and OS X,* for a description of Apple's script-editing application.

The Mac OS X Finder offers file-manipulation and information-gathering functions that are similar to the Finder of OS 8 and 9. The application object model that appeared with the OS X release was virtually identical to the Finder's OS 9 object model. The exceptions were the introduction of two new `window` objects, `Finder` and `inspector windows`, and the absence of any objects that represent `suitcase` or `desk accessory files` (see Chapter 15, *Mac OS 9 Finder Classes* (Mac OS 9) for a description of these file types in OS 9). The Mac OS X Finder dictionary also has some evolving new type definitions (e.g., icon view options, list view options, column). Expect the commands and objects that you can use with the Finder to change and evolve as Apple engineers gradually adapt Apple-Script to the Mac's significantly new underlying system architecture.

The rest of this chapter describes some ways to work with files, folders, and disks with the new Mac OS X Finder application.

Working with Files, Folders, Disks, and Windows in OS X

As in OS 9, a file, folder, and disk (but not a window) are `item` objects in Mac OS X. The code in Example 32-1 returns a list of all the files and folders that are in the current logged-in user's Desktop folder. Unlike OS 9, OS X only displays the contents of the Desktop folder of the currently logged-in user. OS 9's displayed desktop unifies all of the desktop folders of the startup disk and any other local volumes that contain a System Folder. For example, in OS 9, if you have two boot-able volumes—"MacDiskA" and "MacDiskB"—then the desktop items that you see represent any file or folder that was created in or moved to the desktop, regard-less of which disk has been the startup disk.

By contrast, the Mac OS X Finder only displays (on the computer desktop) the contents of the current logged-in user's Desktop folder. Everything else is an icon sitting on the Dock or viewed through a Finder window. For example, if I log in as "brucep," then my desktop folder is located in the following directory: *startup disk:users:brucep:library:desktop* (or, as this folder path would be depicted by the

Unix-based Darwin sub-system, */users/brucep/library/desktop*). So if I have a file in my desktop folder at this directory location called *newfile.txt*, this file is displayed on the OS X desktop only when I am logged in. If a user with a login name of "brynne" logs in to the computer, then the OS X Finder will only display the contents of Brynne's desktop folder.

Example 32-1: Getting References to Finder Items

```
tell app "Finder"
  get items
end tell
```

As you can see from Example 32-1, when you script the Mac OS X Finder, you use the `tell app "Finder"`... as you would with Mac OS 8 or 9. Once you have a reference to an `item`, then you can get a substantial amount of information about that file, folder, or disk. In fact, you can grab all of the available information about an `item` by taking a look at its new `properties` property, as in Example 32-2. `properties` returns a `record` data type, which is a collection of key-value pairs separated by curly braces ({}). Example 32-2 includes a sample return value for the `properties` property.

Example 32-2: Getting All of an Item's Properties

```
tell app "Finder"
(* if there is an item in the Desktop folder then get its 'properties'
property
*)
if ((count of items) > 0) then get properties of item 1
end tell

(* Sample return value:
{class:disk, name:"Mac OS X", index:1, container:folder "Desktop" of folder
"bruceper" of folder "Users" of startup disk of application "Finder",
disk:startup disk of application "Finder", position:{250, 43}, bounds:{218,
11, 282, 75}, kind:"Volume", locked:false, description:missing value,
comment:"", size:missing value, physical size:missing value, creation
date:date "Thursday, March 15, 2001 3:05:49 PM", modification date:date
"Friday, March 16, 2001 5:07:01 AM", icon:missing value, URL:"file://
localhost/", icon size:-1, owner:"root", group:"admin", owner privileges:read
write, group privileges:read write, everyones privileges:read only, container
window:missing value, capacity:3.420332032E+9, free space:1.844187136E+9,
ejectable:true, startup:false, format:Mac OS Extended format} *)
```

The `properties` property of the `item` object includes a lot of information about the access privileges for that file, folder, or disk, which the `item` object does not include in Mac OS 9. These properties include:

owner
> This returns a string username (e.g., "Brynne") that represents the logged-in user who owns the item.

group
> This string identifies the group that has special access to the item, as in "staff."

owner privileges

> This returns one of the following four constants: read only, read/write, write only, or none.

group privileges

> This returns one of the following four constants: read only, read/write, write only, or none.

everyone's privileges

> This returns one of the following four constants: read only, read/write, write only, or none.

Finally, the item also has a new url property in Mac OS X. For a file, the return value for this property might look like: `"file://localhost/users/brucep/library/desktop/newfile.txt"`.

Making New Files and Folders

As in Mac OS 9, you can make new files and folders with Mac OS X and Apple-Script by using the Finder's make command. Example 32-3 creates a new folder called "NewFolder" in the Desktop folder of the currently logged in user.

Example 32-3: Making a New Folder in OS X

```
tell application "Finder"
   make new folder at desktop with properties{name:"NewFolder"}
end tell
```

You can also create new files like aliases with the new Mac OS X Finder. One Finder quirk that has been corrected in OS X is the necessity to use the syntax make file at... as opposed to make new file at... when code is making a new file. Under OS 9 and its predecessors, you generally have to use the make new... syntax when making everything but file objects. Example 32-4 asks the user for a file reference, using the *choose file* osax, and then creates an alias to that file with the default name of "[file name] 2." In other words, if the original file is named "newfile," then the alias is named by default "newfile 2."

Example 32-4: Making a New Alias File

```
tell application "Finder"
   set f to (choose file with prompt "Choose the alias's original file")
   make new alias file to f
end tell
```

Working with Finder and Inspector Windows

The Finder uses Finder windows to graphically navigate the filesystem.

The Mac OS X release renamed the file-viewer windows of the Mac OS X Public Beta to Finder windows, but the Finder dictionary also refers to Finder windows as "file-viewer windows," so we will also occasionally use the file-viewer term.

Figure 32-2 shows a Finder window in column view. With AppleScript, you can get references to any open Finder windows (these refs look like "Finder window id 2" in Script Editor), and you can make new file viewers and specify their target file or folder. The Finder `application` dictionary (which is called "The Finder") includes a description of the new `Finder window` class. A `Finder window` object inherits some of the window's properties (e.g., `id`, `position`, `bounds`) and has its own `target` attribute. The `target` is a reference to the deepest file or folder selected in a `Finder window`. For example, if you were examining the contents of your *Documents* directory in a `Finder window`, then its `target` property would be:

```
folder "Documents" of folder "brucep" of folder "Users" of startup disk ¬
of Application "Finder"
```

If you want a less unwieldy form of reference than the latter target-return value, coerce the return value to a `string` (so it looks like `"Mac OS X:Users:brucep:Documents"`). Example 32-5 first gets a `list` of references to every open `Finder window` (if there are any). For each member of this `list` (i.e., a collection of `Finder window` objects), the script gets the `target` property. This is a settable property, as the script demonstrates in Example 32-6.

Example 32-5: Examining a File Viewer Window via Script

```
tell application "Finder"
   set fv_wins to (every Finder window)
   repeat with w in fv_wins
      get target of w as string
   end repeat
end tell
```

Example 32-6 makes a new `Finder window` and establishes the directory *startup disk:System:Library* as its target. When you run the script in Script Editor, the Finder displays the new `Finder window` and makes it the active window.

Example 32-6: Making a Finder Window

```
tell application "Finder"
   set fv_targ to folder "Library" of folder "System" of startup disk
   make new Finder window to fv_targ
   (* sample return value: Finder window id 6 of application Finder *)
end tell
```

Inspector windows (or Info windows as they are specified under the Aqua Human Interface Guidelines) are new `window` classes in OS X and in the Finder dictionary.

You can view the Finder's dictionary of commands and classes by dragging the Finder icon to the Script Editor icon, or by choosing Open Dictionary... in Script Editor's File menu, then selecting the Finder's icon in the resulting dialog window.

These windows are revamped Get Info windows that are undoubtedly familiar to users of Mac OS 8 and 9. The user displays Info windows by selecting the file, folder, or disk and then typing *Command-I* or choosing Show Info from the Finder's file menu. Figure 32-3 shows an inspector window.

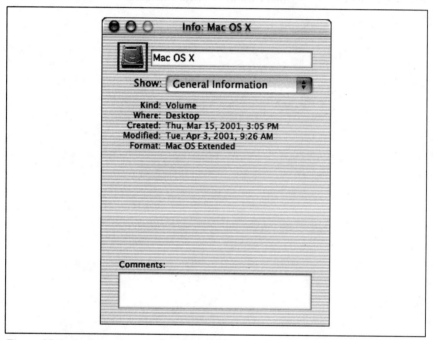

Figure 32-3: An inspector window for a folder

You can get references to all of the open inspector windows (if there are any) by examining the Finder application's window elements, as in Example 32-7. The AppleScript return value for an open Info window looks like `inspector window "Info:Mail"`.

Example 32-7: Displaying an Info window's name

```
tell application "Finder"
    activate
    set nameList to name of windows
    repeat with nm in nameList
        if nm contains "Info:" then
            display dialog "The name of the open Info window is: " & nm
```

Example 32-7: Displaying an Info window's name (continued)

```
      end if
   end repeat
end tell
```

A Work in Progress

It is important to remember that like Mac OS X itself, scripting the Finder with AppleScript is still a work in progress. To find out what terminology will work in your system, use the Script Editor to examine the Finder's dictionary. Open the Finder's dictionary by dragging its icon onto the Script Editor icon in the Finder, or use Script Editor's File → Open Dictionary menu command.

CHAPTER 33

Scripting Mail

Mac OS X installs a nifty email application called, aptly enough, Mail. Like other email programs such as Eudora or Outlook Express, Mail allows you to get and send email, set up various email accounts, and format email messages in various ways. This chapter describes some of the scripts you can already write, as well as some of the potentially interesting classes that the Mail dictionary contains. Figure 33-1 shows what the Mail app looks like on the Mac OS X desktop. Its icon is the second one from the left on the Dock (in this graphic), which is the repository of file and program icons arrayed along the bottom of the Mac screen.

Setting Up an Email Message

The easiest way for a script to get Mail started on a new email message (but not actually complete and send the message) is to use the *GetURL* command. This command takes as its parameter a string "mailto" URL, which looks like *mailto:bwperry@parkerriver.com?subject=My%20mail*. Mail responds to this command by opening up a new message window and constructing the email according to the string parameter you used with *GetURL*. The result might look like Figure 33-2. Notice that the string parameter itself must be URL-encoded (e.g., %20 symbols replacing any space characters) for the message to be properly constructed.

The new email message window becomes the active Mail window and the front-most window on the desktop if you use the *activate* command, as in Example 33-1. Mail includes a *send* command in its dictionary, for sending the mail.

Figure 33-1: OS X's Mail application

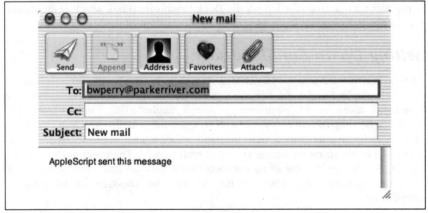

Figure 33-2: A Mail message window displayed by a script

Example 33-1: Using Mail's GetURL Command

```
set theAdd to text returned of (display dialog "enter the recipient's
email address please:" default answer "")
set subj to "scripted%20mail"
set cont to "AppleScript%20sent%20this%20mail."
tell application "Mail"
```

Example 33-1: Using Mail's GetURL Command (continued)

```
    activate
    GetURL ("mailto:" & theAdd & "?subject=" & subj & "&body=" & cont)
end tell
```

Exploring the Mail Application Object

Mail has an application scripting object that represents the Mail app itself. You can get this object's properties with an AppleScript, such as the user's email address (property user email), the software's version, and a true/false property called frontmost (representing whether or not Mail is the frontmost program on the Mac OS X desktop).

Example 33-2 gets the value of some of these properties and displays them to the user, using the *display dialog* scripting addition.

 All the Standard Additions osax are available for AppleScript on Mac OS X, with a few variations compared with OS 9. Appendix A, *Standard Scripting Additions,* describes these variations.

Example 33-2: Query the Mail Application Object

```
tell application "Mail"
    set myemail to user email
    set appname to name
    set mver to version
end tell
display dialog ("the user's email is: " & myemail & return & "the App name
is:" & appname & (ASCII character 13) & "the App version is: " & (mver as
string))
```

Getting Information about an Email Account

You can use an AppleScript to find out information about an account. To do this, you need to get references to the Mail application's account elements. For example, the code fragment: tell app "Mail" to get accounts returns a list type containing Mail account objects.

Finally, Example 33-3 shows how to set up and send an email with Mail and Mac OS X. Mail's *send* command returns 1 if the mail was sent and 0 if the *send* failed.

Example 33-3: Making and Sending an email with AppleScript

```
tell application "Mail"
    activate
    set theContent to "Here's my first Mac OS X email message!"
    set email to (make new compose message at the beginning of ¬
        compose messages with properties {content:theContent, ¬
        sender:"bwperry@mac.com", subject:"test"})
```

Example 33-3: Making and Sending an email with AppleScript (continued)

```
    tell email to make new to recipient at beginning of to recipients ¬
    with properties {address:"bperry@mediaone.net", display name:"bwp"}
    make new message editor at the beginning of message editors
    set the compose message of message editor 1 to email
    send email
end tell
```

CHAPTER 34

Executing Scripts with the Terminal App

In a dramatic departure from prior operating systems, but a welcome one for many Macintosh scripters, Mac OS X comes equipped with a command-line interface (CLI) to its underlying filesystem and applications. In a throwback to old-fashioned ways of interacting with a computer, a CLI involves entering text commands from the keyboard into a window that contains only a prompt in the form of a solid square cursor, percent sign, or some other symbol. You can access the command line from the Mac OS X graphical user interface (GUI) by executing the Terminal app from the directory *startup disk:Applications:Utilities* (or, in Unix parlance, */applications/utilities/*). This program displays the CLI window. Some users, viewing Terminal as primitive and an unforgivable violation of Apple Computer's rich tradition of visual interfaces, will steer clear of the CLI. (Okay, so the Terminal isn't *that* primitive; you can control the size of its window and the font of its displayed text, among other attributes.) However, Terminal gives you access to system directories and files you cannot see in Finder windows, which is critical for system administrators. In addition, the Unix-derived software you can use from the command line, including the text editors pico, vi, and emacs, as well as the scripting languages Perl, tcl, and awk and all of the built-in BSD Commands (e.g., *ls*, *pwd*, *mv*, *rm*), are often indispensable accompaniments to AppleScript and other familiar Mac tools.

You can even create, compile, and execute AppleScripts from Terminal (otherwise, I might not have included this chapter!). Some scripters might be fond of popping open pico or vi and creating their AppleScripts in this manner, but I still prefer Script Editor. The true power of the marriage of Terminal and AppleScript, however, will perhaps come from the integration of AppleScript with the CLI tools, which Apple Computer has suggested will be included with future OS X releases. For example, I would like AppleScript to be able to get and deal with the return values from the execution of Perl scripts, so that AppleScript's eventual tight integration with OS X and ease-of-use could be combined with Perl's tremendous versatility (e.g., it's much easier to do network/HTTP programming and XML parsing with Perl than with AppleScript). You can already take standard input from a shell script and run this input as compiled AppleScript code, as this chapter's section on the *osascript* command discusses.

The remainder of this chapter describes how to use the three Terminal commands that can be used with AppleScript: *osacompile, osalang,* and *osascript.* Figure 34-1 shows what the Terminal window looks like after the *osacompile* command was used to compile a text file called *s;* then on the next line of the Terminal window, the *ls* command was used to show the contents of the user's current working directory. This directory contains the result of compiling the file *s,* which is a script called *a.scpt,* the default name that *osacompile* gives a script if its *name* option is not used. You can use the *osacompile* command to compile one or more text or compiled-script files into a single script.

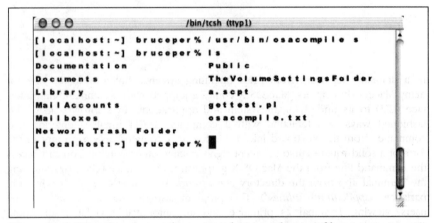

Figure 34-1: Using the osacompile command to compile a text file into a script

osacompile

Syntax

```
osacompile [-l language]  [-o name] [-e save file as execute only] [-d
place the resulting script in the data fork of the output file] [-r
type:id place the resulting script in the resource fork of the output
file, in the resource specified by type:id] [-t the four-character file-
type code for the script (the default is "osas")] [-c the four-character
creator  code for the script (the default is "ToyS")] [one or more files
or standard input]
```

Description

The osacompile program is located in your *startup disk:usr:bin* directory (or, */usr/bin/*). You have to call *osacompile* using the /usr/bin/osacompile syntax.

When you enter a new shell or window with Terminal, the default working directory is the home directory of the user that is logged in. For example, my home directory is called *bruceper*, so when I enter a new shell, the working directory is */users/bruceper/.* You can find the name of the working directory from the command line by using the *pwd* BSD command.

You can provide a filename for the new script by using the optional -o switch, as in:

```
/usr/bin/osacompile -o newscript scripttext.txt.
```

This command-line sequence would attempt to compile the file *scripttext.txt*, located in the current working directory, into a compiled script called *newscript*. The Terminal depicted in Figure 34-1 did not provide a new filename, so the new script received the default filename of *a.scpt*. Type the filenames or paths inside the Terminal window without quotation marks (e.g., `/users/bruceper/ newscript` instead of `"/users/bruceper/newscript"`). In another example, let's say you want to compile a text file in another directory and save the new file in a folder other than the current working directory. You can use syntax such as:

```
/usr/bin/osacompile -o /users/bruceper/desktop/script2 /users/bruceper/
documents/rawscript
```

This command-line sequence takes a text file *rawscript* located in the *documents* folder of user *bruceper* and compiles a new script called *script2* in the same user's *desktop* directory. Are you getting the impression that it is much easier to create and compile scripts inside of a development program like Script Editor?

The *osacompile* command attempts to compile the text file as an AppleScript unless you specify another OSA language with the -1 switch, as in:

```
/usr/bin/osacompile -1 JavaScript rawscript.txt
```

(assuming that a JavaScript OSA scripting component exists on the system). Use the *osalang* command (described later in this chapter) to get information on all of the system's OSA languages. You can specify more than one file argument for *osacompile*, which will attempt to compile all of the given files into one script. For example, one file could be a collection of subroutines, and the other could be a script that initiates some task by calling those defined routines.

You can also pass *standard input* or typed AppleScript code as opposed to a filename to the *osacompile* command. The typed standard-input code has to be enclosed in quotation marks (""). For example, the code:

```
/usr/bin/osacompile -o /users/bruceper/documents/script3 "return (2 *
50)"
```

will cause *osacompile* to create a compiled script called *script3* in my *documents* folder. If you run this script inside Terminal with the *osascript* command, for instance, the return value of 100 (the value returned from the expression (2 * 50)) will show up in the Terminal window.

Standard input is command-linese for characters fed to the shell or command line from an input device such as a keyboard. Standard output is the opposite—characters such as an English phrase that are displayed to the user in the Terminal window. So the scripter can interpret standard input in part as text that they type at the Terminal window prompt.

Examples

You can compile and run the following example from the Terminal command line. It starts with a text file called *rawscript.txt,* which contains a `tell` statement that targets the Finder. The script just returns the number of items (count items), such as files and folders, contained by the logged-in user's desktop folder. This text file is compiled into an AppleScript called *newscript,* which is located in the */users/bruceper/documents/* directory. If you run this script on the command line with input such as `usr/bin/osascript  newscript` (assuming that the current working directory in the Terminal window is */users/bruceper/documents/*), then the script's `integer` return value (e.g., 8) will be displayed as standard output on the command line:

```
(* command line input in Terminal window:
[localhost: ~] bruceper% /usr/bin/osacompile  -o /users/bruceper/
documents/newscript  /users/bruceper/library/desktop/rawscript.txt
*)
(* contents of rawscript.txt *)
tell app "Finder"
    return (count items)
end tell
(* Example return value in Terminal window: an integer like '8' *)
```

osalang

Syntax

```
osalang [-d only print the default language] [-l list the name and
description for each installed language]
```

Description

The *osalang* command lists the computer's installed OSA-compliant languages (i.e., languages that use Apple events to communicate among applications). In the newness of Mac OS X, this command may only return the output in Figure 34-2, "AppleScript" and "Generic Scripting System." Using the -d switch will only print the default language, while the -l switch prints each language in long format (which is still pithy considering the output of Figure 34-2).

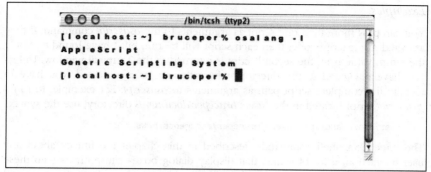

Figure 34-2: Executing osalang in a Terminal window

osascript

Syntax

```
osascript [-1 language] [one or more files or standard input]
```

Description

The *osascript* command attempts to execute the files that are passed to the command as arguments. If you do not use the -l switch and the arguments do not look like filenames, then *osalang* attempts to execute the text arguments as standard input, dynamically run as an AppleScript. Now where else can you generate an AppleScript like that?

By default, *osascript* runs the text files or standard input as an AppleScript, but if you use the -l switch, you can specify another OSA language for it to use. Like *osacompile* and *osalang*, you have to use the syntax */usr/bin/osascript* to call this command. Figure 34-3 is a Terminal window in which the following command has been entered:

```
/usr/bin/osascript "return (65 * 87)"
```

The *osascript* command runs this code phrase just as if you had entered the script into Script Editor, compiled it, and run it. The expression return (65 * 87) returns the value 5655—the product of 65 and 87—to the Terminal window as standard output.

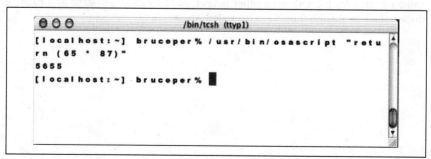

Figure 34-3: Dynamically running standard input using the osascript command

Examples

You can pass more than one script as arguments to the *osascript* command. If they are valid AppleScript code, then each script will be run, but I have found that only the return value from the second script is returned to the Terminal window. Unless you have navigated to the directory where the scripts are located, you have to identify the complete script path as arguments to *osascript*. For example, to run a *newscript* script located in the */users/bruceper/documents* directory, use the syntax:

```
/usr/bin/osascript /users/bruceper/documents/newscript
```

The three OSA shell commands described in this chapter are finicky about any user interaction; a lot of scripts that display dialog boxes cause errors with these shell commands. However, The following example, when run from the command line with *osascript*, did successfully display a dialog window after activating the Finder and making it the frontmost application on the desktop:

```
tell app "Finder"
    activate
    display dialog "Hi there"
end tell
```

The following example describes two separate scripts and the *osascript* command sequence that ran them. Only the return value from the second script—called *roundit* (all it does is round a real number)—is displayed in the Terminal window:

```
(* command line input in Terminal window:
[localhost: ~] bruceper% /usr/bin/osascript/users/bruceper/documents/
getitems/users/bruceper/documents/roundit
*)
(* source code of first script: getitems *)
tell app "Finder"
    return (count items) (* return the number of files, folders, other
desktop items *)
end tell
  (* source code for second script:roundit *)
round 3465.6
(* return value from Terminal window: 3466 (the integer returned from the
second script) *)
```

The OSA-related Terminal commands, particularly *osascript*, hold much potential for integrating AppleScript with more complex shell scripts, such as passing the value of variables formed using other languages like Perl to *osascript* and running these values as though they were compiled AppleScript.

CHAPTER 35

Scripting TextEdit

Mac OS X installs a handy and scriptable word processor called TextEdit. You can find it in the */Applications* directory or by typing *Option-Command-A* when the Finder is active and double-clicking TextEdit from the resulting Finder window. TextEdit is not as feature-laden and bloated as Microsoft Word, nor as limited in functionality as SimpleText. It is useful for creating simple text documents where you want to control the font and color of the text, but more complex publishing tasks than this probably are not appropriate TextEdit jobs. Figure 35-1 shows TextEdit on the Mac OS X desktop.

It is likely that the TextEdit's available AppleScript commands will change with new Mac OS X releases, so this chapter will focus on TextEdit's major commands (e.g., *count, open, save*) and text-related classes. The TextEdit scriptable task that immediately comes to mind is creating a new file, opening it in TextEdit, and then creating the file's contents. Example 35-1 creates a new file using the Finder app then has TextEdit open the file and place some text into it.

Example 35-1: Opening a New File in TextEdit

```
set fol to (choose folder) (* use the 'choose folder' osax to ask the user to
choose a folder; this osax returns an alias type *)
set nm to the text returned of (display dialog "Choose a file name:" ¬
default answer "") (* have the user create a name for the file with the
'display dialog' osax *)
tell application "Finder" -- The Finder is better at making files
    set fil to (make new file at fol with properties {name:nm}) (* store the
new file in variable 'fil' *)
end tell
tell application "TextEdit"
    activate -- make TextEdit the frontmost app
    open {fil as alias} -- 'open' command takes a 'list of aliases' parameter
```

Example 35-1: Opening a New File in TextEdit (continued)

```
   set text of document 1 to "First sentence of this new document." (* write
a line to the file *)
end tell
```

This script first gets a folder (for storing the new file) and a filename from the script user, using the *choose folder* and *display dialog* scripting additions.

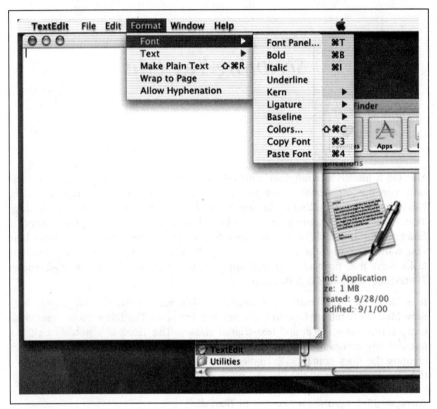

Figure 35-1: TextEdit and its Format:Font menu

 There are variations on the use of some AppleScript scripting commands compared with OS 9.0, such as the *new file* osax being changed to *choose file name*. Appendix A, *Standard Scripting Additions*, describes these commands and differences.

The script then makes a new file using the Finder's *make* command with the user's chosen filename (for the sake of brevity I have left out the usually required checks for the cancellation of these dialogs or for the possibility that the user did not enter any text for the filename). Then TextEdit is made the frontmost or active application (i.e., *activate*), and it opens the new file. The TextEdit *open* command takes as its parameter a `list` of aliases. The code fragment `open {fil as alias}` first coerces the `file` object to an `alias` and then stores this `alias` in a single-item `list` that is passed to the *open* command. Just leaving the `fil` variable as a `document file` object (which is what the Desktop's *make new file* command returns), as in `open {fil }`, will generate an error in TextEdit. This happens because its *open* command takes a `list` of aliases as its parameter, not a `list` of `document file` objects.

The TextEdit app has `document` elements (see the TextEdit classes section in this chapter). The following code would return a `list` of all open TextEdit documents (i.e., TextEdit windows visible in the Finder or on the Dock):

```
tell app "TextEdit" to get documents
```

The final line of Example 35-1 sets the `text` property of the first TextEdit `document` (`document 1`) to a `string`: "First sentence of this new document." In TextEdit, `document 1` is the front window that would appear on the desktop if you activated TextEdit by choosing the program in the Dock or by clicking on one of its windows.

TextEdit

The rest of this chapter describes each text-related TextEdit class and gives examples of how to use them in your scripts. As always, to keep up-to-date about any scriptable program on your computer, use Script Editor's *Open Dictionary...* menu item to view the software's dictionary of commands and classes. Chapter 2, *Using Script Editor with OS 9 and OS X,* describes application dictionaries.

Dictionary classes

attribute run
> A subdivision of a block of text, an `attribute run` is a group of characters that all have the same attributes, such as font or size. An `attribute run` is just a different way of abstracting or grouping parts of a text block. For example, if the first paragraph of a document's text has some characters that are 12 points in size and others that are 18 points, then getting the `attribute runs` of that paragraph would return two separate chunks of text in a `list` (one group would be 12 points in size and the other would be 18 points). However, getting paragraph 1 of that text would return one chunk of characters of different sizes. In other words, the paragraph would contain the two `attribute runs`. The following example gets every `attribute run` of a document's text (a `list` containing three `attribute runs`). The first line of the text contains the characters "hi here is some more text k," but the last "k" character is in a different font and size than the sentence's other characters. Consequently, the "k" and its following carriage return character is considered a separate `attribute run` then its preceding characters. The return value of the code `every attribute run of text of document 1` is at the bottom of the script displayed within comment characters:

```
tell application "TextEdit"
    activate
    every attribute run of text of document 1
```

```
(* returns a list of three attribute runs:
{"hi here is more text ", "k
", "
Meeting notes:
Wednesday, October 11, 2000 12:58:16 PM"}
*)
end tell
```

The following are `attribute run` elements:

character
> An `attribute run` can contain characters, such as:
>
> > (count characters of attribute 1 of text of document 1)
>
> If an `attribute run` is "Hi here is some text" then the latter code fragment would return an `integer` 20, or the number of characters in the sentence. See the `character` class.

paragraph
> An `attribute run` or chunk of text could contain one or more paragraphs, as in (count `paragraphs` of `attribute run 1 of text of document 1`). See the `paragraph` class.

word
> An `attribute run` or chunk of text can contain one or more words, as in:
>
> > (count words of attribute run 1 of text of document 1)
>
> See the `word` class.

The following are `attribute run` properties:

font string
> Each `attribute run` has a font property, as in `Arial`. Code such as:
>
> > font of attribute run 1 of text of document 1
>
> returns a `string` such as `Geneva`.

color color
> Although appearing in the TextEdit dictionary, the `color` property (representing the color of the text in the `attribute run`) was not accessible in the Mac OS X.

size integer
> The `size` property is accessible from code such as `size of attribute run 1 of text of document 1`. It represents the size of the first character in the attribute run's text.

class integer *(read-only)*
> This attribute returns the word `string`.

character
> A `character` object is what you would expect it to be, a single character inside of a word or `string`. The following example returns the first word of a document as a `list` of `character` objects. If you instead used the following code then the return value would be a `string` like "F":

```
get character 1 of word 1 of text of document 1
tell app "TextEdit"
    get characters of word 1 of text of document 1
end tell
(* Example return value:
{"F", "i", "r", "s", "t"}  *)
```

The following are **character** elements:

attribute run

The code:

```
attribute run 1 of character 1 of text of document 1
```

usually returns the character itself as a **string**, as in N. See the **attribute run** class.

character

It doesn't make sense for a **character** to have a **character** element, however, the following code returns the **character** as a **string** (e.g., "j"):

```
character  1 of character 1 of text of document 1
```

paragraph

A character's **paragraph** element returns itself. So if the character is "j," then its **paragraph 1** element returns the **string** "j."

word

A character's **word** element returns itself. So if the **character** is "j," then its **word 1** element returns the **string** "j."

The following are **character** properties:

font string

Getting the **font** property returns a **string** like Helvetica, representing the character's font.

color color

Accessing the **color** property of a character object returns a data value such as «data RGB FFFF433951F7».

size integer

Trying to access the character **size** property returns the font size of the character, as in 14.

class integer *(read-only)*

The class property returns the word **string**.

document

A document object represents an open TextEdit document, as depicted in Figure 35-1. You can get a reference to one or more documents by grabbing the TextEdit application's **document** elements, as in **tell app "TextEdit" to get documents**. This code returns a **list** that looks like:

```
{document 1 of application "TextEdit", document 2 of application
"TextEdit"}
```

The following example gets the various properties of a document. You can view the values of these properties using the Event Log of Script Editor. This example shows some Event Log output at the bottom of the script:

```
tell application "TextEdit"
    set doc to document 1 (* the front document is stored in doc
variable *)
    (* a document's properties revealed *)
    doc's path -- the Unix path
    doc's modified
    doc's name
    set txt to text of doc (* returns the content of the document
if any (if the document is empty, returns an empty string "") *)
    set parcount to (count of txt's paragraphs)
    set wdcount to (count of txt's words)
    (* Event Log output:
    get document 1
    --> document 1
    get path of document 1
    --> "/Users/bruceper/Documents/newfile.rtf"
    get modified of document 1
    --> 0
    get name of document 1
    --> "newfile.rtf"
    get every text of document 1
    --> "Hi, I'm pleased to be the first paragraph of this
document. My font is \
    Verdana."
    *)
end tell
```

The following are document elements:

text

The text of a TextEdit document can be seized with code such as:

```
tell app "TextEdit" to get text of document 1
```

You can also write to a document, without using the *open for access*, *write*, or *close access* scripting additions, by using code such as:

```
set the text of document 1 to "My chunk of text"
```

This code shows how to append text, such as a date string, to an existing TextEdit document:

```
tell app "TextEdit"
    set cr to ASCII character 13 (* use as a return or new line
character *)
    set tmessage to cr & "Meeting notes:" & cr & ¬
    ((current date) as string)
    set docs to documents -- docs contains a list of open
TextEdit documents
    repeat with d in docs
        if ((name of d) contains "memo log") then (* only add text
to "memo log" file *)
```

```
                    set text of d to (text of d) & tmessage (* append the
            text stored in var tmessage to end of file *)
                    (* the path looks like "/users/oneuser/library/desktop/
            myfile.rtf" *)
                        set pth to path of d
                exit repeat
                    end if
                end repeat
                display dialog "the memo file is at: " & pth
            end tell
```

The following are document properties:

path string

This property returns a string that looks like *"/users/oneuser/desktop/
myfile.rtf."* This Unix-style pathname identifies where the document is
stored on the computer. The back-slash ("/") character that begins path
says "begin at the startup disk or root." The standard disk, file, and folder
delimiter for AppleScript, the colon (":"), is still used by many Apple-
Script commands (such as *choose folder*) to represent where the file is
stored. If the TextEdit document has not yet been saved, then its path
property returns nothing in OS X, not even an empty string (""). You can
set the path property of a document (this will not raise an error in my
testing), then use TextEdit's *save* command to save the file to the new
path.

modified integer *(read-only)*

This property returns 1 if the document has been modified since it was
last saved or 0 if the document has not been modified. The following
example finds out if a document has been saved, then saves the
document (using the *save* command) if the document has unsaved
changes:

```
            tell application "TextEdit"
                activate
                (* if the document has been changed since it was last saved
            its 'modified' property will return 1 *)
                if (modified of document 1) > 0 then
                    save document 1
                    close document 1
                else
                    close document 1
                end if
            end tell
```

name string

name returns a string that is the name of the document file. If you have
just created the document in TextEdit but have not yet saved it, the name
property returns nothing (not even a string such as "untitled"). Trying to
find out whether the document has a valid name (such as by accessing
the length of name to see if the name has more than zero characters)
raises an error at least in Mac OS X. You might try this document name
test in future releases, or use a try block to catch and examine the error.

Chapter 7, *Flow-Control Statements,* describes error trapping with the `try` statement.

`class integer` *(read-only)*
> Accessing the `class` property for the `document` object raises an error in Mac OS X.

`paragraph`
> A `paragraph` object is a chunk of text that is terminated by a new line or paragraph character. You can set the paragraphs of a document's text with code such as:
>
> ```
> tell app "TextEdit" to set paragraph 3 of text of document 1 to ¬
> "new paragraph"
> ```

If you try to `get paragraphs of text of document 1`, for example, and the `document` does not contain any content, then a script error is raised. An easy way to find out whether a TextEdit `document` contains any text yet is to check the length of the number of words in the document, as in the following example:

```
tell app "TextEdit"
    activate
    set l to (text of document 1)
    if (length of l) > 0 then
        set notEmpty to true
    end if
end tell
```

The following are `paragraph` elements:

`attribute run`
> A `paragraph` can contain one or more attribute runs, which are chunks of text that share attributes such as font and size. For example, if a `paragraph` contained two bits of styled text that had different fonts, then each of these text chunks would be considered an `attribute run` within a `paragraph`. See the `attribute run` class.

`character`
> Paragraphs can contain one or more characters (unless the `paragraph` is only an empty `string` and return character). You can get all of the characters of a `paragraph` inside of a `list` with code such as:
>
> ```
> tell app "TextEdit" to get characters of paragraph 1 of text of
> document 1
> ```
>
> The return value would look like:
>
> ```
> {"a", " ", "v", "e", "r", "y", " ", "s", "h", "o", "r", "t", "
> ", "p", "a", "r", "a", "g", "r", "a", "p", "h"}
> ```

`paragraph`
> Paragraphs do not contain other paragraphs (philosophically), but the TextEdit dictionary still lists `paragraph` as an element of the `paragraph` object.

word

A **word** is a series of characters unbroken by a space character. You can get all the words of the paragraph inside of a **list** with code, such as:

```
tell app "TextEdit" to get words of paragraph 1 of text of
document 1
```

This kind of code phrase can be very handy in searching for letters, symbols, words, or phrases inside of text. See the **word** class.

The following are **paragraph** properties:

font string

This property returns the font name for the first character of a paragraph, such as **Helvetica**.

color color

This property returns the **color** object for the first character of a paragraph, with a return value in Mac OS X 10.0 that looks like «data RGB FFFF433951F7».

size integer

The **size** property is the size of the font of the paragraph's first character.

class integer

This property returns the word **string**, not an **integer** as the dictionary definition specifies.

text

text represents the body or content of a **document**. The whole chunk of content will be returned as a **string** from code such as:

```
tell app "TextEdit" to get text of document 1
```

If the **document** does not yet have any content, then its **text** element returns an empty **string** (""). Once you have the **text** in memory, you can get or set the values of its characters, words, or paragraphs. The following example finds out whether the existing content of a **document** contains the word **Copyright**; if it does not, then **Copyright** 2001 is appended to the end of the document:

```
tell application "TextEdit "
    activate
    set cr to ASCII character 13
    set txt to text of document 1
    set wd to (words of txt)
    set len to length of wd
    if (len > 0) then
        if wd does not contain "Copyright" then
            set (text of document 1) to txt & cr & "Copyright 2001"
        else
            display dialog "copyright included"
        end if
    end if
end tell
```

The following are **text** elements:

attribute run

> **text** can contain one or more **attribute runs**, which are chunks of text that share attributes such as font and size. To get the **attribute runs** inside of **text**, use code such as:
>
> ```
> get attribute runs of text of document 1
> ```
>
> If the **text** does not have any **attribute runs**, then this code returns an empty **list** (ᜮᜭ). See the **attribute run** class.

character

> **text** can contain zero or more characters. You can get all of the characters inside of **text** with code such as:
>
> ```
> tell app "TextEdit" to get characters of text of document 1
> ```
>
> This returns a **list** of characters that looks like {"a", "b", "c"} (it will be a giant **list** if the document has a lot of text). You can also get a range of characters with the following syntax:
>
> ```
> get characters 3 thru 17 of text of document 1
> ```
>
> This code raises an error if the **document** does not have 17 characters. If the **document** is empty, then the following code returns nothing (at least in OS X), not even an empty **list**:
>
> ```
> get characters of text of document 1
> ```
>
> See the **character** class.

paragraph

> **text** contains zero or more paragraphs, which are delineated in TextEdit by paragraph marks or new line characters. You can get a **paragraph** count for a **document**, for instance, by using code such as:
>
> ```
> count paragraphs of text of document 1
> ```
>
> See the **paragraph** class.

word

> You can get all of the **words** of a **document** with the code:
>
> ```
> words of text of document 1
> ```
>
> This returns a **list** of words that looks like {"list", "of", "words"}. See the **word** class.

The following are **text** properties:

font string

> This returns a **string** such as "ArialMT." This **string** is the name of the font of the text block's first character. In other words, if the first character of the text of **document** 1 is of the font "ArialMT" and the second character is "Apple Chancery," then the code phrase **font of text of document 1** returns "ArialMT."

color color
:   This property will raise an error if you try to access its value from a text object, but you can get the color of individual characters in text. See the **character** class.

size integer
:   This property will return an **integer** representing the point size of the text's first character (such as 14).

class integer *(read-only)*
:   The TextEdit dictionary identifies this property's return value as **integer**, but my testing reveals that it returns the word **string**.

word

A **word** (e.g., "sentence") is a series of characters unbroken by a space character. A **word** contains a **character** object. The syntax **words of text of document 1**, for example, will return a (potentially long) **list** of words. The space characters separating the words will be left out of the **list**. This syntax makes it very easy to search a document's words for a specific word, as in

```
Set found to ((text of document 1) contains "Copyright")
```

The following is a **word** element:

character
:   This element is a subdivision of a **word**. For instance, the following code returns all of the characters of the document's first **word** as a **list**, as in {"F", "i", "r", "s", "t"}:

```
    characters of word 1 of text of document 1
```

See the **character** class.

The following are **word** properties:

font string
:   This property will return a **string** like "Helvetica."

color color
:   This property will return a **color** object representing the text color the return value in Mac OS X looks like «data RGB FFFF433951F7».

size integer
:   This property will return an **integer** representing the point size of the text's first character (such as 14).

class integer *(read-only)*
:   This property returns the word **string**.

application

This class represents the TextEdit application itself. In TextEdit's dictionary, you can find the TextEdit **application** object described under the TextEdit Suite (Chapter 1 describes AppleScript dictionaries). The **application** has four properties or attributes (i.e., the value of its **name** property is "TextEdit"). You can get references to all of TextEdit's documents with code such as:

```
tell app "TextEdit" to get documents
```

The following example queries the property values of the copy of TextEdit running on the machine where the script executes. You can view the output (the property values) in Script Editor's Event Log window. Display this window by typing *Command-E* when Script Editor is the frontmost application, then make sure that the checkboxes labeled "Show Events" and "Show Event Results" are checked.

```
tell application "TextEdit"
   frontmost
   name
   version
(* Example Event Log output:
   tell application "TextEdit"
      get frontmost
      --> 0
      get name
      --> "TextEdit"
      get version
      --> 0
   end tell
   *)
end tell
```

The following are `application` elements:

document

TextEdit can have zero or more open documents. Each one of these documents is considered a `document` object with its own properties or attributes. Each open `document` is indexed from front to back in the manner of `document` 1 (the `frontmost` `document` if you make TextEdit the active application), `document` 2, and so on. For example, to count the open documents use:

```
tell app "TextEdit to count documents
```

To close an open `document`, use:

```
tell TextEdit to close document 1
```

(or whatever its index is). See the `document` class description for a demonstration of how to get a document's properties.

window

A TextEdit `window` is a desktop `window` that is showing a TextEdit document. You can get references to all the names of the open TextEdit windows by using the code:

```
tell app "TextEdit" to get name of windows
```

This code returns a `list` that might look like:

```
{"newfile.rtf", "newfile 2.rtf"}
```

The latter `list` contains the name of one `window` (i.e., the filename of the `document` contained by the `window`) as a `string`.

The following are **application** properties:

frontmost **integer** *(read-only)*
> This property returns 1 only if TextEdit is the active application (if you click on a TextEdit window then TextEdit becomes the active application); it returns 0 otherwise.

name **string** *(read-only)*
> This property returns "TextEdit."

version **integer** *(read-only)*
> This property represents the application's version number, which returns 0 in Mac OS X 10.0.

class **integer** *(read-only)*
> Getting the **class** property caused a script error with TextEdit and Mac OS X.

color
> **color** objects have just one property: **class**. Most of the other **TextEdit** classes, such as **character**, **word**, **paragraph**, and **text**, have **color** properties that can be queried using AppleScript. They return **data** value types, as in «**data RGB FFFF433951F7**».

The following is a **color** property:

class **integer** *(read-only)*
> The TextEdit color object has a class property whose value is «**class RGB** ».

PART VI

Appendixes

APPENDIX A

Standard Scripting Additions

Scripting additions are a powerful element of AppleScripting that give it almost infinite extensibility. These code libraries live inside the *startup disk:System Folder:Scripting Additions* folder in OS 9. Figure A-1 shows what their icons look like. Known among the scripting cognoscenti as osax (singular form, standing for Open Scripting Architecture Extension) or osaxen (a plural form), the scripting additions give you commands you can use almost anywhere in your script. Ever since Mac OS 8.5, Apple Computer has bundled a number of the most useful scripting additions into the Standard Additions file and installed this file with your operating system. In Mac OS X, the filepath for the Standard Additions file is */System/Library/ScriptingAdditions/StandardAdditions.osax*.

Name	Date Modified	Size	Ki
Desktop Printer Manager	Wed, Aug 5, 1998, 3:00 PM	80 K	sys
FileSharing Commands	Mon, Aug 30, 1999, 3:00 PM	24 K	scr
Keyboard Addition	Thu, Sep 23, 1999, 3:00 PM	16 K	scr
Keychain Scripting	Mon, Sep 13, 1999, 3:00 PM	64 K	app
MonitorDepth	Tue, Aug 2, 1994, 3:00 AM	4 K	scr
Network Setup Scripting	Mon, Sep 13, 1999, 3:00 PM	212 K	app
Remote Access Commands	Mon, Aug 30, 1999, 3:00 PM	100 K	scr
Standard Additions	Thu, Oct 21, 1999, 3:00 PM	180 K	scr
URL Access Scripting	Mon, Sep 13, 1999, 3:00 PM	28 K	app

Scripting Additions — 9 items, 8.52 GB available

Figure A-1: Scripting addition files in OS 9

In Mac OS X, if you want a scripting addition to be available to all users, then the administrator (the first user who installs Mac OS X, or somebody she designates as administrator) should place it in */Library/ScriptingAdditions/*. This administrator should first create the *Scripting Additions* folder if it does not yet exist. If you want a scripting addition to only be used by one user, place it in this directory: */users/username/library/ScriptingAdditions/*. You can create this directory yourself, in a particular user's *Library* folder, if the *Scripting Additions* folder does not yet exist there.

The Standard Additions include the following scripting additions:

ASCII character	*mount volume*
ASCII number	*new file (OS 9 and prior OSes)*
beep	*offset*
choose URL	*open for access*
choose application	*open location*
choose file	*path to*
choose file name (OS X only)	*random number*
choose folder	*read*
choose from list	*round*
clipboard info	*run script*
close access	*say*
current date	*scripting components*
delay	*set eof*
display dialog	*set the clipboard to*
get eof	*set volume*
handle CGI request	*store script*
info for	*summarize*
list disks	*the clipboard*
list folder	*time to GMT*
load script	*write*

Figure A-2 shows the Standard Addition's dictionary in Mac OS 9.

Any programmer, not just Apple's, can create a scripting addition. This mechanism has spawned numerous third-party osaxen (i.e., those not developed by Apple), which allow you to parse HTML or XML in scripts, use regular expressions in searches, negotiate a directory tree and do something with each encountered file (the *walk folders* command of Jon's Commands), and initiate many other tasks that you would otherwise have to program with your own code in AppleScript or not be able to accomplish with a script at all. Examples of some of these third-party scripting addition files are Akua Sweets, Jon's Commands, and XML Tools. The site *http://osaxen.com* contains an osax database.

How do scripting additions work in Mac OS 9? When you use a command in a script, the application that ends up receiving the command depends on the

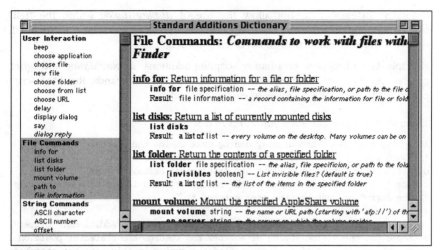

Figure A-2: Standard Addition's dictionary window

command's script context. The command or Apple event could be sent to one of the following targets:

- The app identified in the "tell" block that contains the command. In other words, if AppleScript encounters:

```
tell app "Photoshop 5.0" to do script "New_gif"
```

then the script will send the *do script* command (or Apple event) to Photoshop. If the command inside the `tell` block could not be found in the program's dictionary, then AppleScript would look elsewhere for the command's handler, such as in the contents of the Scripting Additions folder.

- A subroutine that you have included in the script. If you have defined a subroutine called "TimesTwo" in your script and the command *TimesTwo()* appears in your script, then your script subroutine will handle the *TimesTwo()* call.

- A script object that has been loaded into the script where the command was used. See the *load script* description in this chapter and Chapter 9, *Script Objects and Libraries*, for more information on script objects.

- A scripting addition file.

When AppleScript searches for the target of a script command it looks, among other places, inside the *Scripting Additions* folder for an application, an application alias, or a scripting addition file. For example, I have used the *display dialog* scripting addition in code samples throughout this book. This displays a modal dialog to the user and optionally allows you to request them to enter some information into a text field before they dismiss the dialog box by clicking a button (or before it closes if you specify that the window disappears after a certain number of seconds). The reason you can just randomly include *display dialog* in your script (with some exceptions explained later) is that AppleScript will search the *Scripting Additions* folder for the recipient or handler of this command and find it within the *Standard Additions* file in Mac OS 9. Some applications, such as

ColorSync Extension, do not allow the use of *display dialog* within the "tell" blocks that target them (e.g., `tell app "Colorsync Extension"...`). You will receive a "no user interaction allowed" error message.

Example A-1 shows how two handy scripting additions, *display dialog* and *offset*, can be used in a script that involves different types of commands. Read the script comments to find out the targets of each command.

Example A-1: Using Standard Additions in a Script

```
(* AppleScript finds the display dialog osax inside the Standard Additions
file, so you don't have to use any tell statements *)
display dialog "Enter your first and last names" default answer ""
set names to the text returned of the result (* names is set to a string like
"Bruce Perry" or whatever the user enters. *)
(*
AppleScript also finds the offset command inside Standard Additions.  Offset
searches for one string inside of another and returns the character position
as an integer or zero if it doesn't find the string(in this case the searched
for character is a space character). We are using it to locate the space
character that separates the first and last names.
*)
set sp to (offset of " " in names)
(*
The first name is pulled out of the string by getting all the characters up
to but not including the space character that follows the first name
*)
if sp ≠ 0 then (* if a space character is found, there must be at least two
names in the string *)
set first_name to characters 1 thru (sp - 1) of names
    tell application "BBEdit 5.1"
        activate
        (*
        'insert text' is a BBEdit command, so it receives the 'insert text'  ¬
        Apple event.  'Insert text' will put the names string in the front ¬
        BBEdit  document.
        *)
        insert text names
        (*
        the display dialog command will not be sent to BBEdit, even though it ¬
        is included in BBEdit's "tell" block.
        *)
        display dialog (first_name as text)
    end tell
end if
```

As an AppleScripter, you will become very fond of some osaxen and use them *all* the time. You will also discover new ones and realize "hey, this makes scripting web page downloads (or whatever) much easier!" This chapter describes the commands and classes included with the Standard Additions collection found inside the *startup disk:System Folder:Scripting Additions* directory in OS 9. Again, the Mac OS X path for this file is */System/Library/ScriptingAdditions/StandardAdditions.osax*. This group of scripting additions is installed with Mac OS 9 and Mac OS X. The classes described in this chapter are objects returned by certain commands, such as the `file information` object (a `record` type or associative array in AppleScript) returned by the *info for* command.

Standard Additions

Dictionary commands

adding folder items to `alias`

This is a Folder Action command covered in the "Dictionary commands for Folder Actions suite" section of Chapter 26, *Folder Actions Extension*.

ASCII character `integer`

This command returns the ASCII character associated with the number provided as a parameter. For example, ASCII character 80 returns the string "P."

ASCII number `integer`

You can find the ASCII number of a character by using code, such as `ASCII number "P"` (this returns an integer of 80).

beep `integer`

This makes the beep sound `integer` number of times, or once if a parameter is not included.

choose application

This command opens the choose application dialog box, which only lists the programs running at the moment. Figure A-3 shows this dialog. Figure A-4 shows what this dialog looks like in the OS X release. The following example lists the running applications, then opens the user's choice. Note that *choose application* also displays faceless background applications that the user cannot interact with (they can quit some of these apps, however).

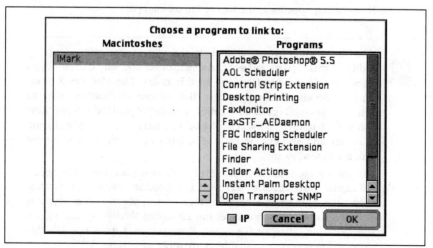

Figure A-3: The OS 9 choose application window

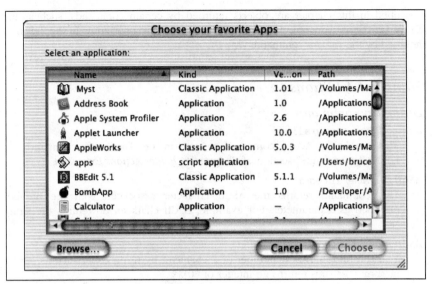

Name	Kind	Ve...on	Path
Myst	Classic Application	1.01	/Volumes/Ma
Address Book	Application	1.0	/Applications
Apple System Profiler	Application	2.6	/Applications
Applet Launcher	Application	10.0	/Applications
AppleWorks	Classic Application	5.0.3	/Volumes/Ma
apps	script application	—	/Users/bruce
BBEdit 5.1	Classic Application	5.1.1	/Volumes/Ma
BombApp	Application	1.0	/Developer/A
Calculator	Application	—	/Applications

Figure A-4: The choose application window in OS X

```
try -- capture error if they choose a 'background only' app
    tell (choose application application label "Choose one program"¬
    with prompt "Here are the running applications") to activate
    on error errmesg
    display dialog errmesg
end try
```

application label string

This string appears at the top of the application list.

with prompt string

This string appears at the top of the dialog box.

Mac OS 9.1 adds two parameters to the *choose application* scripting addition: multiple selections allowed and as class type (these are described elsewhere in this note). The Mac OS X Standard Additions dictionary alters the *choose application* osax to remove the application label parameter and add three new optional parameters: with title, multiple selections allowed, and as type. with title lets you specify the title for the dialog window, as in:

   choose application with title "Choose your favorite Apps"
multiple selections allowed is a boolean value that if true, allows the user to choose more than one application. as type is designed to let the scripter get the *choose application* return values as application, alias, or file types. However, in AppleScript 1.6, this return value was only available as an application type.

---

choose file

This osax opens a dialog box, allowing the user to choose a file to open, which can then be stored in an **alias** variable, as in:

```
set f to (choose file with prompt "Choose a file on the local disk")
```

If the user presses the Cancel button on the *choose file* dialog instead, then an error is raised, and the script terminates. You can catch this error (error number -128) with a **try** block and thus allow the script to resume, as in the following example (Figure A-5 shows the choose file window):

```
try
    c_file() (* call the scripts c_file subroutine which uses the
choose file osax *)
    on error number ern
    if ern = -128 then (* the user clicked the cancel button on the
dialog box *)
        display dialog "User cancelled"
    else
        display dialog "An unknown error occurred with file choosing."
    end if
end try
on c_file() -- define the subroutine
    set f to choose file
    display dialog (f as text) -- display the file path as text
end c_file
```

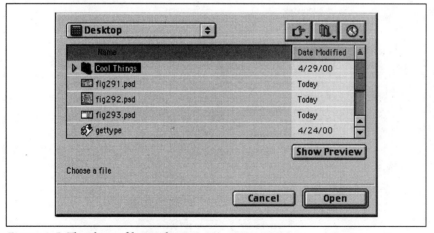

Figure A-5: The choose file window

with prompt string

This optional labeled parameter allows you to include a message or prompt with the dialog box:

```
choose file with prompt "Choose a file on the local disk"
```

`of type list`

You can restrict the file types listed in the *choose file* dialog with this labeled parameter, as in:

`choose file of type {"TEXT"}`

choose file name

This Mac OS X osax replaces the *new file* osax of AppleScript in Mac OS 9.0.4. *choose file name* is also available in Mac OS 9.1. This scripting addition displays a dialog box to the user. The user can then create a filename and a location for a file that does not yet exist (a `file specification` object is created and returned from this command). The return value in Mac OS X looks like:

`file "Mac OS X:users:bruceper:library:desktop:mydbfile"`

In effect, a `file specification` is like a template for a file that you will create in the future. Figure A-6 shows what the *choose file name* dialog box looks like.

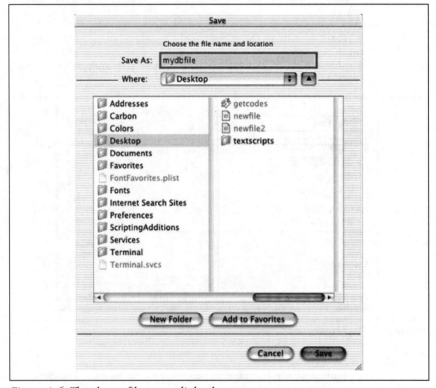

Figure A-6: The choose file name dialog box

`with prompt string`

This prompt or message appears on the dialog box, as in *choose file name with prompt* `"Please choose the location and name for a new file"` default name *mydbfile*.

default name string

> If you want the *choose file name* dialog box to be displayed with a default *file name* already entered in the "Save As:" text box, use this parameter.

choose folder

> Use this command if you want to interact with the user and get them to choose a directory or folder. For example:

```
choose folder with prompt "Choose a folder to save your files in"
```

with prompt string

> This optional labeled parameter adds a message to your dialog box so the user knows why your applet is producing the dialog box in the first place. See the *choose folder* example.

choose from list list

> Lots of AppleScript commands return lists as data types. This handy scripting addition allows you to show the user a list of items in the form of a dialog box. Figure A-7 shows this window. The user can then choose one or more items from the list (depending on whether multiple selections are allowed). When the dialog box is dismissed, the script receives a list of the selected items as a return value:

```
set fruitList to (choose from list allFruits)
```

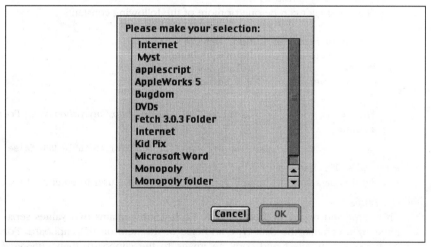

Figure A-7: The choose from list window

with prompt string

> Use this optional labeled parameter to add a message to the top of the dialog box.

default items list

> If you included this optional parameter, then the list of strings will be initially selected in the dialog box (if firstFruits was a variable that contained a list of strings):

```
choose from list allFruits default items firstFruits
```

OK button name *string*

You can give the OK button your own label, as in:

```
set fruitList to (choose from list allFruits OK button name
"Submit fruits")
```

cancel button name *string*

You can give the Cancel button on the dialog box your own label, as in:

```
set fruitList to (choose from list allFruits cancel button name
"Not now")
```

multiple selections allowed *boolean*

If you want to give the user the option to make more than one choice in the dialog box's list, then set this labeled parameter to **true**.

empty selection allowed *boolean*

If set to **true**, this labeled parameter allows the user to click the OK button without any **list** items selected and not raise an error.

choose URL

This command opens up the Network Browser and allows the user to choose a URL involving any of the network services (as constants) identified in the first labeled parameter.

showing list *of constants*

This parameter can be one or more of the following constants:

Directory services	News servers
File servers	Remote applications
FTP Servers	Telnet hosts
Media servers	Web servers

The return value is a **string** URL, as in *http://my.yahoo.com*. For example:

```
choose URL showing {Web servers,File servers} editable URL false
```

editable URL *boolean*

Set this parameter to **true** if you want to allow the user to enter a URL.

clipboard info

This command returns a **list** of lists. Each **list** contains two values separated by a comma: the data type and size of the item on the clipboard. For example, if you select and copy an image to the clipboard, then *clipboard info* would return a value such as {{picture, 14368}}. The second number is the size of the picture in bytes. If you selected and copied the word "HI", then this command would return {{string, 2}}, which is a string two bytes long. If you copied some styled text, for instance (i.e., text that has a certain font), then the clipboard information return value would involve more than one **list** inside the outer **list**, such as {{string, 65}, {styled Clipboard text, 42}.}

```
for class
```
Use this optional labeled parameter if you only want to see clipboard information of a certain data type:

```
clipboard info for string
```
Use the keyword for followed by the name of the class.

close access (file reference number, alias, *or* file specification*)*
Use this command to close access to a file you are reading from and writing to.

closing folder window for alias
This is a Folder Action command covered in the "Dictionary commands for Folder Actions suite" section of Chapter 26.

current date
This command returns a **date** object of the form:

```
date "Wednesday, May 24, 2000 8:50:06 AM"
```
You will use this scripting addition all the time! Since the return value is a **date** object, you can get the various date-related properties from it, such as the *time string* ("8:50:06 AM"), day, month, and year. See Chapter 3, *Data Types*, and the description of the **date** data type. The following example shows how to display various attributes of the current date:

```
set theDate to current date (* osax returns a date object and stores
it in theDate *)
(* get various date properties *)
set d to day of theDate
set m to month of theDate
set y to year of theDate
set ts to time string of theDate
set mesg to "Here's info about today:" & return & ¬
"time: " & ts & return & ¬
"day: " & d & return & ¬
"month: " & m & return & ¬
"year: " & y & return
display dialog mesg
```

delay integer
This useful osax delays the script processing for integer number of seconds, as in delay 5. It is similar to the *sleep* function in Perl. There are many reasons to delay a script for a few moments, such as dealing with the unpredictable download time of web documents. You might want to pause a script as a browser attempts to download a page before the script reports an error in the download. By the way, use the *download* scripting addition to download web pages using AppleScript. *download* is covered in Chapter 18, *URL Access Scripting*.

display dialog
This is one of the principal ways an applet can interact with the user, either by displaying a message or any script-processing results, or by requesting them to enter text in an edit field. *display dialog* may end up at the very top

of your "indispensable scripting addition" list. This command can optionally add an edit field for receiving text entries from the user by including the `default answer ""` parameter (passing an empty string to this labeled parameter displays an edit field with no text in it). *display dialog* has five optional parameters. For example, you can automatically make the dialog go away with code, such as:

```
display dialog "I disappear after five sec." giving up after 5
```

display dialog returns a `dialog reply` object, which is just like a `record` data type. Chapter 3, *Data Types* describes the `record` type. See the `dialog reply` class description in this chapter.

default answer string

> Include an empty `string` (as in default answer "") to display an empty edit field to the user, or include a non-empty `string` as a default value for the edit field. The `string` can be up to 255 characters long. If you do not include this parameter, then the dialog box does not have an edit field.

buttons list

> You can add up to three of your own button labels to the dialog:

```
display dialog "Enter one of your names" buttons ¬
{"first","last","middle"} default answer ""
```

> The first button in the list is the dialog button on the left, and the next listed buttons are displayed left to right. If you do not include this parameter, then the dialog box has two buttons: Cancel and OK. You can detect which button dismissed the dialog by testing the `button returned` property of the reply, which looks like:

```
{text returned:"bruce", button returned:"first"}
```

> In other words, the return value of *display dialog* is like a `record` data type, which gives you access to the returned text and button.

default button number *or* string

> You can specify a default button that will have a dark border around it signifying it can also be activated by pressing the return key. If you do not include this parameter, then the dialog box has two buttons: Cancel and OK. Identify the default button by its `string` or order in the buttons list. In the following example, Keep It is the default button:

```
display dialog "how much of a reimbursement do you want?" ¬
buttons {"Send It","Keep It"} default button 2
```

with icon number, string, *or the constants* stop, note, *or* caution

> You can display one of the standard Apple dialog icons with this parameter. The dialogs are Stop (number 0), Note (1), and Caution (2). (See Figure A-8.) As an alternative, if you specify the name or number of an icon (as in `with icon 9`) stored as a resource in the script file or current application, then AppleScript displays that icon in the dialog box. AppleScript searches the script file, the current application (i.e., the one identified in a `tell` statement), and the System file, in that order, for the icon resource.

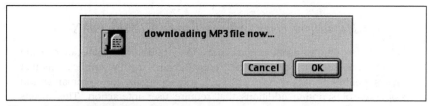

Figure A-8: Display dialog with a Note icon

giving up after `integer`

This command usually displays a modal dialog, meaning that it is the frontmost window, and the user has to dismiss it to access any other windows. Since the scripter is never sure about the context of script execution (what if the applet is executed over a network and the machine happens to be unused at the moment?), it is often a good idea to make the dialog box disappear automatically after a reasonable period, such as several seconds. For example:

```
display dialog "Are you there?" default answer "Yes" giving up ¬
after 10.
```

get eof

This command returns the length in bytes of a file's contents, as in:

```
get eof (alias "macintosh hd:desktop folder:myfile.txt")
```

The return value is an **integer**. *get eof* does not return the size of the file on disk, just the number of bytes of data that can be read from the file using the **read** osax. See the *info for* scripting addition for getting the actual disk size of the file, as in:

```
(size of (info for theFile))
```

See the *open for access* command for a description of reading and writing to files with AppleScript.

handle CGI request `string`

If you are using the Mac as a web server, you can use AppleScript and the *handle CGI request* scripting addition to process Common Gateway Interface (CGI) scripts. In older implementations of Mac Web CGI programs, you had to define a handler using raw syntax such as «on event WWW?sdoc»... but this has changed with the new Standard Additions. CGI scripts are used in web applications that process HTML form data, among other web-related tasks. When the web user submits the form to the web server, the CGI script intercepts the form and processes its data. The `string` parameter contains the path of the CGI program on the server, which might look something like */cgi-bin/myCGI.acgi*. The following example shows what the structure of a *handle CGI request* CGI looks like. The web server generates most of these parameter values, and you will not have to look at them in your CGI program. They are the equivalent of what Unix CGI programmers call environment variables, which are data the web server generates reflecting information about the web page request.

Handling User Interaction with Mac OS X

Due to Mac OS X's Unix origins, only the applications that can execute AppleScripts, such as Script Editor, Script Runner, and the applications that have a built-in Scripts menu, will load and recognize the commands and properties of scripting additions that require user interaction. This means that, according to Apple Computer, an application such as TextEdit will not display a dialog if you use a *display dialog* command inside a TextEdit `tell` block:

```
tell app "TextEdit"
    activate
    display dialog "Hi" -- this code will fail to display a dialog
end tell
```

Apple Computer suggests two strategies to deal with this Mac OS X issue:

1. Execute scripts with Script Runner. Chapter 1, *AppleScript: An Introduction*, describes the Script Runner. Script Runner is designed to execute the scripts saved as compiled script files (as opposed to Mac OS X applets). To work around this user-interaction problem with Mac OS X, you do not need to change a script that already runs under Mac OS 9.1 as long as it is saved as a compiled script and is executed by Script Runner.

2. Alter scripts to bring the script applet to the foreground when using *display dialog*. The script applet will display the dialog, then the script can return any other applications, such as TextEdit, to the foreground. Here is a simple example that does not do anything special with TextEdit but offers a solution to the user-interaction problem described by this sidebar:

```
tell app "TextEdit"
    activate
    set userName to my showDialog() (* call the script's
showDialog handler *)
end tell
on showDialog()
    tell me to activate (* bring the applet itself to the
foreground *)
    set theResult to (the text returned of (display dialog ¬
    "Enter your name please" default answer ""))
    tell app "TextEdit" to activate
    return theResult
end showDialog
```

This applet temporarily leaves the TextEdit application context to call a user-defined handler, which displays a dialog and gets some user input. Then the applet activates TextEdit again.

```
on handle CGI request the_path ¬
    searching for query_string ¬
    with posted data post_string ¬
    of content type mime_string ¬
    using access method acc_string ¬
    from address ip_string ¬
    from user user_string ¬
    using password passw_string ¬
    with user info info_string ¬
    from server serv_string ¬
    via port port_string ¬
    executing by path_string ¬
    referred by ref_string ¬
    from browser agent_string ¬
    using action cgi_string ¬
    of action type typ_string ¬
    from client IP address ipc_address ¬
    with full request req_string ¬
    with connection ID id_integer
end handle CGI request
searching for string
```

This is the data that follows the "?" character in the URL when the HTTP GET method is used. For example, the entire URL for sending form data might look like: *http://www.formcorp.com/cgi-bin/myCGI?first=Bruce&last=Perry*. searching for would contain the string "first=Bruce&last=Perry."

with posted data string

This contains the data sent with the POST HTTP method. This string could look like "first=Bruce&last=Perry."

of content type string

This is the Multipurpose Internet Mail Extensions (MIME) type for the data sent to the CGI program. For example, the MIME type for a web page is "text/html." The MIME type for form data sent with an POST HTTP method is "application/x-www-form-urlencoded."

using access method string

This string is either "GET" or "POST."

from address string

This labeled parameter contains the IP address of the entity making an HTTP request to the web server. For example, if the person sending the form data to the CGI program has an IP address of "24.169.24.11," then the from address string contains this value.

from user string

If the user is being authenticated on the web server for security reasons, then this string contains the username.

using password string

If the user is being authenticated on the web server for security reasons, then this string contains the password of the user.

with user info string

> This string may contain additional user information such as an email address.

from server string

> This is the name of the server application sending the request.

via port string

> This string is the TCP/IP port number of the server, such as "80."

executing by string

> This string is the path to the CGI script, as in */cgi-bin/mycgi.acgi.*

referred by string

> This is the URL from which the user linked to the CGI program. For example, this could be the web form the user filled out before they submitted the form to the CGI program, as in http://www.formcorp.com/form.html.

from browser string

> This string contains the name of the user agent or browser the web user is using.

using action string

> This string also contains the path to the CGI program, as in "/cgi-bin/mycgi.acgi."

of action type string

> This string returns one of these values: PREPROCESSOR, POSTPROCESSOR, CGI, or ACGI.

from client IP address string

> If the client has his own IP address (for instance, if he is a client on a Local Area Network), then this string contains that address. An example is 192.168.0.5.

with full request string

> This is the full request sent to the server. It might look like *http://www.formcorp.com/cgi-bin/mycgi.acgi?first=Bruce&last=Perry.*

with connection ID integer

> This integer parameter represents the server-to-client connection.

info for alias, **file specification,** *or* string *path to the file or folder*

> You can grab a bunch of information on a file or folder, as long as you know its directory path, which you can pass to this osax as a string. For example:
>
>   info for "macintosh hd:desktop folder:"
>
> The return value is a record that looks like this:
>
>   {name:"Desktop Folder", creation date:date "Thursday, December 07,
>   1995 10:48:10 AM", modification date:date "Thursday, May 25, 2000
>   9:36:22 AM", icon position:{-1, -1}, visible:true, size:311307,
>   folder:true, alias:false, folder window:{0, 20, 1024, 768}}.
>
> You can use the *path to* scripting addition to fill out the details of an unknown file path.

In AppleScript 1.5 and later, *info for* now returns the size of a file or folder as a `real` data type (e.g., even "0.0" is given as the size of an empty folder using *info for*), rather than an `integer`, in order to accommodate the files or folders that are greater than two gigabytes in size.

For instance, if you know a file called *cgi.txt* is on your desktop, then the following code returns information about that file, such as its creation date and size:

```
info for ((path to desktop as text) & "cgi.txt")
```

The full pathname of this file might be *macintosh hd:desktop folder:cgi.txt*, but the path to osax saved you some writing. The *info for* scripting addition returns the following type of `record` value:

```
{name:"cgi.txt", creation date:date "Thursday, May 25, 2000 9:36:22
AM", modification date:date "Thursday, May 25, 2000 10:03:19 AM",
icon position:{832, 92}, visible:true, size:2807, folder:false,
alias:false, locked:false, busy status:false, file creator:"R*ch",
file type:"TEXT", short version:"", long version:"", default
application:alias "Macintosh HD:BBEdit 5.0:BBEdit 5.0:BBEdit 5.1"}.
```

list disks

This scripting addition returns a `list` of disk names mounted on your desktop. An example return value is:

```
{"Macintosh HD1", "H2gig", "HF2gig", "scratch"}.
```

list folder `alias, file specification,` *or* `string` *path*

This command lists the items in a folder, as in:

```
list folder "macintosh hd:myfolder"
```

The return value is a `list` of strings. The following example lists the contents of the desktop folder (it also uses the path to osax):

```
list folder (path to desktop) (* returns folders and files as a list
of string names *)
```

load script `alias`

This command loads a script object into the script that contains the *load script* statement. The loading script can then use that script object's properties and methods as though the loaded script was a locally defined script. Chapter 9 describes script objects.

The following example loads a script object called `DateLib` and stores the object in a variable, `dlib`. It then calls that script object's `parseDate` method by using the statement `dlib's parseDate` (i.e., the `parseDate` method of the `DateLib` object, a reference to which is stored in the `dlib` variable). This method takes a `date` object and `boolean` variable as parameters and returns a reformatted date `string` that looks like "05/25/2000." If the `boolean` parameter is `false`, then the date `string` does not include leading zeros (the latter `string` would be "5/25/2000"). The following example includes the definition of `parseDate` so readers can examine the `parseDate` definition, but this method is already available from `DateLib` via the `dlib` variable:

```
(* use the path to osax to get a reference to a file on the desktop
*)
set dlib to load script (path to desktop as text) & "DateLib"
dlib's parseDate(current date, true) (* returns a date string such as
"05/25/2000" *)
(* parseDate definition *)
on parseDate(theDate, leadingZeros)
    local mydate
    local new_date_str
    try -- return "0" if the theDate or boolean parameter is invalid
        set mydate to theDate
        set month_part to my getMonthInt((month of mydate), ¬
        leadingZeros) as string
        -- getMonthInt method is defined in the DateLib script
        set day_part to (day of mydate) as string
        set year_part to (year of mydate) as string
        if leadingZeros then
            if (day_part as integer) < 10 then
                set new_date_str to (month_part & "/0" & day_part & "/" ¬
                & year_part) as string
            else
                set new_date_str to (month_part & "/" & day_part & "/" ¬
                & year_part) as string
            end if
        else
            set new_date_str to (month_part & "/" & day_part & "/" & ¬
            year_part) as string
        end if
        return new_date_str
    on error
        return "0"
    end try
end parseDate
```

mount volume string

Use this osax to mount a volume on your desktop from a remote computer. The on **server** labeled parameter is the only required parameter when using the AppleTalk form of mount volume (see the upcoming note on the TCP/IP form of mount volume). You have to add the Apple Filing Protocol (AFP) prefix ("afp://") if you are connecting with the volume via TCP/IP.

on **server** string
> Specify the file server name with a **string**, as in on **server** "StacyMac". This parameter is required.

in **AppleTalk** zone string
> Specify an AppleTalk zone with a **string**:

```
mount volume "macintosh hd" on server "StacyMac" in AppleTalk ¬
Zone "graphics_dep" as user name "powerpc1" with password ¬
"#go9$4r"
```

as user name string

    If the user has to be authenticated with a username and password before mounting a remote volume, these parameters can be included with the *mount volume* osax. Pass the username as a `string`:

        `as user name "powerpc1"`

with password string

    Include a password as a `string` for the user identified in the `as user name` parameter, or omit this parameter for guest access.

The *mount volume* command takes the following form when mounting a volume over a TCP/IP network:

    `mount volume "afp://user:password@192.168.0.2/MacHD"`

The command uses the Apple Filing Protocol (`"afp://"`), followed by the user name and password separated by a colon, the @ sign, the IP address of the server, and the name of the volume you want to mount. In Mac OS 9.1, mount volume will look in the Keychain for the user name and password information if you have left this information out of the mount volume URL, as in mount volume `"afp://192.168.0.3/Mac HD"`.

---

moving folder window for `alias`

    This is a Folder Action command covered in the "Dictionary commands for Folder Actions suite" section of Chapter 26, *Folder Actions Extension.*

new file

    new file allows you to request a `file specification` from the user and then use that file spec to save a web page downloaded with the *download* osax (see Chapter 18). This osax displays a common Save As dialog box that allows the user to navigate to a directory and save a file. A `file specification` reserves a path and name for a file, even though the file does not yet exist. The following example gets a file spec from a user then downloads a web page to it:

AppleScript 1.5.5 on Mac OS 9 altered this osax and changed the name to *choose file name*. See the *choose file name* description.

    `set fspec to (new file default name "home_URL.html")`
    `tell application "URL Access Scripting" to ¬`
    `download "http://www.parkerriver.com" to fspec with progress`

with prompt string

    You can add a message to the dialog box with this command.

default name string

Give the `file specification` a default name (the user can change this):

```
set fileSpec to (new file default name "myfile").
```

offset

This handy string-manipulation command finds the first occurrence of one `string` inside of another and returns the 1-based position of the interior `string` as an `integer`. It returns 0 if the `string` is not located inside the outer `string`. For example, `offset of "a" in "and"` returns 1, because the "a" inhabits position 1 in the word "and." The following example shows how to use the *offset* osax in a function that checks to see if a `string` begins with "<," ends with ">," and has at least one character that is not a space character inside these tags (An actual HTML or XML tag-validation function would have to do much more than this demo subroutine!):

```
checkTag("<html>") -- call the function with a string parameter
(* function definition *)
on checkTag(str)
    (* initialize booleans  and string length variable *)
    set openTag to false
    set closeTag to false
    set notEmpty to false
    set len to length of str
    if (character 1 of str) = "<" then set openTag to true
    repeat with c in (characters of str) (* examines each character in
    the string *)
        set offs to (offset of c in str) (* what position does the char
    have in the string ? *)
        if offs = len then exit repeat (* we check the last string char
    after the repeat loop, so exit here *)
        (* if the character is not the first or last character and not
    a space then the tags do not just surround a space character *)
        if (offs > 1 and offs < len) and (ASCII number c) ≠ 32 then
            set notEmpty to true
    end repeat
    if character len of str = ">" then set closeTag to true (* check
    last string character *)
    if openTag and closeTag and notEmpty then ¬
    display dialog "It's not empty and has opening and closing tags."
end checkTag
```

`of string`

Specify the `string` you are looking for with the of keyword, as in:

```
offset of "a" in "animal"
```

`in string`

Use the in keyword to identify the outer `string` you are searching for the inner `string` with, as in:

```
offset of "a" in "animal"
```

opening folder `alias`

This is a Folder Action command covered in the "Dictionary commands for Folder Actions suite" section of Chapter 26.

---

open for access `alias`

Use this osax to open a file and read and/or write to it. If the `open for access` parameter is a `file specification` for a file that does not yet exist, then a new file is created. This is a primary scripting addition for file input and output so you are likely to use it often. This scripting addition is closely related to the *read, write,* and *close access* scripting additions. You should close access to a file when you finish with it so you do not block any other operations that need access to that file. The following example reads a chunk of text from a file, then closes access to the file. *open for access* returns a file-reference number, which can be used with *close access* and other commands:

```
(* this script uses the path to, open for access, get eof, read, and
close access scripting additions *)
set theFile to alias ((path to desktop as string) & "write.txt")
set fref to (open for access theFile)
set tsize to (get eof theFile)
read fref as string from 1 to tsize
close access fref
```

write permission boolean

If you want to write to the file, use the `write permission true` parameter. Otherwise, you get an error that write permission is not allowed. In other words, `write permission` is `false` by default.

open location `string`

This osax opens the URL, such as a web page (*http://my.yahoo.com*) or FTP site (*ftp://park:.......@12.16.160.221/*) in the application you have selected in the Internet control panel or in the Internet Config application. For example, if Netscape 6 is your default browser then `open location "http://my.yahoo.com"` opens that page in the Netscape browser.

error reporting boolean

If you include the `error reporting true` parameter, a dialog box reporting errors is displayed.

path to `constant` *or application*

path to returns the path to folders or applications, depending on the parameter you use. You can use one of the following constants to get the path as either an `alias` or `string` to a common location such as the desktop folder:

At Ease applications	At Ease documents
apple menu	application support
control panels	control strip modules
desktop Preferences	modem scripts
editors	desktop pictures folder
Folder Action scripts	extensions
fonts	frontmost application
internet plugins	Help
launcher items folder	keychain folder
plugins	modem scripts
printer drivers	printer descriptions
scripts	printmonitor
shared libraries folder	scripting additions folder

```
stationery folder            speakable items
trash folder                 shutdown items
temporary items folder       startup items
voices folder                users folder
```

Or, you can get the path to a running program by specifying the application, as in:

```
path to application "BBEdit 5.1" as string
```

You can get the path as an `alias` (which is the default—you do not have to specify as `alias`) or a `string`.

as alias *or* **as string**

> Since an `alias` return value is the default, `path to desktop` returns an `alias` path, as in:

```
alias "macintosh hd:desktop folder:"
```

and:

```
path to desktop as string
```

returns a `string` type, as in:

```
"macintosh hd:desktop folder:"
```

 The OS X Standard Additions file added a `from...domain` optional parameter to the *path to* scripting addition. For instance, using this parameter, *path to* provides the location to the desktop folder based on the domain you specify. The *from* parameter can take any one of the four constants: `System domain`, `local domain`, `network domain`, or `user domain`. For example:

```
set dpath to (path to desktop from user domain)
```

The latter code phrase returns a value that looks like:

```
alias "Mac OS X:Users:bruceper:Library:Desktop:"
```

Whereas if you used the `local domain` parameter, the return value might be:

```
alias "Mac OS X:Library:Desktop:"
```

---

random number **number**

> You can generate a random number with this osax, optionally including an upper-limit number, as in:

```
set num to (random number 100)
```

If the upper-limit value is a `real` number, as in `random number 100.0`, then the random result will be a `real` type. A `real` number type has a fractional part or decimal point, whereas an `integer` type does not. (see the description of the `real` data type in Chapter 3). If the upper-limit number is an `integer` or whole number, then the result will be an `integer`. Finally, if the upper-limit number is omitted, as in:

```
set num to random number
```

---

then you will get a **real** number between 0 and 1 that looks like 0. 408063409023. The result will have a scale of 12, meaning that there will be 12 digits on the right side of the decimal point. The following example chooses a random number that could help pick a card in a playing-card game by generating a random number between 1 and 52:

```
cardNumber() -- call the method defined below
on cardNumber()
    set cd to (random number 100000) mod 52 + 1
    return cd
end cardNumber
```

from number integer *or* real

You can produce a random **integer** or **real** within a range of numbers, such as:

```
random number from 100.1 to 500.3
```

If you include this **from number** parameter, you have to use the **to number** parameter as well. The latter code returns a number such as 319.675894353425. If you included two integers, then the return value will also be an **integer**. If either one of these numbers is a **real**, the result will be a **real**. For example:

```
random number from 100 to 200.5
```

returns a **number** with a decimal point and fractional part (i.e., a **real** number).

to integer *or* real

Specify the upper level of a range with the **to** keyword followed by an **integer** or **real**. If you use the **from** parameter with **random number** then you have to use this **to** parameter. If the number used with this parameter is a **real** then the random result will be a **real** data type.

with seed number

Use this parameter if you want to produce a random number that steadily increases in value. The following example shows the random numbers generated by using a seed that increases by one each time the **random number** statement is executed:

```
on ranNumber()
    set counter to 0
    repeat 5 times
        set counter to counter + 1
        set num to random number with seed counter
        log num
    end repeat
end ranNumber

(* results from Script Editor's event log *)
random number with seed 1
--> 0.293460940421
random number with seed 2
--> 0.500003913185
random number with seed 3
--> 0.603275399567
```

```
random number with seed 4
--> 0.706546885948
random number with seed 5
--> 0.758182629139
```

read reference number, `alias,` *or* `file specification` *for a disk file*

Use this command to read bytes from a file. Use the keyword **read** followed by the file reference, such as an `alias` or the number returned by the *open for access* command. Generally, you get the amount of readable data from the file first with the *get eof* command, as in:

```
set theSize to (get eof theFile)
```

This command returns an `integer` number of bytes. Then you can read the first half of a file, say, with the code:

```
read theFile from 1 to (theSize div 2)
```

Close the file after you have finished reading it with:

```
close access theFile
```

using delimiter anything

This optional labeled parameter specifies the value you can use to separate the chunks of read bytes or text. For instance:

```
read theFile using delimiter return as text
```

uses a **return** character as the delimiter. This code returns a `list` in which each line of the text file is a `list` member, as in:

```
{"Hi readers this is a short bit of text.", "Separated by a
line."}
```

You could use this parameter to read from a tab- or comma-delimited file, for instance, and then transfer the values into a database-management system. The **as class** (e.g., **as text**) parameter is required if you use **using delimiter**.

using delimiters list

You can use more than one delimiter to generate a list of read-in values, as in:

```
read theFile using delimiters {",",";"} as text
```

This reads in values separated by either a comma or a semi-colon and returns these values as the members of a `list`. The `list` does not contain the delimiters; they are just used to separate or delimit each value. The **as class** (e.g., **as text**) parameter is required if you use **using delimiters**. This parameter is optional.

as class

Use this optional parameter to specify the data type of the return value. Use **as text** or **as string** unless you are reading in a series of numbers, dates, or other valid alternative data types. The following example reads three lines of numbers separated by tabs and stores them as integers in a `list`. You could take those numbers and use Apple-Script to put them in a database. The code uses the **before return** labeled parameter to prevent AppleScript from reading in a `return` character and trying to convert it to an `integer`, which would raise an error:

```
set theFile to (open for access (path to desktop as text) & ¬
"write.txt")
(* we know there are three lines in the data file; you could
find out how many lines there are first by reading in the text
and counting the return characters *)
repeat 3 times
    read theFile using delimiter tab before return as integer
end repeat
close access theFile
(* return values look like:
{233,244}
{265,234}
{10,9}
*)
```

for integer

Use this to specify the number of bytes to read from the disk (`for 20`, for instance). This code reads 20 bytes from the file. If you omit this labeled parameter, then *read* reads to the end of the file. You get an error of type "End of file error" if the `integer` parameter exceeds the number of bytes in the file. For example, `read theFile for 50` would return an error if the file has only 40 bytes of data. If you use *read* in a `repeat` statement, then the `read` statement sequentially reads through the file and does not just read the same line over and again.

before string

If you want to read up to but not including a character (such as a period "." or `return` character), use code, such as:

```
read theFile before return or read theFile before "."
```

If you know how many lines are in a file (pretty easy to find out in a programmer's editor such as BBEdit or HomeSite), you can use code, such as the `read theFile before return` in a `repeat number_of_file_lines` times statement, and AppleScript will neatly read the file line by line. This parameter is optional.

until string

Unlike `before string`, `until string` reads up to and includes the `string` character, as in:

```
read theFile until string "."
```

This code returns the "." with the other file values.

from integer

You can specify the number of bytes the read should start from, as in:

```
read theFile from 20
```

(which starts reading from and including the 20th byte). If you omit this labeled parameter, AppleScript starts reading from the beginning of the file or from the byte after the last-read byte. Use the `from integer` parameter with the `to integer` parameter to read a range of bytes from the disk file. This parameter is optional.

to integer

Stop the read at this byte position, as in:

```
read thefile to 100
```

This code reads the first 100 bytes of the disk file. Use this parameter with the `from integer` parameter to read a range of bytes, as in:

```
read theFile from 50 to 100
```

removing folder items from `alias`

This is a Folder Action command covered in the "Dictionary commands for Folder Actions suite" section of Chapter 26.

round `real`

This osax rounds a `real` number (such as 45.65) to an `integer` and, of course, returns the `integer`. For example, `round 45.65` returns 46, because by default *round* rounds to the nearest `integer` (i.e., `round 45.45` returns 45).

rounding up/down/toward zero/to nearest

You might want to specify `rounding up`, `down`, or `toward zero` instead of accepting the default of `rounding to nearest`. For example:

```
round 45.65 rounding down
```

returns 45 rather than the default of 46. `rounding down` and `rounding toward zero` are different for negative numbers. For example:

```
round -0.1 rounding toward zero
```

returns 0, but:

```
round -0.1 rounding down
```

returns -1. In other words, for positive numbers, `rounding down` is the same as `rounding toward zero`. For negative numbers, `rounding up` is the same as `rounding toward zero`.

The Mac OS 9.1 and OS X version of *round* adds the `as taught in school` parameter to the other four parameters. `as taught in school` always rounds 0.5 away from 0. For example:

```
round 2.5 rounding as taught in school
```

returns 3. But:

```
round 2.5
```

(using the default parameter of `rounding to nearest`) returns 2, because `rounding to nearest` rounds .5 numbers to the nearest even number. However:

```
round -46.5 rounding as taught in school
```

will return -47, rounding the real number argument 0.5 away from 0.

---

run script `alias`

You can call a script outside of the running script (i.e., the script that uses the *run script* command) by passing *run script* an `alias` to the external script file. For example:

`run script (alias ((path to desktop as text) & "scr_2914"))`

This code runs a script named "scr_2914" on the desktop. For the `run script` parameter, you can also use a string file path, in other words, without the alias reserved word. Actually *run script* calls the implicit or explicit *run* handler of the script file (see the "Run handler" section of Chapter 8, *Subroutines*). All scripts have an implicit *run* handler (on `run...end run`) that encompasses all statements except for property definitions, function definitions, and script objects. *run script* returns the result (if any) of calling the script's *run* handler. The following example defines a *run* handler that takes two numerical arguments. The first parameter is rounded then a dialog displays whether the result is even or odd; the second parameter is simply returned to the calling script. The code used to call this script is identified in comment characters at the top of this example:

```
(*
run script (alias ((path to desktop as text) & "scr_2914"))
with parameters {345.45, 45.6}
*)
on run {num, num2}
    if (class of num is real) then
        if ((round num) mod 2) = 0 then
            display dialog "A real number rounded to even integer."
        else
            display dialog "A real number rounded to odd integer."
        end if
    end if
    return num2
end run
```

`with parameters list`

You can optionally pass parameters to the script you want to call. If the *run* handler takes two or more parameters, you can specify them in the form of:

`run script scriptAlias with parameters {345.5,233.4}`

But if the *run* handler only takes one argument, a line such as:

`run script scriptAlias with parameters {345.5}`

will pass the `list` type as a parameter as opposed to the single numerical argument (at least under AppleScript 1.4). You can work around this condition by making sure the *run* handler takes its single argument and handles it as a `list`.

`in string`

You can specify the scripting component to use, such as in "JavaScript" (if you have installed the JavaScript OSA component from Late Night Software) if you want to use a component other than the default component.

The default component I use in Script Editor is none other than AppleScript.

say anything

This command says the text parameter to the *say* osax in the voice that is configured in the Speech control panel. You have to install the Speech Manager extension in the *startup disk:System Folder:Extensions* folder for this osax to work. Once it is working, you can even use it for debugging by saying the value of certain variables. The following example uses this osax to say the value of a variable each time it completes an iteration in a **repeat** loop:

```
checkVars() -- call the method defined below
on checkVars()
    set v1 to 1234567
    repeat with n from 1 to 5
        (* This will say something like "5 times around the value is 3"
*)
        say (n & " times around the value is " & (v1 mod n) as text)
    end repeat
end checkVars
```

displaying string

This parameter displays text in the SpeakableItems feedback window if you have the SpeakableItems extension installed.

using string

You can specify the voice you want to use, such as "Deranged" or "Hysterical," as in:

```
say "This project is disintegrating!" using "Hysterical"
```

waiting until completion boolean

The default is **waiting until completion** true, which does not return from the call to *say* until the speech has been uttered. This is important when you are using *say* in a **repeat** loop, since you do not want to move on to the next loop of **repeat** until the speaking voice has finished its speech. Chapter 7, *Flow-Control Statements*, describes the **repeat** loop.

scripting components

This command returns the scripting components installed on your machine as a list of strings. An example return value is {"JavaScript","AppleScript "}.

set eof file reference number

You can add or truncate the bytes in a file opened with the *open for access* osax (see *open for access*). The following example reduces a file to only its first 15 bytes. A file has to be open with write permission or this osax returns an error.

```
set theFile to (open for access (path to desktop as text) & "write. ¬
txt" with write permission)
set eof theFile to 15
read theFile
close access theFile
```

```
to anything
```
This required parameter sets the new length of the file, as in:

```
set eof theFile to 10000
```

This file's length is set to 10000 bytes. You can enlarge or shrink a file with this command.

set the clipboard to anything

Use this osax inside of a `tell` statement to paste a program's data onto the clipboard. You have to activate the program before you use *set the clipboard to*. For example, you could activate BBEdit 5.1 then use the code:

```
set the clipboard to (contents of document 1)
```

set volume number

Use this osax to set the sound output volume to a number between 0 (silent) and 7 (full volume).

store script

This osax stores a script object in a file, so you can then run that script using the *run script* osax (Chapter 9 explains script objects). They are essentially AppleScript statements such as property definitions and subroutines enclosed in a `script script_name...end script` block with similar behavior to object-oriented classes the programmer creates. The following example defines a script that resets the computer's volume. The example asks the user where to save the file, using the *store script* osax:

```
store script volume_setter in (new file with prompt ¬
    "Pick a new file for the volume script.")
script volume_setter
    set vol to (the text returned of (display dialog ¬
        "enter a volume number from 0 to 7" default answer ""))
    if vol > 0 and vol < 8 then
        set volume vol -- set the new volume
        beep 2 -- test the sound output
    end if
end script
```

```
in file specification
```
You can have the user create a `file specification` object (a space that the operating system reserves for the new file) by using the *new file* scripting addition. This is a required parameter.

```
replacing ask/yes/no
```
If there is a chance that the *store script* scripting addition will replace another script, specify the saving behavior with this labeled parameter. **ask** displays a dialog asking the user whether to overwrite the existing script file, **yes** saves the script file (over the original if there is one), and no does not replace an existing file.

summarize text or an alias or file specification of a text file

This scripting addition attempts to summarize in an optionally specified number of sentences the text or text file you feed it. For example:

```
summarize alias ((path to desktop as text) & "thyroid1.txt") in 10
```

Summarize returns a `string` summary.

```
in integer
```
Specify a pithy summary, as in:

```
summarize alias ((path to desktop as text) & "thyroid1.txt") ¬
in 1
```

This code attempts a one-sentence summary.

the clipboard

This command returns the contents of a program's clipboard, but you have to couch the osax in a `tell` block targeting the application. After activating the app with the *activate* command, you can use code such as:

```
return the Clipboard
```

This scripting addition returns a `list` type.

```
as class
```
You can optionally specify the return value of this command to a certain data type, as in:

```
the clipboard as text
```

time to GMT

This command returns the difference in seconds between local time and Greenwich Mean Time. You can convert this to minutes using:

```
time to GMT / 60
```

A negative number means that your local time is earlier than GMT (e.g., -14400 is four hours earlier than GMT).

write anything

Use this scripting addition to write data to a file opened with the *open for access* command.

```
for integer
```
You can restrict the write to a certain number of bytes (for instance, if the script was reading from one file and writing to another, and you were not sure of the number of bytes that were read). For example:

```
write theText to theFile for 100 -- write a 100-byte chunk
```

If you do not use this parameter, then all the data in `theText` will be written to the file.

```
starting at integer
```
Use this labeled parameter to specify a position in the file to do the write, as in:

```
write "More text" to theFile starting at 100 (* start writing at
the 100-byte point in the file *)
```

This parameter is optional.

```
to anything
```
This required parameter specifies the reference number (*open for access* returns a file reference number), `alias`, or `file specification` of the

file to write to. The following example uses the *new file* osax to let the user choose the file for writing with the *write* scripting addition:

```
set filespec to (new file with prompt "Pick the new file to ¬
write to")
(* use `choose file name" osax with OS X and OS 9.1 *)
set theFile to (open for access filespec with write permission)
write "Welcome to the beginning of this file." to theFile
close access theFile
```

as class

You can optionally specify the writing of the data as text, a list, a real number, or some other data type. For example:

```
write 292.345 as real to filespec.
```

Standard Additions

Dictionary classes

dialog reply

This record object is the return value of the *display dialog* scripting addition. *display dialog* displays a message in a modal dialog window (i.e., a window that appears in front of other windows), optionally requests the user to enter some text in an edit field, and optionally closes itself after a specified number of seconds. A record is a series of name/value pairs separated by commas and surrounded by a pair of curly braces. The return value for the following example looks like this:

```
{text returned:"Bruce", button returned:"OK", gave up:false}
```

Your return value will only include the gave up property if the *display dialog* command included the giving up after parameter when the command was used, as in display dialog "Tired of me yet?" giving up after 10.

```
set rep to (display dialog "Identify yourself please." default ¬
answer "" giving up after 30)
(*
the variable rep could contain this:
{text returned:"Bruce", button returned:"OK", gave up:false}
*)
```

The following are dialog reply properties:

button returned string *(read-only)*

This property returns the label of the button the user clicked on the dialog. You can get this value with code such as:

```
set theButton to (button returned of the result)
```

text returned string *(read-only)*

This property returns the text (if any) the user entered in the edit field of the dialog. You can get this value with code such as:

```
set theText to (text returned of the result)
```

gave up boolean *(read-only)*

Your script might want to take some default action if the dialog had to dismiss itself because the user failed to interact with the dialog window. For example, the code:

```
display dialog "Enter your name please." default answer "" ¬
giving up after 30
```

closes the window after 30 seconds. If this happens, then the window's return value (a `dialog reply` record) will include the value `gave up:` `true`. `dialog reply` does not contain a `gave up` value if you did not use the `giving up after` parameter with *display dialog*.

file information

This `record` is returned by the *info for* scripting addition. A pretty simple code phrase for getting file information is:

```
set f to (info for (choose file))
```

The *choose file* scripting addition lets the user choose a file, then returns an `alias` type for handling by the *info for* osax. Here is a look at a sample return value:

```
{name:"applescript.doc", creation date:date "Saturday, May 20, 2000
9:57:58 AM", modification date:date "Saturday, May 20, 2000 9:57:58
AM", icon position:{0, 0}, visible:true, size:23877, folder:false,
alias:false, locked:false, busy status:true, file creator:"MSWD",
file type:"BINA", short version:"", long version:"", default
application:alias "Macintosh HD:Microsoft Office 98:Microsoft Word"}
```

name international text *(read-only)*

This `string` returns the name of the file.

size integer *(read-only)*

This number is the size in bytes of the file on disk, such as 23877.

 Mac OS X returns this size value as a `real` data type to accommodate files that are greater than two gigabytes in size.

---

creation date date *(read-only)*

This value returns a `date` object for when the file was created.

modification date date *(read-only)*

This value returns a `date` object for when the file was last modified, such as:

```
date "Saturday, May 20, 2000 9:57:58 AM"
```

file type string *(read-only)*

This value is the four-character Mac file type, as in "TEXT" for text files.

file creator string *(read-only)*

This property is the four-character Mac creator type, as in "R*ch" for BBEdit files or "MSWD" for Word files.

---

default application alias *(read-only)*

This is an **alias** type that identifies the path to the program that would open if you double-clicked this file. For example:

```
alias "Macintosh HD:Microsoft Office 98:Microsoft Word"
```

visible boolean *(read-only)*

Is the file or folder visible? If yes, then this property is **true**.

icon position point *(read-only)*

These are the coordinates for the upper-left-hand corner of the file's or folder's icon, in the form {50,50}.

folder window bounding rectangle *(read-only)*

If the item is a folder, these are the coordinates of the upper left and lower right corners of the folder window. The return value looks something like {557, 90, 880, 332}.

folder boolean *(read-only)*

This is **true** if the item is a folder.

alias boolean *(read-only)*

If the item is an **alias** (rather than a non-**alias** file or folder), this value is **true**.

locked boolean *(read-only)*

If the file is not locked then this value is **false**. You can lock a file by selecting it, clicking *Command-I*, and checking the "locked" checkbox in the resulting window. Its icon will have a little padlock on it, and any changes in the file cannot be saved.

short version string *(read-only)*

The short and long versions apply to the version information in a Get Info window of a file (usually an application). For example, my Script Editor's short version value is "1.4.3."

long version string *(read-only)*

The short and long versions apply to the version information in a Get Info window of a file (usually an application). For example, my Script Editor's long version value is "1.4.3, Copyright Apple Computer, Inc. 1997-2000."

busy status boolean *(read-only)*

If the file is busy or being used by a program, its **busy status** is **true**.

FTP item

This class or object represents a folder or a file on an FTP server. Here's a peek inside a hypothetical FTP object:

```
{class:FTP item, name:"index.html", URL:{class:URL, scheme:ftp URL,
path:"ftp://user_name:.........@12.16.160.221/", user name:"user_
name", password:".........", host:{class:Internet address, DNS
form:"12.16.160.221", port:21, dotted decimal form:"12.16.160.221"}},
kind:"file"}
```

The following are **FTP item** properties:

properties record
> This is a `record` type containing the gettable or settable properties of the FTP object.

name string *(read-only)*
> This `string` property is the name of the FTP item.

URL URL *(read-only)*
> This is the URL object for the FTP item. See the URL class.

kind string *(read-only)*
> This property identifies whether the FTP object is a file or folder.

Internet Address

The host property of a URL object (see the URL class later in this chapter) returns this object, which represents basically an IP address (e.g., 12.16.162.122), a hostname (e.g., *www.yahoo.com*), and a port number (e.g., 80). An example **Internet Address** object is:

```
{class:Internet address, DNS form:"www.parkerriver.com", port:80,
dotted decimal form:"12.16.160.223"}
```

The following are **Internet Address** properties:

properties record
> This property returns the **Internet Address'** properties as a `record` type (although I can only get an empty record ({ }) when attempting to access this value).

DNS form string
> This is the Domain Name System name of the web address or the human-readable form of the **Internet Address** (e.g., *my.yahoo.com*, as opposed to the dotted decimal numerical form).

dotted decimal form string
> This `string` represents the IP address of the **Internet Address**, as in "216.115.105.16."

port integer
> This number represents the port number for the TCP/IP service, as in 80 for the HTTP protocol and 21 for FTP.

URL

This object represents an Internet URL, such as a web, FTP, or newsgroup resource. If your machine is connected to the Web, then the following example will quickly give you the IP address of the web site for which you supply the hostname:

```
set wAdd to (the text returned of ¬
(display dialog "Enter the Web address:" default answer "http://"))
try -- catch user errors entering Web address
    set theURL to wAdd as URL
    display dialog (dotted decimal form of (host of theURL))
    on error
    display dialog "Try me again; you probably mistyped the Web host ¬
    name."
end try
```

The following are URL properties:

properties record
> This is a record type containing the URL properties as name/value pairs.

name string *(read-only)*
> Some URL objects do not have a name property and raise an error if you try to access it. If appropriate, this property represents a name, such as a filename.

scheme constant *(read-only)*
> The scheme can be one of these constants: http URL/secure http URL/ftp URL/mail URL/file URL/gopher URL/telnet URL/news URL/secure news URL/nntp URL/message URL/mailbox URL/multi URL/launch URL/afp URL/AppleTalk URL/remote application URL/streaming multimedia URL/network file system URL/. For example, a web page URL object has a scheme of http URL.

host Internet Address
> The host property returns an Internet Address object (see the Internet Address class). The example under the "URL" section grabs the IP address of a web site by accessing the dotted decimal form property of a URL object's host property.

path string
> This string contains the virtual path on the server, which is often the same as the entire URL, as in *http://www.parkerriver.com/index.html*.

user name string
> An FTP URL often has a username property. For example, the URL *ftp:// my_user_name:mypassw12@12.16.160.221/* has a username property of "my_user_name."

password string
> An FTP URL often has a password property. For example, the URL *ftp:// my_user_name:mypassw12@12.16.160.221/* has a password property of "mypassw12."

web page
This is a class that represents a web page. The following are web page properties:

properties record
> This record contains a series of name/value pairs that comprise the web page's properties. Chapter 3 describes the record type.

name string
> This string is the name of the web page, such as *index.html*.

URL URL
> This is the URL object of the web page. See the URL class.

text encoding string
> This is the text-encoding method used for this page. One encoding method is "application/x-www-form-urlencoded," which is used for form values that are sent from a web page to a server program.

APPENDIX B

AppleScript Resources

Apple Computer AppleScript URLs

Apple Computer's AppleScript web page:

http://www.apple.com/applescript/

AppleScript Language Guide:

*http://developer.apple.com/techpubs/macos8/InterproCom/AppleScriptScripters/
AppleScriptLangGuide/index.html*

AppleScript Finder Guide on developer.apple.com:

*http://developer.apple.com/techpubs/mac/AppleScriptFind/AppleScriptFind-2.
html*

AppleScript Scripting Additions Guide on developer.apple.com:

*http://developer.apple.com/techpubs/mac/scriptingadditions/ScriptAdditions-2.
html*

AppleScript for Developers on developer.apple.com:

*http://developer.apple.com/techpubs/macos8/InterproCom/AppleScriptDev/
applescriptdev.html*

AppleScript for Scripters on developer.apple.com:

*http://developer.apple.com/techpubs/macos8/InterproCom/AppleScriptScripters/
applescriptscripters.html*

AppleScript software development kit:

http://developer.apple.com/sdk/

Entry page for Interapplication Communication on the Macintosh platform:

http://developer.apple.com/techpubs/macos8/InterproCom/interprocom.html

Introduction to Macintosh runtime for Java AppleScript support:

http://developer.apple.com/technotes/tn/tn1162.html

Apple Computer Technical Notes front page:

http://developer.apple.com/technotes/

AppleScript FAQs, Mailing Lists, and Tutorials

FAQ for alt.comp.lang.applescript:

http://homepage.mac.com/dlivesay/aclafaq.html

Beginning AppleScript online tutorial:

http://www.apple.com/applescript/begin/pgs/begin_00.html

AppleScript list server (mailing list):

http://www.lists.apple.com/cgi-bin/mwf/topic_show.pl?id=8

MACSCRPT:

http://listserv.dartmouth.edu/scripts/wa.exe?SUBED1=macscrpt&A=1

Macintosh Scripting Sites

ScriptWeb:

http://www.scriptweb.org/

The AppleScript Sourcebook:

http://www.AppleScriptSourcebook.com

Scripting additions database:

http://www.osaxen.com/

MacScripter.net:

http://macscripter.net

Commercial AppleScript Development Environments

Script debugger:

http://www.latenightsw.com/

Facespan:

http://www.facespan.com/core.html

Scripter:

http://www.mainevent.com

Freeware AppleScript Development Environments

Smile:

http://www.tandb.com.au/smile/

Index

Symbols

& (ampersand)
  & operator, 79
  return constant and, 122
* (asterisk)
  * operator, 80
\ (backslash), 72
[] (square brackets)
  [a] reference to operator, 87
∧ (caret sign)
  ∧ operator, 87
{} (curly braces), 26, 375
  font characteristics and, 376
÷ (division sign), 83, 93
  ÷ div operator, 82
" (double quote), 25
  string data type and, 71
= (equal sign)
  = operator, 84
\ (escape character), 72
/ (forward slash)
  / operator, 82
  in directory paths, xxii
« » (guillemet characters), 56
< (left angle bracket)
  < <= operators, 84
¬ (line continuation character), 23
  in Script Editor, 23

– (minus sign)
  – operator, 82
() (parentheses), 31
  () operator, 80
| (pipe character), 23
  in positional parameters, 155
  in variable names, 104
+ (plus sign)
  + operator, 81
> (right angle bracket)
  > >= operators, 85, 86
' (single quote), 25
_ (underscore), 23
  _ operator, 84
  in positional parameters, 155
  in variable names, 104

A

abort transaction command (Network
    Setup Scripting), 277
accent characters, 115
activate command, 5, 164
active enabler (ASP), 192
active network ports (ASP), 196
ADD (Apple Data Detectors), 325–329
  actions, writing, 328
  Apple Data Detectors control
    panel, 326, 328

We'd like to hear your suggestions for improving our indexes. Send email to *index@oreilly.com.*

Exists command (Appearance control panel), 320
exists command (Network Setup Scripting), 281
exists reference to keychain or key command (Keychain Scripting), 204
exists reference to object command
  ASP, 189
  Finder OS 9, 229
  Sherlock 2, 303
exit statement, 135
expanded constant, 116
expansion constant, 116
expressions
  with comparison operators, 53
  parentheses (()) with, 80
  testing equality of, 78
extension files, 9
extension mapping class (File Exchange color panel), 353
extension mappings, 349
  creating, 349–355
  deleting, 351
extension volumes class (ASP), 192
extensions
  information from, 192
  loading on startup, 377
  security, 201
Extensions folder, 201, 270
extensions folder reference class (Finder OS 9), 270

F

false constant, 116
Favorites option (Apple menu), adding to, 226
feet, converting meters to, 77
file class (Finder OS 9), 253
File Exchange control panel, 349–355
  dictionary classes, 351–354
  dictionary commands, 350
file extensions
  mapping, 349, 353
  searching for, 91
  web sharing and, 399
file information class (Scripting Additions), 470–471
File menu (Finder), 202
file sharing, 193, 196
  turning off/on, 377

file sharing (ASP), 193, 196
File Sharing control panel, 356–362
  dictionary classes, 359–362
  dictionary commands, 357–359
file specification data type, 61
File Transfer Protocol (see FTP)
File Translation panel, 349
file types, 14, 40
  checking before opening ColorSync extension, 339
  deleting, 222
  displaying, 221
  droplets and, 43
  finding, 222
  foreign, 349
  mapping, 349
  OS X, 221
filenames
  creating file specification object, 446
  reserving, 62
files
  audio, 269
  bytes in
    adding/truncating, 466
    reading, 462–464
  closing access to, 449
  creating (Finder OS X), 409
  device link profile, matching, 343
  digitally signed, verifying, 210
  document, 253
  downloading (URL Access Scripting), 311
  encrypting, 201
  executable, droplets and, 42
  executing with Terminal, 421
  existence of, checking, 229
  on FTP server, 471
  image, 339
    closing, 340
    saving with ICC profile, 340
  indexing, 302
    updates to, 304
  information about, retrieving, 62, 454
  information from, retrieving, 470–471
  keychain, 201
  length of, retrieving, 451
    AppleScript V1.5, 455
  moving, 231, 233
  opening, 232, 445, 459
  paths to, aliases and, 52
  permissions, 356–362

Hypertext Transport Protocol (HTTP),
    URL Access Scripting and,
        downloading files, 311
hyphens constant, 117

I

IAD (Internet Address Detectors), 326
ICC (International Color
    Consortium), 339
icons, arranging, 226
id class (ASP), 198
ID reference form, 96
id reference form, 101
identifiers
    naming, 23
    reference forms and, 101
idle handler, 159–161
if statements, 29, 135–137
ignoring statement, 137
Image Capture Extension, 7
image class (ColorSync extension), 347
images, color
    ICC profile
        embedding with, 340
        matching to, 342
        unembedding, 341
    proofing, 342
    synchronizing, 339
index class (ASP), 198
index containers command (Sherlock
    2), 304
Index reference form, 96
Index Volumes window (Sherlock 2), 302
info for osax, 62, 454
    file information class and, 470
information window class (Finder OS
    9), 256
Infrared, 275
insertion points, referring to, 97
inspector window class (Finder OS
    X), 407
Inspector windows, 409–411
integer data type, 62–64
integers
    multiplying, 80
    numbers stored as, 63
International Color Consortium
    (ICC), 339
international text data type, 64
internationalization, language data,
    storing, 64, 74

Internet
    configurations, switching among, 377
    Keychain Scripting and, 209
    searching, 302
Internet Address class (Scripting
    Additions), 472
Internet Address Detectors (IAD), 326
internet location file class (Finder OS
    9), 258
Internet Service Provider (see ISP), 275
IP addresses, 472
    URLs, using as, 396
IP class (DPM), 216
is/is not contained by operator, 92
ISP (Internet Service Provider), 275
it constant, 117
italic constant, 117
item class (Finder OS 9), 258–260
item object command (Finder OS X), 408

J

JavaScript for OSA, 9
JPEG images, 339

K

key class (Keychain Scripting), 207
key objects, retrieving list of, 207
keyboard shortcuts, xxi
Keychain Access, 203
Keychain Access control panel, 201
keychain class (Keychain Scripting), 206
keychain file, 201
Keychain Scripting, 201–209
    dictionary classes, 206–209
    dictionary commands, 204–206
keychains, 203
    counting, 204
    generating automatically, 205
    (see also Keychain Scripting)
Keychains folder, 202

L

label class (Finder OS 9), 261
LANs (local area networks), 275
    (see also networks)
last reference form, 101
left angle bracket (<)
    < <= operators, 84
libraries, 169–171
    of subroutines, 160

About the Author

Bruce W. Perry is an independent software developer and writer. Since 1996, he has developed web applications and databases for various nonprofit organizations, design and marketing firms, ad agencies, and digital-music specialists. Before working in the web field, Perry remained tethered to his portable and desktop Macs while writing environmental law books and newsletters. When not hacking or writing, he loves cycling and climbing mountains in the U.S. and Switzerland. He lives in the Newburyport, Massachusetts area with his wife Stacy LeBaron and daughter Rachel.

Colophon

Our look is the result of reader comments, our own experimentation, and feedback from distribution channels. Distinctive covers complement our distinctive approach to technical topics, breathing personality and life into potentially dry subjects.

The dog on the cover of *AppleScript in a Nutshell* is a Boston terrier. The youngest breed in the American Kennel Club (AKC), the Boston is a cross between various types of bulldogs and bull terriers. Originally bred in England, the breed stabilized in the United States, where it was initially favored as a fighter in the underworld rat pits of the seedier areas of late eighteenth- and early nineteenth-century Boston. By the late nineteenth century, however, people started to admire the beauty of the breed's compact, elegant build—the "American Gentleman," as the Boston terrier is now known, had been discovered.

In 1889, the AKC rejected the Stud Book applications put forth by the "American bull terrier" owners only to accept the breed in 1893 under its new name, Boston terrier. Today, its gentle yet playful and protective nature combined with its willingness to be trained make it a popular family pet—especially, of course, in Boston, the metropolitan area in which O'Reilly maintains a large editorial and production staff. Though the Boston terrier's fighting days are in its past, the sportsmen and women at Boston University evoke the breed's heritage each time they take the field or ice.

Catherine Morris was the production editor and copyeditor, and Matt Hutchinson was the proofreader for *AppleScript in a Nutshell*. Linley Dolby, Colleen Gorman, and Claire Cloutier provided quality control. Interior composition was done by Catherine Morris, Edith Shapiro, and Sada Preisch. Nancy Crumpton wrote the index.

Ellie Volckhausen designed the cover of this book, based on a series design by Edie Freedman. The cover image is an original illustration created by Susan Hart. Emma Colby produced the cover layout with QuarkXPress 4.1 using Adobe's ITC Garamond font.

Melanie Wang designed the interior layout based on a series design by Nancy Priest. Anne-Marie Vaduva converted the files from Microsoft Word to FrameMaker 5.5.6 using tools created by Mike Sierra. The text and heading fonts are ITC Garamond Light and Garamond Book. The illustrations that appear in the book were produced by Robert Romano and Jessamyn Read using Macromedia FreeHand 9 and Adobe Photoshop 6. This colophon was written by Sarah Jane Shangraw.

Whenever possible, our books use a durable and flexible lay-flat binding. If the page count exceeds this binding's limit, perfect binding is used.

How to stay in touch with O'Reilly

1. Visit Our Award-Winning Site

http://www.oreilly.com/

★ "Top 100 Sites on the Web" —*PC Magazine*
★ "Top 5% Web sites" —*Point Communications*
★ "3-Star site" —*The McKinley Group*

Our web site contains a library of comprehensive
product information (including book excerpts
and tables of contents), downloadable software,
background articles, interviews with technology
leaders, links to relevant sites, book cover art,
and more. File us in your Bookmarks or Hotlist!

2. Join Our Email Mailing Lists

New Product Releases

To receive automatic email with brief descriptions
of all new O'Reilly products as they are released,
send email to:
ora-news-subscribe@lists.oreilly.com
Put the following information in the first line of your
message (*not* in the Subject field):
subscribe ora-news

O'Reilly Events

If you'd also like us to send information about trade
show events, special promotions, and other O'Reilly
events, send email to:
ora-news-subscribe@lists.oreilly.com
Put the following information in the first line of your
message (*not* in the Subject field):
subscribe ora-events

3. Get Examples from Our Books via FTP

There are two ways to access an archive of example
files from our books:

Regular FTP

- ftp to:
  ftp.oreilly.com
  (login: anonymous
  password: your email address)
- Point your web browser to:
  ftp://ftp.oreilly.com/

FTPMAIL

- Send an email message to:
  ftpmail@online.oreilly.com
  (Write "help" in the message body)

4. Contact Us via Email

order@oreilly.com
   To place a book or software order online. Good
   for North American and international customers.

subscriptions@oreilly.com
   To place an order for any of our newsletters or
   periodicals.

books@oreilly.com
   General questions about any of our books.

software@oreilly.com
   For general questions and product information
   about our software. Check out O'Reilly Software
   Online at **http://software.oreilly.com/** for software
   and technical support information. Registered
   O'Reilly software users send your questions to:
   website-support@oreilly.com

cs@oreilly.com
   For answers to problems regarding your order
   or our products.

booktech@oreilly.com
   For book content technical questions or
   corrections.

proposals@oreilly.com
   To submit new book or software proposals to our
   editors and product managers.

international@oreilly.com
   For information about our international distributors
   or translation queries. For a list of our distributors
   outside of North America check out:
   http://www.oreilly.com/distributors.html

5. Work with Us

Check out our website for current employment
opportunites:
http://jobs.oreilly.com/

O'Reilly & Associates, Inc.
101 Morris Street, Sebastopol, CA 95472 USA
TEL   707-829-0515 or 800-998-9938
          (6am to 5pm PST)
FAX   707-829-0104

O'REILLY®

International Distributors

UK, EUROPE, MIDDLE EAST AND AFRICA (EXCEPT FRANCE, GERMANY, AUSTRIA, SWITZERLAND, LUXEMBOURG, AND LIECHTENSTEIN)

INQUIRIES
O'Reilly UK Limited
4 Castle Street
Farnham
Surrey, GU9 7HS
United Kingdom
Telephone: 44-1252-711776
Fax: 44-1252-734211
Email: information@oreilly.co.uk

ORDERS
Wiley Distribution Services Ltd.
1 Oldlands Way
Bognor Regis
West Sussex PO22 9SA
United Kingdom
Telephone: 44-1243-843294
UK Freephone: 0800-243207
Fax: 44-1243-843302 (Europe/EU orders)
or 44-1243-843274 (Middle East/Africa)
Email: cs-books@wiley.co.uk

GERMANY, SWITZERLAND, AUSTRIA, LUXEMBOURG, AND LIECHTENSTEIN

INQUIRIES & ORDERS
O'Reilly Verlag
Balthasarstr. 81
D-50670 Köln, Germany
Telephone: 49-221-973160-91
Fax: 49-221-973160-8
Email: anfragen@oreilly.de (inquiries)
Email: order@oreilly.de (orders)

FRANCE

INQUIRIES & ORDERS
Éditions O'Reilly
18 rue Séguier
75006 Paris, France
Tel: 1-40-51-71-89
Fax: 1-40-51-72-26
Email: france@oreilly.fr

CANADA (FRENCH LANGUAGE BOOKS)
Les Éditions Flammarion ltée
375, Avenue Laurier Ouest
Montréal (Québec) H2V 2K3
Tel: 00-1-514-277-8807
Fax: 00-1-514-278-2085
Email: info@flammarion.qc.ca

HONG KONG
City Discount Subscription Service, Ltd.
Unit A, 6th Floor, Yan's Tower
27 Wong Chuk Hang Road
Aberdeen, Hong Kong
Tel: 852-2580-3539
Fax: 852-2580-6463
Email: citydis@ppn.com.hk

KOREA
Hanbit Media, Inc.
Chungmu Bldg. 210
Yonnam-dong 568-33
Mapo-gu
Seoul, Korea
Tel: 822-325-0397
Fax: 822-325-9697
Email: hant93@chollian.dacom.co.kr

PHILIPPINES
Global Publishing
G/F Benavides Garden
1186 Benavides St.
Manila, Philippines
Tel: 632-254-8949/632-252-2582
Fax: 632-734-5060/632-252-2733
Email: globalp@pacific.net.ph

TAIWAN
O'Reilly Taiwan
1st Floor, No. 21, Lane 295
Section 1, Fu-Shing South Road
Taipei, 106 Taiwan
Tel: 886-2-27099669
Fax: 886-2-27038802
Email: mori@oreilly.com

CHINA
O'Reilly Beijing
SIGMA Building, Suite B809
No. 49 Zhichun Road
Haidian District
Beijing 100031, P.R. China
Tel: 86-10-8809-7475
Fax: 86-10-8809-7463
Email: beijing@oreilly.com

INDIA
Shroff Publishers & Distributors Pvt. Ltd.
12, "Roseland", 2nd Floor
180, Waterfield Road, Bandra (West)
Mumbai 400 050
Tel: 91-22-641-1800/643-9910
Fax: 91-22-643-2422
Email: spd@vsnl.com

JAPAN
O'Reilly Japan, Inc.
Yotsuya Y's Building
7 Banch 6, Honshio-cho
Shinjuku-ku
Tokyo 160-0003 Japan
Tel: 81-3-3356-5227
Fax: 81-3-3356-5261
Email: japan@oreilly.com

SINGAPORE, INDONESIA, MALAYSIA AND THAILAND
TransQuest Publishers Pte Ltd
30 Old Toh Tuck Road #05-02
Sembawang Kimtrans Logistics Centre
Singapore 597654
Tel: 65-4623112
Fax: 65-4625761
Email: wendiw@transquest.com.sg

ALL OTHER ASIAN COUNTRIES
O'Reilly & Associates, Inc.
101 Morris Street
Sebastopol, CA 95472 USA
Tel: 707-829-0515
Fax: 707-829-0104
Email: order@oreilly.com

AUSTRALIA
Woodslane Pty., Ltd.
7/5 Vuko Place
Warriewood NSW 2102
Australia
Tel: 61-2-9970-5111
Fax: 61-2-9970-5002
Email: info@woodslane.com.au

NEW ZEALAND
Woodslane New Zealand, Ltd.
21 Cooks Street (P.O. Box 575)
Waganui, New Zealand
Tel: 64-6-347-6543
Fax: 64-6-345-4840
Email: info@woodslane.com.au

ARGENTINA
Distribuidora Cuspide
Suipacha 764
1008 Buenos Aires
Argentina
Phone: 5411-4322-8868
Fax: 5411-4322-3456
Email: libros@cuspide.com

O'REILLY®

TO ORDER: **800-998-9938** • **order@oreilly.com** • **http://www.oreilly.com/**

OUR PRODUCTS ARE AVAILABLE AT A BOOKSTORE OR SOFTWARE STORE NEAR YOU.

FOR INFORMATION: **800-998-9938** • **707-829-0515** • **info@oreilly.com**